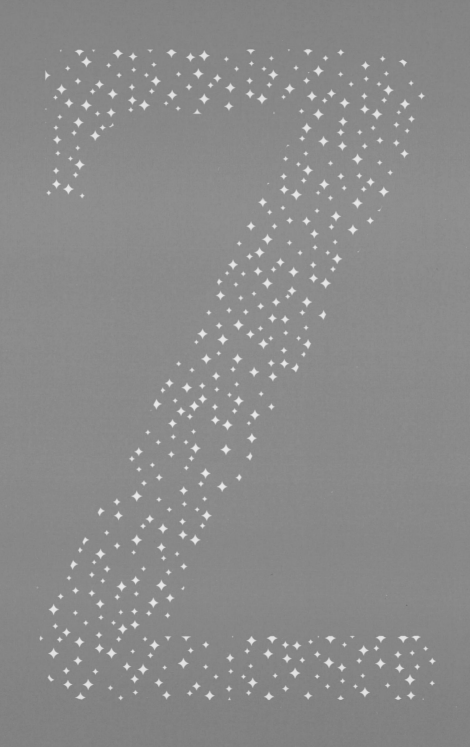

Introducing **The Zap Pack**

Zappos
.com

   6pm.com LLC.

 insights

2011 Culture Book

Zappos!
.com

As defined by our
employees, partners
and customers

Editor in Chief and Aperitifs

Jenn Lim facebook.com/byjennlim | @DHMovementCEO | jenn@deliveringhappiness.com

Designers, Producers and Flair Inducers

Fadhly Bey facebook.com/fadhlybey | @fadhlybey | fadhly@deliveringhappiness.com

Roger Erik Tinch facebook.com/retinch | @tinch | ret@retinch.com

Copy (So We're Not Sloppy) Editors

Kathleen Winkler

Iris Zinck purrformer@gmail.com

Created in cahoots with Delivering Happiness, LLC
www.deliveringhappiness.com

facebook.com/deliveringhappiness

@DHMovement

Printed by Fanny Chen, Orbitel International LLC | fanny@orbitelinternational.com

Vintage Las Vegas Photos used with permission from Las Vegas News Bureau

Hold onto your hat,
2011 Culture Book is off
to the races...

Contents

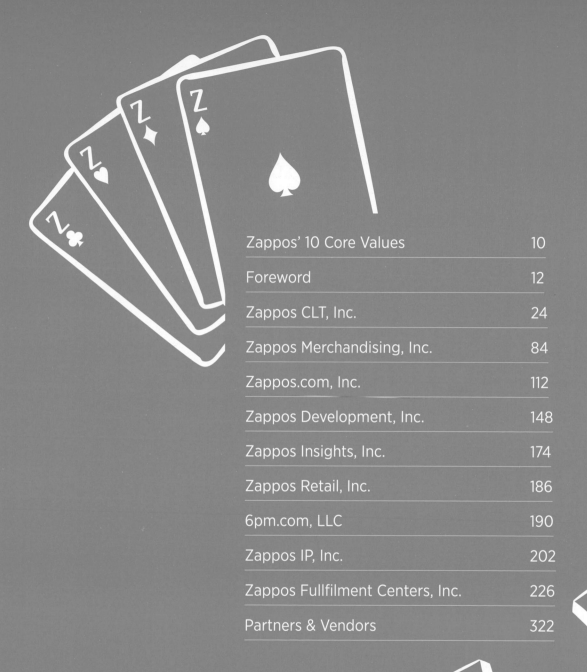

Zappos *Family Core Values*

#3 Create Fun and A Little Weirdness

#1 Deliver WOW Through Service

#2 Embrace and Drive Change

#4 Be Adventurous, Creative, and Open-Minded

Pursue Growth and Learning

#5

#6
Build Open, Honest Relationships With Communication

#7 Build a Positive Team and Family Spirit

#8
Do More With Less

#9 Be Passionate and Determined

#10
Be Humble

#11 Train Elephants to Play Slots

Foreword

The culture book is an annual tradition for the Zappos Family. Every year, I send an email to our employees asking people to write a few paragraphs about what the Zappos culture means to them. Except for typos, it's unedited, because one of our core values is to Build Open and Honest Relationships With Communication.

For us, our #1 priority is company culture. Our belief is that if we get the culture right, most of the other stuff — like delivering great customer service, or building a long-term enduring brand and business — will happen naturally on its own.

In my book *Delivering Happiness: A Path to Profits, Passion, and Purpose*, I write about how a company's culture and a company's brand are really just two sides of the same coin. The brand is simply a lagging indicator of the culture.

Over the past 12 years, we've continuously experienced rapid growth. As we continue to grow and hire new people, we need to make sure that they understand and become a part of our culture. That is the purpose of this culture book — to provide a glimpse of what the Zappos culture is all about to new hires, prospective new hires, our vendors and partners, and anyone else who might be interested.

Our culture is based on our 10 core values:

1) Deliver WOW Through Service
2) Embrace and Drive Change
3) Create Fun and A Little Weirdness
4) Be Adventurous, Creative, and Open-Minded
5) Pursue Growth and Learning
6) Build Open and Honest Relationships With Communication
7) Build a Positive Team and Family Spirit
8) Do More With Less
9) Be Passionate and Determined
10) Be Humble

So what is the Zappos culture? To me, the Zappos culture embodies many different elements. It's about always looking for new ways to WOW everyone we come in contact with. It's about building relationships where we treat each other like family. It's about teamwork and having fun and not taking ourselves too seriously. It's about growth, both personal and professional. It's about achieving the impossible with fewer people. It's about openness, taking risks, and not being afraid to make mistakes. But most of all, it's about having faith that if we do the right thing, then in the long run we will succeed and build something great.

Unlike most companies, where core values are just a plaque on the wall, our core values play a big part in how we hire, train, and develop our employees.

In addition to trying to WOW our customers, we also try to WOW our employees and the vendors and business partners that we work with. We believe that it creates a virtuous cycle, and in our own way, we're making the world a better place and improving people's lives. It's all part of our long term vision to deliver happiness to the world.

Z Girl Blowin' It Up

Of course, the Zappos culture means different things to different people, so I thought the best way for people to learn what the Zappos culture was all about was to hear from our employees directly. Below is the email that I sent to our employees in early 2011:

From: Tony Hsieh
To: All Zappos Employees
Subject: Zappos Culture Book

It's time to put together a new edition of the Zappos Culture Book, to be distributed to employees, prospective employees, business partners, and even some customers.

Our culture is the combination of all of our employees' ideas about the culture, so we would like to include everyone's thoughts in this book.

Please email me a few sentences about what the Zappos culture means to you. (What is the Zappos culture? What's different about it compared to other company cultures? What do you like about our culture?) We will compile everyone's contribution into the book.

When writing your response, please do not refer to any previous culture books, any training/ orientation material, the company handbook, or any other company-published material. We want to hear YOUR thoughts about the company culture.

Also, please do not talk to anyone about what you will be writing or what anyone else wrote. And finally, if you contributed to last year's Culture Book, please do not look at what you wrote last year until after you've written and submitted this year's entry.

Remember, there are no wrong answers. We want to know what the Zappos culture means to you specifically at this point in time, and we expect different responses from different people.

We hope you enjoy the 2011 edition of the Zappos Culture Book!

Tony Hsieh — CEO, Zappos.com, Inc.
ceo@zappos.com, twitter.com/zappos

If you'd like to learn more about our culture, check out our blogs at:
http://blogs.zappos.com

You can also learn more about the Zappos Family at:
http://about.zappos.com

Our job openings are available online at:
http://jobs.zappos.com

Also, we offer tours of our offices in Las Vegas. You can schedule a tour at:
http://tours.zapppos.com

2011
CORPORATE
Challenge

2011
CORPORATE
Challenge
OPENING
CEREMONIES

2011 CORPORATE CHALLENGE *Volleyball*

ZAPPOS Rocks!!

2011 CORPORATE CHALLENGE
Swimming

2011 CORPORATE CHALLENGE
Tug-of-War

LEAVE YOUR CHEER HERE!

2011 CORPORATE *Challenge* **CLOSING CEREMONIES**

SUPPORTING
LIVESTRONG
LANCE ARMSTRONG FOUNDATION

ZAPPOS
CELEBRATES
*Livestrong
Day*

ZCLT™

Build a
Positive Team
and
Family Spirit

(Just make sure your feather boa
isn't in your team member's face)

Abby N.
employee since 2007

To me, the Zappos Culture means acceptance. This is the only job where I have been able to be myself and people don't mind it! We thrive on people being individuals and bringing their own piece to the puzzle that is the Zappos Culture. It is one of the main reasons that we are able to have this great culture! I love Zappos!

Adrian M.
employee since 2009

Another amazing year at the most amazing company in the world! I keep asking myself, "WOW! What else could the company do to top that?" Then before you know it, Zappos answers my question with another shot of WOW! I feel so lucky to be part of a company that makes its number one goal to Deliver Happiness to EVERYONE.

I never would have thought I'd be one of the lucky ones to hit the jackpot in Las Vegas, but I did, via Zappos. I'm so grateful for everything, from the friends I've made to all the wonderful perks we are given. I know I can't pay Zappos back for all the happiness it's provided to me and my family, but I can promise to protect Zappos and its culture, and make sure I'm doing everything I can to Deliver Happiness to EVERYONE I can. All the amazing stories are true! Zappos is that awesome. It's more than just a company or an employer. I can honestly say Zappos has changed my outlook on life for the better. I've also learned my lesson. I'm not asking, "WOW! What else could the company do to top that?" From now on I'm saying, "I can't wait to see what we do next!"

I LOVE ZAPPOS!!! :):):)

Alan O.
employee since 2007

The Zappos Culture is what sets us apart from other companies. I believe in all the Core Values and I try to live by them. (Not always easy.) This is where my extended family lives. There are so many different kinds of people here, bringing cultures from all over the world. We work hard and get the job done and then we play hard! Too bad the world in general hasn't taken to heart what we learn here, but it all starts with the first step and I think we are well on our way!!

Alex S.
employee since 2010

So much of our time is spent away from our family. Most people spend at least eight hours a day/five days a week at a job. Some people add to those hours by attending school or any other extra activities outside of the home. Working at Zappos, you don't feel separated from your family; you feel you are part of an extended family. The Core Values are ingrained in the Zappos Culture. When you're at work … you're at home.

Alexa G.
employee since 2008

The Zappos Culture means everything to me! It is so amazing to be a part of such a great company that really embraces its employees and values its culture. I mostly enjoy genuinely setting ourselves apart from other companies and just doing what we do, with smiles on our faces! I could not imagine myself anywhere else and I look at Zappos as more than work. I really enjoy being around my Zappos family and embrace every opportunity that I have to help continue in cultivating our great culture. I have been here since 2008 and we have evolved tremendously! I can't wait to see what else the future holds!

Alexis P.
employee since 2011

I never thought my place of work would be my sanctuary. The place I go to escape. The place I go to have fun. The place I go to see the people I love the most. The place I cry. The place I laugh. The place I worry. The place I love. A world where I can create. A world where I can dream. A world where I can live. This place is Zappos, which just so happens to be my place of work. I have only been here for a short time, but I already have a family. I am already part of a culture. I already have a journey. And it's what I look forward to every day.

Alicia J.
employee since 2009

The Zappos Culture has made it possible for me to help myself while helping others. It sounds corny, I know, but our culture has seeped into every part of my life. Our Ten Core Values represent how I've always tried to live my life, and to be in an environment that truly lives and breathes these Values - that's something special. I love Zappos and I love who I've become as a result of working here. Also, the popcorn is delicious.

Alicia S.
employee since 2010

The Zappos Culture means everything to me. I came from my previous employer broken and very well acquainted with the word NO! The first time I stepped through the door, the culture sucked me in and pretty much rehabilitated me. The culture impacts you so much that you carry it home and it pretty much changes every aspect of your life.

Allison S.

employee since 2010

The Zappos Culture means more to me than anyone will ever know. Up until a year ago, I was lost and disheartened. In finding this place, I found another home, another family and a new direction. For the first time, I look forward to "work" and to my colleagues. It still amazes me that every day is different, every person is happy, and I actually look forward to being here. Inspiration and respect are infectious at Zappos and for that I wouldn't trade anything in the world for this place. Thanks, guys and girls. It's an honor to be here.

Allison S.

employee since 2010

What amazes me about Zappos is the attitudes and agendas of the individuals working here. Everyone genuinely cares and wants the best for you. If we are all creatures guilty of building our perceptions of self through the social mirror, how lucky we are to be here. Zappos recruiting hires confident and positive people. While I have learned and grown a great deal from all of my interactions and relationships with my peers, my character has been equally influenced by the people who lead because they understand their own potential. I don't plan on being here forever, but there are many people that will be in my life forever because of Zappos and I am grateful.

Amanda D.

employee since 2010

Customers ask me how it is to work at Zappos all the time. My response is "It's something that I can't even explain." This statement is 100% true. I have been here since July and am still in shock about the ways we do things here at Zappos. I am blessed to work for a company like ours. We are like nothing else I'd ever seen. Being able to WOWÊ our customers, to be able to go above and beyond! Even doing team activities, such as our "Peep Shows." The culture here is still something I can't explain. To me, it's something so great; you have to experience it because no words can describe what it really is like. I love Zappos, and my Zappos family. :D

Amber W.

employee since 2009

The Zappos Culture has given me a better outlook on life. I am so grateful for everything I get to be a part of on a daily basis. To me, our culture means happiness, positivity, enrichment and growth. The Zappos Culture brings me out of my shell and helps me feel connected to like-minded folks! I feel genuinely happier knowing that I'm apart of such an awesome family. I hope that shows when I speak to our customers and interact with my co-workers. Cheers!

Amy B.

employee since 2011

Before starting at Zappos, I had heard it was a great place to work, and I knew I wanted in. But while I thought I knew why, I actually didn't yet understand it. Sure, there are the goofy parades, fun events, and great benefits, but those weren't it. After only a few weeks in my training class, I figured it out. When I'm at Zappos, I feel respected and trusted. I don't worry that I'm not doing my job right, or that I'll get in trouble for doing whatever it takes to make a customer happy. In fact, I really just don't have to worry any more. Being respected and trusted makes me want to offer the same courtesies to everyone else, and I can really see the positive effect the Zappos Culture is having on my life already. I think I've found my forever home!

Amy M.

employee since 2010

To me, the Zappos Culture is about being a better version of yourself ... It is about accepting others for what they are and going above and beyond to make everyone around you smile.

Amy S.

employee since 2010

When I started at Zappos, I had no idea what I was about to be involved in. I didn't know that when I walked through those training room doors, my life would be forever changed! (That may sound kinda corny, but it's true!) Working here is like no place I've ever worked, or even been at for that matter. I am so happy to be at work every day. Sometimes it feels like coming to work is actually a break from life (and who doesn't need that, right?)!!! Our Ten Core Values are what we live by. I wish more companies and more people would incorporate these types of behaviors into their lives! The world would be a much happier and much more relaxed place if they did! :-)

I can't imagine ever leaving Zappos. It makes me shudder to think about it! We work hard and our customers are FIRST!!! But we also have fun, sometimes too much fun, at least from what I can remember! ;-) I have made some amazing friends and relationships over the past 12 months and I hope it never ends! Cheers ...

Ana G.

employee since 2010

What does the Zappos Culture mean to me? It means a lot of things. It means I can randomly start dancing at my desk and nobody will think it is weird. It means my entire team can show up to work in pajamas and we wouldn't be out of place. It means we can take a celebratory shot after breaking a record and it wouldn't be out of the norm. Ultimately though, it means my home away from home, because that's exactly what this place has turned into. I've made great friends, not only with my co-workers but also with some of my customers. Sometimes I can't separate them from my real family. Looking forward to many more years with my newfound family! <3

Ana S.

employee since 2009

To me, the Zappos Culture means diversity. I'm always amazed when I look around and see the level of diversity we have and, more importantly, how accepted we all are. Needless to say, having a diverse group of folks often leads to educating each other in our differences and helping promote tolerance. I continue to feel blessed, privileged and honored to be part of the Zappos family.

Andre N.

employee since 2008

The Zappos Culture means the world to me. I could not imagine working anywhere else. I'm thankful for all of the opportunities and freedom we have at Zappos. If someone has an idea, they are fully empowered to run with it. We can reach out to anyone in the company and someone is always willing to help. As we continue to grow as a company, I find myself growing along with Zappos, both personally and professionally. I cannot express how grateful I am to be a part of this company, and I am excited to see more changes and growth for many years to come!

Andreas W.

employee since 2010

When I think of the Zappos Culture, I think of this huge interdependent community. We all look to each other for inspiration and support. I love the fact that every time a new idea is presented, it comes from our own company. I'm amazed at how we always reinvent the wheel at Zappos. There is never a dull moment when it comes to our culture. You are never alone when you want to start something new. Every time I mention that I have new idea for something, a lot of people come to me offering their gifts and talents. There's never a dull moment with Zappos!

Andrew T.

employee since 2008

This is my third year with Zappos and I love our Culture. I am very proud to say that our emphasis on the importance of every person in the Zappos family is ideal and has been the key to the success of our company. The Zappos Culture is unique and should be emulated in part or as a whole by more companies, as this will benefit the company and customers they serve. What makes our Culture different is the openness and the genuine care we have for each other and our customers. They may be our external or internal customers. Zappos is a great and happy place to be. This will be the last company that I will work for. Thank you, Zappos, for everything.

Angela R.

employee since 2010

I love working at Zappos! What other company embraces individuality so much that they make it one of their core values?!! Core Value #3 "Create Fun and a Little Weirdness!! No, we are not brainwashed, like some people might think. We are just genuinely happy to work for such an awesome, fun company! I have never heard anyone ever say they liked their job. I am happy to say that I don't just like my job - I freaking love it!

Anonymous

employee since 2008

Zappos is a unique place to work; I feel truly blessed to be part of such a great company. The Zappos Culture is what makes us so unique and has helped the company grow from a young, relatively unknown company, to one of the leaders in the online retail world. In short, Zappos = Awesomeness!!!

Anonymous

employee since 2003

One of the best things about this job is the Zappos Culture. Without it, I probably wouldn't be as happy as I am. I loved my job from the first day I walked through the door. It's amazing how fast the company is growing now: so much opportunity, so much more to learn. I know a lot of people feel the same way. That's why we have to keep it and protect it.

Anonymous

employee since 2010

Zappos has changed my whole work perspective and outlook. At most other jobs, employees may feel the need to change once they walk through the office doors. They're this happy and loving person at home, but once at the job their whole demeanor changes. Here at Zappos I've been allowed to bring my personality with me every day. I'm given the opportunity daily to be myself. The Zappos Culture has even spilled over into my everyday life outside of work. I'm now more creative, more adventurous, more loving and giving. Thank you, Zappos.

Anonymous

employee since 2009

What does Zappos mean to me? I was asked this question when I was still in training over a year ago and fortunately, my views have not changed much, except for the better. Zappos has been a great place to work and very forgiving when times got hard for me.

The Zappos Culture means fun and excitement. You never know what the day has in store for you. I have made some great friends here. I wouldn't change my experience at Zappos for anything. Thank you!!

Anonymous

employee since 2010

The Zappos Culture is everything! From something that most people would think is minor, like holding the door open for someone else, or asking how someone's day is going, to wanting to be a better person outside of work. It's something that can impact so many people in a good way!

Anonymous

employee since 2010

The Zappos Culture has changed my life. It's changed my outlook on having to wake up every morning and leave my family to make a living. When I leave my house, I don't dread a 9-5 job that leads me nowhere. Instead, it's like I walk through the doors and instantly I'm greeted by smiling faces and an atmosphere that is matched at no other workplace.

I look forward to going to work. How many people can say that?? I feel good knowing that the opportunity for advancement is always there and definitely encouraged! If I ever feel that I want move to another department, our supervisors encourage us and are happy to see us accomplish our goals.

With the lack of micro-managing and the empowerment that each individual CLT representative has, it's comforting to know when I arrive at work that I have what it takes to take care of our customers the way I would like to be taken care of. All companies should adopt the way Zappos trusts its employees. It gets things done and everyone is happy, including myself! Thank you, Zappos!!

Anonymous

employee since 2010

I love being in Zappos land because it connects me with the human heart, and helps me to open mine. It's not perfect, but it gives me purpose, and it feels real. And for that, I am grateful.

Anonymous

employee since 2010

I love Zappos! This is my first call center experience and the job, overall, is amazing. I enjoy coming to work. The Zappos Culture is what sets us apart from the rest. It is important to put our culture first, especially as we continue to grow, so we can be forever amazingggggg!

Anonymous
employee since 2010

The Zappos Culture = Individuality, Happiness, Fun, Friendships, Weirdness, Creativity, Teamwork, Customer Service, and Personal Growth. I feel completely blessed to have this opportunity to work for an amazing company while being able to be myself.

Anonymous
employee since 2009

What can I say??? I love Zappos! I have loved it since day one! I am happier! I have a new, extended family and tons of POTLUCKS! In all seriousness, it is the best place I have ever worked in my life!

Anonymous
employee since 2006

When I think of what the Zappos Culture means to me, "uniqueness" is my immediate thought. There is no other business I know of that encourages fun, provides free food and enjoyment while you are doing the job you were hired to do, as well as all the opportunities for career growth. Like the customers I speak with on the phone, "I love Zappos."

Anonymous
employee since 2010

Zappos is a great place to get some Culture. Since I have been here, everyone makes this job seem more like an adventure and I never know what new fun adventure is coming. These people are fanatics about supporting one another. If you have an idea, share it. This is the first place that allowed me to feel this way. If you came here and did not share your ideas, it would be your fault that we never took the awesome ride that you could have helped to provide.

Anonymous
employee since 2004

The Zappos Culture = Family and Fun

Anonymous
employee since 2008

The Zappos Culture is like nothing else I've ever experienced. Everyone is caring and helpful. I am never afraid to ask questions or be myself. We are all encouraged to express who we are. I feel very much at home and happy here. My co-workers are like family. I am extremely thankful to have the Zappos Culture in my life.

Anonymous
employee since 2010

When I think of the Zappos Culture, I think of life's direction! In life there are so many twists and turns, some of which you can control and some over which you have no control at all. That being said, it's a big help to have daily reminders of the importance of life directions. This is where the Zappos Culture comes in for me, like being "Passionate and Determined (Core Value #9). I've enjoyed using the 9th of the Ten Core Values for this whole first year since I've been part of the Zappos family. I have grown not only by improving myself and my understanding of my job, I have become passionate and determined to make the best I can out of my own life and the lives of all those around me. I'm very happy to be apart of the Zappos family and look forward to many years to come sharing all of the Zappos Ten Core Values with everyone I come in contact with.

Anonymous
employee since 2010

Being a part of the Zappos Culture has allowed me to see that work does not have to be just work. I enjoy coming in every morning knowing that, for the most part, people here are happy and friendly. I never dread the thought of "Monday morning" the way I have at other jobs. My only dread is getting out of bed, but who doesn't dread that? I never leave feeling defeated from the day's events. I am able to go home a happy person and enjoy my time with my family.

Anonymous
employee since 2010

The Zappos Culture means having fun every day, losing some but winning a lot. All of us at Zappos have tiger blood flowing through our veins, and we try to pass that awesomeness on to everyone we can.

Anonymous
employee since 2010

The Zappos Culture is the freedom to be yourself and to enjoy being who you are and doing what you do. Complete acceptance, and super weird!! The Zappos Culture is knowing how to have a good time and how to enjoy every part of life, whether at work or home. The Zappos Culture is AWESOME!

Anonymous
employee since 2009

All the little things that people do for you. How understanding people are and how they do not look at you as if you were crazy because you might be a little different than what they are used to. They actually want to know more about you. Everything we do here is different than what you will find anywhere else!

Anonymous

employee since 2010

Zappos delivers WOW through the services we provide every day. Zappos has embraced me for who I am and has driven me to change for the better. Zappos has Created Fun and a Little Weirdness (Core Value #3) every day that I have come to work. Zappos has pushed me to be more adventurous, creative and open-minded. Zappos has encouraged me to pursue growth and learn skills. Zappos has allowed me to build open and honest relationships by letting me communicate and be heard. Zappos has given me the chance to build a positive team and family spirit with my co-workers. Zappos has taught me what it means to Do More With Less (Core Value #8). Zappos has made me be more Passionate and Determined (Core Value #9) about my goals. Zappos has made me become Humble (Core Value #10), despite the great journey it has taken me on so far.

I wear these words around my neck every day and I smile when I think about this verse: "Bind them continually upon thine heart, and tie them about thy neck. When thou goest, it shall lead thee; when thou sleepest, it shall keep thee; and when thou awakest, it shall talk with thee. For the commandment is a lamp; and the law is light; and reproofs of instruction are the way of life." (Proverbs 6:21-23)

Anonymous

employee since 2010

Workin' at Zappos means I don't spend 40 hrs a week pickin' up dog poop. Not that dog poop isn't awesome, it's just not my thing.

Anonymous

employee since 2004

To me, the Zappos Culture means to work hard, have fun and make friends.

Anonymous

employee since 2010

The greatest feature of the Zappos Culture is that we can all really be ourselves here. Even better than that is that we can be ourselves, more than we are even outside of work. This is because at Zappos, we're able to flourish in both a work sense and a personal sense at the same time. As far as I know, there aren't too many places where that would even be a possibility. To sum it up, the Zappos Culture is unlike anything else you'll experience. When you walk in the building for the first time you think, "How can anyone being doing any work here?" Only after immersing yourself in the culture and talking with the people who work here can you understand how it could possibly work. And then, when you actually do work here, you come to completely understand how that delicate balance of crazy and fun mixes with actually getting stuff done. The way that we work here may not be for everyone. But it's perfect for those of us who do work here and we'll always do our best to maintain and grow this very unique work environment.

Anonymous

employee since 2010

Only a few months in and I can definitely say Zappos has made a big impact on my life. Moved here right out of college from the east coast, and I would not change it for the world!! I have been given the gift of not only a great company but also an awesome family!! Thank you, Zappos!

Anonymous

employee since 2010

The Zappos Culture: friendship, individuality, and honesty, working hard, passion, trust, teamwork and customer service.

Anonymous

employee since 2008

I love that we have the opportunity to visit our warehouse in Kentucky. Learning all the different departments and job functions really elevates the amount of respect we have for our Zappos co-workers.

Anita B.

employee since 2009

WOW! Another great year at Zappos!

Anna C.

employee since 2007

I've been with Zappos for over three years, and still find it one of the best companies to work for. The people that work here are great!

Anna C.

employee since 2010

When walking through the hallways at work, almost every person that you pass will greet you with a warm smile or an enthusiastic hello, whether they know you or not. This act of genuine kindness always puts me in a good mood, and really exemplifies what the Zappos Culture means to me.

Anthony S.

employee since 2008

At a time when millions of Americans are out of work and questions upon questions are being asked about the "state of the economy," I happen to work in a Utopian bubble, a place that expresses only confidence about the future that lies ahead of us. I work for a company where cooperation between employees, departments, and the community around us is the norm! I am so fortunate to work here, a place of dreams and ambitions - a place of hope. Thank you, Zappos, for all of the benefits you provide us all, for the support you offer without hesitation, and for giving us a workplace worth coming to every morning.

For all of those reading this book, I hope the Zappos Culture can inspire you, just as we were inspired from day one. Cheers to making the world a better place, one day at a time.

Ashlee A.

employee since 2007

The Zappos Culture means being a family. Our Culture is unique; we're able to treat each other like a brother, a sister, a mother, a father, and still work well together. There have even been times where my family wasn't supportive of something and almost every Zappos family member I have was right behind me, even surpassing my family as the ones I hold closest. The last times I've cried it's been on a shoulder of a Zappos family member, the last times I've laughed it's been with a Zappos family member. It's impossible to imagine my life without this support and love, and no matter what happens from here, I know that they will always be there for me as a true family.

People have asked me where I work, and when I tell them I work for Zappos, I make sure to tell them I'm part of the family business, so they know that I consider every single one of our over 1,000 employees members of my close family. I love you, Zappos. You were there for my marriage, my two kids' births, and I can't wait to see what happens next!

Ashley JJ.

employee since 2010

If you had told me a year ago that I'd be the type of person who woke up every morning, excited to go to work, I would have said you were cray-zay. (Yes, and I'd say it like that as well.) When I first walked through the doors at Zappos, I was greeted by parades, streamers and noisemakers a-plenty. I knew immediately that this place was different. If I had to describe this place, however, it would not be the parties, or the food, or the decorations; it would be the people. Now when I enter these doors, I am welcomed by my friends, who have become my family without effort,

The #1 thing here is the Zappos Culture. Zappos is unique because our Culture is unique. When you walk in here, you can feel it in the air. It even smells different in here. Maybe it's the food, or all of the coffee we drink ... Or maybe it's the people, emitting Culture through their pores. We're all crazy sometimes. Being here is like a natural coffee buzz. Zappos is our mug, and the people inside make up the espresso. Our culture isn't just an attitude; it's a state of being, a way of life. My Zappos family includes some of the most kind-hearted, weird, fun, interesting people I've ever met. I notice it flooding into my everyday life. The atmosphere here is like no other because of our culture, and I wouldn't have it any other way. What was once just thought of as a job has now become a way of life for us Zapponians.

Ashley T.

employee since 2009

WOW! Almost two years down and I still enjoy coming to work every single day! Where do you find a company like that??? All I really can say is that Zappos has changed my life in so many good ways. I do look at customer service differently and I also value good customer service a lot more! Zappos is not only my employer, they are my family and I would not have it any other way! I cannot wait to see what the next year brings and am so excited to be moving downtown, even though it makes my commute longer! :)

Ashotta W

employee since 2007

Our Zappos Culture makes us unlike any other company in the world. Well, at least, not any I know of. We have something no one else has; we not only come together to give our customers the best service they have ever experienced, we are also like family. People come from all over the country, and in some cases the world, to work for Zappos, and we have one goal in mind - to build a phenomenal company and to give our customers the ultimate Zappos experience. There truly is no company like Zappos. I love Zappos!

Atrell L

employee since 2005

I joined the Zappos family six years ago not knowing exactly what I had stumbled upon. I soon learned that my original goal of finding a place to work had evolved into building a career. The company's Core Values not only affect me at work, but also in my personal life. My life has evolved in so many different aspects since starting to work here at Zappos. The best part about this journey is how much I've grown and the support I have had from my Zappos family along the way. I couldn't have asked for a better home away from home.

Babe B

employee since 2010

What to say about Zappos .... Hmmmm. When I was hired last year, I thought I would know exactly what to write when asked to submit something for the Culture Book for the first time. I was wrong. I've thought and thought for days about what to write, and even debated not writing anything. But after several nudges, here's what I think: I think I feel 90/10 about Zappos. Ninety-percent of the company is amazing, and 10% needs some work. We all know about the non-scripted, empowered decision-making that we have here. The ability to send cards, cookies and flowers to customers without going through ten levels of hell to deliver. This, coupled with the amazing benefits, liberal dress code, parties, parades, free food, unlimited beverages, ice cream, creative team environment, decorations, friendly team competitions, tours, classes, popcorn, vendor freebies, amazing parties and happy hours .... It's almost too good to be true. But it's ALLLLL true! (Don't even get me started about the vat of whipped butter that makes the most amazing grilled cheese "sammiches" in the handy toaster oven in The Bistro .... Swoon!) I'm amazed by the diversity of our family, and how we all see past color, race, age, sex, sexual orientation, religion, and political affiliations. When I see my peers, I see family. And I LOVE, LOVE, LOVE my family. The small 10% that needs improvement is so trivial, it doesn't bear listing in detail. What is important is that Zappos is such a work in progress that I truly believe the 10% is probably on the drawing boards of people here, to be tweaked and improved upon. Hearing the genuine and sincere appreciation that our customers express on the phone, or read online via Twitter/Facebook and blogs makes me so proud to be a part of this family. The comments from charitable organizations that express their appreciation for all that Zappos employees donate and deliver, and the comments from our community about their appreciation for all the revitalization and business that we have sent their way ... It just makes me happy to be a part of this. All of this. I hope next year to be moving the 10% down, and the 90% higher. I'm prepared to roll up my sleeves and pitch in with the rest of the team to focus on our continued growth and improvement. I think that's a realistic goal, and I'm looking forward to seeing what's next.

Beth M.

employee since 2009

The Zappos Culture is all about making friends and turning them into a big, extended family. When I went through New Hire Training, I was amazed at how close our class became. I'd wondered how in the world I'd be able to connect on such a personal level with so many employees. Actually, it's very easy when you treat each other with respect and feel that you can be who you are, without judgment. Be open and honest, and don't put up a wall. The same is true of many of our customers. When you extend yourself, offer help, share personal stories, make that connection, you feel like you've made a friend. THEY feel like part of the Zappos family, so mission accomplished! Do the unexpected to help someone and it comes back tenfold. The culture at Zappos is about being the best person you can be, and spreading that to others. Let loose, take a risk, show your wild side and just have fun!

Betsy C.

employee since 2010

The Zappos Culture is truly AMAZING! It's like nothing I've ever experienced before in the workplace. I've been with Zappos for just about a year and I am so glad to be a part of this awesome family! Everyone is treated the same. No matter what your position, you're a part of this great big family that has a really great time helping our customers, playing, laughing and just being happy! When my friends ask, "Are you working today?" I say no, "I'm Delivering Happiness today!" I LOVE ZAPPOS!

Betty L.

employee since 2004

Wow! Working for Zappos has been amazing. Being around so many people who love what they do is great. The Zappos Culture is very contagious and I am blessed to work for a company that lets you be yourself. I have met many people here and I can assure you that every single person is different. Being able to choose your path and direction within the company is also great. Although we would all love to be at Zappos 24/7, it is not always possible, as some of us have a family at home and other things that that require some of our time. I LOVE that I can balance my personal life along with my extended family (Zappos peeps). I don't consider Zappos just a job, but more of a place where we have fun with what we do. I am thankful to be part of such a great company and look forward to many more years.

Big Uncle Andy

employee since 2010

Zappos is awesome!! The Culture here is amazing! Everybody is always so happy and friendly that it's impossible not to love it here. I have fun every day at work and I wouldn't change a thing. (P.S. The Lions are going to win the Super Bowl this year!)

Brandon D.

employee since 2010

I never, in a million years, thought that a place of employment could have a culture that wasn't bounded by how much money you make for them or how productive you can be. Zappos has been like a breath of fresh air for me. The Zappos Culture gives everyone open avenues to be as cool, offbeat, quirky, inebriated or any other adjectives that could describe the personality traits employees usually leave at home. Coming to Zappos was the first time I have not felt restricted or constricted at work. The sky's the limit.

Brandon L.

employee since 2010

The name Zappos conveys so much more to me than just an online retailer. It was a new beginning for me. Being a part of the Zappos Culture - this family - means more to me than words can express. Being able to provide a level of service that is unmatched simply by treating our customers as family is the best part of being part of Zappos. Being treated like an individual instead of a number continually brings a smile to my face and a to my heart. Thanks, Zappos!

Breanne F.

employee since 2010

To me, the Zappos Culture means loving what you do, loving the people you work with and loving the environment you work in each and everyday. I love Zappos!

Britney C.

employee since 2010

The Zappos Culture has definitely brought me out of my shell. I was always silly and crazy at home, but never felt I was able to completely be myself at work until I came here. I feel at home here, which is awesome because my work and personal life have finally been able to intertwine and become one! I'm obsessed with the potlucks, infectious happiness, self-expression, and friendship here. Nothing's better than food and good friends ... at work!

Bryan B.
employee since 2009

There are few instances when something becomes so ingrained in a city that it starts to shape it, but I truly believe that Zappos has managed to change many aspects of Las Vegas. It's much deeper than casinos and local companies emulating what we do, or having our name splashed across a high rise and local events. Zappos has managed not only to initiate change in the future of Las Vegas, but to sustain the changes it brings. Although the path is still far from concrete, one thing that is certain is that Zappos has enabled Las Vegas to become more than what it is known for, and I'm truly excited to see the metamorphosis.

Bryan F.
employee since 2010

Please take a moment to use your most creative imagination possible. Close your eyes and imagine a life in which your work and leisure are one. A place where your co-workers are like family whom you look forward to seeing everyday. This is a place to share your ideas, to grow, to learn and to be yourself (seriously). Because of the Zappos Culture, I don't go to WORK - I go to LIVE! Some people try to insist it's just a dream within a dream, but to that I say "NAY!" This is real; this is the Zappos Culture, and I thank God every day to be part of it.

Cameron B.
employee since 2011

Last year I was on the outside looking in at the Zappos Culture as a temp. Now I'm officially a Zappos employee!!! This is such a great feeling!! I'm "Hella" (Nor-Cal word for extremely) excited about this opportunity and the great things that I can do to make this company grow bigger and better, also with the help of my class -"CLASS 102, aka FWWOWB, aka Friends with WOW Benefits." We will help with the progress of our company and Deliver Happiness throughout our lives.   "I shall either find a way or will make one." - Anonymous

Camilla J.
employee since 2009

The thing I love most about the Zappos Culture is that we build teams and family spirit wherever we go. We could be giving out free shoes to inner-city kids, having a block party on Fremont Street or drinking at a happy hour. We will always invite everyone to join in on the fun and make them feel welcome. That's just how we roll!!!

Candace S.
employee since 2006

This has been an especially difficult year for me personally, and yet through it all, my Zappos family has provided me with great friendships, genuine concern and support. The Zappos Culture has been difficult for me to explain or put into words in the past, but this year has truly reinforced how important our Zappos Culture has been for me. Let me pass it on for others to feel warm and fuzzy!

Carla A.
employee since 2010

My whole life I worked at jobs where I did not "fit in" and I just was not pleased with where I was. Then I found Zappos. Now I am delighted to say with a gigantic smile "I work at Zappos!" to anyone and everyone who asks. On top of all this, my husband says that I am now a "pleasant and joyful person." I am lucky to be here every day and be part of such an astonishing company.

Carol T.
employee since 2008

The Zappos Culture is a friendly, spontaneous and creative atmosphere that brings out the best in all of us. We learn from and with each other and grow both personally and as a company.

Catherine M.
employee since 2009

The Zappos Culture is about WOWing!! Zappos is one of the most amazing places to work. We have a Culture that stands alone. We are constantly building positive team and family spirit and we always "Create Fun an Little Weirdness" (Core Value #3). If you are without family here, think again. Zappos goes above and beyond to make you feel welcome and the friends that you make here are not just friends they are FAMILY! Being part of the Zappos family is the most amazing feeling. We are able to express ourselves and just be us. I am blessed to be here and to learn the difference between working for a company and working with a company. Being on a CLT team is having the opportunity to get to know someone you may have not known before and somehow you wonder where this person has been. Our teams are unique, each expressing our team spirit in how we are able to greet our visitors. We could have a parade, blow a whistle or shake a noisemaker. On my team we shake our ÊÊmonkeys but we always try to make people feel welcome. Seeing the smiles on their faces means we have accomplished our goal! I have been here almost two years now and hope to be here a lot longer. You never know what tomorrow will bring, but you can bet it will always be Creative, Fun and a Little Weird (Core Value #3), with the best family spirit behind it! ZAPPOS ROCKS like chicken and biscuits! WOW!!!!!

Chelsea P.

employee since 2010

Working at Zappos has truly been a blessing. I don't know where I would be right now if it weren't for this amazing company filled with amazing people! I have grown tremendously, gaining confidence in myself to do the things that I am passionate about. I also met an amazing man! How great is that?! Zappos, I will love you for life!

Chelsea S.

employee since 2007

The Zappos Culture has allowed me to experience something new professionally and personally every year I've been here. I have learned a lot about myself as well as others. I enjoy helping others strive to accomplish their personal and professional goals (no matter how big or small), just as others helped me achieve mine.

Cheree H.

employee since 2004

There is no culture like the Zappos Culture. I started working for Zappos in August of 2004 and not a day goes by that I don't look forward to coming in to work. I know I have never felt that way about any other company that I have worked for in the past. It has been amazing to see and be a part of the growth at Zappos: So many changes and company growth! But the one thing that never changes is the culture. I'm truly blessed to be a part of such a great company where you can grow and choose your own path. Thank you, Zappos, for everything and I look forward to many more years to come! I <3 ZAPPOS!

Cheryl R.

employee since 2009

Zappos has changed my life and made me a better person. The Zappos Culture has inspired many people and businesses to embrace what it means to have great customer service and learn to listen to their employees. I truly am in love with my job and can't ask for anything more!

Chez V.

employee since 2009

The Zappos Culture is like infectious laughter. It is unique, captivating and even if it doesn't make you laugh, it'll make you feel good! It is just amazing and I am so happy that I experience it every day I work.

Christiane T.

employee since 2010

The Zappos Culture allows each of us to be who we are and know that we are accepted and valued for that. It bonds us all together as family - one that is a little bit weird and completely awesome.

The Culture allows us to express ourselves both individually and as a whole. There really isn't anything like it, and it almost seems as if it shouldn't be able to exist. If I didn't work here, I wouldn't believe that so many people from different backgrounds, interests and passions could come together and have such a great time working and playing.

Christina C.

employee since 2007

What I really recognize is that I'm more in love now than I was four years ago when I first walked through the door at Zappos. And I was pretty darned smitten then!

Christina L.

employee since 2008

The Zappos Culture is everywhere, all the time! It's in is the interactions we have with one another, the positivity we express in the work place, the childlike love we have for our co-workers, the friendship, the fun, the aura, and the air we breath at Zappos! After three years at Zappos, the Zappos Culture means more to me than ever! It is the reason why I love to come to work every day. It motivates me to be the best co-worker, friend, and lead that I can be! We don't just believe in the culture, we are the culture and we love to share it with everyone we come in contact with! Peace and Carrots!

Christine B.

employee since 2008

Time flies when you're having fun. I'm edging up on another anniversary with Zappos. With all the growth and change in the company, it's really cool to be considered a veteran employee with three years under my belt. I'm so proud of all the changes that I've seen and have had a hand in initiating. The Zappos Culture, to me, means being excited about what's around the corner and looking forward to the changes ahead, especially with the move to the downtown offices coming up. I can't wait to see how we grow as a company and community in the years to come.

Christine M.

employee since 2010

I heard so many great things about Zappos before I was hired here that I was a little skeptical about how true they could really be. I mean, who really enjoys coming to work??!! Well, everything I heard was definitely right and even more amazing. I have made life-long friends here and I have never worked in such a fun and happy environment. Zappos has not only changed my perspective of what happiness is, it has changed my life outside of work as well. I feel blessed to be working for the best company ever!!

Christopher K.

employee since 2010

To be honest, when I started at Zappos I knew it was an amazing place to work, but I thought that maybe they were over-hyping it. How could a place be so amazing it would affect me in and outside of work? I have been here for five months now and I can honestly say my life is changed forever. The amount of positive energy this place produces is ridiculous. You get up in the morning and want to go to work, and leave with a smile on your face. It has made me appreciate service elsewhere and want to spread positive energy beyond these walls. What Tony and all of the Zappos family have created here is truly amazing, and I'm thankful for every day that I get to spend here. It makes me happy knowing I'm helping push our culture forward!

Christopher R.

employee since 2010

What can I say about Zappos that hasn't already been said? I can honestly say this is the best place I have ever worked, and I have never been happier. I look forward to going to work every day, and I no longer feel stuck in a rut. What I really feel can be summed up in three simple words: I Love Zappos!

Christy C.

employee since 2010

For me, the Zappos Culture is being surrounded by great people. Every day, I get to work with people who truly care about me and drive me to be better. We work together to help each other and our customers. It's amazing to be encouraged to be yourself, and enjoy the diversity of everyone around you. I am WOWed every day that I come to "work." How many people are lucky enough to be able to say this?

Clarence R.

employee since 2008

To me, the Zappos Culture boils down to camaraderie. It's going that extra mile every time the opportunity arises. After a few years of doing this, it's amazing how many friends you will have.

Cody B.

employee since 2007

The Zappos Culture means comfort, it means home. Because of the Culture here we are encouraged to be ourselves, which is amazing. Often you find yourself working some place that wants you to be you, but only if you conform to a very small box. Not at Zappos. We don't even have a box.

Our Ten Core Values don't define us; we define them! Our differences, idiosyncrasies and similarities make us who we are as a whole, which is one awesome group of people. We = the Zappos Culture.

Corey S.

employee since 2008

Work hard, play hard.

Crystal H.

employee since 2010

Before moving to Las Vegas about two years ago, I had never even heard of Zappos. I was actually referred to Zappos by a family I had just met when I moved here. During the application process, I decided to see what Zappos was all about. After reading about the amazing Zappos Culture, I knew instantly that Zappos was the place for me. I was impressed by its Ten Core Values because they so closely matched my own. I mean, what other company has "Create Fun and Little Weirdness" (Core Value #3) as one of its values?

Right then and there I knew that this was not just going to be some company that I would dread working for every day, and to this day (a little over a year later) it still isn't. I love you, Zappos! <3 <3 <3

Crystal M.

employee since 2005

I love working at Zappos because the company's Culture is different from anywhere else I have worked. We all believe in the Ten Core Vales and implement them on a daily basis. It is the One Team/ One Dream theory, where we all work together for the good of the company. That is what makes our culture what it is today. We are one big family.

Crystal S.

employee since 2009

The Zappos Culture is about loving what you do every day and who you're doing it with! Zappos has become my second home, and my co-workers have become my second family. I can't see being anywhere else!

Daniel R.

employee since 2010

At Zappos I am given the opportunity to be myself in all aspects of my job. I enjoy the family and team spirit and the encouragement I get on a daily basis, to name just a few things. All of these things are what the Zappos Culture is to me.

It's rare these days that you see a company treating its employees like real people, instead of numbers on a spreadsheet. I'm so happy that I can contribute my ideas and what I want to be doing, both professionally and personally in my life, to Zappos. And being able to work in such an amazing environment is a blessing that I would never give up. My advice for the reader of this book: Always keep a positive mental attitude. Don't worry! Be happy!

Darlene K.

employee since 2008

What does the Zappos Culture mean to me?? Let me count the ways!!

Number 1: Freedom to be my own boss basically. I love being able to make my job so much easier and my customers so easy to talk to. I love having "one-on-one" conversations with my customers, like they're old friends or family.

Number 2: I really do like having so many different connections with my Zappos family members as well. Every day is an experience, with contests and interactions with many people.

Number 3: The fact that we are growing so quickly. I have an opportunity to meet more new friends and co-workers and to share my knowledge with those fresh new faces eager to pass the Zappos Culture even farther in their world.

Number 4: I am super-excited about our future here at Zappos. Looking forward to all of the changes and new challenges that lie ahead. Well, I believe this will wrap it up.

There's just one thing left to say: My future is looking so bright, I gotta wear shades!!

Dani G.

employee since 2010

In one word, the Zappos Culture is Groundbreaking. I never knew that such a work place could exist, where everyone has a common goal and we are all determined to achieve it. I'm sure that, like everyone else, when I started working here I thought this place was beyond unreal. I had to have been dreaming, because for the first time in my work history I did not fall asleep in a training class and I actually enjoy coming to work day in and day out. It's almost been one year since my hire date and it's seems like I just started yesterday, which proves that time really does fly when you're having fun. Zappos has been the answer to a lot of my prayers about wanting a job that is fulfilling and about knowing that you have a true purpose. Everyone who knows me outside of the office can tell you that I am a Zappos cheerleader. Everyone knows I absolutely LOVE my job and Zappos, and now I don't mind going home from work every day and having my daughter ask me, "How was work today, mom?" I can smile and tell her how awesome my day was and even share something funny that happened at work, rather than giving her the frustrated and annoyed sigh that many people who do not work at Zappos give when asked that question. The happiest place on Earth? Maybe not, to those who don't work here. But to us Zapponians, it doesn't get any better than Zappos.

P.S. Also, Hello Kitty Lovers unite at Zappos.com :)

Dail T.

employee since 2007

Zappos is always encouraging employees to grow and learn and we are given all the tools we need to achieve our goals. The Zappos Culture always puts a smile on my face and makes it a pleasure to come to work each day.

Dana C.

employee since 2007

Zappos is the best place that I've ever worked. I hope that I get to retire with this company and my Zappos family. :-)

Davy J.

employee since 2006

The Zappos Culture is unique. It brings the best out of everyone who works here and walks through our doors. I started back in October 2006 and each day has been AMAZING! My job isn't just a nine to five - clock in and out and on my merry way. I truly feel like this is my second family and I enjoy every second of being here. I could try to describe our culture till I am blue in the face, but I think I will leave you all with: Zappos Kicks A$$!!!

Deborah H.

employee since 2006

The Zappos Culture inspires. It inspires us to be better people. It inspires us to be better parents. It inspires us to be better listeners, to be better teachers. It inspires us to be a better company. The Zappos Culture inspires us to be better.

Deborah N.

employee since 2010

What does the Zappos Culture mean to me? Gosh, how do I explain it? It's a workplace full of humanoids, with energies that are positive and supportive in every way. It's the training, the atmosphere, the hard work and dedication that surround me. It's the growth potential, the education, the laughter and the entire HAPPY work environment. It all just blows my mind! I am grateful to be in a place that is so balanced yet crazy at the same time. What an amazing journey this has been for me so far, and I look forward to the ever-changing, ever-expanding journey ahead of us. Thank you Tony, Fred, Carl and Nick and Alfred too!

I am grateful to be in a place that is so balanced yet crazy at the same time. What an amazing journey this has been for me so far, and I look forward to the ever-changing, ever-expanding journey ahead of us. Thank you Tony, Fred, Carl and Nick and Alfred too!

Denise M.

employee since 2009

I find myself wanting to write about Zappos' Core Values again. To me, they are still basic rules to live by. I am still passionate and determined (a quality my dad once called stubborn), fun and weird and pursuing growth and learning. I have learned how to better embrace and drive change, build open and honest relationships with communication and to do more with less. All of these not just here at Zappos, but at home as well. To me, the Zappos Culture is also family. I have become so close with so many people. Zappos is my family. We share our stories, we laugh together, we cry together, we celebrate together and are more than just BFFs; we are family. And I love my family! ÊÊ(Attached is a picture of the lovely flowers my Zappos Family sent when I was recovering from surgery)

Derek C.

employee since 2007

A single person cannot define the Zappos Culture. Rather, it is a self-perpetuating concept that continues with each and every individual who contributes to it.

With everyone empowered to bring forward their own ideas, exude their different personalities and inspire others with their passions, the Zappos Culture grows stronger as we grow as individuals and, as the company grows as a whole.

Derek N.

employee since 2010

The Zappos Culture took me by surprise. When I joined the company in November 2010, I confess that I had a very skeptical and cynical view of corporate culture in general. I'd worked for other companies with similar value systems that were never present in the day-to-day work environment. It always seemed like everyone liked to talk about values but not live by them.

From my first day of training, I could actively see all Ten Core Values at play, not just in the general workplace but also in the way my peers did business. It was so foreign to me that a company would not just encourage my growth but also wouldn't want me to be anything but myself. The idea that they really want me to be my weird, nerdy and blue-haired self at work was amazing to me. Zappos represented all the things I didn't even know I was looking for in a company.

On a more personal level, the Zappos Culture also means a second chance at happiness in a new town. I moved to Vegas about five years ago, and frankly, I had always hated it. While I met tons of local people who were wonderful, there was nothing I was passionate about here. All of that changed when I began working for this company. Every day my fellow Zapponians teach me more about "the fourth C" ("Community") and the wonderful potential of the town Zappos calls home. I look forward to many more years of Delivering Happiness.

Diana M.

employee since 2010

To me, the Zappos Culture means opportunity; the opportunity to grow professionally as well as personally. The opportunity to be myself without fear of reprimand. The opportunity to speak with so many people from so many places and not feel hurried to finish any conversation. The opportunity to use each Core Value for work and at home in my personal life. Thank you, Zappos, for each and every opportunity!

Diana O.

employee since 2005

To me, the Zappos Culture is AMAZING! It's one of a kind in a warm, fuzzy, loving feeling kind of way. :) It's a culture of happiness and family love and values. It's a special Culture that we have worked hard to build and to love and protect, like a marriage. :)

After being here for five years, I still see it and can feel it. I see our Zappos Culture in the smiles on everyone's faces, the friendly hellos and the sincere "How are you doing today?" It's a great feeling knowing that I can come to work and not think of it as work. This is a home away from home. It's wonderful knowing that I can feel welcomed and protected in happiness and family. It's great to know that I work with a team, a family, that shares the same goals in life: success, happiness, and growth in whatever aspect that may be, both professional and personal.

The Zappos Culture is so many things that, honestly, it makes it difficult to pin down in words exactly what it is. Some may say it is family, values, honesty, openness, teamwork, joy, and determination. Others might say its motivation, a way of life, and love. But all in all, everyone is right. Our culture is motivating what we do and making us want to pass it on to everyone we encounter. Pay it forward. Our Culture is a way of life and family orientated and a determination to become the best we can be and to grow into anything our little hearts desire, either at work or in our personal life. However one might define it, our Culture truly is worth a thousand words, plus some, and I'm grateful that I get to experience it. If it weren't for our culture and Core Values, I think we wouldn't be who we are today. It has allowed us to grow into an amazing company with an amazing family and a future of abundant opportunities, and I can't wait to see what lies ahead!

Diane H.

employee since 2009

The Zappos Culture has become a part of my life. I love to live our Core Values. Not only do I utilize them in my daily life at Zappos, I have incorporated them into my personal life as well. I truly believe they have made me become a much better person. I thank Zappos for this unbelievable opportunity to bring such positive thoughts into my life. I LOVE ZAPPOS!

Dina D.

employee since 2010

Every time I walk into the Zappos offices, I do two things. First, I rub the jade pendant I purchased when I came to Las Vegas for my interview, and then I thank God, Buddha, and the universe for this amazing opportunity.

Zappos is the kind of company I've always dreamed of working for. It is a company that actually practices what it preaches when it comes to treating employees like family and their customers with respect, not like just another sale. This is the most positive and nurturing environment I've ever been part of. Here I'm encouraged to be myself with my co-workers and customers (thank goodness for Core Value #3) instead of sounding like a script-reading robot. If I could choose a theme song to express my feelings for Zappos, it would be Jennifer Holliday/Hudson's "And I Am Telling You, I'm Not Going." My journey towards employment with Zappos took me two years and 1800 miles (Core Value #9 to the maximum!) and six months later, I still end every text message to my mother with: "I love my job!"

Dominique S.

employee since 2010

The Zappos Culture means that I am empowered to make a difference! I am not only empowered at work, but in my everyday life Ñ to make an impact on my community, as well as on people around me.

For instance, I was at the mall one day and had just approached the entry to one of the department stores, when a woman started to come out. I stopped and took what was only a few seconds to hold open the door and she was so shocked. She said, "Thank you so much! I'll get the other door for you." She was taken aback by what should be common courtesy. However, in most people's daily lives, this is something that does not occur. My point is that it felt good to make an impact on someone, so much so that she too felt the desire to hold open the door for me. It is now a story that makes me feel warm and fuzzy to tell.

I hope who ever reads this book is inspired by our Zappos Culture. Maybe you will take what you learn to make a difference and have a positive impact in your life and your community!

Donna G.

employee since 2004

Zappos continues to amaze me after six years! With the tremendous growth of our company, we are still able to maintain our Zappos Culture. It contributes to the happiness and level of customer service we provide our customers and each other. It is a privilege and honor to say, "I work for Zappos."

Donna H.

employee since 2005

I can sum up how I feel about Zappos in two sentences: Without doubt, working at Zappos has been the second most enriching experience of my life to date. (The first was the birth of my daughter.) Nothing else comes close.

Donna P.
employee since 2010

My journey with Zappos has not just been the discovery of an amazing place to work, but a journey of self-discovery. The Ten Core Values. Goals. Sessions. Amazing, kind, hilarious co-workers/ FAMILY members. Mentors, ambassadors. Along the way, all of those things have helped me on my path to becoming the person that I am: happy, more compassionate, more patient and kinder to myself. After only eight months here, I know this is where I am supposed to be. I look forward to an amazing future with a company I love. I want to help it grow while keeping the Zappos Culture strong! And I will, with the help of the wonderful/crazy group of peeps that I have adopted as my Zappos family!

Duke C.
employee since 2005

To me, the Zappos Culture is about participating and contributing in efforts to further enhance the dynamic environment that we strive to preserve and grow. I'm grateful that I have the opportunity to work with passionate and creative individuals that really motivate, inspire and push me to my limits.

Dyan D.
employee since 2008

The Zappos Culture has meant everything to me for the past three years. It's what wakes me up and gets me to work and it's what helps me throughout the day. When you can laugh and smile through a phone call and realize that you made a difference in someone's day, or even walk through a store wearing a Zappos shirt and see people smile, it shows the culture is really contagious. I couldn't be any happier to have been accepted by my Zappos ÊÊfamily.

Dylan M.
employee since 2007

The Zappos Culture is a community effort that nourishes the best aspects of everyone it touches.

Ebony M.
employee since 2007

Okay, family is our thing. I will try to keep it short this year. I have gone from Ms. Ebony R. to Mrs. Ebony M., from a mother of two to a mother of three now, not to mention how a member of my Zappos family saved the day at my wedding! These are people that I work with every day, hang out with after work, and invite to life-changing events. Before I worked at Zappos I would never have invited a co-worker, lead, supervisor or manager to anything outside of work. Most companies are all business, which Zappos is as well, but we also have a family vibe going and we love to spend time together. As I have said for the previous three years, I love this place and would not want to be anywhere else.

Elisabeth B.
employee since 2010

I don't know any other company that gives employees the opportunity to truly go above and beyond for their customers. I love that we get customers who take the time out of their busy day to call back in and want to speak to the representative who made their day.

Zappos has given me a truly rewarding experience that I wouldn't be able to get anywhere else. Zappos has changed my life and I am happy to work with so many wonderful people here. Thank you to everyone here at Zappos!

:] ????? SONG TIME! ?????? ? D is for Dynamite ? M is for magical ? C is for cant be beat! ? R is for ridiculous, just like this song!

Strawberry Pretzel Salad:
• 2 cups crushed pretzels
• 3/4 cup butter, melted
• 3 tablespoons white sugar
• 1 (8 ounce) package cream cheese, softened
• 1 cup white sugar
• 1 (8 ounce) container frozen whipped topping, thawed
• 2 (3 ounce) packages strawberry flavored gelatin
• 2 cups boiling water
• 2 (10 ounce) packages frozen strawberries

Directions:
1. Preheat oven to 400 degrees F (200 degrees C). 2. Stir together crushed pretzels, melted butter and 3 tablespoons sugar; mix well and press mixture into the bottom of a 9x13 inch baking dish. 3. Bake 8 to 10 minutes, until set. Set aside to cool. 4. In a large mixing bowl cream together cream cheese and 1 cup sugar. Fold in whipped topping. Spread mixture onto cooled crust, 5. Dissolve gelatin in boiling water. Stir in still frozen strawberries and allow to set briefly. When mixture is about the consistency of egg whites, pour and spread over cream cheese layer. Refrigerate until set.

Efrain F.

employee since 2010

Zappos truly goes above and beyond to make all employees feel valued. Most places have the "just be glad you have a job" attitude, but not Zappos. I feel appreciated every single day for my hard work. Thank you all!

Eileen K.

employee since 2010

Culture is a way a life here at Zappos. It is something we put before everything else. It is the thing that sets us apart from everyplace else. We do so many amazing things here at Zappos, and everything that we do has to do with our culture. I love that our company believes in something so strongly. It's not just talk; it's the real deal!

Eileen S.

employee since 2009

Being at Zappos has had a positive effect on my life. It has made me a much happier person in general, both in and out of the workplace. And I have met many great friends here that I know I will keep for life. That alone is worth so much to me. What can I say? I love Zappos and wake up every day thinking how lucky I am to be part of such an amazing company. I can't imagine being anywhere else.

Erica P.

employee since 2011

Growing up, I was the weird kid. Zappos is a place where I feel comfortable being weird. Everyone here has their quirks and they are all proud of them. Every day, I feel encouraged to embrace others' weirdness as well as my own weirdness and to grow with it. It's an environment where people can just be themselves and that alone gets me pumped and excited to go to work every day. The many brilliant, unique people make the Zappos Culture and family unique.

Erik L.

employee since 2007

It won't surprise anyone familiar with our Ten Core Values, but the Zappos Culture means change. Every company goes through changes; people come and go, product lines expand into new areas, and processes get refined as people learn from experience. In the Zappos Culture, everyone expects change and welcomes it. I don't think there are many other companies that offer the internal mobility we do. If you have the will, the skill, the desire and the talent, you can go just about anywhere at Zappos.

Erika P.

employee since 2007

Unsolicited messages from my team members ...

"And you know that we love/like you to death! No one will ever be able to replace you ... and we will always hold you in the highest regard no matter what position you hold :)"

"I just wanted to say thanks for all that you do for us always, but especially today when I was not feeling very well. It really meant a lot to me that you went the extra mile to be concerned about my health, checked with scheduling for availability, got my trainee a better mentor today, gave me great advice on my attendance, adjusted my schedule/lunch, etc. When you're sick, you want to be pampered. Thanks Ômom' for taking care of me today!"

The Zappos Culture is about making the <3 *warm* and *fuzzy*!

Eva C.

employee since 2010

The Zappos Culture, to me, is the passion that everyone brings. Each of us brings a little spice to the culture. We are all a little different but the culture just wouldn't be the same without just that one person. I'm inspired by everyone, every day. Seeing the opportunities to grow here and the freedom to make it happen is amazing. Working with people who are really genuinely happy for your success is amazing. I love coming in to work every day to get a taste of everyone's spice and to add a little spice of my own!!

Faby G.

employee since 2005

Today is life - the only life you are sure of. Make the most of today. Get interested in something. Shake yourself awake. Develop a hobby. Let the winds of enthusiasm sweep through you. Live today with gusto. - Dale Carnegie

Gerald M.

employee since 2008

Working for Zappos is AMAZING! Just coming to work daily is an adventure and the day can go in so many different directions. Just last week, I got to go to a wine tasting during work! It certainly made the rest of that day fun and interesting. The best part is that whenever I feel any stress or pressure, I just think of previous jobs and circumstances and realize how lucky I am to be a part of this incredible organization. It immediately changes my attitude. Zappos tries to embrace everything and attempt to make it better, always taking good care of us with benefits and perks. I am proud to be a part of it all. Just a mention of whom I work for always brings delight and questions.

Last but certainly not least are all the amazing people that I get to call friends and co-workers, who inspire and motivate me!

Gina W.

employee since 2007

The Zappos Culture is second to none in the corporate world. One of my favorite things about working here is that we're encouraged to provide Open and Honest Communication (Core Value #6) through feedback. That is rare in corporate settings, in my experience. Also, if it's determined to be the best thing for the business, you'll see your feedback implemented.

I also love that we're focused on customer service and that we inspire other companies to value their employees like Zappos does. I LOVE Zappos and hope this is my last job EVER! =)

Giovanna W.

employee since 2007

Zappos has helped make my life sort of surreal! I am a bass player and vocalist who has traveled around the world singing and playing, performing my music. However, my life changed when my mom slipped through the veil from this life to the great beyond in 2006. Four months after that event, I started working here at Zappos, never thinking for one moment that I'd be here for more than a few months or so, or of how much of a part of my life Zappos would become.

Fast forward to four plus years, and I can only think of ways that I've been enriched here during that time. Even though I'm a musician/actress working as a customer service representative, Zappos still managed to find a way to bring my life as an entertainer into my everyday work life! "That's a nice deep fryer!" is what I exclaimed as the "Zappet Giovanna" in one of the many commercials they ran last year. How surreal did that become?! The laughter I experience with the customers it is my pleasure to serve is one thing that has pulled me from the grief of losing my mom to being the woman I am now, with laughter as an everyday staple served up in large proportions by the customers, Zappos and the co-workers who surround me.

My many thanks to Zappos for helping me become the me that I am!

Grace A.

employee since 2010

Zappos is not only life-changing, it's world-changing. It's a company that operates as all companies should operate. And it's nice to know that employees, customers and potential customers are given the recognition they deserve.

Our company cannot operate without our employees; happy employees mean happy customers, and happy customers mean a happier world. The Zappos world is one in which I enjoy living.

Gregory R.

employee since 2008

Culture here at Zappos means coming through the doors and seeing what America could have been, and also seeing the hope of what America can become with the opportunity to be part of a family filled with diversity. The sincere smiles, hugs and laughter that permeate the company (family) are the most important part of the Zappos Culture. I have been here since 2008. Being infused in the Zappos Culture has been the most enjoyable work experience I have ever had.

Harmoni S.

employee since 2010

How can I possibly express in this tiny space how much the Zappos Culture means to me? How do I convey how I feel like I'm a part of something bigger, that I belong to a community, that I'm connected to something? I have no idea.

Heather W.

employee since 2010

To me, the Zappos Culture means a lifestyle I can live by that makes me a better person. Here at Zappos, our lives are guided by Ten Core Values. By living these values we learn to make the best of almost any situation. We Do More With Less (Core Value #8). We become nicer, happier people. We ultimately become better people.

The Values encourage us to set goals and help us achieve them, not just in our work life but in home life as well. The Zappos Culture is the best thing that has ever happened to me personally and the customer-service industry as a whole.

Heather W.

employee since 2010

Zappos has been a blessing to me in more ways than one. When I started here I never could have imagined how much of an impact a new job could have on my life. The first time I read the Core Values, I thought, "That is what I already live by!" I just knew that this would be the start of something amazing. I have met people here that I know I will be my friends for my entire life. The support that I have gotten from fellow employees has been incredible. This has been true through though bad times, like when my father passed away, and good times, like when I got married and gave birth to my first child. I have grown as a person because of this place and the people here.

I now live wanting to constantly do the right thing, push myself to be better and do more to help others reach their full potential. I am better, and my family is better because of Zappos and all the opportunities that I have been given here. I cannot imagine working anywhere else and I believe that I will work at Zappos for the rest of my life.

Hector G.

employee since 2006

All I can say is that Zappos had changed my life forever. I am really honored to work for this great company. The Zappos Culture is unique and you can work and play at the same time.

Helen D.

employee since 2008

My favorite thing about working at Zappos is how well everyone gets along. That was my first impression of Zappos and it has lasted.

Helene T.

employee since 2008

It's been an awesome ride for me here at Zappos, one I'll never forget! I've learned to go after what I'm passionate about and go for the gold. Tony has taught by example, but most of all with his humility. I've built a special bond with my Zappos family throughout the years. It's a bond that will last a lifetime.

Holly F.

employee since 2006

After four years here, the Zappos' WOW continues. Working for a company that encourages self-expression and self-actualization is an immense blessing. All the pithy lines out there couldn't sum it up. Thank you for the tremendous growth opportunities and the co-workers that have become family, as well as for giving me the space to emulate Joseph Campbell by "following my bliss."

Holly K.

employee since 2007

To me, the Zappos Culture means getting to be the person I really am and the freedom to come to work in my PJs! :)

We're encouraged to be ourselves, which makes for an amazing work environment. Our Culture is what makes Zappos more than a job. We are empowered and told to run with it. I've seen our company change and grow and excel in my four years here, and none of this could have been done without our Culture.

Ingrid M.

employee since 2010

Zappos is just FABULOUS! It is an amazing company to work for. YAY, Zappos!

Izzy P.

employee since 2010

The Zappos Culture means a lot of different things to me. Barnabe Bear sitting on my desk and collecting random swag. Having yummy potlucks with butter mochi and jello cake. Not being afraid to try new things and new opportunities. Conversations over analyzing Glee and Pretty Little Liars. Randomly singing at my desk and my teammates joining in. Ten-pound bars of Toblerone and having a parade for it. Saying Justin Bieber is a reason to call 911 in a game of Scattergories. Wearing super-cute giraffe print shoes to work. But most of all, feeling blessed to come to work each day, calling Zappos my family, and experiencing a Culture that is rare.

Jackie W.

employee since 2010

I have always been a spiritual person, but being here at Zappos has taken me to a whole new level! I did not know there was a company/career/opportunity that existed in this world like Zappos. I'm so grateful for this opportunity! Zappos literally saved my family's life.

When I was allowed to step into this new world, I was surrounded by much love, allowed to be "off" a bit (being yourself on a scale of 1-10), was given the opportunity to grow mentally and professionally in my position, was given a feeling of importance and (did I say?) surrounded by a second group of people who gave much love, all in one place!! This is absolutely overwhelming! My family and I truly thank this company and I will continue to do my part to make sure that Zappos gets 100% of me until I'm 95 years old! (I'm not going home. LOL) :-)

Jackie Y.

employee since 2008

Being at Zappos for three years has been a unique experience. Words can't even explain how much my life has changed because of Zappos, not only professionally but also personally. I started here at age 19 and, in a sense, I feel Zappos and I grew up together. At this point, I thank Zappos for everything and for allowing me to grow with them. It's been an amazing ride and I'm glad to be a part of it. Our Zappos Culture is untouchable. The Core Values we have really bring us all together as a family. I look forward to the up-coming horizons for us!

Jaime S.

employee since 2007

I recently picked up a new hobby - photography! There are three C's that create a good photograph. They are color, clarity, and composition. You can take one away and still have a really good photograph, but if you have all three, your photograph will be groundbreaking!

The Zappos Culture is a lot like photography. I've learned that you can have Community involvement and good Customer service, but without Culture, that third C is missing. That leaves you with a good company or a decent photograph, but imagine what you could create with all three C's! You could change a company into a family or change a photograph into a fine piece of art! That's what the Zappos Culture means to me.

James D.

employee since 2010

The Zappos Culture is as unique and special as it is unorthodox and it is oftentimes misunderstood. I personally have found it to be life changing in and outside of the office. I encourage anyone unfamiliar with our Culture's practices to immerse themselves entirely in it and try to not come out a better person. One of the most important reasons our Culture works and is so fun and appealing to everyone is because we all believe in it and go out of our way to make it work, not only for ourselves but also for our co-workers and friends. We love our Culture because we are the Culture. :)

James H.

employee since 2009

I love the Zappos Culture. It is like working with your close friends and family. I would not give it up for the world! The Zappos Culture ROCKS !!!!!!!!!!!!!!!!!!

Jane J.

employee since 2005

The Zappos Culture is symbolized in a positive and happy way. It is all about the relationships and trust we share. The interactions between us daily, whether very brief or lengthy, help us continue to grow our Zappos family. The energy at Zappos has changed my outlook on life and has enhanced it to a point that is richer and fuller. It has been a real treat for me to spread the love of Zappos!

Janet P.

employee since 2009

I love the EMPOWERMENT I am given here at Zappos. I am trusted to make my own decisions when it comes to taking care of our customers. This allows me do my job peacefully and harmoniously. It's a great feeling to know that your opinion really matters.

Our voices are heard at Zappos. We receive surveys about almost everything that happens in this company. They take our thoughts and opinions into consideration, and many decisions are made based on them. Other companies I have worked for in the past were more like dictatorships. "Do what we say or else!" "Your opinion means nothing!" Thank you, Zappos for always hearing me out.

Since I've been a part of the Zappos family, I have learned that a great way to "Build a Positive Team and Family Spirit" (Core Value #7) is with FOOD! Potlucks to be exact. I would love to share a recipe for you to enjoy:

Super Duper Fast & Easy New Mexico Chili
- 4 cups unsalted beef or vegetable stock
- 4 to 5 small red onions
- 4 cloves garlic, chopped
- 4 cups kernel corn
- 4 to 6 fresh jalapeno peppers, sliced
- 2 (28-ounce) cans crushed tomatoes
- 2 (16-ounce) cans kidney beans, drained
- 3 tablespoons chili powder
- 2 lbs lean ground beef or turkey (or you can omit for veggie chili)
- 1 cup shredded Monterey jack cheese

Heat a large dutch oven over medium heat. Brown meat with onion and jalapenos. (Save some fresh red onion and jalapeno slices for a garnish.) Add tomatoes, garlic, beans, chili powder, corn and the stock. Lower heat and simmer for 30 minutes. (This can also be made in a crock-pot and slow-cooked for 4 hours). Season to taste with salt and pepper. Ladle the chili into serving bowls and sprinkle with cheese, onion, and jalapeno slices. Serve it HOT! Makes 12 servings.

Jasmine K.

employee since 2006

If you asked me five years ago what the Zappos Culture meant to me, I'd look at you as if you were crazy and not know how to answer. But that all changed the moment I set foot in Zappos. Although we've grown quite a bit since I started, one thing definitely remains true ... our company's Culture is like no other. It's really hard to put into words how dynamic and special our Culture is. It's something you have to experience - see, feel, be part of. So for any of you reading this who haven't come by for a tour, what are you waiting for? I promise it will be a breath of fresh air and something you've never experienced before. :-)

Jean D.

employee since 2006

The Zappos Culture is amazing. It has changed me and made me more aware of what I am doing and saying, even when I am not at work. It has brought out the fun and creativity in me. I love working here! I love the balance of fun and work - something that most companies have no idea about. I can't wait to see what the future holds for Zappos. Every day I tell myself how lucky I am! Thank you for letting me share this amazing journey with you all!!

Jeffrey L.

employee since 2006

I love you, Zappos. Thank you! 'Nuff said.

Jen B.

employee since 2010

I <3 Zappos! :D

The Zappos Culture means
- considering co-workers friends and family
- having a Lunch Buddy
- knowing stuff :)
- being more than happy to help
- WOWing the socks off people
- building pyramids for your friends
- sharing your overly absurd laughter
- cutting hair for Lucy, Daryl, and Vivica
- painting pottery dragons
- being okay with letting people know the real you!

I feel blessed to be employed with a company that sees Culture as a keystone.

Jenn D.

employee since 2009

I feel truly blessed to work for a company like Zappos! The amazing Zappos Culture that has been cultivated here has made me a happier person, both at work and in my personal life. When you first step inside, you are treated like part of a family ... a very quirky family, but a family nonetheless!

Jennifer M.

employee since 2007

The thing I love about Zappos is the freedom to be yourself. Keep rockin' it!

Jennifer G.

employee since 2010

To me, the Zappos Culture means having an amazing workplace that you walk into every single day, and not being upset that you are going to work. You have a family here, not just a job. You love talking to your customers and your co-workers. When I heard about all the great things about Zappos before I worked here, I thought to myself "I want to work there! They have an amazing Culture, a positive team and a family spirit!" Almost like love at first (web)site!

Jennifer T.

employee since 2011

I am blessed beyond measure to be working in a company that values ME as much as I value them. I truly feel appreciated and heard. I am encouraged regularly to think beyond today. I have been here a grand total of six weeks and I'm having the time of my life! I'm so happy to put to use the customer service skills I've developed over the years. I am making fast friends of all my co-workers. I can't help but smile when I think of my new Zappos family.

I love the Zappos Culture. It is realized when we are all allowed the freedom to be ourselves. Zappos allows me to participate in being a part of this culture just by being myself. I love our Ten Core Values, as they reflect all that I love, know, and promise to live by as a Christian.

Thank you, God, for bringing me to Zappos!!

Jennifer W.

employee since 2007

"Home is not where you live, but where they understand you." - Christian Morgenstern

Jenny A.

employee since 2010

I walk through the same double doors five days a week. You might think that this could get old, but it's absolutely not the case. Once inside those doors, my senses go into complete overdrive. First, I'm swept inside by a blast of air that fosters my abilities. I can hear the buzz of a contagious energy that engages my mind and encourages my potential. I can see the cohesive nature in which we all come together that inspires me to do more. Lastly, I can taste the endless supply of Red Bull and the savory smells that float up from the bistro that fuel my body. Zappos gives me the opportunity for success, growth and reaching a potential that I never knew possible. Thank you, Zappos, and thanks to all the people that built you.

Jess L.

employee since 2010

The Zappos Culture is walking into the building and feeling at home. While walking through, you are saying hello to all your friends and family, giving a great big smile that will hopefully be contagious.

Jessica B.

employee since 2006

I've been working at Zappos for five years and I have to say, we're family. Every day, I say hi to people in the hallway, and being able to confide in my co-workers means a lot. I like coming to work. I want to work hard and help propel our company forward. We work hard together and we have a great time doing it. Together as a team - I think that's the driving force behind the Zappos Culture.

Jessica C.

employee since 2010

The Zappos Culture is being able to have a desk that looks like the Hello Kitty section of the Sanrio store without people thinking you're weird. It's being able to wear your UNLV Rebels t-shirt any day of the week just because you can. It's going through the whole day in wet clothes because you participated in a water balloon fight on your lunch break with your classmates. It's futilely attempting to slide an Oreo cookie from your forehead to your mouth while playing Minute to Win It and not being at all embarrassed about it. It's decorating your friends' desks for birthdays, weddings, promotions, etc. It's a place where the supervisors sit behind you and sing songs in Spanish (which they're currently doing). Pretty rad. These are all things that most companies wouldn't allow you to do, but are all things that Zappos encourages. I could go on and on, really, but the point is that the Zappos Culture has completely changed my life and I'm so grateful for the new relationships that I build here, every single day.

Jessica F.

employee since 2007

To me the Zappos Culture really is about service and sticking by the Ten Core Values. I've been with the company over three years now and I am still amazed at how dedicated Zappos is to their customers and employees.

I've had jobs with other retail places in the past and was always limited by policies or "managers on duty" for approval to get the customers what they need. At Zappos, I love being empowered to do what is best for our customers without the hassle or wait. I love that we are encouraged to think outside the box and get to know our customers. And I absolutely love coming into work and being surrounded by my Zappos family!

Jessica K.

employee since 2009

O.k., let me start by saying ... Zappos is not a job, it's a family!! I have met some of my best friends at Zappos and I continue to meet more. I am very lucky to not only have a job in this economy, but also to work for such an awesome company!! I am lucky to have met some of the nicest people in Vegas and to have made such awesome connections. Zappos allows us to be ourselves (which is amazing). I don't have to hide my tattoos :) Thanx, Zappos! Rock on!!

Jessica O.

employee since 2005

The Zappos Culture is definitely different than any other company I've worked for. This is the company I have worked for the longest in my entire career. I'm ecstatic that this ever-evolving company Culture is consistently making everyone and their ideas feel welcome.

Jessica P.

employee since 2009

The Zappos Culture means being my fun and a little weird self even at work! Whether it's nerf gun wars, glitter bombs, Easter baskets for Nevada Children's Cancer Foundation, writing messages on the culture Wall, building castles around co-worker's desks, peeps (the candy) shows, Project Mayhem, and the list goes on and on. It's building meaningful relationships with our co-workers through fun and weird events. It's pooling our resources and donating to causes we believe in. It's what keeps us coming back to work each and every day, because work here isn't like work at all. We get to hang out with our family, WOW customers and (at the end of the day) be the best person that we can be, inside and outside of Zappos.

Jewel R.

employee since 2007

Our Zappos Culture is truly transforming! What I mean is that it has changed the way I conduct myself personally, even outside of the Zappos walls. I've become more service-oriented and humble, more excited to learn and grow, more passionate about having fun and doing the things I love. It's a motivating place to work.

Zappos WOWs not only our customers but me as well. I am very thankful to be a part of this company! Four years and counting, baby!

Jim C.

employee since 2006

When I joined the Zappos family in 2006, the only thing I knew about Zappos from my initial visit and interview was that there was something special going here and I wanted to be a part of it! Once I started, I received nothing but support, encouragement and complete acceptance. I was home! For the first 25 plus years of my working life, I never even thought about company culture because it didn't exist! Coming home to Zappos and being a part of this family made me feel as if I could achieve anything!

Right out of training, I sat down with my first team leader and shared my goals with him. To my delight, a flood of support and guidance helped me to reach my goals. The support and guidance has never stopped, even after almost five years! I'm so proud to work at Zappos. I love my Zappos family and all I want to do is give back all of the encouragement and support I received. I'm also proud to say that both of my sons have joined the Zappos family, so my happiness is complete! Thank you, Zappos!

Jim G.

employee since 2005

I'm approaching six years at Zappos and it's never felt so good! I started working here when I was 19 years old and it's good to say that I've grown into who I am today due to Zappos. Zappos is more than a job, it's a way of life. What's to come this year?!

Jina B.

employee since 2011

Considering it has only been about six weeks since I've started with Zappos, you would think I wouldn't have much input to contribute in regards to the Zappos Culture. And you'd be totally and utterly WRONG.

It's amazing how much I've learned and experienced in just six short weeks. LESS than six weeks, 38 days to be exact (yes, I actually counted ... and it took me a while because, contrary to popular belief, not all Asians are good at math. Is counting even considered math???).

So, it's been 38 days and I haven't even gotten out of incubation yet but I can already see how much the Zappos Culture is affecting my personal life. The culture, for me, really shined through in our New Hire Training class. Our class was probably (and easily) one of the most inappropriate, crude, loving, caring, wild, and intensely bonded classes that Zappos has ever seen. I know that is a lot to claim, but we really were quite the group. Just ask our trainers. In the four weeks we spent together we became a true family. We were there for each other through birthdays, deaths, legal matters, breakups, hookups, drunken mishaps, and so much more.

In that time and in the days since we graduated, my class (and everyone else I've met here) continues to WOW me; drives me to change; allows me to be fun and even a little weird; makes me adventurous, creative, and open-minded; drives me to pursue personal growth; allows me to build open and honest relationships; has helped me build a positive family-like spirit; taught me to do more with less; showed me how to be passionate; and shown me the art of humility. And that was just 38 days!! There is still so much more to come and I can't wait until I lose count.

Jo L.

employee since 2007

What I continue to love about the Zappos Culture is that it is has each of our unique stamps upon it. We start with our Core Values (which, by the way, were made up from input from the employees rather than top-down). We are then free to use our imaginations to interpret and express ourselves! I've never had Tony or anyone tell me how to express the Zappos Culture. When I remember the times I've given input or listened to others give ideas, we just took up a torch and ran on the fuel of our own inspiration. Fun stuff. :D

What is the Zappos Culture? It's each of us. :)

John B.

employee since 2010

The word culture comes from the Latin cultura, stemming from the verb colere, meaning "to cultivate." Here at Zappos, it truly is the employees who carry the burden to drive and cultivate our Culture. The really fun thing is that sometimes the drive to change the Zappos Culture spills over to other things in life. Maybe you feel the need to volunteer for a good cause, or maybe you desire improvement in your struggling city, or maybe you wish to simply change peoples' daily moods for the better. Do it! Holla!

John D.

employee since 2005

I can't believe it's been over five years since I started working for Zappos. Both Zappos and I have changed quite a bit since my first day. One thing that has not changed is that at-home feeling I get every time I walk in the front door. Family and friends and, of course, excellent service is the glue that keeps us all together.

A wise man once said that one person can make a difference but together we can change the world. I believe this because I for one can feel the impact of positive change! It's great to be part of the Zappos family. Maybe next year you can join us!

John K.

employee since 2009

I've been with Zappos since November of 2009, and the most amazing thing to me is how working here has changed almost every facet of my life. When you go through training, they tell you that your outlook will change and that your interactions outside work will be different, but it's hard to believe. Then, after working here for a while, you start to realize that leaving work every day feeling proud, or happy, or even just leaving work not stressed out infiltrates your interactions with everyone else in your life. You find yourself smiling more. Suddenly, you have more patience and empathy in situations that may have previously riled you.

After working as part of the FACE team that helps answer Tony's emails, I found out that this doesn't just happen to employees. The customer that had an awesome experience talking to us may pay that happiness forward. The businessperson that watched Tony speak may take what he said to heart, and try to make his business a happier place. It fills me with pride to know that what we're doing is more than just selling shoes; we're Delivering Happiness, one person at a time, and I get to be a part of that.

John M.

employee since 2010

What the Zappos Culture means to me is freedom and responsibility at the same time. It is the freedom to be myself and to grow as an individual by developing my work skills and building personal relationships along the way. Along with that freedom comes the cherished responsibility to make sure this Culture stays successful and our company thrives. Our Culture is almost an organic, living entity. What is happening here has improved my life outside of work, because it has encouraged me to use our Core Values on a personal level. This has strengthened my relationship with my family and improved the way I approach strangers and people I meet throughout my days.

Jonathan L.

employee since 2007

The Zappos Culture has been exciting lately! Over the last year, my relationships with many of my friends have become stronger, and I've had a bunch of really, really cool experiences. But what's really exciting is how palpable the sense of higher purpose has become. For one, Zappos Insights has been growing as people and organizations are more and more interested in Delivering Happiness as a business model. So awesome! The move downtown though ... that will be amazing! I'm excited to see how we affect the area, and I'm looking forward to spending more time out there! This is going to be a great time to be a part of the Zappos family.

Josh P.

employee since 2008

When I'm asked where I work and what I do, I find myself at a loss of words. It's hard to describe Zappos to people without looking like a liar. To be completely honest, I think it is hard for people to believe that a place like this really exists. I've learned a lot over the past few years while being a part of the Zappos family but, most important, I have learned that I have a voice and my opinion counts. I appreciate learning this at Zappos because I've applied it here at work and also in my personal life. Zappos helps me grow more and more each year and I'm really grateful for being a part of such a wonderful team.

Joseph R.

employee since 2010

I have been at Zappos for six months and I am still as excited as I was on my first day in training. When I applied for employment at Zappos I was unsure what my workday would be like and tried to keep an open mind about what tasks I would be asked to perform. What I did bring to Zappos was a dream. My dream was to work in an environment where ideas and creative thinking were encouraged and where those ideas would never be snubbed by an oppressive, hierarchical management. My dreams have come true, more vividly than I ever could have hoped. There are no closed doors here. There are no lengthy forms or reports that need to be submitted for review if you want to change something. We are empowered to take our ideas as far and as high as we wish and have readily available assistance on the way. How wonderful and rare it is to work for a company that supports and thrives on the success of its employees, not only on a professional level but on a deeply personal level as well. It's called the Zappos family and it's not just lip service.

Here's a scavenger hunt to see if you really work somewhere special. Collect the following: A ride to work tomorrow. A warm hug. A slice of homemade cake. A toy elephant. Some help moving furniture. Someone to go to a movie with. A random object from the CEO's desk. Someone willing to let you shave his head bald. A hand puppet. A round of applause. Someone who would trade shirts with you. A toy Oscar statue. And 100 high fives. At Zappos, all this would take less than ten minutes!

Judy A.

employee since 2010

The Zappos Culture is contagious! It's not just a Culture, it's a way of life! Customers and other companies are amazed at how we can be professional, efficient and still have fun at work. (We don't see Zappos as just a workplace, but that's the general idea out there.)

We can be a little weird, creative, be ourselves, and get the job done while spreading our contagious happiness around. It's really great!

Julez Z.

employee since 2010

I love my Zappos life. It has truly changed me. Where else can I pursue my true love as a makeup artist but also spend time with our awesome customers? The Zappos Culture means freedom to grow, knowledge that we gain from our peers and our company, and understanding that it's OK to make mistakes; we learn from them. We love what we get from our Zappos family: creativity being fed, needs being met both personally and professionally. ÊTLAÊ Zappos Fam!

Joselito H.

employee since 2010

The Zappos Culture reminds of me the Tardis. If you're wondering what exactly a Tardis is, it is an amazing machine that can take you through time and space. On the outside the Tardis looks like an old English Police call box, but on the inside it is larger than all three of our buildings. It contains bedrooms, bathrooms, kitchens, pools, closets, libraries and so much more. It has everything you can think of and even those things you can't think of. Every day with the Tardis is a different experience. It can be crazy, it can be boring, it can be frustrating, it can be amazing. Every day is always different and always memorable. Now as amazing as the Tardis can be for a machine, it can also understand and change. The Tardis isn't just an object, it is a dynamic force that can change lives. The Tardis is awesome to have in your life. That is what the Zappos Culture means to me.

Justin 'Jay' A.

employee since 2009

Working at Zappos is truly incredible and the Zappos Culture is everything to us. We're not your average corporate office/call center. We mix play thoroughly into our work. One of my favorite unusual things is that we had a giraffe at one of our vendor parties. A REAL FREAKIN' GIRAFFE! You can read all the entries in the book and articles you can find, but you really can't understand it until you see it in person. Yes, that's my secret way of telling you to take a tour of our awesome office.

It's been a quick year and a half since I started working here but I've grown so much as a person and I've become totally part of the Zappos family!

Justin F.

employee since 2009

Zappos has meant more to me every year that I have been here. I have been given a huge opportunity to continue to grow and learn at this company. I never thought that this would be my third entry into our Culture Book.

Since the last time I wrote my entry, so much has happened for the good. There is still no company out there that I can remember that does what we do. I get to come to work and be with close friends and be a part of something that is different and amazing. I have had people simply smile at me because of the place I work. We have an ability to share our Zappos Culture with all the different people we come in contact with over the phone, email or just shopping at a store. I defiantly continue to believe that this will be my last place of employment. I get to learn every day, get into eating competitions, and who knows what will be in store for me until next year? I love this place.

Justin H.

employee since 2009

I feel like I could write volumes on the Zappos Culture, but I'll keep it brief: To me, our culture is the most important thing we have. It's what binds us all together as a family. It's what enables us to be the best at what we do, and at the same time it's what motivates us to improve and evolve. It keeps us grounded. It's a way of life more than anything. Without the Zappos Culture, we'd be just another company. We wouldn't have the amazing collection of happy people that work here day in and day out. Being at Zappos has brought me more amazing experiences and life-long friends than I can count. I can't imagine being anywhere else.

Kandis Y.

employee since 2010

The past year has been pretty amazing. In April 2010 I packed my bags and moved from my comfy home in Northern California to try out a new adventure here in Las Vegas with Zappos. I wouldn't change it for anything. In the past year I have learned a great deal about myself and grown as a person. I used to think I was happy, but I have found a new level. I have built some amazing relationships that I am so thankful for.

Though I miss my family back home, I have found another family I didn't even know I had. Friends that no matter where we go I will always appreciate. Every day I consider myself lucky. I am very thankful to be a part of Zappos and look forward to the next round of adventures.

Kara H.

employee since 2008

I have worked for a few companies that had a business culture, but until I started working at Zappos, I had no idea what having a company culture actually meant. Not only is the Zappos Culture something to work by, you also start living by it when you are not at work. After working for Zappos for about three years, this Culture has become part of my everyday life. What gets me is when people visit our office and take the tour; the response that we get about their experience is incredible. When they talk about how much fun they had experiencing our culture and how they plan to go back to their businesses and start to incorporate what they learned, it makes me feel really good to be a part of it all.

Karen H.

employee since 2011

ZAPPOS!!! It is such an amazing place. My journey with Zappos started in March 2011. On my first day, I was extremely nervous. What should I wear? What would it be like?

Each and every person that I have met at Zappos has been kind, supportive and funny. I already consider all of the people that I have been in contact with family. Long-time Zappos employees kept saying they were waiting for the other shoe to drop when they first started working at Zappos, but it never has. Even though I have been with the company a short time, I can confidently say that I do not believe the other shoe will ever drop.

Kari Z.

employee since 2007

What can I say? Zappos is amazing! I have grown up with the company. I started working here when I was 19 years old and almost four years later, I can say that I am still happy and even more WOWed than I have ever been before!

Over the years, Zappos continues to give to employees and always asks for our input. What do we want? What do we think should change? Why and how? Ultimately, we are given the freedom to communicate openly about everything that happens here. The happiness that we create within our work environment immediately translates to the work we do, both with our co-workers and customers. My favorite thing about my job is coming into work, knowing that we have a warm, welcoming environment and that everybody is willing to do his or her part. There is no doubt in my mind that our company will continue to flourish with our same goal in mind: Delivering Happiness!

Karla C.

employee since 2010

For me, the Zappos Culture means that I know every day when I get to work I will be greeted by smiling faces, sounds of laughter and happy people who are not only my co-workers but also my family. I know that I can lean on all of my team members and management for support. Zappos gives me the opportunity to be myself, progress at my own pace, and dream big. This is a Culture of happiness, growth, friendship, and dreaming. There is never a bad day at work when you work at Zappos!

Karla D.

employee since 2010

WOW!!!! I have made it a full year since starting at Zappos and it seems like it was just yesterday. This place is truly like family, with everyone always willing to lend a hand or an ear. It is amazing to be able to be yourself every day and be around people that care.

Zappos is all about customer service. We strive to make this company the best it can be. I am so grateful to be able to work here. Thank you, Tony!! Thank you, Zappos!!

Katheryn G.

employee since 2007

What can I say? I love Zappos. I have been here for over three years and Zappos just gets better with time.

Kathy R.

employee since 2010

I love working at Zappos. I've been here for a little over a year now and It's been a wonderful experience. It feels great to work for a company that makes life easy, and it also makes our customers very HAPPY! I love my Zappos FAMILY! I enjoy every minute of my day!

Katie P.

employee since 2011

To me, the Zappos Culture means everything. What other company can you work for that encourages you to bend the rules? I can honestly say that this is the ONLY job that I look forward to coming to. When my alarm goes off at five in the morning I actually want to get up and not hit snooze 10 times. This is the only company that has encouraged me to be me, encouraged me to do WHATEVER it takes to make the customer happy, and the only company that makes me feel like I'm actually a part of a family.

Kelli A.

employee since 2010

To me, the Zappos Culture means that I'm not only providing service at work, I'm also treating everyone outside of Zappos in a way that makes them feel WOWed by me. I think it's super-important to remember that the way we behave and treat others (good or bad) is always noticed! Also, the Zappos Culture means I can be my silly self and nobody will think I'm weird ... Well, maybe just a little!

Kelly W.

employee since 2010

This is my first year being able to contribute to the Zappos Culture Book, as I have only been with Zappos a little over a year. It would be an understatement to say that I have so many things I would like share about how the Zappos Culture has affected me personally, but it would be at least five pages long! So, after writing many versions of this entry, I have finally decided to share just one story that I feel is a prime example of how amazing and life-changing our Zappos Culture is.

Around my seventh month of employment, I was hearing about some new program the company was rolling out call "Wishez." There were rumors going around that this program would allow any employee to make any kind of wish they wanted. It sounded ... well ... a little unreal. Since I had been around just long enough to know that Zappos was the kind of place where "unreal" things happened, I started seriously thinking about what I would wish for if I could wish for anything. When the program was rolled out, I got on the site, and made my wish. Let me tell you, it was a doozie! I was going to move my 18-month old son and me into our own home. I had almost no furniture and, as a single mom, buying new wasn't really an option for me. So I wished for furniture. To be honest I thought maybe someone would donate a used couch or something like that to me. Never in a million years did I anticipate Zappos taking me shopping to furnish my entire condo! Yes, that's what I said ... the whole SHEBANG!

Zappos had already made my life amazing and now I can honestly say they changed my entire life. They helped me provide the kind of home my son deserves. That is what the Zappos Culture represents to me!

Kellye T.

employee since 2010

Zappos has been such an amazing blessing for me. I am so grateful to work for a place where I come in and leave with a smile on my face every day. I have been fortunate enough to have created many life-long relationships and plan to make many more during my adventure! Zappos' Ten Core Values have not only helped my growth as an employee but also as a person. The Zappos Culture is apparent on a daily basis in random acts of kindness and cracking jokes all the time, which really makes our Culture unique. Zappos will always have a special place in my heart and I can never give enough thanks. Thank you Zappos, friends, and customers. You truly rock!! Peace and Love.

Kelsey W.

employee since 2010

There are not enough words in the English language to express how amazing Zappos is or how grateful I am to work here. Since I started, everyone has been welcoming and I felt comfortable from the first time I walked through the doors. Working for Zappos is a different experience from other companies. No two days are the same and it is definitely not a job I dread coming to in the morning. The people I've met have truly been the most genuine, kind-hearted people in the universe, and they have really become great friends. I love Zappos and all of the people, experiences, and knowledge I have gained from working here!

Kevin K.

employee since 2010

To me, the Zappos Culture is all about creating the happiest environment in the world for our employees, our vendors and our customers. We're encouraged to be who we are. We are encouraged to be different. It's a rare thing to find. To me, the Zappos Culture is about being more than just part of a company, it's also about being part of a family. I come into work every day excited to see the people I work with because they all hold a very special place in my heart. That's what Zappos and its Culture is all about.

Kevin T.

employee since 2008

As years go by it gets harder to write these Culture Book entries without saying the same things I said in previous years. Zappos is my family now. I spend more time with everyone here than with my own family. Thank goodness my wife works here or I would hardly get to see her. (LoL!)

On a serious note, I have always liked how supportive everyone here is. No matter if it is work-related or not, someone always has something positive to tell you. They are also there to help push you to step out of your box and do things you didn't think you could have done. Overall, this has been the best company I have ever worked for.

KMac

employee since 2007

I remember when I first got the job at Zappos my mom kept telling me it was too good to be true. We both kept waiting for reality to set in. It never happened. The crazy thing is that it just keeps getting better!! I've been here for almost four years and I can't believe that every year I seem to be happier ... What?!?! Now I have family and friends that work here and my mother is next on the list, haha!

Kristen F.

employee since 2010

"We are all a little weird and when we find someone who's weirdness is compatible with ours, we join up and fall in a mutual weirdness and call it love." - Dr. Seuss. That's what the Zappos Culture is all about!

I caught Zappos fever the first day I walked into training and I've never looked back or thought twice about it. Whether I'm at work, or not, I live my life by our Core Values; living and breathing these values within our office is what makes us one big, ridiculously happy family. In the short time that I've been at Zappos I've built some of best and strongest friendships with my co-workers. They aren't just people I enjoy seeing and talking with at work, they're the same people I'll call to spend time with on my days off. I love and respect Zappos and the Culture we live by because they teach us to respect people for who they are and what we can accomplish as a whole.

P.S. I LOVE ZAPPOS!!

Lacie J.

employee since 2010

After thinking about the Zappos Culture, no other job I've had has such a culture. Usually it's just clock in, work and clock out, no contributions. I left daily feeling unfulfilled and dissatisfied with how business was handled (or not handled). Now I come to work knowing I have the power to help people and make them happy. If I can make people laugh or smile even for just two minutes out of their day, goal achieved. What is more rewarding than that? We are encouraged to have fun while working at the same time. We work hard and play harder. I love it! I'm thankful to be a part of the Zappos family!

Lailonnie H.

employee since 2008

Recipe for Zappos Culture: One teaspoon of "greatness," one positive attitude and personal motivation, a sense of purpose and direction = 100% job satisfaction. One half a cup of humble pie, three full cups of honesty and integrity. A willingness to learn at work. Unlimited amounts of "confidence and higher self esteem." One cup of gratitude, a focus on giving rather than receiving and making others feel valued and appreciated.

Laura C.

employee since 2007

I fell in love with Zappos from day one. Four years later I am still in love. I have had many opportunities here and have met many wonderful people who I now consider friends and family. This is my home away from home and I am truly happy to wake up every morning, loving my job. <3

Laura M.

employee since 2005

The Zappos Culture, to me, means that you enjoy your day not just at home but at work. You are among family and friends.

Laura S.

employee since 2010

I love it here at Zappos! The people I have meet here have become true friends in the short time I have been here. We are a family, we go through ups and downs together. I am currently working the 4:00 am to 1:00 pm shift and I enjoy getting up every morning to come into work. I know that it is going to be a fun-filled day, all the while being able to WOW our customers. I like the ability to give my all to my customers and if I can make them laugh or smile, it makes my whole day. I have never worked at a place like this. If other companies were run like Zappos, there would be a lot more happy people in the world!

Lauren "eLGato" G.

employee since 2009

Zappos is AMAZING! Throughout my journey here, I've had the opportunity to meet people from all over the company, all of who have diverse backgrounds. Each of us has a story. What's striking about each of our stories is the common thread that we all share - Zappos saved us from something else in our lives. To me, the Zappos Culture is everything: It dictates who we are as a business and it shapes who we are as individuals. Being a part of such an amazing movement makes me want to be a better person each and every day. I mean, how many other things in our lives can we actually say that about? Zappos does that for me and I am truly blessed to have the opportunity to express my gratitude.

Lauren C.

employee since 2006

Each year I can honestly say that I am growing into a more well-rounded person thanks, in large part, to the growth and development that I am gaining every day from working for this AMAZING company. I have worked for Zappos for five years now and, looking back at who I was and who I have become, I am very proud of the person I have evolved into. I have always felt that our Core Values were ones that I shared outside of work. However, living and breathing them every day has challenged me to take my relationships to a new level outside of Zappos as well as here at work. I am so thankful for the life lessons learned and I believe the friendships I have developed here at Zappos will last me a lifetime. I look forward to the next five years and beyond, and I can't wait to meet the new me.:)

Lauren E.

employee since 2010

Here at Zappos, we are encouraged to be true to ourselves. On any given day, you can find an expression of this walking past our decorated cubicles or listening as we greet our customers. We have many different people here from all walks of life, and we are all part of this fun, weird family. We work and play together and I can personally say that I have met many kindred spirits. We laugh and have fun, but we are all here to deliver WOW and take pride in what we do. I have never worked in a place like this, and I can't wait to see what happens next. It's a wild ride!!!

Lauren P.

employee since 2006

I have been with Zappos for the past five years and it has been the best five years of my life. Zappos has completely changed me as a person and I have made many lifetime friends that I am grateful for. When I first started working here, I was a very shy person and I always had a hard time making friends. With each passing year, I have become less and less shy and really started coming out of my shell. I have had the privilege of working with some really great teams within CLT and have gained a great deal of knowledge working with each one.

I will be leaving Zappos to attend graduate school in San Francisco this coming January and I want to reflect on what makes the Zappos Culture different from any other company. From the minute I walked through the door on my first day, I felt like I belonged here. I didn't ever feel judged and I believe that everyone accepts others for who they are. I always come into work with a smile on my face and never dread my work day. The countless Zappos events I have attended over the years have allowed me the opportunity to meet new people, make new friends and reconnect with friends I already have. The Zappos Culture is something that sets us apart from other companies. It's not often that you will walk into an office and find that everyone working there is happy. At Zappos you will find just that - individuals all around the office who genuinely love their job. I will be forever grateful to have worked for a company like Zappos and am glad that I was able to witness the culture that we strive for.

Lesley L.

employee since 2011

As a brand new employee I'm struck by how completely genuine, friendly, encouraging and fun everyone is at Zappos. I've yet to ask for help and not receive multiple offers of assistance. The Zappos Culture is zany, fun and very hardworking, but also one that really embraces differences in personalities, ages, and skill levels, thought processes, and ideas! I can honestly say that I've never experienced anything like it before anywhere. I'm definitely lovin' it!!

Letha M.

employee since 2007

It has been three years and I still continue to be WOWed on a daily basis by my co-workers, customers and the company. What an awesome feeling it is to get up each day looking forward to coming to work.

Lillian H.

employee since 2010

The Zappos Culture has truly been life changing. I have never had a job that I was actually excited to go to until I started at Zappos. Gone are the days of knots in my stomach while driving to work! I feel this vibe of positive energy when I walk through the doors, and I feel like I'm part of something special. Zappos lets you be yourself, no matter how odd or silly you are! When I started working here, it was as if everything else in my life started falling into place. When I'm in a great mood, great things seem to happen, and even if great things aren't happening, I'm able to look at things with a positive perspective. I've cried here, laughed here and loved here. I cannot imagine where I would be without my Zappos family.

Linda H.

employee since 2006

I owe Zappos so much for the happiness in my life. Many of my personal goals have been reached because I became part of this family. I think "family" best describes my part in this group of people. I'm so happy to see what good things will come in my life. I'm afforded so many things here. The list is endless. Expect big changes outta me! Go Zappos!

Linda R.

employee since 2007

Core Value #7: "Build a Positive Team and Family Spirit." That means being tolerant and kind to others. Listening attentively and silently to each other. Being non-judgmental and open to different opinions and points of views. These are the things it takes to be a great team member and build a positive family spirit. At Zappos, we all respect each other and build relationships upon our differences.

Lisa H.

employee since 2006

Ever since I started at Zappos, I knew it was a great place to work. From Day 1, you are supported in whatever career path you choose to take. Zappos has become a second family to me. This became very apparent to me early in 2011. In January, my daughter gave birth to my first grand-daughter. My Zappos family gave me cards and gifts for the baby and offers of baby-sitting. Everything was going great. Then in February, my father was rushed to the hospital and was not expected to make it. My Zappos family surrounded me with love and concern. My lead and supervisor told me that they were there to support me and help me through this tough time. Four days later, my father passed away. I informed my lead and supervisor that I would need to take the bereavement time off. Both of them texted me and told me that if I needed more time to let them know. Zappos even sent my family flowers. When I came back to work, my co-workers had left me several cards and my lead and supervisor asked me how I was doing and gave me hugs. They also told me if I needed to talk, no matter the time, they were there for me. Two weeks later, I had to go pick up my father's ashes and it affected me more than I thought it would. I texted my lead and supervisor and told them I couldn't come to work and the reason and they told me not to worry about it. Later that same day, I received texts from both of them telling me they were thinking about me and sending me strength.

I will be forever grateful for all the support I received from my Zappos family. I never had a favorite Core Value before and I've tried to embrace them all. Now I do have a favorite: "Build a Positive Team and Family Spirit." (Core Value #7) I truly believe I work for the best company with the best people.

Lisa R.

employee since 2010

As I'm only a couple of weeks away from my one-year anniversary, I feel like I'm still a newlywed. A friend of mine suggested I apply here at Zappos, saying it was a fun place to work and like nothing I had known before. As I was out of work at the time, I thought, why not? After I passed all of the intensive testing and the interviews (and I now know why they have that in place, because they truly do get the cream of the crop!) I was hired. This past year has really flown by in a haze of meeting many amazing, creative and talented individuals.

Nowhere I have ever been has there been such a comfortable mesh of personalities. I'm on my third team right now and all of the Leads have been supportive in helping me obtain my goals. (Goals I set, not a pre-set charted course.) I look forward to my continued learning and growing and will continue, of course, creating "Fun and a Little Weirdness" (Core Value #3)!! Until next time …

Lisette M.

employee since 2010

I want to share what our Zappos Culture means to me. It has changed me in many positive ways and has also inspired me in my daily life. I am proud and excited to answer the phone every day and to be able to share with our customers a little bit of our culture when they call us. I am grateful to be a part of the Zappos family. Our Culture means so much to me, but the one thing that stands out when I think about it is our FAMILY SPIRIT.

Lycette C.
employee since 2010

Culture is a huge part of my every day life at Zappos. I never realized how having a culture could have such a big impact in and outside of work. I am so proud to share our Culture with friends, family, and customers because it's what sets us apart from everyone else. Culture can be many things. At Zappos, you never know what to expect because every day is completely different, which makes it very interesting here and such a fun environment. The Zappos Culture, to me, means fun, definitely a bit of weirdness and happiness!

Marco N.
employee since 2010

Look at you, in your little undies!

Marcus H.
employee since 2010

The Zappos Culture that this company instills in its family members (more than just employees) is nearly impossible to describe in words. To me, it's more of a feeling. When you walk through those glass doors, you aren't thinking of clocking in to a normal routine, already yearning to end your day. Instead, each day is a true adventure holding countless surprises. The second you set foot in the building, you're consumed by the positivity and happiness exuded by everyone around you and it's truly contagious. Having adopting the Zappos Culture in my everyday life, I have come to grasp the true meaning of the word passion. Being surrounded by such diverse and extremely talented individuals who have honed their skills through art, music, communication, food (God, I love pot lucks ...) or other skills, I have been able to dig deep and pursue my passions full throttle without ever needing to look back.

Maria E.
employee since 2006

The freedom to be yourself and to show family spirit at work is an amazing feeling. I feel blessed to be part of such an amazing company ... It's literally like no other. The company's passion and dedication to growth and inspiring us to be happy in everything we do is simply the best. Just shows you how we as a team are going to take Zappos to the number one spot. Fortune 500, we're coming to get it!

Marina M.
employee since 2007

The Zappos Culture is a guide to living, both inside and outside of work. Other companies may state their core values and their mission, but rarely do they live it out like Zappos. I like that our Culture has been constant since day one. It never fades away and never will. We are treated equally and I love that. It makes me enjoy my job even more, and the fact that our customers say what a good experience they have makes it even better. We are one big family and you can talk to anyone, completely open door.

Marissa G.
employee since 2007

As each year goes by, I become more and more content with being a part of Zappos. This is my second family for sure and I have become very attached. The people here are wonderful! I remember when I was going through some hard times and lost everything. Zappos took me to the furniture store and filled my entire apartment up with furniture. I almost fell out of my chair when I was told the great news. True care for employees is something that I never experienced before I found Zappos.

There are a variety of schedules to accommodate life outside of work. There are constant changes and surprises, which makes it that much more worthwhile to work here. Every day you can look forward to something new. I love the fact that there is so much room for growth within the company and our Leads, Sups and Managers will make sure we get where we are trying to go. Our benefits are out of this world. The free food and drinks, medical, dental, vision, and prescription coverage speaks for itself. I love to be able to surprise another employee with a recognition bonus. Our "zollar" store (I am a huge fan) rocks hard core. We have team buildings, in-office parades and company picnics. Our floor-wide potlucks are endless.

The best part about being part of Zappos is that I am able to be myself, and not anything less or more than who I really am. I can wear what I want, do my hair how I want, smile when I am happy and cry when I am sad and not be judged for it. I never have a day that I say, "I don't want to go to work." It actually doesn't feel like work. I will be with Zappos forever and a day!

Marko C.

employee since 2008

The Zappos Culture is showing who you really are! Whether it's waking up and just throwing clothes on and going to work, or whether you're going to work after the club. You can be who you want to be and look as lazy as you want doing it! It's just awesome that you don't have to pretend to be someone else while you're at work. You get to be you 24/7! I must say that it's the best job I've ever had and the people here are amazing and quite entertaining! It's different from a lot of other places, but that's a great thing! I love Zappos!

Marlene K.

employee since 2005

I've spent majority of my 20's with Zappos and learned so much along the way about business and about life. The Zappos Culture, to me, has always been about the people, and I feel very fortunate to have grown up with this ever-innovating company and culture. Looking forward to the next decade of this journey.

Mary T.

employee since 2007

Zappos is not just a company, it's my second family! I have been here for some time now and would not want to be anywhere else. I have such a great time working that I forget I am actually working. I consider myself blessed. =)

Matt D.

employee since 2011

To me, the Zappos Culture is the realization of what can occur when good people meet good business. "Work hard and play harder" is a phrase that may be thrown around a lot, but there are very few places where it carries some weight. The Zappos family not only exemplifies that phrase, it also lives by it. Because of this environment we're able to form tight bonds with our co-workers. When you can honestly say that you are friends with your co-workers out of preference and not convenience, you know that you work at a special place.

I have been nothing but impressed with the respect and appreciation I've felt since Day 1. Zappos has taken the correct philosophical approach to business by trusting their employees and customers, and removing a framework of "don't do this," replacing it with Ten Core Values to live by. Companies that follow this business model (or at a minimum, this business philosophy) are sure to go far, and I'd advise anyone who is in the job market to look past the dollar signs and into the company culture. I did just that, and I haven't looked back yet!

Matthew F.

employee since 2010

The Zappos Culture is the culmination of a positive and enjoyable work environment. This company is literally built around its Culture, which embraces and celebrates the changes we all face every day. While we remain humble, it is difficult not to be filled with pride when discussing a culture that truly brings people together.

Maura S.

employee since 2003

The Zappos Culture is what gets me out of bed every morning. It and the people that contribute to it are motivating, inspirational and fantastic. Bottom line - I wouldn't work here if it weren't for the Culture.

Mel C.

employee since 2009

Zappos is an amazing place to work. Our Culture is unlike anything I've ever experienced at any job before. Where else can I dunk my CEO or pie my supervisor in the face?? I love my job!

Melanie M.

employee since 2009

My excitement about working at Zappos grows every day! I am excited to come to work and know that I have awesome opportunities within this company! I appreciate the true friends that I have made here. I especially felt the love this winter when my mom got really sick and was in the hospital for some time with heart trouble. I did not know if she was going to get better. Just knowing that my Zappos family was here to lean on meant so much to me! Fortunately, she is doing much better now. I am truly blessed to be here!

Melissa C.

employee since 2006

The Zappos Culture is Joy, Happiness, and Laughter combined with blood, sweat, and tears!

Michael A.

employee since 2008

As a nearly three-year employee of Zappos, this is a very different environment than I am used to. I have worked in various types of retail businesses for most of my life, so I appreciate the time and effort that leads and supervisors are willing to give me to make me a better person and a better Zapponian. I appreciate the benefits and things we receive for working here. I am looking forward to our changes as we move downtown and appreciate the effort the company is making to make Las Vegas a better place to live and work.

Michael B.

employee since 2010

As soon as I started working at Zappos, I knew that it was a great and positive place to be. The energy here is astounding and when I come to work every day it's not a chore. The Zappos Culture is like no other that I've ever experienced. I've had friends with whom I've worked at previous jobs, but the culture is what separates Zappos from other places. This is more than just a job to me. It's slowly becoming a way of life inside and outside of the workplace. I've become an even more positive person now that I've become part of the Zappos Culture.

Michael S.

employee since 2009

The Zappos Culture is all about being passionate in life. Passionate about helping others, passionate about leading your thinking with positive thoughts, and also about sharing happiness in the most creative and positive ways. The Zappos Culture, to me, means that I am spreading happiness and cheer to those around me no matter where I am or what I am doing ... whether it's at Zappos, at home, or out on the streets interacting with people who pass by. Life is all about the people you meet and the bonds you build. Our relationships in life are what matters most and Zappos has shown me ways that I can make the best out of each and every relationship with friends, family and the world.

Michael S.

employee since 2010

To me, the Zappos Culture is a direct injection of happiness. I never thought a place like this existed until I started working here. I can honestly say I enjoy waking up and coming to work every day. I have built relationships with people here who I can say with confidence will be lifelong friends. ZapposÊ has raised my quality of life. I am forever grateful and this really is the happiest place on earth.

Michelle C.

employee since 2010

The Zappos Culture feels like when a best friend or close family member welcomes you into their home. You kick off your shoes, put on some comfortable clothes, relax and feel free to be yourself. You immediately feel relieved, comfortable and safe. That is how I have felt since day one here at Zappos. The Zappos Culture is what makes us a family. A family that cheers you up when you're having a bad day. A family that is there to cheer you on when you accomplish something and encourage you when you struggle to reach a goal. This is everyone's dream job. Zappos takes every employee under its wing, guides and nurtures them, and gives them the knowledge they need to have the career they want. Zappos and its culture mean so much to me because I have never in my life had a job that encourages me to express myself and my opinions to help better the company as a whole. Nor have I ever met anyone who has a job that values them as an employee/family member like Zappos does. I feel that Zappos and its culture are providing me with the opportunity of a life-time and I will never take that for granted. I was born with only one sister, but since being at Zappos, I have many sisters and brothers.

Michelle F.

employee since 2010

The Zappos Culture is driven by creativity. For me, that's what culture means. The freedom of expression is a huge tool in ensuring that we are in constant evolution. It's also a profoundly spiritual experience that allows people to feel pride in being creative, feel joy in connecting to others creatively, and feel triumph when using creativity to overcome obstacles. The Zappos Culture is one that encourages creativity, and that's why I'm here.

Mike D.

employee since 2010

Oh Zappos, you are my good friend. You had me at orientation! You complete my workday. Like a good friend, you are fun, you make me feel better when I am down, you give me reasons to be excited, you help me improve myself and you do not judge me when I make mistakes. Seven months in and I am still amazed by the things that I get to see and do here and I think it will continue for a long time. You have not let me down in times of stress, you have given me the motivation to get up in the morning and have something to look forward to at work. You have given me reasons to laugh in so many ways, you have surprised me and WOWed me as well. P.S.: my belly says thanks for the food! So that's what I got for now but ... I'll be back!

Mike D.

employee since 2011

I just arrived here at Zappos two weeks ago for my training. Even if I don't make the final cut, or for whatever reason my time here doesn't last as long as it will take to publish this book, I can truthfully say that this place is pretty badass. I've never had this much fun working anywhere and I hope that this is the beginning of a long and wonderful career.

MP

employee since 2005

I love Zappos! That love grows every day and helps me contribute to the Zappos Culture. What does that culture mean to me? It means being myself, having fun, working hard and reaching my goals. Our Culture enables everyone who works at Zappos to enrich the lives of all of our customers as well as anyone we come into contact with. We Deliver Happiness and we really want everyone to be just as happy as we are. Thank you for making me a better person and the world a better place to live in!

Naima "Boba Fett" B.

employee since 2010

I came from the land of the cubicle coma (urbandictionary.com/cubicle+coma) and then, just as Dorothy stumbled upon the land of Oz, I stumbled upon Zappos. Zappos is a place where I can wear my Boba Fett helmet around the office and be high fived for being a little weird, not ostracized for it. It's a place where, with the help of my team, I can build a headless horseman (complete with horse), a giant goal post, and a Skee-Ball game (complete with ball return) entirely out of cardboard boxes and hot glue, and be applauded for my creativity, not punished for wasting time.

The Zappos Culture is everything that traditional corporate mentality SHOULD be. I can't tell you how many times I've been told about an alleged "open-door policy" at other companies, only to find the opposite. At Zappos, I got an email directly from Tony wishing me a happy birthday, followed by some rather dry, but greatly enjoyed math jokes.

The Zappos Culture means taking the time to make someone feel appreciated (or actually being appreciated yourself), whether it be our customers via the VIP program, our co-workers through the employee recognition program, or even ourselves, when leads ask if we want something from the break room when the phones are busy during the holidays.

The Zappos Culture = being HAPPY at work!

Naomi S.

employee since 2010

I moved to Vegas for my job and for a new start in life, only knowing one person here. When I started at Zappos, I felt very alone and scared. It didn't take long to make friends within my training class and with those already working on the floor. Since I started a year ago I now have many friends (90% here at Zappos) and I'm not lonely anymore. I have my Zappos family!

A lot of things have happened in the short time I've been here - some good, some not so good. Through it all, my Zappos family has been there. They've celebrated my accomplishments and mourned my losses. I walked in here feeling like a peon, but now I feel loved and appreciated. It doesn't matter if you're a supervisor, manager, lead, or just a regular CLT member, everyone is treated the same and shown the same respect and appreciation. I love my job and I never want to leave!

Natalie L.

employee since 2010

I honestly cannot say enough about how much of a positive impact the Zappos Culture has had on every aspect of my life! I am so lucky to work in an environment where I feel appreciated, valued and encouraged. I feel truly grateful to work for this fantastic company and I have met such amazing people here! It's super refreshing to walk around the office and see so many smiling faces! I look forward to coming to work, which is something that relatively few people can say. I am in love with this place!

Nikisha P.

employee since 2006

The Zappos Culture is phenomenal!! I love how diverse the company is.

No'l B.

employee since 2007

Once upon a time, before my first sunrise, there was a choice that lay before my eyes. Go with the flow or swim upstream - one of two extremes. I'm in a groove and you don't approve, go on and look the other way. These are opening lyrics to a song I wrote called "It's Just a Phase." While these lyrics describe my life perspective, they also reflect how closely aligned they are to the true Zappos purpose. We are here to Deliver Happiness, which sometimes leads to tough choices. No matter what your passion is in life, Zappos supports you in your journey, even if it takes you in a direction that you never expected. Life is all about phases, so embrace and drive the change your journey brings.

Pamela A.

employee since 2009

Almost two years at Zappos and I am still as happy as when I first started here! It is just amazing that I cannot have a bad day here - because everyone, even people that don't know me, try to make me smile or just get my mind in a positive state. Our customers even have that effect on me if I am having a bad day.

It is motivating when we have our all-hands meetings to see everything that Zappos does for our community and that it is going to be a part of in the future. I simply cannot wait to move to downtown Las Vegas to start the Zappos experience there! They will not know what hit them. I am happy to see what is still in store for me and glad I am still employed by the best company ever!

Pamela C.

employee since 2010

The Zappos Culture, to me, is being allowed to be myself. It's the way we act and care about one another. It's having fun at work and loving our jobs. I laugh every day at work and we can be as weird as we want, and nobody cares. Zappos encourages all of us to socialize and become one big family. I feel very fortunate to work here, especially when customers call and are so impressed with our company and, of course, with Tony. He is an amazing and humble person.

Patrice C.

employee since 2007

I can't believe I have been part of the Zappos family for four years! The time has absolutely flown by. The Zappos Culture is so positive that it naturally becomes part of you. You feel energized and motivated every day. I look forward to sharing my day with fellow employees. Feel the change - bring a little Zappos zest into your life.

Patricia S.

employee since 2010

I believe in the purpose of The Zappos Culture and family is everything! I am grateful to have both!

Paul C.

employee since 2010

Working for Zappos is AMAZING!! Before I worked here I used to dread coming to work every day. Now I actually look forward to going to work. It's a great job with great people! Zappos is much more than just a job; it's a family! Everyone takes care of each other and genuinely cares about each other! The Culture that Tony has created here is incredible. I hope other companies notice how happy everyone is here and that they try to incorporate some of our culture to make their work environment better. I have never said that I loved my job before and actually meant it! I can say that now! Whenever someone asks me where I work, my reply is always the same: "I work for Zappos! The greatest company in the world!"

Peg Leg Meg

employee since 2010

I have been a member of the Zappos family for six months now, and our Culture is truly amazing. It embraces each individual's unique personality while also placing high importance on our Ten Core Values.

I remember the first time I walked into Zappos. I was going through the hiring process and had to come in for some testing. I thought, "Wow. This place is definitely not like any traditional office." It was loud. People were walking in and out. Everyone seemed happy, stopping to say hi and carry on a conversation, knowing each other by name. When I came back a second time for my interview, a brief tour of the call center upstairs was included. My excitement was heightened. This time I thought, "Zappos is like the perfect high school." Again, it was loud. Everyone seemed happy. There were decorations galore. These included, but were not limited to, colorful streamers and a bubble machine that was emitting bubbles in the row visible from the creatively painted conference room that I interviewed in.

Even now, six months later, I would say that Zappos is like the perfect high school. There isn't a dress code. We're all able to express our unique style by dressing the way we want. Everyone is "popular" and involved in "extracurricular" activities, whether it's during or outside of work. We aren't scared of our lead or any other superior. Rather, we view them as friends. They help us become the best person that we can be. They do this in a variety of ways: helping us to deliver WOW to every customer (internal & external), to embrace and drive change, to pursue growth and learning, etc.

Now, I could go on and on talking about how great it is at Zappos and how much I love coming to work here five days a week. Instead, I will end my thoughts with this: The Zappos Culture = Pure Happiness!

Peri G.

employee since 2006

Zappos is the best place to work by far. Our culture shows who we are!

I'm excited to go to work every day so I can be part of the Zappos way!

We live and breathe our culture with all that we've got.

So it's easy to see why being part of the Zappos family is the perfect spot!

I never thought that my workplace would feel like a home, but Zappos has done a great job in proving me wrong!

Porsha P.

employee since 2008

I want to invest in the company like they have invested in me. Corny, but we are going to have an amazing future together! Forget a key, the doors are always open for my creative juices to flow. I am flying through. Overjoyed, my heart cries out in happiness! My husband and I are very thankful!

Pua M.

employee since 2010

Anything "BZ" (before Zappos) is irrelevant and a huge BLURRRRR because I'm the HAPPIEST I've ever been in my life! I love Zappos! NUFF SAID! ;)

Quintaye P.

employee since 2006

Thanks for five great years, Zappos!!!! Looking forward to the next five!!!! Thanks for all that you've done and continue to do for me.

Ranielle R.

employee since 2009

Theodore Roosevelt once said "Far and away the best prize that life offers is to work hard at work worth doing."

Zappos isn't about making sales or profits; to me it's about Delivering Happiness to all that surrounds us. And without even realizing it, it changes you as a person, makes you a better version of yourself. I can't describe our culture in words, but I know it's what makes everything we do worth doing.

Reandra aka ReRe

employee since 2008

I cannot believe that I have been with the company now for three years!!

I never thought that my workplace would feel like a home, but Zappos has done a great job in proving me wrong!

Rebekah N.

employee since 2006

I am so happy that I found Zappos in October of 2006. In the four-plus years I've been here, I have made a lot of lifetime friends that I also think of as my family. When I wake up each "morning" (I work in the afternoon) I thank God that I found a place that treats its people as people and not as numbers. I love my Zappos family! How many people do you know who would have more people they work with at their wedding than blood relations? Well, now you know of at least one. The majority of people that came to my wedding in 2009 were Zappos people. Mind you, there were about 50 people at the wedding. They celebrated the best day of my life! I've also gone through some bad personal times and Zappos has always been there for me. My Zappos family has rallied around me and supported me. They gave me a shoulder to cry on and the strength to keep going. The Zappos Culture, to me, is coming to "work" to spend my day with family ... to be at my desk and laugh with those around me as well as the customers on the phone. The Zappos Culture is to not be afraid, to be myself and to know that I am accepted for who I am.

Regan H.

employee since 2011

The Zappos Culture is a feeling of acceptance and generosity. Zappos is an environment in which the culture is full of high energy and support for one another and the company, as well as our customers. Our Culture here at Zappos is one of service. We serve each other and our customers to make life a more beautiful and fulfilling experience, full of happiness. This is what the Zappos Culture means to me.

Rian C.

employee since 2009

I never thought that my job could change my life, but it has. I can honestly say I am a better person because of Zappos. The people I have met have become my family. They have helped me though hard times and smiled with me though good. I am very blessed to be apart of the big business of LOVE!

Richard S.

employee since 2010

The Zappos Culture, to me, means "coutureness." It's so couture to be able to pursue growth and learning. It's so couture to be happy. It's so couture to be humble. It's so couture to be part of Zappos!

Ricki M.

employee since 2004

I will celebrate my seventh anniversary as a Zappos employee this year, and the longer I am here, the more impressed I am - with the company, the Culture and all the great plans for the future. Zappos has grown from a small company with great benefits, and a fun atmosphere, to a larger company with fantastic benefits, and an incredible culture that might never develop anywhere else without a great deal of effort.

When I'm out and about town, sometimes people notice my security badge and ask me about working at Zappos. I tell anyone who will listen about the fact that we rank sixth among the 100 best places to work in the USA. They want to talk about the wonderful customer service they have either experienced, or heard about. They want to talk about Tony's book, an appearance on television, or a rumor they have heard. Yes, those rumors are true. I believe it's possible to change the way the world functions from frowns to smiles - from skeptical to impressed - from annoyed to accepting, one smile, one kindness, one service at a time.

You don't think so? Hide and watch. Better yet, put on a smile, embrace changes you never thought were possible, and join us.

Rita S.

employee since 2006

Wow! It's time again to share our thoughts on the Zappos Culture, Core Values and goals. Our Zappos family has grown so much this past year. The kind of growth we are experiencing makes it even more important to welcome the new members of the tribe into our Culture. And for those of us who have been here for a few minutes, we need to make sure we are awesome examples of our Core Values. When all is said and done, it is the Zappos Culture and Core Values that attracted most of us to our path at Zappos. Working at Zappos and being inspired by my peers and encouraged by the Core Values has helped me find the confidence I needed to step out of my comfort zone and achieve goals that I wasn't sure I could obtain. I am very grateful and profoundly appreciative of Zappos.

Rob S.

employee since 2004

At Zappos, we treat others as we wish to be treated. We share love, life, and laughter. We work hard while playing hard at the same time. We are all aligned on our mission to live and deliver WOW.

Personally, I've found a place where the goals of the business match up well with my own belief system. Strive for excellence. Be engaged. Build relationships. Improve every day, and continue to feed your passions. The Zappos Culture is our ultimate team accomplishment. It's become what we have today due to the collective efforts of everyone here. It will take all of us to preserve the wonderful environment we've built. Our Values will be our guide. We won't let up!

Robin A.

employee since 2010

WOW! What a place to work. What does the Zappos Culture means to me? Every day, I actually enjoy coming into work. My co-workers are always happy. Every six months, we switch teams and it's like forming a new family. But I still have the close friendships from my old team. It's like my family keeps growing.

My Zappos family is never critical or passes judgment. People are accepted for who they are - faults and all. We all support and encourage each other to pursue our goals. I'm looking forward to going upwards in this organization.

Robynn J.

employee since 2010

I started with Zappos August of 2010, and have been nothing less than amazed from the moment I entered the Zappos lobby. This place is filled with warmth and friendliness. It's safe to say that we are all genuinely motivated and excited to come to work on a daily basis. The one thing that I will always cherish is the way we are able to build relationships with each other. Although I have not been here for long, I can truthfully say that the relationships I have built with some of the Zappos peeps I've met will last for a lifetime. I am forever grateful for the opportunity to work around entertaining, exciting and excellent people.

Rockne H.

employee since 2009

Well, it's been another great year at Zappos. Some pivotal moments that I will remember include beating our previous year's ranking for one of the best companies to work for, the announcement of moving our corporate offices to a new downtown location and Zappos CLT's very first All-Hands Meeting!

This year has been a blast and continues to solidify my faith and passion for this company. The Zappos Culture is a huge reason for why we continue to amaze both our customers and our employees. Every single person in this company contributes to a picture-perfect atmosphere that keeps beating all odds. I am so blessed, so fortunate, so privileged to be a part of something so wonderful. Whenever I have the opportunity to write one of these Culture Book entries, I can't help but shed a few tears, as my dreams have already come true: to live a happy life. Zappos has been a HUGE part of that success. I remain forever grateful.

Roni R.

employee since 2010

I learned about Zappos in college when I did a business report on the company and by the end of my report I had decided that Zappos was my future home. The day I turned in my paper, I started tracking down ways to become part of Zappos. How can I be part of this company? Every day, I'd go to work and tell my co-workers I'll be leaving soon to work at Zappos. Now that I'm here I have to say, this is not what I was expecting. It's only like a trillion times better.

This isn't just a job, it's part of my lifestyle. The Core Values are part of our daily life, both within Zappos' walls and at home. So many places say you shouldn't bring your personal life to work or bring your work life home. At Zappos, home and work are one in the same. In college I majored in Ornamental Horticulture - a degree that has no place in a call center. However, because of the unique Culture I have been able to bring an unrelated passion to the work environment.

Zappos is, seriously, the Hogwarts of my life - a magical place where lasting friendships are made.

Rosario S.

employee since 2006

The Zappos Culture is unique. Its uniqueness is the reason why companies from all over the world come to Las Vegas to learn and embrace the Zappos Culture.

Ruby A.

employee since 2008

Wow! I have been with Zappos for almost three years and I have never worked with a company where I wanted to apply their culture to my every day life. The Zappos Culture has brought out the best in me. Thanks, Zappos!

Ryan I.

employee since 2007

To me, the Zappos Culture means a lot of things. It's tough to write a few words about it without going into a long speech. Over the years, new meanings have been added to my definition. The big one this year is trust! In a perfect culture, trust can go a long way. I got a chance to experience this first-hand this past year by having my peers trust in my abilities to take the lead in projects. Culture, baby, it's what's hot on the street!

Sabrina C.

employee since 2010

SOOO, I would like to start off by thanking my mother! (Just kidding, haha!) But seriously I felt like I'd won some type of award when I got the phone call that Zappos would like to hire me! Long story short, I am truly happy here and excited to continue my journey at Zappos.

Sam B.

employee since 2008

The Zappos Culture means having fun, taking pride, and truly enjoying what you do. Working here allows you to keep an open mind about absolutely everything. The ideas that flow throughout the call center are amazing. Not many people can say they honestly love coming to work every day.

Scott J.

employee since 2008

Another great year at Zappos! Made a lot of new friends, and my lovely wife was hired. One of my favorite things about our Zappos Culture is that it encourages us to bring our friends and family members into the company. I have worked at places where this was actually discouraged, if not outright forbidden. I've never understood that. I have found that it just helps our culture that we have our spouses, siblings or children working in the company. It provides existing bonds to expand on, and helps us stay connected to our own families, instead of leaving them for eight hours every day, and only seeing them to eat dinner with, etc. Thanks, Zappos for providing us with this opportunity!

Scott K.

employee since 2004

This year was a bit more challenging for me. I had a lot of back and neck issues that were bothering me both physically and mentally. Where does the Zappos Culture fit into this equation? Folks have been very supportive, just like a family. My manager and various co-workers were always trying to help out with suggestions, doctor referrals, or just words of encouragement to help me feel better. I don't think that I would have experienced this at any other company besides Zappos and that's why I love it here! Go Core Value #7, Build a Positive Team and Family Spirit! :)

Sean H.

employee since 2009

The Zappos Culture, to me, is in essence, a template to live by. Each of the Ten Core Values is key, not only when it comes to working at Zappos, but to living a positive, productive, and worthwhile life.

I feel truly blessed to have had the opportunity to make the connections and build the relationships that I am so fortunate to possess in my workplace. These connections and the people who form them are all a byproduct of our amazing Culture here at Zappos.

Sean M.

employee since 2006

The Zappos Culture means taking a long lunch with a co-worker to go visit a team member in the hospital and not having this become an issue. It means being able to express yourself in your mini-world and no one thinking you're crazy for having a dragon on your desk! It means being able to take ideas that you would never have thought to create at other companies and tell your supervisor, who then tells you to run with it and the next thing you know, you've helped to make your department and your company just a little bit better. The Zappos Culture means acceptance, creativity, family spirit, and appreciation for contributions. When I first started here back in 2006, I never would have imagined that I would still be here five years later and that I would be a part of a management team here. I was literally about to move to Austin, Texas when I got this job, and once I experienced what the culture here is really about, I stayed. I have had the opportunity to grow in my career here, to learn new things and to contribute to the betterment of my department, which creates an incredible feeling of being a part of something bigger than myself. I can thank the Culture here for helping me to become more than I was when I started. Thank you, Zappos, and thanks to my fellow team members who make coming in each day easy and a joy! You know who you are! ;)

Sean P.

employee since 2008

When I look at the big picture, the Zappos Culture means many things to me: hardworking, fun, loyal, etc. But if I can put it in one word, it would be "Amazing."

Sean-Pierre W.

employee since 2010

Soooooooooo. The Zappos Culture is unlike any other in the known universe. In the short time I've been here, the folks have completely embraced and accepted me. All the people here are nice and understand that we as individuals make up the tapestry that is the Zappos Culture. I can be a little loud at times, and not everyone is like me. We are not all crazy and all over the place. Some people are quiet. Not only is that OK, it's encouraged! We work as a team and respect each other's individuality. That's what makes us so cool. We don't force everyone to fit into a single corporate mold. We encourage them to be themselves, find something within the company to be passionate about, and become the best employee they can be. Happy people are the best equipped to make other people happy. That is a fact!

I don't know if this is what you're looking for, but I just opened a page and wrote from the heart. Enjoy!

Shannon C.

employee since 2008

Core Value #7: Build a Positive Team and Family Spirit.

Zappos is my extended family. I cannot say enough wonderful things about the people here. They look out for you, share your joy, and always have your back. I am truly blessed to be employed at the most amazing company ever!!!!!

Shannon M.

employee since 2007

Hands down, Culture means ZAPPOS! I have learned and grown so much from working here. I have learned to truly appreciate great customer service! I smile and try and make my day and everyone that I come in contact with brighter. Zappos is a truly AMAZING company and I'm SO blessed to be a part of the awesome growth daily!!

Sharon R.

employee since 2007

I LOVE our culture at Zappos. It's a place where I am encouraged to have a most fabulous day - one to look forward to and not dread like many jobs I've had throughout the years. A place where you feel like you are visiting an extended family. A place where Creating Fun and a Little Weirdness (Core Value #3) is encouraged to keep the atmosphere upbeat and enjoyable for everyone.

Zappos always has open and honest communications with the employees; we are invited to submit our opinions, suggestions, and feedback into the final decision-making changes that will affect us - both large and small - in our work environment. This is truly a unique and much-appreciated bond between the executives and the employees. Everyone has a voice at Zappos, and we are encouraged to use it! Now for me, that's a really BIG WOW!

Thanks, Zappos for saving my life from a dull, dreary, unappreciated, stressful job and giving me this opportunity to look forward to each new day as an employee of Zappos!

Shaun S.

employee since 2010

The Zappos Culture, to me, means family, friends, fun. I've met more people and made more friends in the last eight months since I've been here than I have anywhere else I've worked. The way we are treated, how we are empowered to do the best that we possibly can, the friendships we make ... the list goes on. You would have to smash me with a wrecking ball to get me to leave. ZAPPOS FOR LIFE!

Shawna M.

employee since 2010

I feel that the Zappos Culture is surreal. You would never believe how unbelievable (I said that on purpose) this Culture really is. It's like being in a dream that you never want to wake up from. Everyone is so pleasant to be around. It's like they secretly have "happy gas" in the air conditioning vents. There is a sense of family here and that's what I love. Although I may not be familiar with everyone here just yet, I know that they would definitely help me if I needed it because that's just how things are here. In just the year that I have been with Zappos, I have made long-lasting friends and I have finally found a job where I can wake up and say "I cannot wait to go to work today!"

Shay T.

employee since 2010

The Zappos Culture, to me, means having good times with great friends. What better way to celebrate a friendship than with SANGRIA?!!! ENJOY!!!

Fruity Sangria

This simple sangria requires some patience, but minimal effort. If served at a party, guests will delight in nibbling on the wine-flavored apple and pear chunks remaining in their cups after their sangria has vanished.

Makes 18 glasses
15 minutes preparation
Difficulty: very easy
Ingredients:
8 cups (64 fl. oz) dry red wine
8 cups (64 fl. oz) apple juice
1 small grapefruit, cut into eights
1 medium orange, sliced thin crosswise
1 medium lemon, sliced thin crosswise
1 small pear, diced
1 medium apple, diced

Preparation: Combine the wine, apple juice, and grapefruit pieces in a large pitcher. Mix well, cover and refrigerate overnight. The following day, add the orange and lemon slices to the wine. Refrigerate for a further three hours. Add the pear and apple to the mixture and allow to stand for another hour to absorb the flavor fully. Mix well and serve over ice.

Shayleen H.

employee since 2009

Words cannot describe just how blessed I feel to work here. I am immersed in our Culture all the time by waving, smiling, laughing, and hanging out with genuine, sincere, and amazing people. Knowing that I can do all of this PLUS get things done, be there for my team, and help Zappos grow to the next level is awe-inspiring. We may play hard, but that is only because we work twice as hard with smiles on our faces.

What is real for me is that Zappos is more than a call center. It is a place of acceptance, ability, and potential. As each month passes, I find new things to fall in love with and more things to be proud of. From the excitement of new hires, to the recognition of the city, Zappos continues to make me feel as though I am in a dream. I don't think working here will ever be "real" to me, and I like it like that ...

Shea G.

employee since 2010

What does the Zappos Culture mean to me? It means being able to grow into the person I want to be, both professionally and personally. The feeling of support that I received from the moment I walked in to new-hire training is just amazing! Everyone was telling me that I was capable of amazing things and that nothing should hold me back. You hear it a lot, but the people here really do feel like family. Zappos is, by far, the best company that I have ever worked for!

Sheena B.

employee since 2010

No words can truly describe the Zappos Culture. Whether you realize it or not, you eat, breath, and sleep the culture the moment you step into those front doors for the very first time. It's part of your life and there is no turning back.

To this day I can remember when I first walked through those doors to interview for a Customer Loyalty position. I thought to myself, this is not like any office I've ever been in. Streamers hanging from the ceiling, all the conference rooms having their own theme, employees' desks decorated to fit their personality, and most of all, laughter throughout the building. You feel the presence of just pure happiness.

I was originally hired in June of 2009. I left the company in January 2010 to further my education in a different state. Parting ways with everyone here was completely different than any other job I have worked for. Every person I connected with had soon after became a family member to me and they kept in touch, whether it was a five-minute phone call, a text message, or even Facebook. Regardless the miles apart, I felt the individuals I connected with were just down the street.

When I returned to Las Vegas, I was jobless. I went on a long, exhausting hunt for a job but nothing measured up to what I was really looking for. Zappos had set the highest standards. It felt like it was going to be impossible to find a company that could measure up to Zappos. I risked it all and emailed every single person I knew to help me return to Zappos. Of course, with open arms, everyone I contacted responded and was willing to help me in every way possible to return to the company. Well, long story short, I am back. I can't even put words together to explain this amazing family I have here. This may be the real world, and it's said that you're on your own. But here at Zappos headquarters, there is no such thing as loneliness. I am so blessed to be a part of this company and proud to call myself a Zapponian!

Sherri-Lei S.

employee since 2010

My journey began months before being hired at Zappos. I left Hawaii to see the world and my first stop was the ninth Hawaiian Island (Las Vegas). Guess that wasn't too far. I had the opportunity to stay with someone and really learn about who I am, what I want, and where it would lead me. I would ride the double-decker bus from one side of the valley to the other just reading books and taking pictures. I read books for inspiration, self-education and laughs, and one awesome book was called Delivering Happiness by Tony Hsieh. This was my first interaction with the company. All I knew was the puppets on the commercials that just cracked me up. Realizing that I was staying a few blocks from Zappos HQ and my friend had just started working there, it intrigued me that people could be so happy and crazy. When I walked by, people had the friendliest smiles and that scared me. It wasn't a job ... it was a cult.

Needless to say, I applied and am now part of this CULT!!! I'm so blessed to be a part of this Zappos Culture. It's everything that we all strive to have at a job: flexibility, mobility, encouragement, co-worker support ... the list is endless. The supervisors don't have offices, Tony sits outside in the bay area and the CEOs, CFOs, COOs, whatever Cs and Os socialize with everyone. To be where I am at this time of my life Êmight very well have to do with many prayers and positive vibes from back home in Hawaii. The new relationships created during training, teams and departments are amazing. I share with anyone who wants to hear about my job. When friends from Hawaii come to Las Vegas, I tell them that taking a tour at Zappos should be on their bucket list. I'm humbled for having the opportunity to provide WOW not only to customers but also to friends, family and co-workers. This isn't just a job for me, it's a destiny that has the power of creating a "Hawaiian" legacy. AND I DO NOT TAKE THIS FOR GRANTED. 100th Training Class April 2011 (6-months)

Sheena G.

employee since 2008

Zappos has become my second family and I owe it all to the Culture we have grown. I have been fortunate enough to build relationships with some amazingly intelligent, inspiring and exceptional people who don't hesitate to help me when I'm weak and allow me to spread my wings when I am strong. I am floored every day by the fact that these awesome people actually want to hear my ideas, take them into consideration and truly care about what I think. I have never felt so lucky to belong to such an outstanding group of people, united with a common goal to push the envelope and constantly strive to make things better. And the best part is, I get to contribute by just being myself! What more could anyone ask for?

Sofia K.

employee since 2009

Zappos is my home away from home. I love that everyone is accepted for who they are, no matter how different. Also, I have never worked for a company that does so much for their employees. Zappos throws amazing parties and provides outstanding benefits. I can't imagine ever working anywhere else again.

Stacey S.

employee since 2010

The Zappos Culture is a living, breathing thing that I've seen extend beyond the walls of our offices. Zappos has fed my soul in a way that no other job has before. I feel at home every time I walk through the doors here or spend time with my Zappos family. I'm happy and that has come to mean more to me than any other gift I can be given. "Happiness always looks small while you hold it in your hands, but let it go, and you learn at once how big and precious it is." - Maxim Gorky

Stacy H.

employee since 2006

The ABC's of Zappos: Ally Booze Customer Developing Energy Food Groups Humbleness Inspire Journey Kentucky Laughing Moving Nevada Optimization Parties Quarkey Reaching Service T-shirts Unity Victory Wow Xenodochium Yoicks Zap-tastic! - I heart Zappos.

Stephanie C.

employee since 2007

I LOVE coming to my job each day. Thank you for allowing me to be a part of the Zappos Culture and teaching me that I can do anything. My Zappos family is one talented and amazing group of people and I am so fortunate that this is my job.

Stephanie H.

employee since 2010

One word that really sums up our Culture at Zappos is WOW!! The happiness I have found at Zappos has spilled over into my personal life and has allowed me to become a happier person. I cannot thank Zappos enough for this opportunity!

Stephanie H.

employee since 2007

I have been here four years and still stand by that the Zappos Culture is like no other. Every day I come to work with a smile on my face because I'm excited for all the fun and crazy things that I'll experience that day. I love being part of a company where I can be myself, wear whatever I want and shave the CEO's head! I have made lifetime friends at Zappos and feel blessed every day to be here. I can't imagine my life without Zappos! :)

Stephanie T.

employee since 2006

Another wonderful year here and it is hard to believe that it's almost been five years! The Zappos Culture couldn't mean more to me than just being myself. I come to work every day not feeling like I'm doing a job, but making people happy and spending time with friends I think of as family. I don't think there is anything else like it out there and I hope to continue to be myself at work and "Create Fun and a Little Weirdness" (Core Value #3)!

Stephanie W.

employee since 2004

The Zappos Culture is like being at home with family and friends. It's a place where you are encouraged to be whomever you aspire to be. Urged to be more, do more, expect more. Community involvement. We are cherished for what we contribute to the world. Our voices and opinions are valued and appreciated. We have a great balance of working hard and playing hard. It's an amazing feeling to wake up each day and be happy to go to work! I've worked here for around seven years, and to this day I feel blessed to be a part of the Zappos family!

Stephen A.

employee since 2011

Energy, happiness and great expectations! It's easy to write an entire book on the Zappos Culture (in fact, we're doing that right here!) but I can sum it up in those three concepts. There's a vibrancy about Zappos that makes it impossible to be down, even when you're tired. You don't even have to fight being tired - the natural energy and excitement you find at Zappos do it for you! I leave here happier every day than I was when I started, which is really saying something. Everyone smiles at you, waves at you, offers you a helping hand. It's impossible to not be happy. And finally, Zappos produces great expectations. We are all here to do great things and we are all here to get Zappos to great places. It's the perfect combination that makes Zappos Zappos.

Tabitha J.

employee since 2009

I have been with Zappos almost two years now and I am excited to say I am still in love with my Zappos life!! This has been the best experience, ride, journey I have ever had and I am truly thankful for all the friends and family I have gained over time. The Zappos Culture is truly an experience like none other! I see myself being here for many, many years to come!

Taisha T.

employee since 2006

I've been here for almost five years and there's never been a dull day!! You never know what to expect and someone is always pulling a prank on someone else! The Culture here is more than our Ten Core Values ... It's a lifestyle. :) I don't know anywhere else you can go from work to wine tasting and back to work. LOL! Zappos is truly in a league of its own. Thanks for everything!

Tama C.

employee since 2007

The Zappos Culture is so fantastic that it is becoming a worldwide phenomenon! Many individuals and companies come to visit and experience the fun, weird, crazy, and absolute "sane" way we live our Culture. In turn, they head home embracing the Culture to share with others. How many businesses can inspire this type of chain reaction? Want to see a parade while having a free lunch, at the same time you're working? I've never seen another place where this can happen. This type of joy at work automatically makes you spread it into other areas of your life. This type of freedom allows us to positively influence others, and allows us to concentrate fully on making our customers happy.

I'm extremely proud to be a Zapponian, and extremely happy to be here. I wouldn't want to be anywhere else.

Tamara H.

employee since 2010

The Zappos Culture creates a place to work that doesn't seem like work. It is trying your best to help customers and co-workers to have a great day. It is having the ability, power, and freedom to use your best judgment to do what you feel is right. The Zappos Culture allows you to be yourself, express your creativity, and have fun. Zappos employees, as well as our great customers, create the Zappos Culture.

Tami L.

employee since 2007

Culture at Zappos truly comes down to one thing ... YOU! Everyone at Zappos is responsible for our Culture. That means participating in events, bringing forth ideas, being open to new experiences and change, dressing up on crazy dress days, lending a hand to Zappos family members, finding ways to be involved with the community and support charitable events/causes, and as simple as saying hello and smiling when greeting one another. I am fortunate to be a part of the Zappos family and feel responsible for protecting our culture and making it even better for future Zapponians.

Tamika C.

employee since 2010

The Zappos Culture, to me, means family and growth. I have never experienced a place like this in my whole life. It means building relationships inside and outside of work.

Here, we are very close, and everyone is here for everyone else. We are always being encouraged to try new things and to grow, both personally and professionally. It is great to come to work at a place where everyone knows your name even if you are not that close. To me, the Zappos Culture means stepping outside of the box. I absolutely love it here!!!!!

Tammy R.

employee since 2009

WOW, I can't believe I will have been here at Zappos two years come July. I am still blown away by the Zappos Culture and the wonderful people here. This environment is like no other I have ever experienced. It brings the term "family" to a whole new level. Most people develop a friendship with co-workers, but here you truly bond as a family. Your family members will be there to support you and help both in your professional and personal life, which, in my eyes, is more valuable than any amount of money! This is something I have learned from my own personal experience, which has helped me through some difficult times. I feel very blessed to know that I have such a wonderful support system at work in my Zappos family.

Tamra J.

employee since 2008

Wow, where do I even start? Zappos has taken me under its wing and guided me through this amazing journey I am on. I love everything about the Zappos Culture down to the little things. As you're walking down the stairs on your way into the building, someone ahead of you will hold the door for you. If there's a line in the bathroom and you have to go really, really bad (I'm pregnant, don't judge!) people will let you go ahead of them. If you're having a rough day, someone is always there to talk to.

We truly have a second family here at Zappos. Someone is always here to lean on no matter what you're going through. The biggest thing is that Zappos gives you the time to build relationships with your fellow team members. Thank you, Zappos for always having my back and giving me every opportunity possible!

Tanai M.

employee since 2008

The Zappos Culture means so much to me. It has changed my whole outlook on life and helped me become a better person. it has taught me to be more open and giving to others. I have also learned to make wiser choices because I now think of the effect that I have on people and how the little things we do can make a big difference in someone's life.

Tanya S.

employee since 2010

I have only been at Zappos for just under a year (July 2010) and I have loved every minute of it. I like that when I come into work at 4:00 am ... which most people would not be okay with ... I am just fine with it. My team members make it FUN to come into work. They are also more like a family than co-workers. I absolutely LOVE my job ... well if you can call it "a job." I mean, who else can say, hey guys I am going to go take a nap in the nap room. See you in 30 minutes.

I <3 Zappos!

Tara M.

employee since 2008

I am now 22 years young and have been with Zappos since I was 18. Over the last three years, I have not only grown as a person but have had the amazing opportunity to become an adult with this company. It has shaped me. Zappos has helped me become more independent because we all know that we have the power to change things if we are passionate about it. I have learned life-altering skills, such as compassion, open-mindedness, acceptance, not resisting change (even though this one can at times be difficult) and, above all, how to embrace my creativity and not be afraid to let it shine. The people that work in this company have become my family and support system, not only inside the company walls but also throughout my everyday life. We may all come from different beliefs, backgrounds, cultures and ethnicities, but in the end we are all one, family. This company looks past everything on the outside of a person and looks within. This past year, 2010, has been nothing short of amazing. The experiences I have had with my Zappos family and the interactions with people daily that need assistance on the phones have all made me the person I am today. Zappos brought out such passion within me.

We all have a light within us that burns, but within the walls of Zappos we are all granted the opportunity to let the light shine bright together as one in unity to create a light for all the world to see. With this light, I feel that we can change the world, not only with our shoes and other products, but also with our views and happiness!

Tasha G.

employee since 2005

The Zappos Culture, to me, is exceptional! I've been with the company for almost six years now! This isn't just a job for me, it's my family and my second home! Watching the company evolve into what it has become has been truly amazing. I'm constantly being introduced to new people and ideas and I'm learning something new every step of the way. I cannot express enough how proud I am to say I am part of this amazing company and I know that the best is yet to come!

Teinesha I.

employee since 2010

Nothing you have heard has prepared you for the Zappos Culture. Bring gum, an extra pair of socks, a bottle of Tylenol, flippers and a bow and arrow. Leave your worries at the door.

Thomas S.

employee since 2007

The Zappos Culture, to me, is like being part of one big family environment. I've made many lasting relationships with my fellow employees. I truly care about them and they feel the same about me. The Culture is what makes me really enjoy being a part of the Zappos family. I've never had as much fun working for a company as I have with Zappos. There is never a dull moment here. It still amazes me that our CEO Tony not only attends our happy hours, but also will even have shots with us and sometimes is the one pouring them. Zappos is simply amazing!

Tiffany L.

employee since 2005

The Zappos Culture is simply amazing! It is sometimes hard to describe because of all of the amazing things it encompasses! It is family, it is diversity, it is being who you want to be and not being afraid to take risks. It is coming together and being aligned when working towards a common goal. It is about a higher purpose and truly making a difference in the world. It is about touching people's hearts and souls and becoming a better person for it. It is about amazing opportunities, growth, joy, laughter, tears and wonderment. It is something I am truly humbled and honored to have the chance to be a part of and I can't say thank you enough. It is ours to participate in, contribute to and propel forward! Here's to the future, my fellow cultivators of WOW!

Tiffany P.

employee since 2010

One of the reasons the Zappos Culture is so great is because it is such a large and important aspect of the entire company. How you act, work, learn and play is all centered around our culture, which makes Zappos a wonderful, unique place to be. Everyone is encouraged to display his or her personality, whether it is through specific activities, cubicle decorations or even appearance. It is fun, not only to be able to show your own distinct style, but to see the various things from everyone else's imagination around the office.

Zappos made me more open to new ideas and change. I have learned that it is okay to put myself out there and show people what I really believe in. In order for the Culture to work for you, you have to be able to put your whole heart into it and embrace everything for what it is. The Culture is not just what you do for eight hours a day - it includes all aspects of your life, and you have to be able to let it in. I feel so lucky to be able to experience this.

Tom S.

employee since 2008

The Zappos Culture means that I get to work with over a thousand peeps who all have the same Core Values and who share the same Big Picture vision I do. Every one of those over a thousand peeps is a unique individual with different backgrounds and experiences, but in the most important area of Core Values, we are very much the same.

Tony F.

employee since 2009

In my one and a half years here at Zappos, I can honestly say that it is by far the best place that I've ever worked. There is a very high priority placed on personal growth, learning and progression within the company. We have been successful in attracting a lot of talented people of all ages and from every walk of life.

I am very impressed with the generosity of the company, especially when it comes to taking care of employees. One great example of this is in the area of health benefits. I have worked in a few major industries, and this is by far the most generous benefit package of anywhere I have worked. Another impressive area of the operation is the way that our customers are treated. We have by far the best customer service of anywhere that I have shopped, whether it's online or bricks and mortar operations.

I'm very excited about our transition to the downtown area of Las Vegas as I worked there for many years and have recently realized how much it has changed for the better. More culture, entertainment, dining and shopping. I can't wait to be part of the downtown community!

Tree

employee since 2007

The Zappos Culture has changed my life. I look at the world differently because of our Culture. I have grown as a person because of the opportunities I have been given at Zappos. I have learned so many new skills and mastered different tasks. Every day it is a joy to come to work, to be with my Zappos family. Our customers share our passion and are so much fun to speak with.

Here is my definition of the Zappos Culture: C = Customers, who are part of our Zappos family! U = U come first, externally and internally. L = Love me some Zappos. T = Tony Hsieh rocks. U = U choose your destiny at Zappos. R = R you ready to Wow? E = Everyone loves Zappos!

Tyler D.

employee since 2010

This has been my first year at Zappos, and it has been a wonderful experience. The Culture here is amazing, and it has warmed my heart and shown me what a great company can accomplish when everyone works together. I am grateful to be a part of Zappos, and I hope to be around for many years to come!

Tyson W.

employee since 2009

My time at Zappos is best expressed not just by our subjective understanding of happiness, but also by a companywide drive to reach a state of perfect satisfaction, fulfillment and geniality. I found this idea of living and employment to be closer to Martin Heidegger's later works on the human condition. He felt happiness was too convoluted, too vague by 20th and now 21st Century standard definitions. And it is through the adoption of the Greek word eudaimonia (a contented state of being happy and healthy and prosperous) that I find a better definition to explain the culture, goals and work environment here. The Zappos Culture reflects a deep happiness, birthed as a habitat for our fellowship with being, serving as a predicated musical in accordance with our preponderance of vitality.

Valerie D.

employee since 2010

It is really hard to put into writing my thoughts about Zappos. It isn't so much a thought as a feeling, but I am going to try my best.

From the day first I walked in the door, I knew my life was going to change. The Zappos Culture is out of this world and has not only changed my outlook on a work environment but has changed my life outside of Zappos. I was immediately taken in as a family member and was embraced. Each and every Zapponian practices the Ten Core Values and that is what makes Zappos a step ahead of the rest. To me, the Zappos Culture not only incorporates the Core Values but also love, family and trust. Zappos has made my life better and I can honestly say I am thankful for this company!

Veronica J.

employee since 2005

The Zappos Culture ... is. :)

Veronica M.

employee since 2010

I love, love, LOVE working at Zappos! I've even got my husband talking about how wonderful Zappos is. The best part of Zappos is the friends and family I've made here.

We moved out to Las Vegas not knowing a soul and I can honestly say that I have made lifelong friends I now consider my family. I'm so excited to know that I will continue to grow and learn with Zappos. It will never be "just a job." Louis Khan once said, "Even a brick wants to be something." My something is Zappos. :) I am blessed to be part of this company. Thank you!

Victoria P.

employee since 2010

In order to explain what the Zappos Culture means to me, I would like to tell a brief story of the journey that led me here. I was born into an amazing, kind family; a mother, father and brother. I had a very enjoyable academic career and began working at age 16, despite my parents' hesitation. I really enjoyed my first job, which was in the food industry, as I was fortunate to have worked for some very kind and fair people. I entered college and began working for a company that had beliefs similar to Zappos. Those beliefs changed over time, but I was still able to make it work. I had the pleasure of being in a college course in organizational behavior with a brilliant professor who taught me an interesting lesson. He taught me about several companies and, most importantly, about this idea of company culture. I was sold on his teachings and believed that one could be nice and still be successful. Many years later, I had a chance encounter with an intriguing customer who rekindled the spark that my professor had stoked. I had been married for a couple of years by this time. My husband worked for a company named Zappos and had been introduced to the company by some close friends. He constantly told me how much he enjoyed working for Zappos. He finally convinced me to interview and I again saw a spark. I was very lucky and was hired by Zappos in 2010.

By now, I am sure you are asking if I have a point to this story and the answer is yes. Zappos has confirmed my belief in my family's, professor's, and customers' teachings. People can be nice, hold others accountable, respect individuality while embracing teamwork, and still be a part of a successful business. This is what the Zappos Culture means to me. I would like to thank all of the remarkable people I have met along the way. I would also like to thank my new friends and family here at Zappos for exemplifying the company culture. I am even now able to thank the not-so-positive influences I have come across throughout the years because I appreciate what I have here at this company even more. Simply put, I enjoy coming to work!

Vincent Q.

employee since 2010

The Zappos Culture, to me, means not having to be somebody I'm not. I can be as kooky as I'd like to be without fear of being judged or held back. While I'm not the loudest, social or outgoing being there is, there is still a place for me at Zappos. On my very first day here, I thought to myself "Great, what have I gotten myself into? There's no way for me, being as quiet as I am, to ever survive here! I'm a married guy with a wife and a six-year old; I should've had this job 10 years ago." Well, eight months later, I turned out to be wrong. Not only am I surviving, but thriving! All my co- workers (or should I say, my family) have been more than accepting and accommodating. Every lead I've had has been encouraging and made me aware of my potential here. Zappos is not just a job, but a gift. There's not one day that I don't look forward to coming to work. My co-workers are awesome. Helping our customers is rewarding and there's always something new happening here. So essentially, for me, Zappos is what I've been looking for my whole career and I'm glad to be here.

Vinny V.

employee since 2008

Zappos … It's been almost three years and I'm still feeling lucky to be a part of all this. Collectively, we are all the Zappos Culture. Our everyday interactions are the Zappos Culture. Our Ten Core Values are a great foundation for our culture. It's really amazing to work for a company that not only cares about its customers, but also about its employees. I believe that being cared for tends to make you care a little more as well. =)

I appreciate being able to work with so many awesome people. Many people along the way have helped me, and I am trying to do my part by giving back as well. Since I started working at Zappos, my life has only changed for the better. I'm sittin' nicer than I have ever been. I'm very thankful for coming across Zappos' path.

Thanks for reading our Culture Book!

Viola H.

employee since 2007

The Zappos Culture means that we are a family. We not only work together, but we look out for one another and help one another whenever possible. We are all able to have unique personalities and we respect each other.

I am proud to wear my Zappos shirt in public and am honored at how many people know who we are. They come up to me and ask questions about the company. Many can't believe how great it is to work here, but when I am finished talking about Zappos, they want to work here too! Zappos IS the greatest place to work!!!!

Wendy Z.

employee since 2010

The Zappos Culture has had a great impact on my life and the way I view my co-workers. Having worked for "corporate America" and then been blessed enough to join the Zappos family, I have discovered it's a complete 180 degrees from anything I've ever experienced. Fun and weird? Done and done. Team and family spirit? Done and done. Open and honest relationships through communication? Done, done and DONE! I could go on and on and on for pages and pages about how spectacular the Zappos Culture is. For me, it's about being myself, being happy in what I do, and being happiest with who I am.

William L.

employee since 2010

Zappos is a home away from home. I'm a transplant from Michigan and have only been in Las Vegas for about a year. I had no family and only a couple of friends when I first moved out here. But, through working at Zappos, I've been able to gain both friends and family. The Zappos Culture encourages us to foster relationships with people from work through team building activities, corporate challenge sporting events, happy hours and the continuous cycling of the teams through which we move.

Yoshi

employee since 2010

The Zappos Culture is like bacon. It makes everything amazing!

Zachary W.

employee since 2010

Culture, to me, is valuing certain qualities fitted towards a common goal. Some of Zappos' best qualities are based on customer service, and that dedication to our customers is supported by our culture. Our Culture is the ability and desire to make a positive connection on any level approached with every person. Our Culture is the way we handle our drive to bridge the gaps and access the hearts of our customers. Our Culture is friendly and open, genuine and simple, classy and weird, nerdy but popular, successful and growing, busy with work but partying. I guess you could say that, in a way, the Zappos Culture is how we do business.

Zerina P.

employee since 2008

The Zappos Culture, to me, means family! We argue, we disagree, we cry, we laugh. However, at the end of the day, this is not my job, it's my family!

...WHAT HE SAID

Z MERCHANDISING
Happy Hours

VERY
HAPPY
HOURS...

ZLCT
Recognition
HAPPY HOUR

OREO
Art Contest

2011 ZAPPOS

Family Picnic

PIE
Your Boss
DAY

THE AMAZING
Easter Hunt

Zappos Core Value #2

Embrace
and
Drive Change

**(Although building a robot to play
roulette might be a bit much)**

Aaron T.

employee since 2005

The Zappos Culture is continually changing. I never come into the building knowing what to expect. Some days it's a parade, or a prize raffle, or basketball in the office. Other days, it's a pine car derby or a scavenger hunt. There's always some element inserted into the atmosphere of this building that creates that loose, relaxed, fun environment that's become so characteristic of this company. Every year I write something different in these books, but the core of our culture remains the same: delivering the best service to our customers, having fun doing it, and letting us be ourselves in the process. It will continue to evolve as the years pass, and I'm grateful that I get to be a part of that evolution.

Aila M.

employee since 2009

I love coming to work; it is a happy place and full of friends, laughter and fun. It is also always challenging, hard work, brain-stretching, learning. We can tackle and enjoy the challenges and win because we have our Zappos family to support us. I wouldn't want it any other way!

Alana P.

employee since 2006

The Zappos Culture is captivating and unconditional to every person who walks through the door. No matter how big the company gets, the pulse of what has made the company successful has remained the same. This company has made me realize that happy people create the solid foundation for a company's achievements. Every day I'm reminded of how lucky I am to work for this amazing company.

Alesha G.

employee since 2004

The Zappos Culture has provided me with a career I love, as well as friends who are my family that I can go to for anything. It is a life that I never imagined I would have. Moving to Las Vegas seven years ago, I really didn't know what I was signing up for other than to become a merchandising assistant and eventually a buyer. But now, I'm a part of something bigger. I finally made my goal of becoming a buyer last year and am involved every day with people from different teams working together to make Zappos even better. Being here at Zappos, living the culture every day makes me feel like I'm part of something bigger and it's because of the culture that everyone here wants to be involved and take this company to the next level. I'm proud to be a part of it and couldn't imagine doing anything else.

Alison C.

employee since 2008

The freedom of possibility and open opportunity. What I love about Zappos is that you are free to be yourself and you are surrounded by a support team that enables you to continue to grow and become the person you want to be. The "pipeline" classes are amazing, and what other company pays you and allows you the time to continue to grow and learn? If you have a great idea about how to improve the business, to streamline a process, or to create a brand new concept, Zappos allows you to present it and then own it and make it a reality. Regardless of your position within the company, you have a voice. You truly have the ability to make a difference for yourself, your co-workers and Zappos' customers!

Alison D.

employee since 2011

I have found a true home at Zappos. I have always felt that I am slightly quirkier than the average person, but here I am plain vanilla, comparatively speaking. Coming to work means experiencing the culture that has crept into every facet of this awe-inspiring company. My job makes me happy, as do my team and co-workers. I hope that the Zappos way of life becomes like a Kudzu vine and takes over the world.

Alyssa B.

employee since 2011

Just a few months ago, I decided to move across the country to work with Zappos. "Lucky" does not adequately express the feeling I have about working here. I feel fortunate to work with such amazing, genuine people. Since I started working here, the meaning of work has changed dramatically. The passion that everyone here has is contagious and I can honestly say I am happy and super-fortunate to come here every day! :)

Amber R.

employee since 2005

I have been coming to work at Zappos every day for the last six years and I am still as excited as I was when I walked through the doors for the first time. My friends have turned into family and I have found myself along the way - a job that turned into a career I never knew I wanted. I know I am one of the lucky ones! I count my blessings each day and working at Zappos is definitely at the top of the list! No other company has made me feel this way and I am convinced no other could.

Andrea L.

employee since 2007

Whenever someone asks me where I work, I always say "Zappos!" with great pride. Immediately, smiles appear on their faces and they proceed tell me how lucky I am to work for such a great company. Of course, I already know this and I thank my lucky stars every day. It's amazing how happy employees affect their work every day.

Anonymous

employee since 2005

What a ride it has been so far! I've been here for over five years now and it has truly humbled me, in terms of all the successes we have had. Although the Zappos Culture is a key ingredient of our professional success, the importance of our culture has had a far greater effect on me personally. The culture keeps our relationships close and, as my boss would put it, "friendlier than most." As the company grows, the teams within each department seem to have created and maintained their own culture or sub-culture. Our team, in particular, has had the experience of gaining many new members. One would think that those changes would be challenging, in terms of forming new relationships. However, it has not been difficult because of our culture, which provides an environment in which we look forward to being involved in on a daily basis. As for the past, our culture is the cause of eternal friendships formed and unforgettable experiences engraved in our hearts. This is what the Zappos Culture means to me today. Tomorrow will bring another story.

Anonymous

employee since 2004

Simply, the Zappos Culture is found within every one of the Ten Core Values that we strive to live by on a daily basis and in how we interpret them while still being true to ourselves. Delivering WOW Through Service (Core Value #1), Embracing and Driving Change (#2), Creating Fun and a Little Weirdness (#3), Being Adventurous, Creative and Open-Minded (#4), Pursuing Growth and Learning (#5), Building Open and Honest Relationships Through Communication (#6), Building a Positive Team and Family Spirit (#7), Doing More With Less (#8), Being Passionate and Determined (#9), and Being Humble (#10). It's up to each of us to spread and promote these Core Values to keep the Zappos Culture alive. If you should ever lose your way, always look back to these Ten Core Values and you will find your way home to the Zappos family.

Anonymous

employee since 2010

To me, the Zappos Culture means having the opportunity to enjoy and love what you do, where you work, and the people you work with. I come to work excited to be here and eager to learn something new every day. I'm truly blessed to work at a company that puts so much effort into ensuring its employees are happy.

Anonymous

employee since 2007

What does the Zappos Culture mean to me? Our culture is unlike anything I have ever experienced before. I feel lucky and very fortune to be a part of the Zappos family! I have been at Zappos for four years now, and these have honestly been the best four years of my working career! I have made some really great friends and met wonderful people. We are all like family! I would never ask for anything else! :)

Anonymous

employee since 2010

The Zappos Culture means you get to be who you want to be ... not only professionally but personally. We are encouraged to step up and be leaders, planners, or just ourselves, whoever that is. This environment allows individuals to thrive. Not only are we encouraged to grow professionally, we are encouraged to be better people. We are more kind, we open doors for people, say hello when we pass someone in the hallways, and we give back and participate in fundraisers. We are challenged to do more and be better people. In return, we are better to our vendors, partners, and co-workers.

Ashlyn B.

employee since 2009

This is my second entry in the Zappos Culture book and it's been an amazing year. I feel blessed that I was given the opportunity to work here and to be a part of something so special. Everyone here is truly happy and I haven't ever had a bad day at work or a day when I felt like I didn't want to come in. Everyone here is my family and the longer I work here, the more my family grows and the more my love for everyone here grows. It's truly a special place and it's so cool when you meet someone who has heard of our company's culture and they have a zillion questions. They are in awe that you are part of such an amazing company. I love my job and everyone here is my family. I feel like I am a part of something bigger than myself, and that feeling is impossible to define in words.

Avneet S.

employee since 2009

The best thing about the Zappos Culture is that, not only are you working with friends and truly happy coming in to work, it is also what happens when you randomly see a Zapponian on the street and you instantly connect. The reason for that connection isn't necessarily because you are friends or you work together; it's because you share the same values. It is difficult to find that connection anywhere else, and that is just one of the many reasons for my happiness. More than a workplace, this is a place for creativity, freedom and building relationships.

Betsy D.

employee since 2010

Yeah, runnin' down a dream that never would come to me workin' on a mystery, goin' wherever it leads, runnin' down a dream
— Tom Petty

Tom Petty said it best, but Zappos makes it possible for me.

Braden M.

employee since 2006

I moved to Las Vegas with the intention of saving up some money to complete school. My sister in-law worked here in customer loyalty and she was able to get me an interview at Zappos. I was hired to man the lunchroom, which afforded me the opportunity to meet everyone at the company. Almost immediately, I knew that I wasn't moving back to Arizona. The people were too nice and the opportunity was too great.

Five years later and I am buying shoes for the outdoor division and couldn't be happier. Zappos has pushed me to grow both personally and professionally, light years beyond traditional education. I truly believe that every day I am at Zappos I am a better, happier person.

Bridget D.

employee since 2009

"Happiness is a direction, not a place."
— Sydney J. Harris

Brooke J.

employee since 2005

Company culture can make or break a company. Zappos would never have advanced this far without our culture. The company genuinely cares about its customers and employees. We all follow the Golden Rule. I think the main reason we are all so happy and motivated is because we truly care about the customer and employee experience here. The work atmosphere is unparalleled. The office is relaxed and fun. We work hard, but definitely have many hearty laughs throughout the day. Work can be fun!

Cameron G.

employee since 2005

The Zappos Culture, to me, is about friendships, life-changing experiences, uncontrollable laughter, "ah-ha!" moments, finding higher meaning and being professional, yet casual. It is also about doing what is right, learning from mistakes, discovering the positives, using your instincts, taking risks, evolving and recognition. It's about having a voice and being heard, team effort, taking charge and being the change. It's also about having heart, about unexpected generosity, spontaneous adventures and endless opportunities.

Carla L.

employee since 2006

What I love about the Zappos Culture is that it's constantly evolving. Everyone is willing to pitch in when it counts; it truly is all about teamwork and achieving our universal goal: the best customer service around! I can still proudly say that, to this day, I have not experienced great customer service consistently with any other company. I also love how everyone is committed to evolving the company's culture. There are always fun, new ideas that people come up with, whether it's getting to know another team because they wrote funny details about themselves on a shamrock, and the unsuspecting team had to guess who wrote it. (The prize was a beer when you guess correctly!) Or whether it's a scavenger hunt where everyone in the entire company to signs up for the corporate challenge. The Zappos Culture is precious to each one of us and, thankfully, no one is willing to let it fade! Zappos really is the best company ever! I look forward to seeing how its culture evolves this year!

Casey C.

employee since 2008

Zappos is great! Where else can you have wine tastings, parades and bbqs and still call it work? I love my co-workers and that they have become like my family. I feel very lucky to work here.

Cat S.

employee since 2008

The Zappos Culture is definitely one of a kind and something I've never experienced anywhere else. Our culture has become a huge part of my life, both inside and outside the office, and it is something I value because it is so special.

Cathy T.
employee since 2007

This is my fourth entry for the Zappos Culture Book and what the company means to me. Simply put, I love waking up and coming to work to be here with the craziness and excitement that comes daily, whether it is from my co-workers or vendors. I feel truly blessed to work here. Our passion is exemplified in our culture daily. This magical culture is the breeding ground for productive and happy people, and it makes work creative and fun.

Catie S.
employee since 2008

Giggling and work. Lots of giggling and work. My mother used to tell me as a child "stop giggling like an idiot" but I haven't stopped giggling like an idiot. So take that, Mother! I get the opportunity to work with amazing, talented people every day. Everyone is dedicated to making Zappos a flawless place to work, and without all the people I work with, Zappos wouldn't have the culture that it does.

Christina Q.
employee since 2010

To me, the Zappos Culture means providing a place where I can express myself and challenge new possibilities at work, and to go above and beyond my expectations. The support of all of my co-workers has made coming into work rewarding. I can't express how honored and grateful I am to be working with such a great company!

Christopher P.
employee since 2004

Zappos means everything to me. I never dreamed of working for a company that could motivate and inspire me as much as Zappos does. The idea of Zappos being "a calling" for me, "the last place I'll ever work," or simply "a place I love coming to every morning" are all emotions I have and felt since my first week here. It's easy to call this place amazing. What seems so difficult for other companies, but so easy for Zappos, is the culture, which is held together by so many great people who live and breathe our Core Values ... the people that influence and inspire me every day and the people I consider my family and best of friends ... people who care because they do. I love this place! :)

Claire S.
employee since 2007

It's been four years and I still smile on my drive into work each morning. I feel blessed to come into an environment every day where I feel supported, challenged, empowered and cared for. Being part of the Zappos family really feels like home and I am excited to see where the future will take this powerful company and its wonderful people.

Courtney B.
employee since 2010

To me, the Zappos Culture means the opposite of typical corporate culture. You are listened to, valued, and taken care of. You enjoy coming to work every day. Your teammates become your family. You are empowered to excel at your position in the manner that you see fit. You are given freedom to prioritize. You are given freedom to take initiatives. You are given freedom to go outside to the temporary carnival and get your face painted if you need an afternoon break. Excellence is expected - even demanded - but mistakes are also understood. Most importantly, it's about being part of something bigger than yourself and bigger than the bottom line, and that breeds fulfillment.

Dana Z.
employee since 2009

It has only been a year and a half and I feel like I have been with the Zappos family since the beginning! The most amazing thing to me is how we are surrounded by so many people from all walks of life, yet we have this special thing in common - our culture. What I love most about Zappos is being able to get involved with so much more than what we call jobs. I feel like I have found a place where I do have to work, but where I am also making a difference in people's lives - whether it is through helping people within the company or volunteering for the many projects that we do throughout the community. We are making a difference!

Dave H.
employee since 2009

The Zappos Culture, to me, is about being part of something that encourages me to be the best version of myself. We work hard, we play hard, and we make sure that everyone we interact with - either at work or just out there in the world - gets to enjoy that feeling right along with us! And with any luck, it makes them a little happier.

David C.
employee since 2006

The Zappos Culture is involved with everything we do. Whether we are interacting with fellow employees or communicating with vendors, our culture always comes through, and those who come in contact with it know it's something special. I'm always amazed at how many people come through our office on tours that heard about our culture and wanted to see it first hand. The fact that so many people want to experience what we have here speaks volumes about the importance and uniqueness of the Zappos Culture.

Deborah W.

employee since 2009

When people find out where I work, the reactions are quite remarkable!! Most of the time I get a smile or a laugh! When I question their reaction, most say that they are customers, have read Delivering Happiness or have seen something on TV about Zappos. They ask, "Is Zappos really like what we have heard?" My answer is "Yes!" Then they tell me, "You are so lucky to work there!" My answer is "Yes, you have no idea how fortunate I am!" Every day is a new experience and it is a pleasure to be associated with a company that Delivers Happiness to so many.

Dee C.

employee since 2007

I love Zappos! I love Zappos! I love Zappos! No really, I truly love my company. There has been no other company like it for me. I have an awesome team and they have all become my family. I still love walking in the doors every Monday morning, ready to go. Where else can you come to work and never know what you are going to see that day? A guy dressed in a hot dog suit; boys running around in super-hero costumes with a large camera following them; a person wearing enormous Sherpa-lined boots; pie-eating contests; dunk tanks; monkeys hanging around what people know as our executive team. It is a world in and of itself when you walk in our doors. WOW! We are so lucky to help continue to grow the Zappos Culture. We live our jobs and we love every minute of it. I wouldn't trade it for the world. I <3 Zappos!

Dena M.

employee since 2006

The Zappos Culture means freedom to me. Freedom to be myself at work, not cookie cutter and scripted. Freedom that allows me to seize opportunities to help me grow, personally and professionally. Freedom to embrace my co-workers' quirks and attributes, and them mine. Freedom to speak my mind, and the freedom to come to work and contribute to something greater than myself with a positive purpose. In this economy, I'm lucky to have a job. Even luckier to be able to build a career at a company that lets me be me.

Derek F.

employee since 2008

Three years ago I sat down with ÊÊDr. Vik and let him know where I wanted to be in five years. Turns out it only took about two. I pursued growth and learning at my own pace and did it with a smile because I was truly happy doing it! I get to work at the greatest company, doing what I love. I couldn't be happier and I know that the good times are going to keep rolling in.

Eileen T.

employee since 2002

Zappos has a work hard, play hard culture! Everyone is focused on what is best for the company and not just their particular area. There is no distinction between work life and personal life, since we are all passionate about what we do. We are our own competition, since we're constantly working to make sure our services are the most innovative in the market for our customers. We are never discouraged and always looking for a solution to any roadblock.

Eiron M.

employee since 2010

The culture here at Zappos is unlike anything that I have experienced before. We are truly allowed to be whomever and whatever we want to be!

Elisa N.

employee since 2009

The Zappos Culture, to me, is all about learning and the relationships we build while doing it. We work with a family of people that want to help us succeed and are always willing to give a helping hand. We have a broad mix of personalities, yet they all mesh. We have fun in and out of the office. I love it!

Emily B.

employee since 2009

When I was studying at UNLV to follow a career path in Education, I already knew there would be days I would dread at work. Luckily, I chose a different path, which led me to Zappos! To me, the best part of Zappos is their support in helping us follow our passion. Last year my Culture Book entry was part of our Customer Loyalty Team department, since that is where I started my journey at Zappos. With the progression plan Zappos has created, I have been able to follow my dream of one day becoming a buyer with the best leadership one could have and great classes to teach me all I need to know. When I started working here, I never imagined I would get so much from my "job."

Erica W.

employee since 2004

I am honored to continue driving the Zappos Culture - treating people the way we would like to be treated. Conducting our business in a partnership manner with our brands, co-workers and customers. Working hard and having fun doing it. Being free with ideas and turning those ideas into reality through partnerships developed and connections made internally and externally. The Zappos Culture is making our dreams come true.

Estela B.

employee since 2010

I've been at Zappos for almost a year now and I can't begin to quantify how many ways my life has improved. Before coming to Zappos, the thought of actually enjoying my job, let alone looking forward to coming in, was only a pipe dream. Now I could never settle for less. Working for a company that recognizes hard work and fosters creativity is something that I'm truly grateful for.

Fred M.

employee since 1999

Wikipedia defines culture as follows:

• Excellence of taste in the fine arts and humanities, also known as high culture
• An integrated pattern of human knowledge, belief, and behavior that depends upon the capacity for symbolic thought and social learning
• The set of shared attitudes, values, goals, and practices that characterizes an institution, organization or group.
I think they missed something in these definitions with regards to the "Zappos Culture."

Zappos Culture (aka Family Zappos) A place that provides love, support and encouragement. A place you have to experience to truly believe. A place like no other. One of the best places in the world to work.

Galen H.

employee since 2004

Let me just say, WOW, what a year!

I broke my neck in August of this year at my 38th birthday party. I had to have three surgeries, was in a halo brace for 75 days and was out of the office from August 13th through December 26th. On ÊÊthe day of my accident, I remember Tony telling me I was going to be OK while we waited for the paramedics to get to my house. I remember Fred Mossler and Steve Hill leaning over my bed after my second surgery telling me that this was one hell of a way to get out of MAGIC. I remember being in the rehab hospital and having many people from Zappos come to visit and wish me well. I remember Tony coming to the rehab hospital and visiting with me as I learned how to walk again. I remember the outpouring of support over Facebook from many, many people from Zappos. I would not have recovered as fast as I did if it hadn't been for the outpouring of love and support from everyone at Zappos. The support, the caring and love they showed me is a testament to the Zappos Culture.

Graham M.

employee since 2006

The Zappos Culture is constantly evolving and always new, but the thing I love most about it is that I truly love the people I work with. I like just talking to them. Getting to know them. Helping them work through things. We've been working on a specific project in Merchandising over the last month. We've got a room of very passionate people, many of whom disagree with each other strongly. It's been pretty heated at times. The thing about it is that we all really care about this place and this company we're part of, and if that weren't true, things would never get so heated. My hope for the future of our culture is for us to grow and find ways to harness these passions for incredible improvement as a company.

Heather C.

employee since 2007

In essence, the Zappos Culture is the Golden Rule: Treat others as you would like others to treat you. We live it every day and it is evident in all that we do.

Heaven T.

employee since 2006

Unfortunately, there's not enough space for my entry to get into all of the inside jokes and random pranks that go on at Zappos. I can tell you that it's what I look forward to every day and I'm extremely happy. Stop by Steve P.'s desk and ask him to tell you about his knee!

Jared F.

employee since 2009

When I think about all the fun I've had at Zappos, I'm still shocked that we have created such a great environment. Even before I worked at Zappos, I knew I wanted to find a company to work for that valued not only profits, but also its impact on the community and others. Zappos is amazing! Have a good summer and see you next year.

Oh, and the worst part of ÊÊthis photo is that I didn't have to buy anything for that themed happy hour costume.

Jarett A.

employee since 2008

Asking "where to begin" implies that the Zappos Culture is describable. That we are able to do what we do everyday in a continuously evolving culture makes me feel truly blessed. Having a super "rad" and "funner" community to be part of - one that is also our workplace - is unheard of in the fashion industry. It's exciting, it's exhilarating, it's ... the Zappos Culture. We uphold every foundational Core Value and with a constant family mentality. It's unprecedented and I think that's why so many people are interested in what goes on in here! It's hilarious because everyone always asks me "How do you guys get any work done there?" Simply put, the culture is the epitome of the work hard, play hard philosophy. As McDonald's famously exclaims, "I'm lovin' it!"

Jay A.

employee since 2009

This is my second year at Zappos and my second entry in the Zappos Culture Book. I have to say that my thoughts at year two are very different than year one. In year one, I was a little skeptical about the Zappos Culture and what it would mean to me. But from the viewpoint of year two, I can tell you it is no joke! The culture here at Zappos is wonderful and you can really make it your own! I have never worked anywhere with stronger or better relationships. I think of everyone as friends and in many cases, best friends. So, I am going to call them Zapfriends! So, here is what I have I done in the past year with my Zapfriends:

• I have thrown my very first wedding shower/ bachelorette party
• Attended a wedding in Louisiana, bringing a Zapfriend
• Attended a 50th birthday party
• Attended a 40th birthday party
• Attended a 30th birthday party
• Won the fist pumping contest at the Zappos Jersey Shore Day and scared a lot of female Zapfriends
• Was detained in Canadian customs with a Zapfriend (that's a long story)
• Celebrated 6pm.com's first million dollar day
• Dressed as a Kardashian, as a pirate and as a nerd
• Referred, hired and housed a Zapfriend for eight months (and yes, we are still Zapfriends)
• And finally, hired my first Zapfriend ...

All with my Zapfriends.

Jeanne M.

employee since 2006

H Having a group of extended family and lifelong friends
A And working in a dynamic environment where the fun never ends!
P Pursuing personal and professional growth that I never could have dreamt of
P Pipeline classes that are rewarding and some of most enlightening time spent
I Independence to make decisions about running big brands
N Not to mention incredible team outings, happy hours and
E Excitement to see all the individual growth of those on my team,
S Since they each inspire me, WOW me, and every day make me beam!
S So looking forward to Zappos infusing our culture in the downtown scene!

Jeff B.

employee since 2006

The Zappos Culture means many things to me, but most important, it means family. I know it sounds pretty corny, but it is true. When I am with my real family I feel comfortable and relaxed. I feel like I can be myself and not hold back at all. At work, I feel the same way. I feel like myself all the time and I do not have to put up a prissy front to anyone. I am encouraged to just be who I am. Without our culture, Zappos would just be another corporate website that sells stuff. I definitely love the culture here. It is a new experience every day ... Oh, and buy clothing from Zappos!!!

Jeffrey E.

employee since 2010

I joined Zappos a little over a year ago and my experience here has truly exceeded my expectations. I have worked for two other great companies that have good cultures, but nothing compared to the culture Zappos has created. It is truly amazing to see Tony and Fred empower the people to build the culture and truly live the Core Values. The company truly does walk the talk. This is very rare in the business world and I am extremely happy to be a part of this family. Zappos has given me the opportunity to run the business and trusts me to make the right decisions for the company. This doesn't happen very often today outside of our company. I look forward to the future growth of Zappos and I am proud to be part of that.

Jenn M.

employee since 2006

Believe it or not, the constant tours, parades, classes, contests - they all start to feel habitual in their own ways, eventually. Our 'it' factor is the family we've created here over the years. Whether it's a personal or professional challenge, the support and compassion you receive with this family is mind-blowing.

Jennifer S.

employee since 2007

The Zappos Culture is like this unspoken thing that ties us together as a team. I walk through the halls every day and have fun interactions with many different people. We are able to be ourselves and the company embraces our differences. I laugh more and more every day I work here and feel lucky to be a part of a higher purpose.

Jennifer T.

employee since 2009

ÊÊ/\\--s--/\\ - - = O =   * \\-----/ This sums up my team.

Zappos allows you to grow professionally and personally. We are given so many amazing opportunities to do the things we are passionate about. Not only are we able to learn from each other and get mentored by great leaders, but we are also able to grow wonderful friendships.

Jessica C.

employee since 2010

Where do I start? I have been here for a little less than a year and I cannot even begin to explain the awesome relationships and experiences I have built already. At Zappos, those around me constantly inspire me. We have the opportunity to take risks, think outside of the box, and turn ideas into a reality. I feel blessed to be a part of a company that truly embraces you for just being you.

Jessica M.

employee since 2009

The Zappos Culture means being able to express ourselves ... to show our differences and know we don't have to hide them. We have the freedom to complete our tasks in various ways that work for us individually and as a team. We are free to be creative, to find "out-of-the-box" solutions. We are not criticized for unusual ideas. We are given the opportunity to develop in a healthy, productive way.

Jessica R.

employee since 2009

Zappos Culture = Freedom. Empowerment. Creativity. Wings (not the kind you eat but the kind you fly with). Humility. Friends. Living for others. An open mind. A chance to shine. Focus. Encouragement. Challenges. Hope. Life. Choices. Adventure. No limits. Smiles. Diversity. Pranks. Embracing change. That whole reply was off the top of my head ... holy moley!

Jim C.

employee since 2004

WOW! I can't believe I'm writing another Culture Book entry! Has it been a year already? Time seems to pass so quickly when you work at a company like Zappos. Well, it's getting harder and harder to write these because I feel like I've said everything I can about our culture, but I'll do my best.
I feel the same way about our culture now as I did "back in the day" when I was hired. Back then I felt like I was a part of something special, something real, and those feelings haven't changed. As the company has grown and evolved, we've managed to keep a grasp on what really matters ... the people. There is no other company in this world that treats its employees the way Zappos does, and you can feel it in the atmosphere when you walk into the building. We are all just people who were hired not only because we could do the job, but also because we all knew Zappos is a special place and it's not for everyone. We are all part of the same breed - people who like to have fun, work hard and reap the benefits of our hard work. As long as I continue to work for this company, I will always know that I am part of something special ... the Zappos Culture.

Joel G.

employee since 2010

Our culture is one of the two things I really enjoy about being at Zappos. The other is ice cream sandwiches. And visiting finance. Wait, that's three. Apparently there are more than I thought.

Corporate culture is a company's personality. If your company were a person, would it be fun, approachable, kind and welcoming yet adventurous and unpredictable? Would people want to hang out with your company after work, maybe hit a happy hour for drinks and play a little beer pong while you tell them the story of how you were questioned by the police and mistaken for a lady of the night? Would you invite your company to celebrate at a local bar downtown, make some bad decisions, stay out until the wee hours and then give them a ride home even though they live on the other side of town?

You spend a lot of your time at work. You should enjoy what you do and the people you do it with. If not, go find the ice cream sandwiches.

Josh S.

employee since 2006

Zappos has always been a cool company to work for. I remember back when I was hired, I really didn't know too much about Zappos, the culture, or E-commerce in general. I remember telling people where I worked, and the response that I would normally get would be, "What is Zappos?" Now-a-days when I mention that I work for Zappos, about 90% of the time I end up feeling like I work with a sort of Rock Star company because of responses like "WOW, I heard/have seen/or know how cool a place that is to work!" Awesome. This is my fourth entry in this lovely yearbook. My original thoughts are pretty hard to come by because of what I have written in prior years. However, this year means a lot to me. Being born and raised in the best city that I know of, Las Vegas, I carry a huge sense of pride for this place (even stamping my body with the most notable icon that we have). In recent months, Zappos announced that we will be at the forefront of the redevelopment of downtown with our move, scheduled for 2012. I couldn't be more excited about the plans that the city has to improve, and the part that Zappos has in the improvement of a part of town that has typically been characterized as run down. And that is what the Zappos Culture means to me.

We could go on all day about family, friends, community, etc., but at the end of the day, Zappos has adopted the city that I love as its own and is planning to give back to it exponentially. Dr. Vik said that it was his time to go when he could step away from Zappos because he knew that the culture would not change one bit. And I feel like it is sort of the same for the Zappos move downtown. The family at Zappos knows how we feel about each other, and now it just seems natural to spread the love to the city that has been so good to us.

Kara T.

employee since 2010

Holy Sh*$! Or, for better words, WOW! I can't believe I've already been here for a little over a year. What they say is right: "Time flies when you're having fun." :)

Of course, I knew the definition of "WOW," but I never really got it until I started working at Zappos. It's amazing how many times I get WOWed, I see people getting WOWed, or I hear the word "WOW" at this place. The Zappos Culture has everything to do with it. It's so refreshing to wake up every morning and get to experience it, live it and love it!!! Best move I ever made was coming to work at Zappos.

Kari M.

employee since 2010

When I was little, I loved the feeling of staying home on a rainy day with my family. This is my first year here at Zappos and when it was raining this past fall, I still had that same happy feeling and I was at work. Weird!

Needless to say, but I will say it anyway, I definitely feel like I am "part of the Zappos Family," and happy to be part of it.

Karrie M.

employee since 2006

The Zappos Culture has become so many things to me over the past four and a half years ... home away from home and friends that have become like family. It continues to be the exciting and constantly evolving company that I dreamed about working for. With the amazing news of our new campus downtown, I can't imagine what the next four years and beyond will hold.

Kate C.

employee since 2010

I moved here from Michigan, and my team pokes fun at my thick Midwest pronunciation of "mom" and my love of lakes, apple pie, hockeytown, Michigan cherries, POP, MSU Spartans and anything else that came from the "high five of America" state. But within days of joining Zappos and the Private Label team I realized I had plenty to appreciate here in Vegas as well. I have a supportive and fun company, an opportunity to do a job I truly love and people to work with that I consider family. So I don't have some of my favorite things from the Great Lakes State but I wouldn't have it any other way. Zappos is my ultimate favorite thing!

Katherine T.

employee since 2006

There is so much that makes the Zappos Culture stand out, but when I really reflect on the most important aspects of the culture, to me it isn't parades or amazing benefits that really make Zappos unique. They are like the special effects in a movie. They add a lot of flash, but the substance is in the story and characters. At Zappos, we are given a sense of purpose and community that drives us in the same direction. We feel empowered to make changes for the better, both at work and in our lives. It is this sense of community that really brings us together as one team, and it is my co-workers who have become my friends and my friends who have become my family that make the Zappos Culture so important to me. We are never discouraged from being ourselves and are able to take time to laugh at the small things so we can focus on what is important. Even when you have days when nothing seems to go your way, you know that going in to work will be what you need to turn your day around.

Kathleen J.

employee since 2008

Three years ago, when I said "Yes, I will be a Zappos employee!" I knew I was on the verge of something great! I didn't realize then how much it would feel like the best decision I've made in my life so far!! Every day I remind myself that we have to be some of the luckiest, most blessed people on this planet. We are members of the Zappos family and we work at the "Happiest Place on Earth." (Sorry, Mr. Disney!)

Kathy K.

employee since 2006

The Zappos Culture is all about letting me be who I am ... letting each of us be who we are. Zappos Culture is unique, in that it not only allows me but also encourages me to build relationships with the people I work with, both inside and outside the building. These are relationships that I know will last a lifetime. I feel special that I am a part of such an amazing company and Culture.

Katie D.

employee since 2011

Today is the first day of my fourth week at Zappos and these past weeks have been a whirlwind. Like most of us here in Las Vegas, I knew about Zappos, especially since my very close friend was an employee. She let me tag along to a couple of the vendor parties and the holiday party, and I always knew this place was special, but never really thought too seriously about working there. At the time, I was working in the Retail Division of a luxury resort-casino on The Strip (my first job out of college) and I was happy there. I had a small number of friends at work, I worked hard, I did very well there, I felt like I had a lot of ownership and I was proud of where I worked.

However, as it happened, this very close friend of mine (the one who works at Zappos) actually became one of my roommates! After she moved in I saw more closely what her life was like at Zappos. She had all these friends at work. Her ability to grow quickly with Zappos was very impressive; she attended lots of happy hours, was able to travel for work all the time, and the list goes on. The bottom line to me was this: she was invested in Zappos and it wasn't so much of a job as it was a lifestyle. (I had heard the stories before, but then I was seeing through my roommate's eyes how different this Zappos really was.) Around this time I developed a very strong fondness for Zappos. There was all this buzz about the company really helping in the efforts to revitalize the downtown Las Vegas scene, and even moving its offices down there! This pulled me in even more! I could not ignore the level of commitment to excellence Tony and the rest of the Zappos family displayed on every level (community, culture, customer service, etc). I wanted to be a part of it, and I knew I could contribute to making it even better. (I know a superb thing when I see it.) One thing led to another and I was lucky enough to be offered a job here in Merchandising. So here I am and I can already tell how right this decision has been for me. I can only imagine the ride I am in for, and I am more than thrilled to experience it!

Kelly M.
employee since 2006

The Zappos Culture is a manifestation of the unique balance of its Core Values within each of our employees. We have our own passions and backgrounds but share the same goals, values and ideals.

Kelly R.
employee since 2006

Dear Zappos,

It's been too long since I have said "thank you" for everything you do. It's to the point where those two words -"thank you" - don't do justice to what's been given to me over the past five years. You have seen me through several phases of life and the culture has always amazed me and meant different things to me. We have changed from Zappos to the Zappos family, and that seems fitting for my Culture Book entry this year.

The first thing I find most amazing is that I had twins on August 4th, 2010, and I was able to spend all 12 weeks with my two babies without ever worrying about my job. You let me check out on August 4th and check back in 12 weeks later. I am so thankful for that. Now that I am checked back in as a mother (huge life change!), Zappos allows me to incorporate my new family into my work life. From dressing the babies up on Zalloween and trick or treating at the office, to the Zappos Family Picnic, the Reid family is part of the Zappos family as much as I like them to be. I am so thankful for that. Zappos, always keep changing and being better than you were the day before! And thank you again!!!

Kevin W.
employee since 2004

Over the past year, we underwent a legal entities project that divided Zappos into several smaller companies. It's fitting that we now refer to ourselves collectively as the "Zappos Family." In a family, you get to see each other develop, face challenges, succeed, and fail, while always providing encouragement and support. It sounds a lot like my time here at Zappos. I feel very fortunate to be a part of this family and can't wait to see what we do together next!

Kristin C.
employee since 2009

You know you've made a profound impact on society when you become a verb, as in "Just Google it." Or " Jen just Hoovered that sandwich." Or "Don't go pulling a Charlie Sheen." At Zappos, we throw the term 'WOW' around a lot. It's one of our Ten Core Values and it is the ultimate desired effect, whether we are dealing with customers, vendors or teammates. Our culture revolves around this term. In my opinion, it shouldn't be too long before 'Zappos' replaces the word WOW, as in, "Come on, guys, we really want to Zappos their socks off." It has a nice ring to it, don't you think?

Kristin J.
employee since 2010

The Zappos Culture means coming to work every day awaiting some adventure. It means coming to work every day knowing I'll be WOWed by something or someone. The Zappos Culture means coming to work every day and being challenged by those around me. It means coming to work every day loving the people I see! The Zappos Culture means coming to work every day and loving what I do! Thank you, Zappos!

Lauren G.
employee since 2006

The Zappos Culture is a large part of my life. I live it everyday at work, outside of work and with my friends and family. Zappos has become a major part of my life; I would not be who I am today without the culture and everything I have learned here. When I look around, I feel lucky that I get to work next to some of my closest friends. There is still so much to learn here and so many opportunities that I feel lucky every day to be a part of such an amazing culture and company! Cheers to Zappos!

Laurie B.
employee since 2010

The Zappos Culture, to me, is both unique and unexpected. I started working here a little over a year ago and was surprised to find happy employees and co-workers who actually care about how you are doing professionally and personally. I believe that the Zappos Culture can be created anywhere you have happiness, positivity, and people around who encourage you to be your best. Zappos encourages employees to be themselves 100% of the time and even gives them the needed support to jump outside of their comfort zone once in a while! Zappos has given me many opportunities that I would have never been given or even dreamed about and I can't wait to experience even more.

Leemarie S.
employee since 2006

The Zappos Culture means having an idea and seeing it come to fruition, bonding with your team after a long day, and laughing so hard you can barely breathe. It also gives you an opportunity to build upon the culture and create something new just by getting involved.

Lindsay R.

employee since 2007

Working at Zappos. What can I say? This place is my first home. This is my fourth year here and it has been quite a ride. This past year has been the most eventful. Not only did I meet one of my best friends here, I married my other best friend, thanks to Zappos. I love the challenges I am faced with daily; they keep me alive. I am so happy to be part of such an amazing team and company. Thank you, Zappos for all that you are.

Marisa R.

employee since 2007

I would say something unique to the Zappos Culture, but that's difficult because there are so many sub-cultures. There is not just one way to be a part of the culture, and since everyone interprets the Zappos Culture differently, it is constantly able to evolve.

Matt T.

employee since 2007

A great thing about the Zappos Culture is that, although things are always changing, the community feels the same. We're a family first and foremost and co-workers second. It's almost like working at a "mom & pop" main street store, but with a thousand family members. Thanks, Zappos for making me feel at home every day!

Megan R.

employee since 2007

The Zappos Culture helps bring out the best version of each employee. It allows us to be ourselves, embrace others for who they are and learn from each other's differences. I wake up every morning and I'm excited to come to work. I'm excited to learn and grow with people on my team. I love my job! I love working in an environment that encourages change and growth as well as fun and weirdness. The Zappos Culture is about being yourself and respecting others. There is nothing more I can ask for in a company!

Megan T.

employee since 2008

The Culture here at Zappos feels like home to me. I am free to be myself with my amazing Zappos family. I truly enjoy coming to work each day. I love the company, I love my job and I love my co-workers. We spend eight to ten hours a day together and then we go out after work and on weekends. Zappos is a wonderful family and home.

Melanie P.

employee since 2010

I think the Zappos Culture means so much to its employees because most of us came from a former job with no culture. When I first started at Zappos I often heard horror stories of my co-workers' former places of employment and how much Zappos means to them because they don't hate having to get out of bed every day. Once they are part of the Zappos family, they actually look forward to coming into work. I felt pretty lucky that I never had a day where I hated walking into my job. For me, the Zappos Culture means so much because I went from a place I liked working at, to a place I love working at. The Zappos Culture made me realize it can always get better. I have had fun at jobs, but I have never had this amount of fun at a job. I have had support at other jobs, but I have never felt this kind of empowerment. I have made close friends at former jobs, but I have never felt that I made an instant family. The happiness I have found at Zappos comes from being surrounded by people who want the same joy out of work that I do, and that is what the Zappos Culture means to me!

Melissa K.

employee since 2010

The Zappos Culture is like a marriage; you have to learn different values and traditions, but once you're in, you can't help but to adopt those principles in your own life. The culture allows you to grow personally and professionally while having fun. I love that I am challenged daily and given the opportunity to make mistakes, while being supported along the way. Typically, work is not something one looks forward to, but at Zappos no day is ever the same, which makes coming into work every day fun and exciting!

Mercedes M.

employee since 2010

I have been with Zappos for almost a year now and I can truly say that I see our Core Values put into practice on a daily basis. There are many things that blow my mind about my job, but the one thing that amazes me the most is the trust that we are given to make decisions. I had never experienced that before and it is a great feeling to have that support. I think of my co-workers not only has friends but as family. I love coming into work every day; you never know what to expect. I'm excited to see the growth and future prospects of the company and happy to be a part of it!

Mica M.

employee since 2007

As I am approaching another anniversary, I have been thinking of all my memories here at Zappos, and I still think "WOW"! The Zappos Culture means opportunity and growth to me. Zappos has given me the chance to dream and turn those dreams into reality. From a merchandiser to a human being, I'm able to fall in love with the things I'm most passionate about. How very lucky I am to be merged into a culture that gives as much back, if not more, than what I put in.

Micheal E.

employee since 2010

The Zappos Culture reminds me of one of my favorite quotes from Mahatma Gandhi, "Be the change you wish to see in the world." I believe that was my mindset when I started at Zappos. How can we be different? How can we be better? What kind of company do we want to work for? Can we make a difference? Today, Zappos still strives to make positive changes. How can a company as large as ours even attempt to make everyone happy? Three little words ..."The Happiness Survey." I have never worked for a company that not only asks how happy you are, but is open to ideas on how to increase happiness. Thank you for that. We really are Delivering Happiness to our customers, our employees and even our business partners. Our culture is amazing and I absolutely feel happy at work. It may be the widespread feeling of appreciation that creates happiness and we, in turn, are kinder to each other. This may be why we feel like being part of a family and have so many friends at work. Everyone should experience a culture like ours at least once in his or her lives. (Come in for a tour.) Zappos is a big change in the business world - a change that I am blissfully happy about and proud to be a part of.

Michael F.

employee since 2007

Culture is hard to define, and that rings true here at Zappos as well. I can tell you that the Zappos Culture is a feeling of belonging and togetherness that manifests itself in the number of employees you see smiling throughout the day. Time just seems to fly by because we all enjoy what we do, and we know that what we do is helping Zappos spread WOW, both here inside our walls and beyond.

Mike F.

employee since 2008

This year Zappos donated enough money to make sure the Las Vegas Corporate Challenge continued on for its 26th year. Many of the Zappos employees, especially myself, look forward to the Corporate Challenge every year. It becomes difficult to play the sports you love once you pass high school and college. When we heard rumors that the games might be cancelled, we were devastated. Then, in typical Zappos fashion, the Las Vegas community and my competitive edge was were WOWed. A company that would do just about anything to meet all of its employees' needs means the that company culture is everything.

Mike N.

employee since 2003

I have to share a very Zappos moment that happened to me when I turned 50 a year and a half ago. It was during the holidays and, after a great day of being on the phones, seeing a Christmas parade by Jeanne's team and having my team sing Happy Birthday to me, I went to the airport to pick up my fianc-e for a very romantic evening. We went to Alize at the top of the Palms and ordered some great food and a really nice bottle of wine from my favorite region of Napa Valley. The waiter came up to me half way through and gave me Dylan M.'s business card and said that my friend was picking up the tab for the bottle of wine. I was floored! I toasted to him from afar and when I got the chance I went over to him and said he was too kind. He responded, "We are all family, Mike."

This really is what Zappos Culture is all about and Dylan was the proud example of that at that moment. I still am WOWed to this day by his kindness and generosity and thought this would be a great entry for the Culture Book. I have thought long and hard about how to thank Dylan for what he did, as it was one of the kindest things anyone has ever done for me, but I feel telling his story is the best way. I am so proud to work for a company that lets people like Dylan shine and spread the Zappos Culture one moment at a time. As I write this I am approaching my eight-year anniversary with this company and it has been a great ride, I look forward to the next eight years.

Monica D.

employee since 2011

Zappos is a gem. It's amazing to have co-workers who help you and care about your progress, who stop whatever they are working on to answer any question. Plus, the social events are fun, with little to no out-of-pocket expense. Not to look a gift horse in the mouth, but the one thing I would change ... more types of cheeses at the free sandwich bar (smoked cheddar, goat and gouda would make my life complete)! I've only been working here for one week, but everyone has made me feel at home and I already know it's the place for me.

Moxa G.

employee since 2009

"Nothing is really work unless you would rather be doing something else." — J.M. Barrie That pretty much sums it up. The Zappos Culture means that this is more than a job, more than a career... it is a lifestyle choice. Every day, there is something new and challenging for me to take on and I can't imagine doing any of these things anywhere else or with any other group of people.

Myra D.

employee since 2008

The Zappos Culture is everything to me. It's the Hello in my Kitty. It's the Stevia in my coffee. It's the hip in my hop. It's the Stewie in my Family Guy. It's the hype DJ in my favorite club. It's the cool down of my workout. It's the cheese on my macaroni. It's the Chocobo in my Final Fantasy. It's the kung fu in my panda. It's the crunchy tempura flakes in my sushi. It's the cool breeze on my summer beach day. It's the Kobe in my Lakers. Basically, it's the best part of Zappos. Not only have you discovered my obsession for food, you have found my obsession with the culture we have here. It's what makes Zappos the best place to work by far. I feel extremely blessed to be part of something so great. I would not trade it for anything in the world.

Natasha P.

employee since 2005

The Zappos Culture means freedom, growth and opportunity. It means creating a space for yourself and trying something new. Being ecstatic when it works, and being able to laugh at yourself if it doesn't. The Zappos Culture says, "Don't stop trying."

Nicole S.

employee since 2006

Zappos Culture is unique and I see it every time we have a tour that comes by and people's eyes light up. We work in an amazing environment that would be chaotic to some (which it is), but it's a great and open space for us to enjoy what we do!!

Nicole S.

employee since 2010

I knew that moving across the country from Michigan to Las Vegas would be an adventure, but at the time, I do not think I had any idea what an adventure it would be to work at Zappos, nor did I know the instant family that was waiting to welcome me!!! My stereotype of a typical corporate retail company stems from my previous experience at a very conservative, traditional Midwestern company - one that did not sponsor happy hours or rent out clubs for fun, lavish Christmas parties. Until I came to Zappos, I had no idea what I was missing out on, nor did I understand the true happiness and excitement that can be achieved in the work environment. I was thrown for a loop when I attended the "All-Hands Meeting" my first day of work, followed by a happy hour. My second day of work was the monthly golf outing with more drinking! The first project that was assigned to me was to decorate the PL team row with a theme. Throughout this first week, I was waiting to dive into my work, and my friends would ask me, "So when are you going to start actually working?" At the time I did not realize that I was learning the backbone and the most important aspect of company ... its culture. I discovered this welcoming and happy environment during my first week and it continues to grow and evolve every day. I think I am still in shock that part of my job is to socialize, build relationships, and have fun!! These past six months of working at Zappos have been amazing and I consider myself very lucky to be a part of this unique, hospitable and happy Zappos family. The culture of Z-happiness lives here in Vegas through every smile, parade, meeting, happy hour and team event, and is around every corner in the building and within every person here at Zappos!!!!

Noel C.

employee since 2006

I happened upon Zappos by accident. I had recently finished college without any idea of what I should do. I had an entry-level job that wasn't a good fit and just received word that I hadn't gotten a job I had interviewed for with another company. That was over five years ago. The job that wasn't a good fit helped me to appreciate everything Zappos is and would be for me. The job I didn't get was for a local home seller and the housing market crashed less than a year later. I originally wanted to work for Zappos to see if it really was like the company I had read about in business books - the company everyone told me "didn't really exist." But it was all true. Zappos was better than what I had read about it. It was a real life business utopia. I started off in the content coordinator department, writing descriptions on the site. Within six months, I was transferred to merchandising as a "merchandising assistant 1" (entry level) and worked my way up to a buyer last year. I have loved every minute of my journey with this company. I'm also proud to say I work for a part of the company that didn't exist when I first started (6pm.com) and am excited to see where I will end up. (I'm sure it doesn't exist yet either.) Thank you, Zappos, for fostering such a creative, exciting and continually evolving work environment that continues to excite and challenge me every day. I love my job.

Paul P.

employee since 2007

The Zappos Culture is one that affects customers internally as well as externally. The respect we show our customers on the phones and through our actions is the same respect shown to our fellow employees on a day-to-day basis. I am happy and amazed to be a part of it for another year. Thanks.

Raven M.

employee since 2008

When I think about the Zappos Culture, what first comes to mind is how to define it. It's about the way of thinking, the traditions, the values, the attitudes, the overall feeling that makes us who we are. When I think about Zappos I think about how our culture sets us apart from the rest, and how we do this continually, breaking the rules and moving forward in an environment that stays stagnant. Our culture is excitement, creativity, and an inspiration for us to "color outside the lines."

Rebecca K.

employee since 2004

It's hard to put my feelings about the Zappos Culture into a few words. I've now worked at Zappos for seven years and the culture has grown into something so far above what I expected that if I wrote down all my thoughts I would have a novel. I specifically love the way Zappos takes care of all its employees. I feel there is a genuine regard for making us feel happy at work and outside of work. Zappos provides small things to its employees that other companies might find insignificant. The Zappos Culture truly stems from these small things. Zappos has found what really matters.

Richard Z.

employee since 2008

The Zappos Culture is like a trip to the hospital.

My youngest daughter, Ava, and I had the opportunity to go to New Orleans with Tony and Jenn on the Delivering Happiness bus tour. We had a blast in New Orleans Delivering Happiness and being tourists. One day, we had the opportunity to volunteer with a local charity to help re-build homes in the 9th Ward for families displaced by Hurricane Katrina. This was going to be Ava's first home rebuild ... she was excited! Early on "volunteer day" we toured the charity's facilities, which included two warehouses, one for office staff and the other filled with donated items to be used to re-build houses. We were happy to see they had plenty of materials to help those in need.

We then drove to the 9th Ward to our project. Our house was a plain, one-story home. Our assigned tasks were simple, like sweeping the floors, mudding and sanding walls. It was super-hot and muggy, but we forged ahead with our jobs. After a quick lunch, Ava noticed several geckos on the outside walls of the house. She managed to catch a couple and attach one to her ear and another to Tony's ear so they resembled dangle earrings. After a good laugh, the owner of the property arrived. She was a lovely grandmother with a thick New Orleans accent that was hard to understand, but by her smiles and hugs, we knew she appreciated us volunteering. Before she left, she turned to us and with complete seriousness said something like we all needed to "go to the doctor." We weren't sure if we heard correctly, but before we asked for clarification she said, "ya'll got to go to the hospital 'cause your hearts is too big for your body." Ava has been saying that ever since.

Robert P.

employee since 2007

The Zappos Culture is a way of life, at work and at home. The culture is honest, friendly, compassionate and (of course) fun! This type of culture is not seen everywhere, but it is easy to spread. Just make someone happy and you have expressed the Zappos Culture. The culture here at Zappos allows everyone to be who they are and be the best they can be.

Rudy R.

employee since 2005

Working at Zappos, is like a dream come true. It is like an adventure. I started in CLT, then move to the "Kan do" department, and after that, I got the career that I wanted. I work for Merchandising and I love it. I feel that it is the Core Values that keep this company the best! I love the friendships that I've built; I love the buying part of Merchandising, and all the learning that we get to experience. I love the people I work for; they are like a family to me. I love that Zappos inspires me to be my best.

When I moved here from San Diego six years ago, my plans were to just pass through. I got a job here, and I haven't left. I love that my CEO wrote a book about Delivering Happiness because working here give me the tools to be quite happy. The Zappos Culture is the heart of our company. Without it, Zappos would be just another company where people can't wait to leave to have fun. We have fun while we are at work. Our Ten Core Values are the roots of our culture. My favorite is #9 ("Be Passionate and Determined"). Every position that I have held during my career at Zappos allowed me to give it my all and I love it. My dream now is to continue to grow with Zappos as I embrace and try to drive change in this amazing job.

Samantha L.

employee since 2010

The Zappos Culture is a way of life! It allows us to push the limits and explore all kinds of opportunities to learn and challenge ourselves. Everyone is unique and determined because we all share one goal - how to make Zappos and ourselves go above and beyond. I am very thankful and proud to be part of this big, warm, fun, weird, and happy family!

Sandra S.

employee since 2011

The Zappos Culture was the main reason that I wanted to work for Zappos. I came on a tour as a guest and saw that the working environment was very positive and that the Core Values were truly a part of everyone's lives. I feel blessed to be a part of this wonderful company and look forward to work every day.

Scott C.

employee since 2010

Although I have only worked at Zappos for about seven months, I have been immersed in its culture from day one. I moved from half way across the country for the opportunity to work here and I haven't regretted it one bit. Before I worked here, my employers treated me as a number rather than a person. In my short amount of time here, I can honestly say that Zappos is much more than a business. All of my co-workers truly care about one another and it makes working here amazing! I am proud to say that our Core Values really do reflect Zappos!

Scott J.

employee since 2002

This will be my ninth year of employment at Zappos; it has been an amazing ride. I can still honestly say I love coming to work each day. Each week provides opportunities to grow our team and to amplify the company's goals. I only expect the coming years to get better and better. We have a huge opportunity to be a part of the downtown Las Vegas project and to become architects of our community; it's going to be a lot of fun. Let's go!!

Shannon E.

employee since 2010

For me, the Zappos Culture means family. Before coming to Zappos I worked in an environment that should have had a team and family spirit, but it did not. I wasn't friends with people at work because it wasn't something people at the company did. When I walked into Zappos the first day, I instantly connected with many people who will be life-long friends. I work on a team that is my family in Las Vegas. I feel supported and encouraged every day. I look forward to coming to work and feel fulfilled and challenged. Although I left friends and family to come to Zappos, I do not feel a void because I have found a new family here.

Sharris

employee since 2010

10.10.10 is a date that truly changed my life. While vacationing in Vegas, I grabbed drinks with a friend who had recently moved out here to work on the wonderful Private Label Team at Zappos. My trip ended up changing my life. A few cocktails later, I learned that my friend's team was hiring and the rest is history. I had one last rowdy and unforgettable weekend with my friends by celebrating my birthday, the Red Wings season opener, and a glorious Michigan State victory over U of M. Hung-over as hell, I packed up two carry-on bags, checked 106 lbs. worth of luggage and left Detroit to embark on a new adventure in Vegas! Zappos is my first job out of college and I can't imagine a better one. I'm fortunate to be a part of such a challenging, supportive, creative, zany and inspiring atmosphere!

Shyloh W.

employee since 2007

I sit here today in a bright pink paisley Loudmouth Golf outfit, surrounded by my 20 team members, who are also dressed in various obnoxious golf attire. We have a team outing today where we will play 'Pub Golf' and each team (four in all) will have to answer questions about other teammates. If they fail to answer correctly, they will need to take a drink. That is not an uncommon team outing here at Zappos! This weekend we have a company picnic to which all families are invited and, as always, it will be over the top! Later this afternoon, I will complete a survey about a summer camp we are putting together for the children of employees here at Zappos and also continue to work on our 'charter school' program intended for the future. Oh, and in between I will manage to tend to business and meet with our folks from Nike who have come to see us in the office. There is never a dull moment here at Zappos and never a day that is the same as the previous one. This is why I love Zappos!!

Steph P.

employee since 2011

When I graduated from college, almost a year ago, I kept hearing this phrase (or one along the same lines), "You'll find a job, work there a year or two and then go somewhere else. People of your generation are at a disadvantage because there are no longer companies where you can both start a career and finish one in your lifetime." Well, if these people had known about Zappos, I don't know that they would have been so adamant. The Zappos Culture is about supporting people in their personal as well as professional growth. It's not just about looking at the bottom line, but about taking that line and moving it up, down, sideways, diagonally, whichever way possible, and then, in traditional Zappos style, adding a shot of some alcohol, even if it is 8:00 am.

Although I have not been employed here for that long, the people I've met, friendships I've formed, experiences I've had ... all within a short time period ... have been incredible. I feel as though I have family when I come in to work and not many people are lucky enough to feel that way about their colleagues! So while I'm trying to stay humble here, "boo" to all of those people who told me I would be in for a long line of jobs, switching companies every two to three years for the rest of my life. Little did they know about Zappos - a company where you determine your own path of personal growth and meet some pretty cool people in the process.

Stephanie C.

employee since 2010

When people ask me how work is, they often get a bit of a glazed-over look. After about 15 minutes of me rambling on about how much I love it and how's it's the best place to work and how much I love the people I work with and how I've never been so satisfied in a job in my life and how I'm going to work here until I'm 90 ... I realize they probably just wanted a simple, "It's good, thanks for asking."

Steve P.

employee since 2008

Zappos means living in the moment, being able to be yourself and constantly being surrounded by people you think of as family!

Steven H.

employee since 2004

The Zappos Culture continues to evolve and grow. Every year we bring new people into Zappos and they become friends and family. Entering 2010, there were many questions about what the changes our partnership with Amazon would bring to our culture. It's a great testament to our teams and leadership that our culture is now greater than ever and our team continues to focus on growing and improving the culture as it evolves. I have worked at other companies but have never felt as fulfilled as I do at Zappos. I look forward to our continuing journey together as we each grow, learn and experience new things together.

Sunday P.

employee since 2010

This is more than a job! The people I work with are family. No matter if things are going great or badly, my team is here. They are the most supportive people that I have ever worked with. How often do you actually look forward to coming in on Monday morning? When people find out that I work here, they always ask if it is really as crazy and fun here as they have heard. I am glad to be able to say that it is ... and more!

Terra E.

employee since 2007

How time has flown! I cannot believe I've been here almost five years and I'm still as excited to be here as I was on my first day! It's been amazing watching us grow as fast as we have. I used to feel I knew majority of the people who work here, but now there are some unfamiliar faces. Even so, they still have the Zappos spirit and still say hello. I think what makes Zappos such a special place to work is that - as big as we have become - we still have a strong sense of family and we really do care about each other. Working with people that you really enjoy being around makes it a fun environment. There is no other place I'd rather be!

Terry I.

employee since 2007

The Zappos Culture is the ability to achieve whatever we aspire to do.

Valencia F.

employee since 2007

The Zappos Culture means being happy. There seemed to be a big movement for Delivering Happiness this past year, and I believe they really worked hard to deliver happiness to employees, vendors, visitors and people across the country with the Delivering Happiness bus. Who could ask for a better company to work for than one that continually strives to make Zappos a place you are excited to work. Our culture is something to be experienced and those who visit us are excited to share with others when they go home. It's contagious!

Vanessa B.

employee since 2011

The Zappos Culture, to me, means happiness! It is a culture you can enter and immediately have a new family and new friends. I moved here without knowing anyone at all and I was not worried. I had confidence that the culture was more than just words. When I came for my interview and I saw it first-hand, it was surreal. I will never forget my first impression, and ever since that day I have been hooked on the Zappos Culture.

Victoria "Tori" B.

employee since 2011

I joined Zappos three weeks ago; this was my first job out of college. When my mom and sister toured the office during my second day, one of the girls on my team walked out with us and told my mom, "Don't worry, she will have an immediate family here." This has definitely been true. Not only am I in the career field that I've always dreamed about, but I also have an amazing new family and home! I'm excited to see what this next year holds.

Zac B.

employee since 2010

My first full year here at Zappos has been one of the best. I can't believe I have been here for so long. Time flies when you love what you do and the friends you are with. Within this year, I made a ton of new friends and it wouldn't be possible without this unique culture. The culture here is nothing like what I've experienced in a workplace before. I don't dread coming into the office everyday because it is so relaxed; I can be who I always am and not have to put on a "mask" when I am here. I enjoy what I do and the people I am around every day. Here's to many more great years at Zappos!

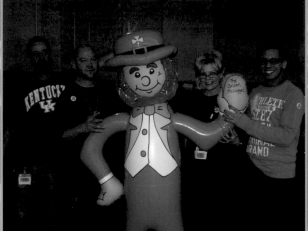

PADDY DOES
Kentucky

Nerd
DAY

ZAPPOS *Speakeasy* PARTY

SPEAK EASY, PARTY HARD

ZAPPOS
SPEAKEASY

ZAPPOS
Speakeasy
PARTY

BOOTLEGGERS, GANGSTERS AND FLAPPERS, OH, MY!

Peep-ing TOM

THE ZAPPOS
FAMILY
Peep Show

peep csi: vegas

DEATH AT A PEEP SHOW

BORN IN BLOOD

Crystal Boehne
Vadenmayer
Lockhart
Mann

Peeps   Peeps

THE THRILLA IN MANILA

ZAPPOS
CASINO

OCTOBER 1ST 1975

KY   ALI

ZFCI

A2 Pack/Ship

peace

3 DAYS OF PEACE
& MUSIC

love

Zappos!
.com

Be
Passionate
and
Determined

(And make sure you're on your horse when the starting gate opens)

Abbie M.

employee since 2005

Every year I write an entry for our Culture Book, and every year I feel like there aren't enough words to describe how I feel about the Zappos Culture. When I sit down and think about it, our culture is like a having a best friend who listens to you when you need to talk. They let you be yourself and accept you for who you are. They keep you in line when you forget that you're at work. ;) They give you relief when you feel stressed out. They believe in you and encourage you to do the right thing for the right reasons. They talk sense into you when you want to be nonsensical. They are happy for you as you grow within our family. They take pride in you. They teach you new things everyday. They open your eyes to the world around you. They give you the benefit of the doubt. They show you how important you are. They offer you an inch, hoping you'll take the mile. They take you to sweet parties and introduce you to fun, new people. They send you flowers and make you smile when you think of it. They show you that there is always a brighter tomorrow. "Friendship isn't a big thing – it's a million little things." – Author Unknown

Adam A.

employee since 2010

Culturally, working at Zappos is similar to working at a family business. We joke and make fun of each other like we are family, celebrate as a family during the great times, and band together as family during the not so great times. The family-like atmosphere is one of the reasons why our Zappos Culture is strong, and we hold it as dear as one of our Core Values.

Alane C.

employee since 2006

Once upon a time there was a little girl who wanted to be a singer when she grew up. So she sang here and sang there and had some fun opportunities and always enjoyed singing, but never really fulfilled her dream of being a "singer." Then one day she went to work for a fun company named Zappos and got an idea that she and two of her co-workers could do a little something to bring others cheer by singing to them for their birthdays. Since then the three women have had many opportunities to sing for different company events, i.e., love songs from one co-worker to another, songs to welcome some Zappos guests, or even singing the Star Spangled Banner to a co-worker who just became a U.S. citizen. They even have videos so others can see and share what they do. So the girl who once upon a time wished to be a singer got to be a singer after all and do her job as well. I'm sure that nowhere else on earth could this have been possible but at the amazing company called Zappos! Thanks Zappos for giving me a great job and fulfilling (in part) one of my wishes in life!

Alexander S.

employee since 2010

If everyone could experience life at Zappos the world would be a better place. I have enjoyed being a small part of the Zappos Culture, and hope that more people are able to get a little taste of it whenever they interact with each of us.

Amy Y. 俞惠

employee since 2010

The first time I read the words, "Build a Positive Team and Family Spirit" –which is one of Zappos' Ten Core Values – I wondered: "Does a family spirit really exist in a company? Or is it just a slogan?" Gradually I found that it was real and I was deeply attracted to it. Not only do members of our China office live and eat together, we are also truly like a family, helping each other and never having to worry about returns. I hope we can keep enjoying this spirit, and continue to create fun and weirdness all the time. O(＿＿)O~

第一次看公司的核心价值最疑惑的就是 build family spirit 这点： 一个公司真的可以有"家庭精神"吗？还是只是一个口号而已？渐渐地，我发现 家庭精神的含义所在并且被其所吸引。一方面，因为我们公司的模式是吃住一起。另一 方面，我们确实像一家人那样相处，互相帮忙，不计较。希望可以一直享受这种 spirit，并且继续 create fun and weirdness O(∩_∩)O~

Andre C.

employee since 2011

I first met and became good friends with several Zappos employees prior to joining the Zappos family. After attending several Zappos events as a guest and touring the facility I was amazed by the strength of the Zappos Culture. During this time, I was working for another company where I battled an intense struggle to bring change. The friends I made at Zappos supported my passion while my employer at the time was doing everything it could to turn me into a "corporate machine," devoid of all passion.

In sharp contrast, the Zappos Culture was full of passionate, young, intelligent, compassionate and motivated individuals. I've always searched for a corporate environment that had a heart and operated less like a machine. The Zappos Culture, built by people, provides the pulse of the company and is the reason why I joined Zappos.

Andrea W.

employee since 2007

The Zappos family has increasingly expanded into a realm of culture! I'm ecstatic about each new day at Zappos. The possibilities are truly endless! Cheers!

Andrew P.

employee since 2009

I like the Zappos Culture because it makes for a better workday. Time goes by so much faster and better than a day at most other jobs.

Anonymous

employee since 2009

The Zappos Culture allows us to live life to the fullest, which also allows each of us to deliver exceptional business results. How, you ask? By asking us to Deliver Happiness to our customers. We all know that making others happy leads to our own fulfillment and happiness and it makes our customers more loyal to us. Zappos also allows us to take risks without being afraid to fail. Other companies create bureaucracy and processes designed to prevent failure, which rarely work anyway. Failure allows us to learn faster and move faster as a business. Zappos also creates a family atmosphere at work that is personally fulfilling as well as highly effective from a business perspective because information flows between various teams and departments at exceptional speeds. I could go on ...

Anonymous

employee since 2007

At Zappos, we do not have a lot of unnecessary meetings, but we do have a lot of happy hours and parties.

Anonymous

employee since 2007

I'm not a writer, but my manager's manager is telling me I have to write something. So this is it. I do love Zappos, just to be clear.

Anonymous

employee since 2010

Zappos Culture: As much as we value it, embrace it and see it in front of us every day, I find that sitting down and writing about it is somewhat difficult. I think it's because our unique and fabulous culture is created through a combination of so many things. It's in the personalities of each person who works here, it's the activities we participate in both inside and outside the office, and, most importantly, it is the Core Values that we each strive to embody. The Zappos Culture results in a work environment like none I have experienced at any other company. Although our culture may not be easy to describe, I am truly grateful for every day I get to be a part of it.

Anonymous

employee since 2003

The Zappos Culture is all about giving. For the customer, give great customer service (free shipping, return shipping, selection and nearly anything desired).   For the employee, give outstanding benefits and a lot of happy hours to booze it up. And 401(k) matching? Yes.

Anonymous

employee since 2008

I look forward to going to work every morning, and to me this is the greatest feeling ever. I absolutely love everything Zappos has to offer, including the people I work with, whom I sincerely consider family. Zappos cares about its employees, their vendors and their customers. They also care about giving back to communities – they support numerous events and the list goes on! I love Zappos! <3

Ashley K.

employee since 2010

Working for Zappos over the past year has been an incredible experience. This is the first place that has challenged me to grow both professionally and personally. I have grown so much since starting here. It isn't just a job. There is so much more to it.

I have never worked with such genuinely nice people before who really enjoy what they do. I am embraced for who I am. Most importantly, I love how everyone gets to share their talents with each other, whether it be art, music, an eye for fashion, great people skills, etc. We encourage each other to strive to be our best.

It's hard not to fall in love with the Zappos Culture. I love being part of this creative, unique family and I am looking forward to being a part of it for many years to come.

Betty H. 黄宇旋

employee since 2010

I am very happy to work at Zappos. I believe that we are more than just a team; we are a family. We take care of each other. What's more, we work together, laugh together and trust each other. Our relationship goes far beyond being just co-workers. That is one of our Core Values "Build a Positive Team and Family Spirit." The Zappos Culture is unique. What makes Zappos different from other companies is its great reputation, spread mostly through word of mouth. With the best service, we always WOW our customers. I am proud of Zappos.

觉得自己身处于在捷步达康工作，很开心！我相信最好的团队应该是不仅仅在工作中是一个 团队，即使大家在工作以外的时间还是有很好的交流沟通。我们不仅仅是一个团队，我们 更是一个大家庭。我们大家互相照顾，互相关心，更重要的是我们互相信任。我们一起工作， 也一起欢笑。我们之间的关系已经远远超出了其他公 司 通常意义上的同事。BUILD A POSITIVE TEAM AND FAMLY SPIRIT. 捷步达康是一个独一无二的品牌和文化，确立了正确的文化，与其他公司的不同之处就是 有很好的口碑，有很好的服务，这都是通过服务让人们感到惊叹：WOW~~~这都是其他公司 做不到的！我为捷步达康骄傲！

Beverly S.

employee since 2005

I just came back from an amazing two-week adventure in Thailand. While I was there, I noticed a lot of signs about happiness. That's when I learned about the Thai's "Sanuk" way of life. Sanuk means finding fun and enjoyment in everything you do. I found it so amazing that an entire culture embraced this way of life. Then it made me think about the Zappos Culture and how we also incorporate this concept into our daily lives.

No matter what it is – from running a scavenger hunt for our new hires to help them learn about departments and processes to hosting a peep show contest – there's always a fun adventure to be found at Zappos. The past six years have been amazing, and I can't wait for what's in store the next six-plus years. When you find the fun in what you do, it doesn't feel like work. It just feels like hanging out with your friends. And because you're with your friends, you have the support to accomplish anything. This is the Zappos way of life.

Bhawna P.

employee since 2010

The Zappos Culture is so unique that it's hard to put your finger on one single thing that stands out. It's always evolving and changing. What I love is that there is no single department that is tasked with creating the culture. Everyone in the organization takes it upon himself or herself to help us take our company to the next level. Often, at other companies, the human resources department drives the events and activities, but here at Zappos, activities and events are spearheaded from every department. What makes it better is that each department invites other departments in, so it truly feels like a family atmosphere. I also like that we are allowed to be ourselves. Our abilities are not measured by how we act around management or whether we are dressed up in our finest clothes. This kind of atmosphere makes us want to contribute as much as we can and makes us feel proud to be part of such a company.

Brad B.

employee since 2010

After working at Zappos for a full year, I believe this company is far and away the best place I have ever worked. The Zappos Culture promotes an atmosphere where we can enjoy coming to work every day and be part of something new and exciting!

Bruce R.

employee since 2006

This is how I would describe ZAPPOS in six words: Zany, Arousing, Passionate, Potential, Open-minded, Successful.

Carrie A.

employee since 2011

Every day, I thank my lucky stars for three things – my family, my health, and my job. I don't even like to label it a "job" or "work" because it is anything but that. I have only been here at Zappos for two weeks, but I already have complete loyalty and a sense of family with those I work with – even with those employees I haven't yet met. For many years, I was convinced that I had gone into the wrong profession, as I was horribly unhappy in past jobs. They truly were "jobs" and "work." However, I've quickly learned it wasn't my profession at all – it was the environment that I worked in that provided no sense of accomplishment, achievement, family, or FUN. Thank you Zappos; I feel as if you have brought me back to life!

Celina E.

employee since 2009

As most people know, Zappos has a lot of great stuff to offer, such as the ability to be yourself, great benefits, unforgettable parties, etc. What I care about most, though, are the people. Some people come into our lives and quickly go away, while others stay and leave footprints in our hearts and we are never the same. I am extremely grateful that the people who work at Zappos have made me a better person and their footprints will always be in my heart.

Chantal Z. 曾春桃

employee since 2010

I first walked into Zappos' China office in September of 2010. I immediately felt its uniqueness. I had longed for a relaxing and free work atmosphere. One of the Zappos Core Values is: "Create Fun and a Little Weirdness." We are allowed to express ourselves freely. In this kind of spirit, jokes become more enjoyable when people laugh together. Another Core Value – "Build a Positive Team and Family Spirit" – is definitely reflected in the China office. Everybody here is positive, kind and patient. For example, they take care of new colleagues, accompanying them to shop for necessities and helping them adapt to life here. Our new colleagues all think we're like a big family and they fit in quickly. When I come to a new environment, I tend to be silent and discreet. Here, my new colleagues all hugged me and I got a lot of help from Mr. Hsieh and Augusta – the golden coach of Zappos. I appreciate that very much. The team practices "Do More with Less" to perfection. When we discuss work, colleagues often come up with good ideas and more efficient working methods develop. It's so amazing! \(^o^)/~ I have a great time working and living here!

我是2010年9月初次踏入美捷步中国办公室的。踏进门口的一刹那就感觉到它的与众不同。 这种轻松自由的工作氛围是我梦寐以求的。美捷步的十条核心价值第三条： "创造欢乐和 一点点搞怪。大家自由表达自己，展现自己。很多时候就是这种轻松自由的环境，笑话变得 更好笑，因为大家一起欢笑。核心价值第七条 "建立积极的团队塑造家庭精神。"在中国 办公室体现得很彻底。大家都很乐观，友善，包容。例如，对新同事全面负责，带他们去 购买生活用品，关心他们在这里是否适应。当然，新同事都觉得这里很像家庭，很快就融入 这个集体了。我到陌生的环境，会比较沉默和小心翼翼。大家都包容了我这种偏内向的性格。 还得到了谢先生和美捷步金牌教练Augusta的步步引导，非常感激他们。这个团队出色地实践 了第八条核心价值 "追求事半功倍"。确实如此，通过集体讨论研究或是某同事灵机一动， 经常会有更快捷的工作方法诞生。这多么令人 愉快啊！\(^o^)/~我在这里工作和生活得很开心。

Charles A.

employee since 2001

Since I started work at Zappos in 2001, I have seen many changes in this company. The days of being a small business that barely anyone had heard of are long gone. Now when I tell people where I work, I often hear an ecstatic "I love you guys!" We've gone from just a few employees who all knew one another, to many employees and it's getting more and more difficult to remember everyone's name. Some things haven't changed though; even from the beginning. I am still proud to work here and I smile when I tell people where I work. Although I may not know the names of all my fellow employees, it's still good enough that we work for the same company. We always treat each with the utmost respect and go out of our way to help one another. I can't help but wonder if this is the way it is at other companies and if it's not, how happy their employees are.

Cheryl Anne F.

employee since 2006

For the past five years I've been spending approximately 30% of my life with the people at work. (Yes, I'm counting all hours, not just waking hours.) Since we're all in the same position of needing to work to survive, why not gather a group of people that enjoy one another's company? I love working at Zappos because I genuinely like my co-workers. It's more than tolerate, more than grudgingly accept, it's genuinely like. Oh, and once in a while we get to work on cool projects, too. =) But even if the tasks at hand are less than rock-star glamorous, or require burning of the midnight oil, at least it's with people who understand me enough to know that:

A. Hoping that each other's faces rot is a sign of team unity, B. When you call me a whore, that really means "thank you for helping me work through a tough issue," C. The level of inappropriate comments is directly proportional to how close we are as a group.

Cheryl L.

employee since 2010

I have been at Zappos for a year now and I LOVE it here!! The Zappos Culture is a dream come true!

I have had jobs I enjoyed in the past, but I absolutely love coming to work here at Zappos every day. The people are awesome, and that stems from the Zappos Culture. There is always something entertaining happening, which makes each day you come to work new and exciting. I love the openness, quirkiness and the over-all family oriented atmosphere of the company. Any time I need assistance, whether it's personal or professional, I know my Zappos family will come through for me. Hands down, it's the best place to work!!!

Chris B.

employee since 2010

As a consultant for the past year at Zappos, I must say that this is the most awesome place that I have ever worked. When I was in Las Vegas I thought I had met the nicest folks. Then I started working at the warehouse in Kentucky and found that they only get nicer in there. The Zappos Culture, to me, means making work a part of your life and making your life a part of work. I am sure I have made friends here that will last a lifetime.

Chris L.

employee since 2010

Being a part of Zappos means that I get to be myself at work every day. My favorite Core Value is #3: "Create Fun and a Little Weirdness" because it embodies who I am.

At my previous places of employment, I felt that I wasn't able to fully express the zaniness that is me. Other work environments can stifle you. At Zappos co-workers get to know the real you, not just some "work version" of yourself that you present to them when you walk through the front door. For this reason I have never felt closer and more connected with a group of co-workers than I have while working here. It truly feels like I am coming to see my family every day. That's why I am honestly excited to go into work. It's something I've never felt any other place that I've worked.

Chris N.

employee since 2010

I joined the Zappos family this year, and it has lived up to everything that I imagined. People here have been incredibly welcoming to wife, my children and me. That Zappos family support has included advice about Las Vegas, fun events and amazingly engaging conversations about "work." There is no doubt that we will continue to evolve our Zappos Culture and business practices as we grow – that is inevitable as we respond to what our customers want. We must retain this family spirit though, among other things. It is at the center of what makes Zappos different from other companies.

Christa F.

employee since 2004

"Culture is a powerful human tool for survival, but it is a fragile phenomenon. It is constantly changing and easily lost because it exists only in our minds." (Copyright 2002-2006 by Dennis O'Neil) After six years in recruiting at Zappos, this quote really resonates with me. There have been so many changes over the years. Some of them have been challenging, some of them a bit painful, but at the heart of it all, the changes have driven us forward in the most amazing ways! The power of the Zappos Culture cannot be easily defined. You have to touch it, smell it, live it, and experience it … And most importantly for those of us here, you have to own it. Culture is indeed a fragile phenomenon. We all play a role in creating it, defining and shaping it, and protecting it. It can mean different things to different employees. But there are two important facts to know. First, the Core Values are the heart of our culture. They are guiding principles, not defined rules. The breadth of interpretation for each of them is vast and it is that vastness which combines to create the rich, unique place that is Zappos. And the Zappos Culture will constantly change and evolve, as it should. It's our commitment to the spirit of our culture and fierce protectiveness of it that will ensure it never exists only in our minds.

Christal T.

employee since 2007

Hooray for Pajama Day every day! … if I want. I am now completely spoiled and this Princess loves it!

Christina K.

employee since 2010

Whenever I'm out of office, I feel like I'm missing out on the fun.

Cindy P.

employee since 2011

Zappos means the freedom to finally be myself 24 hours a day. Which is AWESOME!!!

Craig A.

employee since 2005

Writing an entry for the Culture Book gets harder every year. One of the important things about our Zappos Culture is that employees should never have to worry about being themselves. I think that in a lot of organizations people tend to be very guarded about letting their real selves shine through. Being yourself doesn't mean you can be destructive in your behavior, because if that's who you are, you shouldn't be here. However, you can be as weird and goofy as you are without fear of being described as an oddball. This is the first place I've been where I felt like it was OK to just be me. I can't tell you how liberating that feels and I wish more people would just be themselves. :) Thanks to Zappos, it's pretty much impossible for me to work anywhere else. (I hear a lot of people say that too. Isn't that great?)

Crystal D.

employee since 2008

Do me a favor ... nod your head up and down as if you are reading something extremely profound. Good! Now gasp as if you are having an ah-hah moment. FANTASTIC! Finish it up with a smirk of satisfaction. Yup, that just happened :) Since this is my third Culture Book entry, I thought I would channel Core Value #3, "Create Fun and a Little Weirdness." Zappos means so much to me. It means having jobs like ZCLT, TLC team member, RA intern, or Giving Guru, and the inevitable explanation to my dad that yes, I have a real job. :) Every day brings a new adventure and new excitement! I cannot wait to see how our culture will evolve in the next few years. Zappos, you are one of a kind and I salute you!

Cynthia T.

employee since 2008

"If we bring a little joy into your humdrum lives, it makes us feel as though our hard work "ain't been in vain for nothin'." Bless you all. "
–Lina Lamont – Singing in the Rain

Danielle D.

employee since 2011

Zappos is about appreciating little things every day. Our customers find joy in the simple pleasure of a pair of shoes, and behind the scenes Zappos employees embody that idea. We take every opportunity to turn mundane tasks into moments that are fun and a little weird. Each bigger splash of Zappos Culture – every party, picnic, and game – has its root in the time that we take to laugh with the people sitting next to us.

Debra J.

employee since 2007

To me, the Zappos Culture means that I can come to work relaxed and ready to work hard. I love hard work, but I hate feeling like my neck could be on the chopping block. I never feel like that here. This company has allowed me to grow and expand my life's experience. I am never bored because at Zappos something new is always around the corner. I LOVE IT HERE!

Dennis L.

employee since 2008

Once again, it's on! The Zappos Culture is like the Word; it needs to be spread throughout the world. At this point, I expect everyone I meet to exhibit our culture. I get disappointed when I don't experience it outside of work. "That's not the Zappos way"! Our culture is something I live, eat and breathe, and I try to spread it around.

Derek F.

employee since 2007

WOW! Four years already. It seems like just yesterday I was in class learning about customer loyalty. I still can't get over how excited I get when I'm on my way to work in the morning, wondering what new challenges the day will bring. It really is awesome to love the place you work. Zappos rocks!

Devlyn T.

employee since 2005

After almost six years with Zappos, there is so much I love about our Zappos Culture. What I love most is the support people give to others without wanting recognition or anything in return. I've seen people here do amazing things for their Zappos family members. I've seen inspiring acts of generosity, large and small. I know people who have given their time, their money, or some of their sanity just to help a fellow Zappos employee during a rough time. When I catch myself thinking that human beings are all a bunch of pricks, I remind myself of all the generosity I've witnessed and all the generosity I've received at Zappos. I stop feeling cynical and start feeling inspired. It's hard to be a cynic when you're surrounded on a daily basis by so many genuinely good people who support one another. The experiences I've had at Zappos have made me more optimistic, more open, and more giving. I can't wait to be inspired for another year.

Diana G.

employee since 2005

I was just talking to my sister about the Zappos Culture, and we both realized how much everyone has grown! I don't just mean growing within the company, I mean as people. I been working for Zappos for five wonderful years, and I've seen many of my co-workers getting married, buying a house or starting a family. Because we are encouraged to get to know our co-workers on a personal level, I have been part of special moments in their lives. The best part is that I know I will always have an extended family to share my special moments with as well.

Don N.

employee since 2010

For the past few years, I was living in Louisville and working as a Tax Partner in a public accounting firm – a good job, but I wasn't necessarily happy. I liked the folks I worked with, but the focus was on profits, not necessarily people. When I asked one of my partners how it was going, he would always answer (a bit sarcastically) "Livin' the Dream." In July 2010, I got an email on a Saturday morning about an available tax job at Zappos in Las Vegas. I went on the Zappos website, watched a nine-minute video on the company produced by ABC Nightline and was blown away. I loved the culture, the Core Values, the CLT training, the focus on employees and WOWing customers, the fun and the wackiness. I asked my wife, Cathy, "Could you please come in and watch this video? I am going to leave the room and let you watch it alone and then, you tell me what you think." After nine minutes, she came out and said, "That is a perfect company for you. I couldn't work there, but I know you would fit in!" My wife's parents were in poor health in a Louisville nursing home so I asked her "If this were to somehow work out, could we even consider a move from Louisville to Las Vegas with the shape your parents are in?" She replied "If Zappos is the right place for you, we will make it work."

On November 1st, I was lucky enough to join Zappos and I got an apartment for the short-term. My wife has flown back and forth between Louisville and Vegas about every two weeks, continuing to care for her parents. Personally, it has been a tough six months for us with the separation, the stress of trying to live in two places, and witnessing her parents' failing health. My father-in-law passed away in January. Two months later, my mother-in-law, a huge Kentucky Wildcats Basketball fan, passed away in the middle of March Madness. A few Christmases ago, I had given her these puffy bedroom slippers in the shape of Kentucky Wildcat basketball shoes that she loved to wear while she watched her beloved Wildcats on TV. In her honor, and in celebrating the Wildcats run to the Final Four this year, I wore her slippers to work every day for a week in March.

I don't think there is another place on earth that a tax accountant can wear puffy basketball bedroom slippers to work for a week and no one bats an eye! I love my job, I love my wife, and I love my new Zappos family! Cathy and I are looking forward to getting settled in Henderson. I consider myself the luckiest tax guy in the world. "Livin' the Dream!"

Dr. Larry M.

employee since 2010

People ask me all the time "Is it really that fun there? How can you all be having that much fun at work?" I think what people are missing is that this isn't work. I'm not at a job, I'm at my life and I'm having a great time living it.

Duron P.

employee since 2007

2010 is a wrap! It was another great year with my Zappos family. As I sit here at my new desk, in a newly built space in Building 2290, I think about all the change that has occurred over the past year, how much I'm looking forward to this year and what it has in store: GOOD TIMES!!! Zappos exudes CULTURE inside and out. And soon we'll be spreading this way of life across the world. Slowly, but surely :-) See ya' in 2012!

Ellen W.

employee since 2009

Every day is something fresh and exciting – we are surrounded by creative minds, their passion to release a new invention, and celebration!

Elyse' Granola

employee since 2010

The Zappos Culture is freedom! It is freedom to let your ideas, individuality and creativity flow. It is acceptance and growth. It is believing in the impossible, believing in others and believing in yourself. Zappos Culture is friends that turn into family. It starts with crazy, is shaken with fun, and sprinkled with opportunity. Zappos Culture makes me happy to work! I'm extremely grateful to be where I am, and BEYOND excited about where this adventure will take me! The best part is ... we filter our water. ;) LOVE YOU ALL!

Eric K.

employee since 2008

Liquid tangerines.

Ericka L.

employee since 2007

Culture at Zappos is about working hard and playing hard.

Eva L. 黎玲

employee since 2010

I have served as a remote assistant in the big family of Zappos for more than one year. When I came into our office building for the first time, the word "family" kept flying in my mind. I don't know why, but I know that this amazing feeling comes from my sixth sense.

This is the first job I have ever had. God gave me enough fortune to make me a part of the Zappos family. I am definitely WOWed by the powerful Cculture, by our family spirit, by the democratic working environment and by all of you guys.

I am so proud that I am a Zapponian. I would like to give up everything for happiness – the best part of my everyday life and the best thing I got from Zappos. My favorite Core Value is "Be Humble." This means we are humble to our customers, to our colleagues, to our friends and among ourselves. Being modest makes one improve. We can't receive any respect from others unless we respect others first. Keep smiling and keep being humble.

我在Zappos这个大家庭工作一年多了，主要工作是远程助理。当我第一次踏进办公室的时候，我的脑海里面不停地有一个词在萦绕，那就是 "家庭"。我不知道为什么，但是，我知道 这是一种直觉。这是我人生的第一份工作。上帝给了我足够的运气，所以我才可以成为 Zappos 的一部分。Zappos的文化真的把我震撼了，还有这里的家庭精神，自由民主的工作氛围，以及 这帮快乐的员工们。我为我是Zappos的一员感到骄傲。我愿意付出极高的代价换取幸福——那是每天最开心的时光，也是Zappos给我的最好的礼物。我最喜欢的核心价值是 "虚怀若谷"，对我们的顾客谦逊，对我们的同事谦逊，对我们的朋友以及我们自己谦逊一点。谦逊可以让人 不断改进。如果我们不尊重别人，就无法得到别人的尊重。所以，微笑吧，保持虚怀若谷的态度，保持谦逊。

Fay W.

employee since 2009

Zappos is a unique place. When I first came here, I couldn't believe that this was an office – we could listen to music, joke with one another, and walk around to have some snacks. It is so different from other workplaces I have seen, where people are required to keep quiet during work time. Here, we value the family spirit.

Shortly after I came here, I had the opportunity to interview other applicants. Our recruiting system is very different from those at other companies. We treat our applicants as friends; we share jokes and joys during the interview. We prefer to hire those who seem honest and most likely to fit the Zappos Culture.

Fly L. 赖毅飞

employee since 2010

To me, the Zappos Culture is like signs on a freeway. It keeps me on the right track. I think the Zappos Culture is like backbone to a man; without it, a man can never stand straight. I am not quite sure what other companies' cultures are like. But to me, the Zappos Culture is great. One example is the Core Value, "Create Fun and a Little Weirdness." Other companies may allow you to create fun, but weirdness is usually frowned upon. This makes people restricted. But at Zappos, things are different. If we think it's right to do something, we are encouraged to do it. We believe the things that can make us grow can come in different ways. We are encouraged to try things so we can find the best way.

捷步达康的文化对我而言就像高速公路上能很明确看到的路标牌，沿着文化这条道路去走 就能很容易找到正确的出口。捷步达康的文化是整个Zappos!的脊梁骨，就像人一样，没了 脊梁就不能站立。虽然我不太清楚其他公司的文化是什么，更不能明确的对比起来有什么 不同的方面，但是，以我个人而言，Zappos!的文化就是比较 "大众化" 的。就举例，以 第3条，创造欢乐以及一点点怪异。来说，别的公司或许允许你创造出欢乐，但未必允许你 把怪异，搞怪也带来，这就使个人的一些行为举止受到局限。但Zappos！就不同，你可以 拥有自己的思想来行动，来做自己想做的事情，只要你认为对的就可以去做。

Gagan A.

employee since 2010

Zappos is the best place to work. I now have a reason to go to work every day. I believe the Zappos Culture brings out the best in a person and also gives everyone an opportunity to be what they want. Yes, we can be a little weird too at times :)) but still succeed in our role at Zappos.

George R.

employee since 2009

The Zappos Culture is out of this world! I am still amazed at what goes on here on a daily basis, and the people who ask about Zappos are just shocked. Thanks Zappos! You've changed the way we work, play and live. :)

Grace G. 郭华玉

employee since 2009

In this big Zappos family, every day is bright and fresh. We have lots of stories. I want to express some of my thoughts and feelings. It is a family that allows us to express ourselves freely, which impresses me profoundly and changes me a lot. Being honest and faithful to others is the Zappos way to WOW. Everything in life will speak for it. Each department WOWed us with the best service. With the help of Taylor J. and Richard Hsieh, all aspects of our office are gradually becoming perfect. I am honored to be part of Zappos. The Zappos Culture is alive. Our office is full of laughter. "One loses nothing by smiling at others." The harmonious atmosphere is the foundation of the company's promising future. In order to create a positive team and family spirit we start with ourselves!

在Zappos这个大家庭，每天都生活得如花似锦，有太多的故事吧，现将这回忆用文字来 表达出来。这里是一个自由发挥，自由表达的大家庭，无论是在工作上还是生活上都让我 感触颇深，收获也很多，在这也改变了我的很多想法。WOW "以诚待人，以信为本"给客人 提供优质的服务。生活上的点点滴滴足以证明了这点。伙食组和总务组都为大家提供了 很好的服务，特别是在主任与谢先生的关心和指导下，各方面逐渐成熟和成长着。能成为 公司的一员，感到非常荣幸。Zappos文化是有生命的。办公室时刻都冒出笑声， "你不可能 因为给人一个微笑而觉得丧失了什么，因为它永远都会再回来"融洽的生活环境，是创造 公司明天辉煌的基础，也是一个旅程。 Positive team and family spirit,实现这个 "美" ，必须从身边的事做起。

Hollie D.

employee since 2006

Best work environment, great people, hard work, dedication, challenges, and fun, expect the unexpected. Zappos is all that and more. It is a place where you can be yourself. You can wear what you want, be who you are and not be embarrassed or made to feel bad about it. I wouldn't trade it or change it. It is what it is. It's Zappos, the best job ever!

Israel S.

employee since 2010

Working at Zappos is nothing short of amazing. Zappos loves us and we love it back. I can truly say that the friends I have made here are closer than family. I never want to leave this place. When I wake up in the morning, I look forward to coming to work, have fun while I'm here and then hang out with co-workers afterwards. Where in the world can people do that? Thanks for making my life brighter. I'm glad that I'm part of the Zappos future. March on and make waves!

Jackie A.

employee since 2010

I <3 Zappos!

Jacob P.

employee since 2003

You would think it would get harder to write these things after being here for over eight years now. But I'm happy to report that as time goes by it gets even easier. This time around, though, I think I'll share a little secret with you about my first days at Zappos.

The truth is I never intended to stay here more than five or maybe seven months, tops! I had been through start-ups in San Francisco and thought for sure these guys were going to be like all the others. Well, a strange thing happened around month two. I woke up one Monday morning and for the first time I was excited and looking forward to going to work. In fact, I spent a good deal of my Muni ride thinking about how much I liked working at Zappos. Back then, there wasn't as much talk about culture as there is now. But you could sure feel it in the air. In one way or another, we all knew we were a part of something that was unique and special. Tony, Nick and Fred did a great job of planting the culture seed and like many, I latched on to it.

As a recruiter, I'm always asked to explain what the Zappos Culture is. So much of it is just doing what's right! I think if companies spent time doing more of what's right they would be better off. Do right by your employees, empower them to make decisions and get involved. Encourage your vendors and customers to demand the very best from you. Always look for ways to learn from mistakes. And most important for managers, lose the ego and remember that the people you serve are what matter the most.

What does the Zappos Culture mean to me? Real simple. It's treating every customer, vendor and employee like they are your best friend's grandmother and having a great time while you do it.

James H.

employee since 2010

If Cheers, Friends and How I Met Your Mother met and had a magnificent and glorious baby, that would be Zappos. Everyone would know your name, you would meet friends for life, and you would learn valuable and humorous life lessons.

Jamie N.

employee since 2004

The Zappos Culture is what makes working here such an amazing experience! The culture is inviting, warm, honest, and humble. The people here are truly the best, and the kind of people that become life-long friends. After six years of working at Zappos, I can honestly say there has never been a dull moment. I've had more memories and experiences than one person should be allowed, and I have loved ... and continue to love ... every moment of it.

Jane H. 黄健雯

employee since 2010

I've read the 2008-2010 editions of the Zappos Culture Book since I joined Zappos' China office on June 15, 2009. I am excited that my words will be part of the 2011 Culture Book.

When I first arrived at Zappos, I had thought that it would become my second family. It's not because I already knew somebody here. Actually, most of us came from different provinces. We work and live together. Although we are not related by blood, we have become like family to each other. Everyone has different habits and personalities, but we are also tolerant and respect one another. We have fun and joke around, especially when the Happy Hour comes, . "Play hard and work hard" is our policy. But when it comes to work, we try our best to make it much better than good. I think that we should all be responsible for what we do, since we are grown-ups. We should not just wait for opportunity. We should always improve ourselves and correct ourselves and earn our opportunities.

I have spent my two years after graduation here because it feels like family. I cannot guarantee that this will be my last job. But I do enjoy working here and I am happy here because of the respect and thoughtfulness for others I see. Everyone is true to his or her words. We are not jealous when someone is promoted. We only learn from them how to improve ourselves.

Our leaders often arrange training sessions for us in order to enrich our knowledge, and we have our own little library from which we can learn after work. Each of us has different specialties and we can learn from each other. In addition to work skills, the company also cares about our health and buys us sports equipment. My favorite is badminton. My colleagues tell me I am fast when I play badminton, but I don't appear that way in daily life. I can only say that I speak slowly, but move quickly.

从我09年6月15加入china office 后，08版到10版都睇过 Zappos Culture Book，以家，参与 Zappos China office culture book 的第一版，感觉有滴不知所措……第一次踏足 china office，那阵还没意识到，尼到会成为我的第二个家。点解？！唔是因为相处的人 同我有咩关系而这样讲。确切滴来讲，尼到的人都是来自全国唔同的地方、唔同的省份，大家住系一齐，工作系一齐，虽然是无血缘关系.但相处的模式就跟自己的亲人住系一齐 是一样的感觉。也都因为是来自五湖四海的，生活、作息上的习惯都会有所唔同，这个时候 就需要大家迁就、谦让，但到了Happy Hours那阵，就完全无了隔膜，就算那个系工作上是你的 吖头，就算之前搞得有得有几唔开心。Play Hard Work Hard，平时可以点样讲笑点样大冇大冇细都得，但系工作上，就是需要百分百 甚至是120%的投入。再点讲，我滴离开学校尼个象牙塔，踏足社会了，是一个社会人士了，要为自己的行为负责，机会唔是总要人家比，要自己争取，发现自己有错要改、人家提出 自己的唔足，都要改。唔是下下都有比你改过的机会。是这个家的感觉，我在呢度度过了 毕业后的2年，我唔敢讲以后我还会在逗，但起码以家，我开心、我enjoy！因为在呢度大家 相互尊重，唔会话口头上讲佐就算，而是，大家都会企在对方的立场去思考。有人表现出色、 得到提升唔会去排斥佢，羡慕总会有滴，但更多的是，反思点解人滴做到的，自己做唔到……唔同的人，在学识上都会有所唔同，为佐唔比大家的水平相差太远，老顶还会安排一滴 培训，或者是买滴书等大家可以自己系工作之余自学，office有唔同的人，专长的都会唔同，大家取长补短。公司唔只是睇重工作能力，还注意我滴的健康，购入一些器材，而我 个人就偏好羽毛球， 还有同事话我，平时反应就-100，打球就反应妗快…… 我只能讲，身体反应比语言反应要快。以上是用粤语口语的方式书写的，非正规的国语书写。

Jeff L. 刘家昌

employee since 2009

The Zappos Culture is the standard I use to motivate and restrain myself. Everyone knows the Ten Core Values are simple words with big powers because they are the essence distilled from many successes and life experiences. We should never stop learning the Culture because the learning is endless. No one can say he has fully practiced all Ten Core Values. It takes less than ten minutes to memorize all of them, but it takes a lifetime to fully understand and to experience them. We always say that they are not something just hanging on the wall. I want to add that these Core Values are also not just something printed in a book or a posted on the internet; they are more than just letters, words or numbers. They're the means by which the Zappos Culture is conveyed. The real Zappos Culture is found in every little aspect of our work and life. When we have Cculture training sessions we are learning more than those words; we are learning the soul behind those words. We often say we should WOW others – our colleagues, customers and partners. That's how we practice and spread our Culture. In Zappos' China Office, we treat our colleagues like customers. Every little WOW is appreciated.

There is an old Chinese saying "Don't neglect doing any good thing just because it seems insignificant and don't do any bad thing just because it seems insignificant." In fact, even small things can reveal the culture. We WOW others little by little, like many small streams that flow together to make a river. It is the same when it comes to the relationship between an individual worker and a team. We are a team with a family spirit. Every member's growth strengthens the whole team by sharing and communicating. If we are feeling down, the Zappos Culture comes into play. Our Culture encourages us to be creative and to "Create Fun and a Little Weirdness," which inspires us in our life and work. An article about how we should understand the Ten Core Values said that we should avoid saying that we are already doing very well or even perfectly. This might be very upsetting and can be an obstacle on the road to success. It's what we must get over so we can go further. Like it or not, the path is endless.

"文化"对我的意义就是：激励和约束自身的标准，大家都明白这十条文化的力量是非 常大的，毕竟它们是由很多人从自身成功的经验和生活中精炼出来的，但是我们不是每 个人都能够做到或者做好，对于文化的学习是永无止尽的，因为没有一个人能说"我已经 全学会了文化，这十条我都掌握了?????是的，这十句话很简单，背下来可能不用10分钟，可是你真正去体验和感受它是花一辈子的时间都不够的，我们经常说十条文化不是挂在墙上的，其实我还想说，它也不是写在书上或者贴在网上的，它不仅仅是文字、字符或者数字，这些只是文化传播的导体罢了，真正的文化源于生活和工作中的点点滴滴，每次 我们学习文化或者培训文化的时候学到的不是那几个字而已，真正要学习的是从字里行间体现出来的文化气息和气氛。我们常说WOW，我们自己的员工或对我们的客人和合作伙伴，这种WOW的效果就是很好的口碑和宣传着我们China Office，我们的顾客就是同事，同事 就是顾客，哪怕是一点点小的服务都会得到同事的认可，中国的一句古话 "不以恶小而 为之，不以善小而不为" ，其实往往一些小事情就能体现你的文化，并不是非要做到惊天 动地才能WOW到客人，汪洋大海都是由小川小河汇流而成的，然而也也形同于个人力量和 团队的关系，我们是具有家庭观念的团队，一个人的成长联系着整个团队，一个人的效率 提高了，分享成功，通过沟通、交流，每个人的效率会提高，自然团队的力量也大大提升。 或许在工作和生活中你会觉得萎靡、枯燥乏味，所以是文化鼓励大家创新、搞怪，这是工作 和生活的调节剂，当你不满足于现状的时候，那么你就要想办法去创新，让自己重新找到 激情，对十条文化理解那篇文章中说 "我们永远都不会说：我们做的很好，很正确了" ，这样讲确实比较消极，但是这也可能会成为你前进的绊脚石，这是成长的必经过程和轨迹，不论你喜欢或者不喜欢，这条轨迹 都不会停止。

Jeneen M.

employee since 2006

I agree. P.eace L.ove U.nity R.espect. Thank you.

Jennifer L.

employee since 2010

The Zappos Culture is something more palpable and better defined than what "culture" generally means in corporate America. It's real and not marketing fluff, which means there are pros and cons. For example, I love that we are open, that people are genuine, and just old-fashioned nice, but we're not clones of each other. However, I think it's fair to say that in an organization that draws a lot of generally nice but still strong personalities, there are going to be differences of opinion and issues you can't just hug out (which is great because group-think is boring!). Our culture isn't about frivolity and it's not all about having fun, although there is a lot of that. My friends sometimes think that all we do is party at Zappos – that we don't get any work done! My take on the Zappos Culture is that it's largely based on pragmatism. Who doesn't want to do great work with people you not only like, but who are also your friends? And when issues do arise, wouldn't it be better to face these challenges with people you already know and trust? How much better is your end product when you work with people you naturally jive with or already have this common ground? This is such a wonderfully weird and truly special place to work. It's not that I don't have bad days, but those days are few and far between, and when I take stock of all the great things about working at Zappos, it more than offsets whatever it was that was bothering me that day. You have to take the good with the bad. No company is perfect, not even Zappos, so it's important to maintain a degree of objectivity. However, what I would like anyone interested in Zappos to know is that the culture is real. It's something much more profound than just parades and "class spirit," and it does deliver much of what it promises.

Jennifer S.

employee since 2010

In the past, I thought of myself as a one-woman wolf pack. Then a year ago, when I started at Zappos, I thought, "Wait a second, could it be?" And now I know for sure, I just added to my wolf pack. Us wolves running around the Las Vegas desert attending happy hours and WOWing customers. Now I can't imagine what my life would be like without my Zappos family.

Jenski.

employee since 2008

I've never loved my job so much, nor have I ever before felt like my co-workers were family.

Jerald T.

employee since 2005

WOW! Someday, when I tell people I was one of the luckiest people in the world to work at Zappos in the early days, I can only hope they see the magnitude of what happened. We changed people's lives and saved some people from desolation and despair. When you first see the vision of where we are going it is mind-blowing, but then when it starts to come together you get another WOW moment. I am very thankful for this day and all of the time I have been a part of the Zappos family. Thanks to everyone.

Jessica L. 廖丽芳

employee since 2009

I'm an outgoing person. I love to laugh and communicate with others. I was born and raised in Hubei province, but my hometown is in Hunan province. I love them both. :) My favorite candy is a lollipop and I like different tastes. Eating lollipops makes me feel happy. Another thing that makes me feel happy is to be able to work at Zappos. The Zappos Culture plays a very important role in both my life and my career. I really have grown considerably, both personally and professionally, since joining Zappos.

Those of us who work at Zappos treat each other like brothers and sisters; we are a big family. My colleagues here are full of energy and enthusiasm; we often go to KTV in our spare time. (KTV means karaoke TV, where we can sing songs, play games and drink beer with friends.) I also love all of my US colleagues. The ladies are very lovely and the gentlemen are very handsome and humorous. I like working with them and I have really learned a lot about our Zappos Culture and their lives in America. I hope our China office can help promote the Zappos Culture here and that we can deliver happiness together.

我是个外向活泼的女孩，我喜欢微笑和与人交流。我是在湖北省出生并长大的，但是我的家乡在湖南省，不管怎样，这两个地方我都喜欢。 我最喜欢的糖果是有很多种口味的棒棒糖，我认为吃棒棒糖让我觉得很开心。就像甜甜的糖果一样，另一件让我觉得幸福的事情就是能够在Zappos（美捷步达康）工作，Zappos的文化在我的人生和职业生涯中扮演着很重要的角色。我 真的成长了很多，包括我自身的成长和专业技能上的成长。我喜欢在Zappos工作，我们对待彼此 就像是兄弟姐妹一般，我们是一个大家庭。我在这里的同事们都充满了精力与热情。在我们的 休闲时间里，我们经常去KTV玩。（KTV就是唱卡拉OK的地方，我们可以和我们的朋友们一起唱歌， 玩游戏，还有喝啤酒。）我同样也喜欢所以在美国的同事们，女生都很可爱和漂亮，男生都很 帅气和幽默，我喜欢和他们一起工作，因为我从他们身上真的学到了很多Zappos的文化，以及 知道了他们在美国的生活。希望我们中国办公室可以帮助推广Zappos 的文化，让我们一起奉上幸福吧！ ^^

Jessica V.B.

employee since 2010

Family, friends, and personal growth.

Jessie M.

employee since 2010

To me, the Zappos Culture can be summed up as love and acceptance of all people. You can show your love/acceptance through nurturing, supporting, lifting them up, donations, teaching, learning, aid, assisting – the list is endless. What I do know is that the more you give – the more you will receive. It's our very own "pay it forward" world that is shared daily with others. Everyone at Zappos is driven to give 110% in all they do, and when they finish their task, they give even more! This includes their job duties, friendships, family life, hobbies etc. It totally rocks!!! I love being here, I would say working here, but just being here is awesome! Imagine, getting paid to work here and be with this awesome bunch! I have felt the effects of this love family at home and in the community, and I strive to live up to the 120% club in all I do.

Jim D.

employee since 2011

Try working for corporate finance in a casino and then working for corporate finance at Zappos. I love you,

Jimmy A.

employee since 2005

Hi. I like working at Zappos. Thanks for reading my entry. Bye.

Jimmy C.
employee since 2003

Running with an idea you're passionate about and seeing it through. Trying new things and being allowed to fail. Finding friends at work who will support you in your endeavors. Constant change.

Jong K.
employee since 2010

Not many people can say they've worked for a company listed on Fortune Magazine's Top 100 Companies to Work For, let alone the sixth from the top! I am excited and honored to be part of Zappos, which provides opportunities to help me grow professionally as well as personally, and to work in the comfort of jeans and a T-shirt. (People here think you have a hot date after work or another interview if you are dressed in slacks, dress shirt and dress shoes).

Josh M.
employee since 2010

The Zappos Culture is the reason why everyone around here smiles all the time. Our culture is focused on the pursuit of happiness. It may take some extra effort to focus on your employees' happiness, but I see it paying off everyday. Amazing Zapponians make me smile (and laugh!) daily and that really empowers me to pay it forward. Thank you, Zappos!

Josie D.
employee since 2006

The loyalty we have for this company is awesome. Senior employees have just as much enthusiasm, energy, and spirit as new hires. Together, we strive to maintain our Zappos Culture, which is unique and awesome, and sets us apart from other companies. I'm proud to work for the Zappos family.

K O
employee since 2005

If it ain't broke, don't fix it. But don't stop making it better. Make it not break. Make it go faster. Make it do things no one's seen before. Make it sing. Make it (break) dance. Make it fix itself. Make it exceptional. Make yourself some lunch. You did it! Thanks. OK, keep going.

Kar T.
employee since 2010

The Zappos Culture means creating a place where anybody, no matter how weird and wacky, will be accepted. It is a place where people can genuinely say they are happy and a place where great people can gather and just simply have fun.

Katrina J.
employee since 2006

I Googled "culture" and found this definition: "The beliefs, customs, practices, and social behavior of a particular nation or people." I would like to think that we are now the nation of Zappos. We are not tied down to a particular country. We are a community of ever-evolving people. We respect each others' individuality, and we thrive on our joint beliefs. Together not only can we can change our own lives, but those of the people around us as well. With our culture in place, we can change our world too. Better watch out! There's a Zapponian about!

Keith C.
employee since 2008

Zappos is a really special place to work. I'm going on three years here and it passed by in a blink. Where else can you be creative, be recognized for hard work and love your co-workers like family. I'm pretty lucky to be contributing my talents to the only place I'd want to work.

Keith H.
employee since 2009

What can I say about Zappos that hasn't been said a million times before? It's hard to find words to describe how you feel about this place. Sometimes WOW doesn't even come close to how this place makes you feel. I wish I could think of the word, or maybe the word doesn't exist all. I know that when I see or hear this place, the fire in my heart is overwhelmed with joy and happiness and energy.

Kelly H.
employee since 2008

Zappos is a permission-giving organization. Anyone who has an idea is encouraged to explore the possibilities. In fact, we are not only encouraged but also EXPECTED to run with our ideas; nobody else is going to do it for us. And if we fail? It's another opportunity to learn from our experiences. Zig Ziglar says, "Failure is a detour, not a dead-end street." The Zappos Culture gives each of us permission to try and permission to fail. It's this permission that keeps us growing and thriving!

Kevin F. 丰凯

employee since 2010

I have been working in Zappos' China office for a year. Strictly speaking, this is my first full-time job and I feel really lucky to be here! I still remember the first time I read about the Zappos Culture. I was deeply attracted to it. And then, when I saw that the people in our office and at Zappos headquarters were trying their best to practice the Culture themselves. I was really WOWed. That was when I knew that Zappos had a unique Culture and felt it was the right place for me to work. Here, we live together as a family and we work together as a positive team. What's more, we have a very good relationship with each other, thanks to good communication.

I believe people should keep learning throughout our lifetimes because this is the most effective way for us to grow and to be stronger. We should learn that the more humble we are, the more things we can learn. Since changes always happen in our daily life, it is better for us to embrace them, even to drive them. In order to pursue growth and learning, we need to be adventurous, creative and open-minded. Passion and determination are also important because they give us strength to "Do More with Less" (Value #8) in our daily work. And please don't forget to "Create Fun and a Little Weirdness" (Value #3)!

我在Zappos工作已经有一年了。严格说来，这是我第一份全职工作，并且非常庆幸自己能够来到这里！依然记得，在我第一次了解到公司文化的时候，我就被她深深地吸引了。之后，当我得知我们中国办公室和总部的员工们一直都在努力实践我们的文化，我真的被他们的热情打动了。从那时起，我就认定Zappos和她的文化是独一无二的。同时，我也明白这里就是我一直找寻的地方！在这里，我们像家人一样生活在一起。同时，我们也是一个积极、上进的团队。更重要的是，通过交流我们彼此都相处的非常融洽。我们应该不断学习，因为这是我们成长和壮大的有效途径。当然，我们也要明白一点，我们越是谦虚，学到的东西也就越多！变化常常会发生在我们的日常生活中，最好的方法就是拥抱它，甚至驱动它！为了追求成长和学习，我们应该勇于冒险，敢于创新并且开放思想。激情和决断力同样非常重要，这些能让我们在日常工作中充满力量，从而达到事半功倍。当然，请不要忘记创造快乐和一点点搞怪！

Kiersten S.

employee since 2010

Hmmm ... What does the Zappos Culture mean to me? The Zappos Culture means the most amazing bond with co-workers that you will ever have. Work, good times, family, drinks, laughs and so much more. The culture makes you push yourself harder than you ever have before. You want to work extra hard and do great things for this amazing family.

Kimberly G.

employee since 2010

Before coming to work for Zappos I never thought work was or could be fun. In fact, I dreaded going into the office. My snooze button was my buddy. Putting on my "business attire" every day was something I had become accustomed to and pretty much just accepted. That's what work is, right? I found myself just trying to get through each day without quitting. THEN! I found Zappos. Talk about a life-changing experience! I've met so many genuinely kind people working here. Now work is fun. I look forward to coming in (sometimes in my flip-flops :) EVERY DAY. My best day at a previous job still doesn't even come close to matching a "bad day" here at Zappos. When you love what you do, that joy can't help but spill over into other areas of your life. I've never been more content. I feel like everyone is here for the same reason ... to Deliver Happiness.

Kimmy L. 梁金梅

employee since 2011

Before I came here I had been told that Zappos was a great company that paid special attention to its Culture! But at that time I didn't have the whole picture! I had always felt that profit is the first goal of every company. Anything else is just serving this goal. The first project I learned when I got to Zappos was "UPS." – a project to improve customer service. We need to confirm the status of returned products and determine whether we are ready to refund the customers' money or not. In the beginning, I was a little surprised by this kind of service, as not many companies in China do business this way. When I first started this project, I was also a little confused. Some of the returned shoes seemed worn, but we still gave the customer a refund. I was a little worried about making mistakes that might lead to a loss for the company! Then a colleague taught me that, when in doubt, Zappos' policy was to give a refund! WOW, this is an amazing company! This was my feeling at that time! As the time went by, I became more and more familiar with this unique Culture. The more I know about it, the more I love the company. I am really happy to be here. And I am very proud of our group as well! Just like the first of Zappos' Core Values says, "Deliver WOW Through Service." Zappos is providing superior customer service in order to WOW everyone who experiences it!

记得我还没来之前，Selina就告诉我捷步达康是一个非常注重文化的公司，当时我还没有一个完整的概念，因为之前一直认为，公司的第一目标是盈利，其他都是为这个目标服务的。我来这里学的其中一个项目是UPS，是为客人处理退回来的商品，确认商品回仓库之后给客人全额退款。这一点一开始的时候真的令我很惊讶，因为很少会有购物公司会这样做，真的是以真诚的服务去WOW客人，让客人感受到我们的优质文化和服务。刚开始做这个项目的时候，看到有些鞋子回来的时候是坏的，但是我们还是要全额退款，我退款的时候还是充满疑惑，害怕自己会做错而给公司造成损失，不过小K说是要退的，无论是worn还是defective，我们都要退钱给客人，只要客人把东西还回来。WOW，这真的是非常了不起的公司，当时我是这样想的，后来随着在捷步达康工作时间的增加，对我们公司的很多独特文化有了越来越多的接触和了解，就越发的喜欢和敬佩捷步达康，对自己能在这样优秀的公司里工作真的是无比的高兴和自豪。Just like the first core value says, deliver WOW through service.

Krisy W. 吴洪

employee since 2010

Hello everyone! I have been at the China office for more than one year now. My major was Business English when I was in college, so I wanted to find a job where I could use my English-speraking ability every day. Now I can. And I like working here very much, not only because I can speak English every day, but also because all members here are so lovely and easy-going. Our office is really a big family and everyone is like my brother or sister. I have worked in other companies before, but Zappos is very different. I love the Culture here!

I work with some colleagues in Las Vegas, especially Zappos CLT. I like them very much. They are kind and patient, and they teach us many projects. Thanks for sharing your happiness with us. I am looking forward to knowing more friends from Zappos in Las Vegas.

大家好，我是Krisy，来自Zappos中国代表处。我已经在这里工作一年多了。大学的时候，我的专业是商务英语。所以毕业后，我一直想找一份可以每天都接触到英语的工作。现在 我做到了。我非常喜欢在这里工作，不仅仅是因为每天都可以学习英语，还因为这里所有人 都很可爱，很好相处。我们这个办公室就像一个大家庭，每一个人都像自己的兄弟姐妹。 之前我也有在别的公司工作过，但是Zappos跟它们很不一样。我热爱Zappos的文化。我与 Zappos总部的一些同事合作，特别是CLT部门。我非常喜欢他们，他们都很好，很耐心， 我从他们那里学到很多东西，他们也跟我们分享了很多快乐。我很期待能认识更多拉斯 维加斯的朋友。

Lina L. 林俏萍

employee since 2011

As a trainee, I still have only a little knowledge about the Zappos Culture, but I will try my best to learn more about it from now on. Like someone has said, delivering happiness works everywhere, and I do agree with that. To use some of Zappos' Ten Core Values as examples:

#1. "Deliver WOW through service." No matter whether an institution's purpose is profit or not, it needs to use service to tell the customers that it can be depended on. So providing perfect service will not only deliver happiness to the customers, but also fulfill one's self-confidence. #5. "Pursue Growth and Learning," and #10. "Be Humble." Humility creates a positive attitude to pursue learning and growth. #8. "Do More with Less." This Value is about efficiency. To do more things with less time requires practice, becoming familiar with the work and planning a reasonable time schedule.

由于来捷步达康没多久，所以对它的文化还不是非常的了解。但是我会在接下来的 日子里努力去学习它并理解透它。就像有人说过的，三双鞋的文化理论适用于所有的行业， 对此，我非常的赞同。拿我们公司的核心价值观来说: 1.通过服务来让人们感到惊叹WOW.不管 一个企业是盈利机构还是非盈利机构，它都需要用它的服务来告诉客户，它是非常好的， 是值得信赖的。因此，提供完美的服务不仅能够给客户带去幸福，而且能够满足一个人的 自信心。2. 积极进取和不断学习。虚怀若谷。虚怀若谷就是一种非常好的积极进取，不断学习 所应具备的态度。3. 追求事半功倍。这是有关效率的定律，尝试用更短的时间去做更多的事情， 当然这也是需要更多的练习，并熟练自己所做的工作。很重要的一点，就是要设定一个好的 时间安排表。

Lindsey K.

employee since 2005

Core Value #1, "Deliver WOW Through Service"
A few members on the Development team created the Fitnezz website recently. They did this without us asking for it and it really WOW'ed the benefits team! It was a great service and it really made our lives so much easier!

Core Value #2, "Embrace and Drive Change"
Last year the benefits department went through some changes in the structure of the team and two new employees were added (Celina and Bhawna!!). We have become a very strong group and this wouldn't have been possible if we all didn't embrace and drive the change.

Core Value #3, "Create Fun and a Little Weirdness"
For last year's open enrollment, the benefits team branded our benefits as "Benefits are Hot." We had so much fun running with the idea and making the theme sticky.

Core Value #4, "Be Adventurous, Creative, and Open-Minded"
I recently got the opportunity to go to Kentucky and go through the Hero Academy. It was such a great experience and I can't say enough good things about it. I loved getting to see the unique spins they have on Zappos' Culture out there, getting to travel to a new state, eat a lot of delicious food, meet new people, and learn all about the warehouse.

Core Value #5, "Pursue Growth and Learning"
I am in the process of completing a Certified Employee Benefits Specialist program. Zappos is paying for me to complete this program and I feel very thankful and privileged to be able to do this. It is such an amazing opportunity for me and I am so lucky to be able to continue my learning.

Core Value #6, "Build Open and Honest Relationships With Communication"
There are always a lot of great surveys that get sent out to give people the opportunity to be open and honest with one another. This allows everyone to express their opinion and have a say with what happens in the company.

Core Value #7, "Build a Positive Team and Family Spirit"
My co-workers are like family and they make coming to work every day worth it. This is definitely my favorite part about working at Zappos.

Core Value #8, "Do More With Less"
The benefits team always tries to bring wellness vendors on-site to provide free services, such as classes and screenings, instead of requiring employees to pay for these services elsewhere. We are fortunate enough to work with great vendors who are willing to do this for us and it allows us to offer the best possible benefits with our budget.

Core Value #9, "Be Passionate and Determined"
Recently Zappos started matching 2% of employee contributions to a 401k! This is something that the benefits team has been very passionate about for many years, but we always came across different obstacles that prevented it from being implemented. It is so exciting that this benefit got approved and it shows how being passionate and determined really pays off!

Core Value #10, "Be Humble"
When discussing our benefits with outside companies, it is a very humbling experience to hear their thoughts on how great they feel our benefits are. It makes me very proud to be part of the overall efforts and to be able to work for a company that allows us to offer such rich benefits.

Lisa M.

employee since 2004

Site Manager currently says we have 3,782 employees. One of the 3,782 defines our culture as fun, fast paced and spontaneous. It is cohesive yet allows each person and department to be unique. This uniqueness is what makes me really enjoy my job and don't think I will ever find another legal department that does cartwheels in the hallway.

Lisa S.

employee since 2010

The Zappos Culture means many things to me, but mostly it inspires me to be the best I can be and to continue to contribute and share our culture with others. Zappos is a place you are happy and proud to be part of. We are one big family that cares, shares, encourages and supports one another in all we do. We don't just say we have Ten Core Values. We truly live by them and share our passion for them with others. I am blessed to be part of our Zappos family!!

Liz G.

employee since 2006

Being so far from my family has been hard since I moved to Nevada in 2005, but Zappos has given me a second family in Las Vegas. I have found wonderful friends and feel lucky to have a job that brings me such satisfaction and overall joy. Yay Zappos!

Louie M.

employee since 2006

The Zappos Culture is definitely unique. I always get questions like: "How do you guys get anything done?" or "Do you guys ever work?" It's always a tough question to answer because I really don't know how it's possible to get so much work done and have so much fun at the same time. We have a culture that I think can often be imitated, but never duplicated. We have proven how successful we can be with a lot of hard work and teamwork, like a lot of companies. I believe what sets Zappos apart is that we all strive for happiness and that means stepping outside of what is conventional and allowing all of our employees to be themselves and have the opportunity to play just as hard as we work.

Lyndsey A.

employee since 2010

I love how the Culture at Zappos allows for each and every employee to be themselves, regardless of what that means. I have never felt at home and felt as if I did not have to alter who I was just because I was at work. I think that because everyone is able to be himself or herself. It fosters the growth of real relationships, not just "work" relationships but actual, genuine friendships. I love that I am able to be creative, grow both professionally and personally, be myself and build real relationships with my co-workers.

Maggie M.

employee since 2007

The Amazon acquisition is so 2009! Now the big focus for us as a company is moving the Zappos headquarters to the downtown area of Las Vegas. And let me be frank ... I'm definitely an "uptown" girl. :-) I enjoy the luxuries of gated communities, upscale retail stores, parks to walk my dog through, and a general sense of security in the neighborhood I call home.

At first glance, the downtown area of Las Vegas offers none of these things. I have been in Vegas for six years and can count the number of times I have gone to Fremont Street on one hand. The prospect of spending 80% of my time in downtown Las Vegas isn't ideal. However, when faced with change, Zappos encourages its employees to open our horizons, embrace and drive the change, look beyond the obvious, and to be adventurous, creative and open-minded. I plan to do just that as I prepare to enter the downtown world. :-)

Mahvash A.

employee since 2008

The Zappos Culture breathes life into every minute of my time spent here. It fills my heart with ecstasy and brightens every weekday morning as I get ready to come to work. Silly jokes, pranks, and endless giggles fill in the air around my desk. Hats off to the Zappos Culture for letting us have lots of fun while working. Work just seems to be play here!

Maja L.

employee since 2008

The Zappos Culture means growth in every aspect, as a person and as a professional. It encourages me to change and learn from other people that are there always there to help and celebrate with me.

Mallory J.

employee since 2007

I have realized that I am a different person than I was a few years ago, thanks to my Job here at Zappos! I have had the best time here and wouldn't change it for the world. I have never seen a company with employees as happy as we are here. Everyone really gets along with everyone else and its wonderful. I couldn't ask for a better place to work.

Marcela G.

employee since 2005

I missed the opportunity to contribute to last year's Culture Book because around this time, my husband was in the hospital and he later passed away. As he was getting sicker, I knew I would soon be facing the hardest decision in my life .... Should I move closer to family, as it was now only my son and I, or stay here? I'm not sure how many of you actually know what it's like to lose a partner, a friend, and father. I knew that whatever decision I made was not only going to affect me but the most important person in my life: my son.

The dreaded time of his passing came! What to do next? Well ... here is where I was surprised! I didn't need to go anywhere; I was already surrounded by family! No need to move across country to be close to anyone, my family had been around me all this time! Starting with Marlene, who was there with me in the hospital, making sure I was eating and getting a break. Loren, who on multiple occasions offered to go pick up my son from school so he wouldn't have to be in the hospital. Kelly, calling to check on me. Alfred, taking the time to come and offer his condolences. They respected my space and the time I wanted to be alone, but I knew they were there for anything I needed. The whole team went to a meal-making place and brought us two weeks worth of dinners so we would have one less thing to worry about. I was also surprised to see so many loving faces at the funeral. I knew they were there because they really meant it, because they were feeling my pain. And today, exactly a year later, I am glad I made the decision to stay. If this whole experience has brought anything positive, it has been for me to be able to identify my Zappos family. It is not blood that makes your family; it is the love and support, and that's exactly what you get here. Love and support!! I consider myself very lucky to not only have my blood family but to be part of an even bigger one. I'm proud to be part of the Zappos family. I love you guys!

Marcie A.

employee since 2007

It's bursting with fruit flavor.

Maritza L.

employee since 2006

Culture + Super Rad = Zappos

Mark G.

employee since 2009

I truly enjoy working with my friends every day. This environment is like nothing I have ever experienced. Great place to work, or greatest place work? Zappos Culture is crazy – crazy like a fox!

Mary F.

employee since 2009

I don't know what I could possibly say that has not been said repeatedly. The Zappos Culture is like no other in the world. It is a privilege to be a Zapponian and I just can't imagine working at any other company. In the time that I've been here, I have never heard one employee utter a negative remark about the company or the management. Coming to Zappos each morning makes me feel recharged and I can't wait to see what the day is going to bring. We are encouraged to have fun, be creative and to always expect the unexpected.

May L. 李梅

employee since 2009

Like most of my colleagues, this is my first job. I did not have any work experience before this. It has now been two years since I was a college student. We've seen each other change and grow. Zappos is my second family.

We are very proud to practice the Zappos Culture. Many times we have WOW'ed each other, "WOW! You guys are so different" "WOW! How did you make it?" But to us, those just come naturally. Our colleagues are brothers and sisters; it's what we should do to help and understand each other.

We always try to create a little fun at work while working hard too. And everyone is equal; no one is superior because of his position. We are different from many conventional companies in so many ways. That's all because Zappos' Ten Core Values have made us different so we stand out.

和我的大部分的同事一样，在这里的工作是我的第一份工作，在这之前我没有其他的工作 经验，从一个学生到现在工作已经两年了，在这里所有的人都相互的见证着大家的成长与 改变，对我来说这里基本就是我的另外一个家！Zappos的文化实践对于我们来说是一件非常 自豪的事情，很多人都说："WOW！！！！你们怎么这么不一样，wow！！！你们怎么可以 这样？等等……但是有许多事情对我们同事来说是非常自然的事情，就像我们觉得同事就 应该是兄弟姐妹，相互理解与帮助是很应该的；工作中大家营造出来的轻松氛围也是理所 当然的，但是对待工作有更加高的要求；上司和员工的关系的平等性和和谐性……从中可以 看出我们和其他的许多传统公司有许多不同的地方，因为这些都是我们的10 core values 所要求的，因为有它我们才变得不同与卓越：）

Megan P.

employee since 2006

Reputation is what others know about you. Honor is what you know about yourself. That's how I feel about our Zappos Culture. :)

Melanie B.

employee since 2008

Zappos Culture has the amazing ability to truly bring out the best in people. New employees blossom into people they never knew they were or could be. It's the open and accepting environment that cultivates people's imaginations and creativity. I thought I'd seen every kind of culture imaginable in the Silicon Valley, but being part of Zappos has made me understand and appreciate that there is so much more to work than just doing what's in a job description. Zappos is a way of life. =)

Mia P.

employee since 2010

Always new challenges, new faces and new snacks everyday at Zappos.

Michael H.

employee since 2010

I have only worked here for a few months and could have never imagined such an awesome place to start my career. The only bad thing starting my career here is that I am already spoiled and I couldn't imagine being happy working anywhere else. Every person I have met here so far has been more than amazing. I had high expectations of Zappos and this place has exceeded every one of them.

"Pursue Growth and Learning" is my favorite Core Value (#5) and everyone here is so encouraging with my ideas, no matter how small they are. I have never been to a place that is so accepting and lets you be who you are. The best part is that I already have a full week's worth of Zappos shirts!

Michael M.

employee since 2008

The Zappos Culture is amazing. The feelings of belonging and family are truly unlike those anywhere else that I have worked. Never before have I been around so many people that not only care about who I am as a person, but also about what I want to accomplish. This has made achieving goals a reality, and I truly feel like family.

Michael R.

employee since 2010

The Zappos Culture is so great that sometimes I don't even realize I am at work.

Michelle S.
employee since 2008

Two really cool events took place in my life this past year: hearing that my husband passed the Nevada State Bar exam and getting to meet my favorite rocker, Bret Michaels! The coolest part? My Zappos family had something to do with both of these events!

On the morning that the bar results were to come out, I was at Lake Mead to stake out a camping spot. No matter what the result, we would have a peaceful family weekend. Little did I know that the results had been revealed three hours early. I also didn't know that my team back at Zappos had been keeping the Bar Results page up on a computer. They were almost as anxious as we were! As I was driving a tent pole into the ground, I received a text message from my teammate, Tamra. The message read, "Go check the website! The results are up! He passed!" Before my hand could even stop shaking, before my eyes had a chance to tear up, and before I had even heard from my husband, I received a call from my team. Everyone was cheering and yelling their congratulations! It meant so very much to me that my team cared enough to not only care what the results of the exam were, but to watch for them and to celebrate with me, even though I wasn't there. I knew every one of them was genuinely happy for my family.

Later that month, I learned that Bret Michaels would be performing at the Zappos Rock 'n Roll Las Vegas Marathon in December. I was excited that I would be able to see him perform live again, but I had no idea what would happen that day! Three days before the concert, I had a thought: Since Zappos is sponsoring the Marathon, they might know how I could meet Bret! Zappos had just started a new program for its employees called Wishez. I thought it was worth a shot to share my wish, but wasn't really sure if it could actually happen. I came in to work the next morning and saw an email saying that my wish was granted! I was set up with a Backstage Pass to the concert! I don't think I've said "Oh, my gosh!" and "No way!" so much in my life.

Meeting Bret was one of the coolest things that has ever happened to me. He was so kind and gracious, especially after learning that someone in my Zappos family granted my wish to meet him. (Thanks, Tom!). These are only two examples of how we continually strive to build a positive team and family spirit here. My Zappos family rocks!

Mike A.
employee since 2006

The Zappos Culture represents friendships, hard work, forward thinking, creativity, and the ability to adapt and drive change so that we can live up to the service level promise we make to our customers. It's up to all of us to continue to live and drive the culture that has been the key to our success over the past 12 years.

Mike B.
employee since 2010

It's pretty difficult to put into words what the Zappos Culture means to me, so I'll just provide a few examples of things that have happened within these walls over the past year: a beer bong contest using apple juice (bad idea!), a Spaun parade celebrating his modeling debut, the 12 days of christmahanaquanzika, an ill-advised April Fool's day joke (sorry again, Lisa!), a lesson on portion sizes, shake weights, live HR girls direct to you, and did I mention shake weights? In between all of the fun (it is one of our Core Values, after all), we still manage to get a whole lot of work done! :)

Mike B.
employee since 2010

To me, the Zappos Culture is what drives all Zappos employees to deliver the best customer experience, all while having fun. Because of this culture, I never dread going to work. I look forward to every day and every experience, whether it's working on a difficult problem with my team or shooting a nerf dart across the office and yelling "You're crazy like that glue." The Zappos Culture is what enables me and all Zappos employees to love what we do for a living and, in turn, it's what drives us to deliver the best possible service to our customers.

Mike K.
employee since 2000

The wonderful world of Zappos Culture never ceases to amaze me. Last year I attended CLT training after 10 years of being with the company. Let me tell you, it was an eye-opener for sure. Not only did I meet some very awesome folks, with whom I remain in close contact, but the feeling of connection and building relationships with those joining our family was truly special. All in all our family spirit is strong and after many years of being a Zapponian, it remains true that our culture is something to cherish.

Miki C.
employee since 2006

Zappos is a great place to spend your day. So much so that sometimes you forget you're at work. The combination of doing what you love plus being in such a fun and friendly environment feels nothing like work. :) I've been here for over five years now and the culture is the same as it was when I started, even with all the growth and changes. This shows me how much we truly value our culture here at Zappos.

Millie C.

employee since 2006

One would think, after five years, there would not be anything new to write for our Culture Book, but that is the essence of Zappos Culture. We are always moving, evolving and expanding our universe. We have transitioned from a small private company to a subsidiary of a publicly traded company. We are anticipating a move from our suburban offices in Henderson to a new campus environment. We are continuing to improve our websites and our customers' shopping experiences. While we navigate down these different trails, it's nice to be hiking next to colleagues who are also my friends and family.

Miss Patti C.

employee since 2005

This is the greatest company to work for. Every year is better than the last. I am going on my sixth year with Zappos and it just keeps getting better. The team and family spirit grows stronger every day. It's amazing how our culture has spread. When people find out where I work, they all say the same things. What an awesome place it must be to work, how well we are treated and how much they admire our Zappos Culture. I feel extremely blessed to be a part of this amazing family. I am also very grateful for the freedom, support and knowledge that everyone who is a part of Zappos has given me over these past years.

Nancy T. 谭思思

employee since 2010

WOW! It's really amazing! I have now been working at Zappos for over one year. I have to say I am super lucky. I got the offer immediately after the first interview I had in my whole life. Then I began my first job at Zappos smoothly. I never expected that I would have so many lucky first-time events at Zappos. LOL. Without a doubt, "family" is the best word to describe Zappos' China office. We are a family and our colleagues are lovely, diligent and helpful. We have never been afraid of difficulties and changes because we know we will not fight alone. We are a team, a strong family.

In the very beginning, I was the remote assistant to some of our US colleagues, and I had a very nice time cooperating with many of them. They are nice and patient; we cannot achieve any success without their generous help. We love you and we will keep providing our best service to you. (*^___^*) Now I am very honored and grateful that I got this precious opportunity to be the leader of the Pipeline team in the China office. Each time we recruit new members, we try our best to find those whose culture seems like a good fit. Sometimes we have to refuse talented people for lack of culture fit. However, we have never regretted our decisions. We are proud of our Zappos Culture and we only welcome those who will be able to live by our Core Values. Zappos Culture is powerful! It binds us together. I love working at Zappos!!!!!

Wow!太棒了！我在捷步已经工作一年多了。我不得不说我是一个超级幸运的女孩子。我参加 了我一生中的第一次面试，很快的我被录用了。于是我在捷步顺利的开始了我的第一份工作。 我从未想过我的那么多的第一次都是发生在捷步。LOL^^^^^^毫无疑问，用家庭这个单词来 形容捷步达康办公室是再好不过了。我们就是一家人，我们的同事都那么的可爱，勤奋和乐 于助人。我们从不畏艰险，以为我们知道我们不是孤军奋战的，我们是一个团队，一个强大 的家庭。起初，我作为远程助理服务美国同事，期间我和所有的美国同事都合作的相当开心。 他们既耐心又友好，没有他们慷慨的帮忙我们绝对不能取得任何成功。我们爱你们，我们也将 一如既往的为你们提供最好的服务。(*^___^*)现在我非常荣幸并感激我有这么一个珍贵的机会 来领导中国办公室的pipeline组。每次当我们应聘新成员时，我们都竭尽全力地寻找那些符合 文化的人，甚至有时候我们不得不拒绝很多有才能的人。然后我们从未为我们的决定遗憾过。 我们以我们捷步达康的文化为荣，我们只欢迎那些遵循我们核心价值的人。捷步达康的文化 太有力量了！正是文化把我们联系在一起。我真的非常喜欢在捷步达康工作！！！！

Pam T.

employee since 2003

A friend said to me last week, "I was in a meeting with others from around the company and Zappos' strong culture was a big part of our discussion." When I hear comments like this, or read the weekly CLT Props, I am reminded of how fortunate I am to be a part of our growth. I'm inspired every day by people from around Zappos. Every company has a culture, good or bad. Prior to Zappos, I worked for companies where the culture was negative or indifferent. I left because I was unhappy for a variety of reasons, but primarily because I felt disconnected. When I joined Zappos, I felt "unleashed," given the autonomy to make things happen without having to ask permission. Years later, I still feel unleashed and inspired to do everything I can to keep our culture healthy and evolving. Moving downtown is exciting – what an awesome opportunity we've been handed to continue building our culture and reaching outside of our walls and into the community. It's exciting to be a part of this big movement!

Pati V.

employee since 2006

We are just one big happy extended family. I love it! Our Zappos Culture is like nothing you could ever imagine or dream. There is no place I would rather call my home. We work hard and play harder. I love it!!!

Patricio J.

employee since 2010

Zappos Culture means the ability to think, develop ideas and create initiatives governed by the limits of your own abilities. My life has switched completely. These days I am happy, rejuvenated and eager to go to work. It means creating friendships, pride and being able to relate to people I work with. Nerf gun wars, innovative developing in my field, happy hours and all the support from everyone around the company. Zappos Culture means: chenito, chanchito, hurrah and burrah, alexito magapa, ck, Neo, markinho, "DA FONG", lefty and righty, flaca, the icio brothers, Mego, P.I.T.A, reposado, chiquita, The Tank! and all of you who make this such a special place! Of course this would not be complete with a shot of Tuaca or, as it is usually called, chihuahua shot; chewbaca shot … Pato out!

Patrick S.

employee since 2001

Zappos is just like being Barry Bonds. It means constantly hitting home runs and making people jealous of our rapid growth.

Priscilla G.

employee since 2007

The Zappos Culture is one of a kind. My time here has flown by and without the fun, loving atmosphere that we have here, I don't know how things would be! Culture is a way of living, learned traditions that are passed down from generation to generation, and I feel as Zappos keeps growing we will be able to take over the world! I truly appreciate this company and look forward to many more years!

Rachael B.

employee since 2005

The best way to describe what the Zappos Culture means is that I'm still excited to come into the office every day, even after over six years. :) In the past, I always hopped around to different cities and every time I have a Zappos anniversary, I can't believe how long I have been here! I get bored pretty easily, but at Zappos there are always new people, new ideas and exciting new endeavors we are able to be a part of. I love being a part of the Zappos community and all the opportunities we have. Whenever I talk to friends/family/visitors about what we're doing, I get excited and feel grateful for being able to be a part of it. Can't wait to see where the next six years take us!

Rain Z. 钟荣勋

employee since 2010

Zappos is a company built on a good reputation through high-quality service, which helps maintain social resources like customers and employees. Culture is the soul of a company and the power of promoting the enterprise's development. A company without culture is like a person without soul, let alone development. So we can say that culture is very important to a company. "Create Fun and a Little Weirdness" (Core Value #3) doesn't just mean a smiley face. Our company treats everyone with respect and serves everyone from the bottom of our hearts. Creating fun can be used not only in life, but also in work. It's also crucial to create a happy atmosphere. Emotional waves are inevitable during a long workday. We need a way to release emotions, which can relieve the pressure. Everyone should experience the joy of success and avoid the frustration of failure. We can bring fun into our work, and at times come up with some tricks to share fun and weirdness with our customers.

Zappos通过优质的服务来树立口碑，留住客户员工等资源。文化是企业的灵魂.是推动企业发展的 不竭动力,这是非常重要的。没有文化的企业就相当于没有灵魂的人,而没有灵魂的人还谈什么 发展呢?所以说文化对一个公司是非常重要的！搞怪与创造欢乐,并不是脸上的微笑。我们公司 更是要用发自内心的快乐去感染每一个人和服务每一个人。创造欢乐这个词不只是体现在生活上, 也体现在工作上。因为在工作中营造欢乐的气氛也很重要,在我们长久的工作中难免情绪会有点 波动,难免会有成功的愉快和失意的烦恼,这时我们就需要宣泄情绪,那就是把苦变成乐,我们 可以把生活中的快乐带到工作中,时不时动动脑搞点花样,让客人也感受到欢乐和搞怪。

Ran G.

employee since 2009

I am so thankful to be part of Zappos family where I can express myself as a unique individual and strive to be a better person.

Ravindra A.

employee since 2011

I'm very proud to join Zappos family. I have only been here for a month and I already feel that I've been here for years because I met so many people. Everyone is so nice to each other. I'm a part of very big family. I'm very fortunate to join Zappos as my first job. The culture here is not only positive for my professional life; it will definitely affect my personal life and make it better as well. Thank you, Zappos.

Ray Ray.

employee since 2004

I always look forward to this time of year. The time when I get to share my feelings with so many. Now that I am going on my seventh year here at Zappos, I have seen lots of growth. With this growth, some wonder how our Zappos Culture is affected. Let me tell you first hand, it only gets better year by year. As we grow, I acquire more awesome folks to call my family. I continue to wake up every day excited to come to work. Excited for the smiles, the connections and the knowledge I get to share with our guests and visitors as they walk through the doors for the first time. So if you wonder if the culture has changed any with our growth, yes it has. It has gotten better every year.

Rebecca P.

employee since 2010

When I think about the best moments in my life, it is not surprising to me that coming to work at Zappos makes the list. But it does continue to surprise me every day just how genuinely caring everyone here is. From the moment I applied to work here, I felt truly welcomed into this great big wonderful family. When comparing Zappos to previous jobs, the biggest difference I have found is that when I come into work at Zappos I can just be myself. There is no need to watch my words or pretend to be someone else just to fit in. I find that with the contagious atmosphere of Zappos I not only strive to work harder, I take ownership of it and have loads fun along the way. Every morning I wake up wanting to come into work. How great is that?!!

Renna C.

employee since 2007

The Zappos culture is like a mixtape of my favorite songs. Each has a different effect, purpose, and sentiment. :) "Feel the light upon your face as we draw closer to the sun. We'll live our lives in its warm embrace. We have only just begun." – Adair

Richard H. 谢传刚

employee since 2005

Perhaps the part of Zappos Culture that's most relevant to me is the spirit of work/life integration. This doctrine has guided us in hiring, training and retaining dozens of employees in China, not only to work together or to devote about 20% of their time outside of the office, but also live, eat and play in the same building. In order to maintain the many advantages of offering such a unique environment to prospective employees, we have to relentlessly focus on "culture fit" as the number one priority in every aspect of our activities. The strategy works. The China office now not only has an extremely high level of employee happiness, it has also attracted the attention of some well known MBA professors and students in China who have come to visit the office and participated in some of our Cculture events.

It warms my heart that, for the first time in the company's history, the Zappos Culture Book includes contributions made by employees in the China office, who have been trained by and are working with many of our colleagues in Las Vegas and Shepherdsville on a regular basis. In an effort to communicate with the readers in both the US and China, all the entries are presented in both English and Chinese. They are soooo good and I'm proud of them!

Ron C.

employee since 2011

As I write this, I have been at Zappos just under two months. It really is an amazing place. I was at my previous job for five years and knew less than a dozen people well, but in less than two months here I already have many dozens of people I can call my friends. It is very different to work in a place where everyone is genuinely happy to be here, to help out and teach and do everything you could ask of them. I am so excited for the future now – something I have not experienced in far too long.

Rosalind S.

employee since 2005

Change, passion, growth, learning …. I'm all in!!!! I could never get enough and it's not about to stop!!!! I'm doing what I love! :) Since I started working here at Zappos in the beginning of 2005, I've been on a constant search for something. I'll continue searching because I've realized it's the ever-evolving change you experience throughout life that grows you individually.

Change is ongoing here at Zappos and "Embrace and Drive Change" (Core Value #2) had to be a Core Value. Zappos knows how to develop the best in you, giving you the opportunity to learn, grow and the opportunity to pursue your passions. I've experienced all of this and so much more. Family and love … that's what I have here at Zappos. I have many great friendships that I don't believe I could have found anywhere else. I will say, I have a few lifetime friendships too and you know who you are! So I have to give a shout out to the ZCON Team, KY Solutions and everyone attending the FC Hero Academy and the LV Encounter!!! This is not by chance that we all know each other. Lastly, my good friend Jeffry Daniels from our KY Family for asking the question. "Are you all in?" Yes, I am!!! Blessings!!! :)

Rosanna V.

employee since 2007

I can't believe I've been at Zappos for almost four years now. It's awesome to see that our Culture is still growing and reaching new audiences. I absolutely love seeing the look on people's faces when I tell them where I work. You would think that they're opening up a gift. I must admit I have the same look on my face every day. I love my Zappos fam bam! Holla!

Rowell M.

employee since 2011

The Zappos Culture to me means just being myself. If you ask my family and friends, they'll say that I'm always happy, smiling, quiet and a very nice person. Coming to work is just like having family and friends as your co-workers to help, guide and have fun with while working hard and providing the best customer service. I'm so blessed and thankful for the opportunity to work for Zappos. In my short time here, I've been WOWed with how the company treats its employees and customers. I love coming to work and the experience and training I have received so far will last me a lifetime. As the company grows, I'm so anxious and excited to see what the future holds for me here, both professionally and personally.

Ryan D.

employee since 2010

Zappos is truly the most unique place I've ever worked. All the employees really do act as a family. The only complaint I have about working here for the past year is the 35 pounds I gained from eating all the cupcakes and cake pops around the office.

Ryan R.

employee since 2010

To me, the Zappos Culture is our people. We have the best people from all over the place, all in one building. Each person brings something different to the table, but when you pile it all together, you end up with one huge and wonderful family.

Sam G.

employee since 2009

The Zappos Culture is working hard and efficiently while enjoying a family atmosphere.

Sandeep C.

employee since 2009

Work culture did not mean a whole lot, until I joined Zappos. And now, after one and a half years, I have learned that culture can have huge impact on job satisfaction and motivation. The Zappos Culture, to me, means that I no longer have Monday morning blues. It feels like I am going to work to meet my family and close friends. :-) Thank you, Zappos!!

Sarah B.

employee since 2008

The Zappos Culture is what makes this such a great company. When I first started here in finance, I had no desk, just a tiny little table in the middle of finance area where a sombrero was waiting to be worn ... by me, of course! Half way through the day, Jeneen and a couple others broke out in song and dance. Everyone was so welcoming and treated me like they had known me for years. That's just one example of the many times we've had over the years since I've been here.

The best day overall for me would have to be when I found out I was going to be a single mom. Here's the scene. I'm on maternity leave, cell phone got shut off, power was about to get shut off, and I was driving to the gas station with a new-born in the back seat, crying and hoping I was going to make it. Out of the corner of my eye I saw someone in another car waving at me. I didn't want to look because I was embarrassed that I was crying. After about two minutes of this person waving, I finally decided to look. It was my sister (a Zappos employee at the time). She then followed me to the gas station. She got out of her car and said, "I've been trying to get ahold of you"! I explained why I was not receiving her phone calls. She says, "Everyone at work put together a food drive for you and they all collected money to give to you."

To this day, I still get chills re-living that moment. That is what Zappos Culture is all about. We are not only co-workers, but also friends and family. I've grown really close to a lot of people here at Zappos and I think that's because we are able to express ourselves and be who we truly are, not just outside of work, but at work as well. I'm thankful to be surrounded by such wonderful, non-judging, caring, compassionate people. Zappos, you complete me! ;)

Scott S.

employee since 2008

In three years of working for Zappos and loving every minute of it, I have come to the realization that I feel bad for anyone whose first job is at Zappos. If they leave, it will never be as good!

Sean K.

employee since 2006

Over the past few years, the Zappos family has grown considerably, in terms of the number of employees. What amazes me is how the Zappos Culture has also grown. In fact, the culture is stronger now than ever before. I often think about how fortunate I am to be a part of this and to continue to help build and grow our culture and company. The Zappos Culture may have started as a manifesto but now it has grown into a movement. Thank you, Zappos!

Shannon R.

employee since 2007

This year I actually died and went to heaven. This is because I have been given the great good fortune to serve as the Happiness Hippie for Zappos within the P.E.A.C.E. department. P.E.A.C.E. strives daily to enhance our culture through various programs, events, activities, charitable giving and volunteer engagement opportunities. Since I first arrived at this wonderful company just over four years ago, it has been awesome getting immersed in the amazing culture and helping to protect, preserve, and promote our culture across the company. Our culture is our heart. It is what guides us in our everyday actions and in our business decisions. It is what makes this company a family rather than simply a place to work. It is the embodiment of Delivering Happiness.

Stevie B.

employee since 2010

The Zappos Culture, to me, is my daily interactions with fellow Zapponians. It's going to lunch, happy hours, and hanging out with my fellow co-workers outside of work. It's getting to know one another as fellow workers, friends, and extended family. For me, culture is every employee and the daily contributions they bring to this company.

Susi P.

employee since 2007

Never have I made more friends at any job like I have at Zappos. When you are down, you always have someone there to pick you up. The Zappos Culture, to me, means never having to go through anything alone and a bunch of people willing to be there for you at the drop of a dime. I love all my Zappos friends/family!

Tara J.

employee since 2010

The Zappos Culture means that I can be myself. There is no need for a "work Tara" and a "home Tara." I am who I am, and Zappos is OK with that. You don't ever have to feel like fitting in, because everyone is his or her own person. If someone feels like putting on a performance, planning an event or leading a parade, they do it!

Zappos accepts and encourages everyone's awesomeness. And awesome people make an awesome company.

"The Laser"

employee since 2007

Zappos Culture means that it's OK to procrastinate. For example, Zappos cares enough about what we think to keep a poll open days after it should have been closed. It's fantastic! That being said, page 259 says everything I cannot put into words. It also does it far more succinctly, and with far more elegance than I can muster.

Taylor J. 焦彤彤

employee since 2006

I have been working with the Zappos China team since 2006. To me, the Zappos Culture means family, teamwork, happiness etc. I especially love our Ten Core Values, each of which not only inspires me about how to work as a team and a family, but also brings me a really happy life.

If I persist in practicing our Core Values in daily life, I believe that I can make them part of my thoughts and life. Eventually I have confidence that our company Cculture will bring our team and me from good to being great. I always feel that I am lucky and happy to have a chance to serve such a great company and have Zappos as part of my life.

我是焦彤彤，自2006年以来我一直在捷步达康工作。对我来说，捷步达康的文化对我很重要，它意味着家庭，团队合作，幸福等等。我特别喜爱我们的十条核心价值观。每一条我都是我的最爱。因为我们的核心价值观不仅仅激励我如何团队家庭式的协作，还带给了我一个真正幸福的生活。所以我一直在我们的日常生活中坚持实践我们的河西价值观，我相信我可以让我们的核心价值成为我们思想和生活的一部分。我相信最终我们公司的文化会让我和我的团队从优秀到卓越。我一直觉得能够服务于Zappos.com是我一生中最幸运和开心的事！

Tonya S.

employee since 2010

If I were to compare Zappos to anything, it would be summer camp. When I wake up every morning, I cannot wait to get to work for another adventure. Every day is a new experience, a new accomplishment, and a new opportunity. It's a place where I help make a difference in people's lives while making a mustache on a stick. Work doesn't have to be work, and for me, Zappos is summer camp all year round.

Tim K.

employee since 2008

The longer I work here, the more I realize that the Zappos family does live by the Core Values! I feel lucky to get to come to work everyday.

Vanessa L.

employee since 2007

All my life I wanted to belong to something. I wanted to feel accepted and be surrounded by people that I felt comfortable with. I was never a cheerleader or involved in sports or clubs, I was home schooled most of my life. I was the girl in the back of class who never spoke or had many friends. I don't say this to get sympathy, just to say I am now part of a company where I have found my voice and my calling. The Zappos Culture does this for every person who walks through these doors. I belong to something incredible and I am a part of something that is, in so many ways, changing the world! And, I'm not the girl in the back row anymore. I found a voice and realized it's actually pretty loud! I'm proud to call every person in the company my friend and a part of my family.

Vicky Z. 章玲

employee since 2011

To be frank, when I first saw Zappos, I was immediately attracted to its Culture. I like having fun and a little weirdness. I like being an adventurous, creative and I am an open-minded person. I consider myself very fortunate to be able to do my job in an agreeable atmosphere that is filled with respect and cooperation. Fortunately, Zappos gave me this chance to work here, and made me really feel that we are a family. I believe that our Culture delivers WOW not only to our customers, but also to each member of the Zappos family!

老实说，当我第一眼看到捷步达康时，我就被捷步的文化所吸引。我喜欢欢乐以及搞怪，并且一直想成为一个勇于冒险，敢于创新和开放思想的人。所以，捷步的文化不就是我所追求的吗？我总是想如果我可以在一种充满轻松、尊重和合作的氛围下工作，这将是我巨大的财富。幸运的是，捷步达康给了我这个工作机会，并让我感受到这里就是一个大家庭。我相信，我们的文化不仅能够让顾客感到WOW，而且还会给每一位捷步的成员带来更多的WOW。

Victoria B.

employee since 2007

I am so happy to work for a company that is an innovator in how to treat both its employees and its customers right. It is my hope that all organizations will copy Zappos' business model to spread the happiness virus!

Vincent van de C.

employee since 2010

At Zappos you can be yourself in a friendly environment, meaning that whoever you are, you are able do the best work you can.

Wendy H. 黄佳

employee since 2011

I think the ultimate pursuit of Zappos is happiness, no matter what we have done before. I love "Creating Fun and a Little Weirdness," which keeps my passion for work. I enjoy it. Compared with other companies, there are few restrictions here and it's never boring. You can enjoy the freedom of your mind. The most important part is our family spirit; the communication is sincere and it is always filled with joy.

To me, to be humble is what I strive for and I have never changed that pursuit since I knew about Zappos. The whole company makes every effort to reach "Do More with Less." It's our goal to pursue growth and learning and be creative in our work.

我认为幸福是Zappos的最终追求。我喜欢创造快乐和一点点搞怪，它带给我好心情，让我在工作中 充满动力，我很喜欢公司的这条核心价值。和其他公司相比，这里没有那么多条条框框，思想可以 天马行空，工作中就少一些乏味。最重要的是这里像个大家庭，个人之间的交流不公式化，可以 随时随地创造快乐的气氛。对我而言，虚怀若谷是我最崇尚的，也是我的精神向导。从知道Zappos 开始到现在这一追求就不曾改变。追求事半功倍是我们整个公司及员工都要努力达到的。积极进取 和不断学习以及有创新精神在Zappos我们这个办公室是最常见的。

William A.

employee since 2008

Zappos is a friendly place; it's my family. Well, I've been working for Zappos for three years now, and it doesn't seem that I've been here that long at all. It's a joy to come to work each day knowing the amount of confidence I am given to do my job. I believe the Zappos Culture makes you want to come back every day. My workplace is relaxed and laid back, as are my co-workers. But now I need to get back to work, as I am proud to work for my company.

William H. 黄伟宏

employee since 2009

I am very happy to be part of Zappos! I have been at Zappos for almost two years and I realized I had made a good choice in the first place. I love the atmosphere here; there is laugher everywhere! We work and live like brothers and sisters! With the Zappos Culture, we learned how to serve others, how to innovate and how to drive changes as well! I believe that only if we persist in our commitment to the Zappos Culture, nothing can stop our progress!

我觉得是身处于Zappos之中是一件很幸福的事，我觉得自己当初的选择是非常正确的。在捷步达康 工作了将近两年了，我非常喜欢我们这里的环境，因为我们这里每天都充满了欢乐、笑声，大伙们 都像兄弟姐妹一般开心的在这生活和工作，在学习公司文化带领下，我们懂得服务、懂得创新、 懂得驾驭改变。相信只要我们坚持对Zappos文化的学习，这样就没有任何问题能够阻挡我们前进 的步伐。

William N.

employee since 2010

I wish I could contribute, but I'm contractually bound by my publisher not to release anything through non-sanctioned channels. Thanks for understanding.

Zachary Z.

employee since 2008

In the words of my favorite homicidal robot, Neumann, "This was a triumph! I'm making a note here: HUGE SUCCESS!" Over my three years here, the Zappos Culture has time and time again proven that it means freedom to be me. I can walk down a hallway with a broken laptop keyboard strapped to my lanyard like a medal of honor and no one gives it a second thought. The culture is what gives me the ability to not only enjoy coming to work, but to feel that an extended part of my family is waiting here for me. To me, our culture does not mean just another employee. It means that I am seen and heard, and this means more to me than this jumble of words can express. Thanks for reading! Now it's time to slay the Kraken.

Zack D.

employee since 2006

Zappos has changed my life in so many ways. It has taken me from the streets of New York City to a unique corner of corporate America that has helped me become more professional in both my work and personal life. Zappos has allowed me to engage with CEOs and COOs of other companies. It has put me in an amazing situation, and for that I am blessed to be a part of the family. Until next year, Peace and Love.

2ND ANNUAL
ZAPPOS.COM
Rock 'n' Roll
LAS VEGAS
MARATHON

2ND ANNUAL ZAPPOS.COM *Rock 'n' Roll* LAS VEGAS MARATHON

DELIVERING *Halloween* HAPPINESS

Cookie
**DECORATING
TIME**

NEW HIRE
Graduations

Pursue
Growth and Learning

(For best results, sit next to
Hoover Dam while looking
longingly into the distance)

Abby B.
employee since 2007

Friendship. I have made countless friends at Zappos. Friends that will last a lifetime. We do everything together. We work together, party together, laugh and cry together. I'm amazed at the support and encouragement I receive from my co-workers on a daily basis. I can honestly say that I have true friends here and that simply leaves me speechless ... speechless and happy.

Alex K.
employee since 2005

To me, the Zappos Culture comes down to people. It has to do with how we hire, how we train and how we interact with one another. Because we value this more than most other companies, it creates a Culture of mutual respect, admiration and inspiration.

Alex M.
employee since 2008

I'd like to keep this short and simple by stating that I definitely feel fortunate to be employed during such hard times, with amazing benefits and people I enjoy being around! Thank you, Big Z, for all you do!

Amanda W.
employee since 2007

To sum up, the Zappos Culture in a single entry is impossible. The year. The days. The moments. Each second has brought different experiences into my life. Each word spoken changed my future and solidified my past. And then there are other things that have re-defined my place in the taxonomy of my life. Zappos Culture is impossible to define in this entry.

Amber O.
employee since 2005

After almost six years of working here, I still enjoy coming into work every morning. (Whoa, true story!) Here I am, writing yet another testimonial about what a great place Zappos is. I'm sure there are super-clever and witty things strewn about this Culture Book, but not here. Not this entry. Instead, I'll quote an old customer review that I've kept over the years: "She loved them so much that she decided that when she grows up she was going to go work at Zappos. Thank you for making our daughter want the perfect job for life. We love Zappos." While I'm not this daughter, that pretty much sums up my feelings toward Zappos. =)

Amy V.
employee since 2007

To me, the Zappos Culture means that there is never a dull moment. At most other companies people go to work just to do their jobs, and there is little variation from day to day. At Zappos, there is always something fun to get involved in or something new to learn. The Zappos Culture inspires creativity and turns co-workers into life-long friends.

Andi L.
employee since 2007

WOW, another year! :) Zappos has played such a huge role in my life that I can't imagine anywhere else I would want to work. Our team has become sooooo much like my family, and they have taught me a lot. My teammates have taught me on a personal scale, and Zappos has taught me on a professional scale through pipeline and delphi. :) I'm being paid to learn WooHoo! I am proud to say I work for Zappos. Thank you for everything.

Andrew K.
employee since 2009

Zappos is about being yourself. I really enjoy that about the company. I hope as we continue to grow so we can stay true to these beliefs. PS.: I love cheesecake.

Angela C.
employee since 2006

H is for humbled, when I think of what this company does for me. Y is for you, the people who make working at Zappos worthwhile. P is for pound, every single pound that I have added since working here. E is for everyone who challenges me to be better. R is for relationships, all the beautiful ones established through the years. C is for change that keeps me on my toes. U is for unpredictable, which describes almost every single day at Zappos. B is for blessed, how I feel about working at Zappos. E is for exciting, a combination of C + U S. S is for sexy, how I feel about this awesome sizing data structure. Yeah, I know I'm pushing it with this but I really wanted to use hypercube in my submission :)

Angela H.
employee since 2010

If you had told me a year ago that I would get up at 4:00 AM, drive 60 miles round trip every day, for a third of what I was making at my previous job, I would have thought you were crazy. Yet here I am and loving it! No stress, great co-workers, tremendous benefits, no larger-than-life egos, and a good hard belly laugh several times a day.

Angela K.
employee since 2007

I have to say that over the four years that I have worked at Zappos I have discovered a lot of strengths within myself that I never knew existed. I have found a renewed sense of self and a clearer understanding of spirit. This has to be the greatest job I have ever had.

Angelina F.
employee since 2010

As a newer employee, I'm still figuring out what Zappos Culture means to me. I feel fortunate to be here, to love what I do, and to respect and admire the people I work with. Seems like a good start!

Anne P.
employee since 2008

Zappos continues to be a place that I really look forward to coming to every day. I've made so many friends and learned so much since I started working here that I'm planning on a long future with this amazing company.

Anonymous
employee since 2005

The Zappos Culture is our DNA. It's at the heart of everything we do with genetic i ntent to bring meaning, value and purpose to all those we come in contact with, both internally and externally. We lead by example with hope and wish to inspire others to live by the same code.

Anonymous
employee since 2005

Subtlety is what Zappos Culture is to me. Happy hours and parties come and go. Any company can throw an employee picnic, but you might still stew at your boss, talk behind your co-workers' backs and otherwise dislike your job. Even at Zappos you might initially partake of a few events simply because everyone else is doing so. But here, if not right away, things begin to click. Your boss really does trust you to do your job, you take an initiative that your co-workers support enthusiastically, you make a mistake and it's turned into a rewarding growth opportunity, not a resentful experience. All the smiles and laughter you might have taken for granted at first now seem truly genuine. An invitation to spend time with co-workers after work isn't a chore; it becomes a chance to relax with friends. It works not because Zappos Culture is a company edict, but because Culture here is a byproduct of the trust and respect the company gives you. It's very much organic, and despite the din of our offices, actually it's very subtle.

Anonymous
employee since 2009

Zappos Culture truly means everything to me. It makes for a far more rewarding workday. It makes the position more than just a job or even just a career. I have made countless friends that I will undoubtedly keep in touch with for the rest of my life. I no longer dread coming into work in the morning. The utterly pervasive Zappos Culture creeps into your very being and you start becoming not only a better employee, but also a better person. I feel lucky every day to be a part of something so amazing.

Anonymous
employee since 2005

For me, the Zappos Culture means feeling proud to say I work here. I couldn't say that if my co-workers weren't like family to me, if we didn't deliver the best service possible, and if I didn't feel appreciated as an employee. Compared to other companies I've worked for, I believe that is what makes the difference here – people taking pride in their work. After nearly six years at Zappos, I know that I never want to work anyplace else!

Anonymous
employee since 2010

Zappos to me symbolizes many things. Although it does have its own politics, I have never had the opportunity to work somewhere so cohesive, forward-thinking and fun. I didn't realize these kinds of opportunities were available to me, so I am glad they took a chance on me and I found a rewarding environment.

Anonymous
employee since 2011

I recently joined Zappos and what the Culture here means to me is that it's like being with family. It's a fun and little weird family, but that is the joy of it. The Zappos Culture provides the opportunity to be yourself and have the support of those around you. I love it!

Anonymous

employee since 2005

I have worked at a place where all you heard was "Efficiency," over and over, so that it was depressing on Sundays to think you had to go to work on Monday. It's not like that at Zappos. The photo department has its fun. We do our work and still have a good time. I look forward to going to work even though there are days when it's so nice outside that you hate to go inside. The benefits are great, like not having to worry about bringing food through the gates every day and not having to bring money for the vending machines. I love Zappos.

Anonymous

employee since 2007

It's been a wild ride and I am looking forward to the future here.

Anonymous

employee since 2007

Zappos ... it's home away from home.

Anonymous

employee since 2005

I have worked for Zappos for six years and I have seen a lot of changes, but I have always loved my job and the people I work with. Not many people can say that.

Anonymous

employee since 2009

The best part of our Zappos Culture is knowing that every day is unique, exciting and adventurous. It's rare when a company can simultaneously have a fun office atmosphere while exceeding everyone's expectations. We manage to pull it off and the Zappos Culture is at the core!

Anonymous

employee since 2007

What does Zappos Culture means to me? Hmmmm ... I really don't know where to start.

The company, as a whole, is amazing. The stuff they do for their employees is phenomenal. When I started looking for work after college, I never imagined that I would find a company this awesome. Free lunches, free vending machines, free healthcare (huge plus!!), parties and just day-to-day activities. It's unbelievable. Yet here I am, going on my fourth year, and time has just flown. I've gone through three departments and it amazes me how this place just keeps growing and growing.

Although I do feel more attention should be paid to certain management and departments (training, etc.), the Zappos Culture makes it more bearable throughout the entire building. Knowing that most people here feel they are family and can confide in one another helps too. I know not all families are perfect, and there are always some bumpy roads. The atmosphere here is what gets me through tough times. When I feel like I don't like my job or management anymore, I go back to the Core Values to get me through. They help me to put a positive spin on the situation and make it to another day, because I do feel my job here matters. I feel like I matter. I know things will get better. As long as I live the Core Values every day and try to instill them in others, everything will get better. How could it not?

April S.

employee since 2007

Zappos Culture to me is ... all about the food. Yummy, delicious, mouthwatering delights on my taste buds. And the people around me aren't too bad either. They smell good most of the time.

Ashley F.

employee since 2007

As the Zappos family continues to grow, it amazes me that we still take the time to WOW each other every day. From companywide initiatives like Wishez to the small things our teams do for one another – we truly are a family. I am excited to see what the future holds as we continue to grow and WOW the world. :)

Ashley P.

employee since 2008

The Culture here is unlike anything you could ever imagine! I have been here for three years, yet I am still constantly impressed by how much the company gives back to the employees and the community. LEEEERROY JENKINS !!!

Austin B.

employee since 2010

My, my, my!!! What a difference a year can make in one's life. After graduating college in one of the worst economic times this country has seen (spring of 2009), I would never have imagined finding such a wonderful place of employment. When I started with Zappos in January 2010, I was hired as a video content coordinator, but I have since been fortunate enough to become the supervisor of this wonderful department. I am thankful to be at a place that has really fostered me as I mature into the role and responsibilities. Thanks to Zappos as a company for providing a vehicle and such a wonderful environment. But I'd really like to thank the people of Zappos, because it is the attitudes and work ethics that YOU bring to work every day that really make Zappos what it is. WOW the customer (internal and external) through service, and always stay humble. I'm looking forward to many more awesome years.

Bobbi P.

employee since 2010

The Zappos Culture allows me to express my individuality freely. Be it pink hair, clothes, or just being able to be the huge goober that I am. It's refreshing.

Brooke H.

employee since 2007

Soul. To me, the soul is the core of any being. It is what lifts you up when times are tough; it's what radiates joy when life brings blessings. I see the Zappos Culture as the Zappos soul.

In any job, there are times when you have to make tough choices, deal with cranky people, and sacrifice to get the job done. When things like this arise, the Zappos Culture somehow transforms what could be not-so-fun situations into secondary things that are going on while we're having fun at work. And at the opposite end of the spectrum, during those many times when we have the pleasure of working on an amazing project, it's made that much more exciting because of the fabulous people with whom we get to collaborate. There is never a day I dread coming to work. There are many days where my bad mood is lifted the second I get to work and my team members make me laugh. How many places can you say that about? We are so lucky. Zappos is so full of opportunity ... full of life! And, did I mention, we are all crazy, insane, weird and ... FUN?!?!? There's no place like home.

Brooke L.

employee since 2009

Who would have thought that I'd be able to spend every day doing what I love with people I adore and getting paid for it? I certainly didn't. The people on my team are not only my friends; some of them feel like family. I even met my fiancé here!

It's incredible to be a part of such a creative atmosphere, where your thoughts, ideas and personality are not only accepted, but also encouraged and celebrated. I'm extremely blessed to be a part of the Zappos family and I can't wait to see how things evolve. Zappos goes above and WAY beyond anything we, as employees, could ever dream of as far as giving back and supporting us, and it shines through our service and Culture. :oD

Candyce L.

employee since 2010

I had my interview the day of my birthday. I told my hiring manager that it was my birthday and she went out of the room for a minute and two others came in with a balloon singing (what else?) "Happy Birthday." I heard great things about Zappos, but this memory left a lasting impression.

Captain Pickle

employee since 2007

Zappos Culture is the reason I don't want to work anywhere else again, unless I could change that company's way and make it more like Zappos! Of course, I never get tired of bragging to people about our free lunch and vending machines, but it's the small group activities that make me enjoy my days. Taking 20 or 30 minutes out of your workday to have an Easter egg hunt, a rock-paper-scissors tournament or a simple trivia game can brighten your day and make you feel like a kid again. Just because we are all grown-ups at work doesn't mean we can't have fun too! Culture Culture Culture Culture Culture Culture Culture Culture Cuultuuure!!! That was my Culture Cheer. Sincerely yours, The Captain of The Pickles.

Carla B.

employee since 2006

What does Zappos Culture mean to me? Well, it means that I am part of a family here at work, and since I am an only child, that means a lot. My co-workers are my best friends and I know that I can count on them to be there if I need them for anything. I have worked in a few places but they have never been like Zappos. As with any job, there are ups and downs, but here we learn and grow from those. I have seen Zappos change in many ways, but never has it forgotten the Core Values that have been set, even when we partnered with Amazon. I must say, "Way to go, Tony," for not letting things change here, and thank you for giving Zappos the Core Values that we have and letting us grow with them.

I can say that my company's CEO is just a cool man that had a dream and went for it. I am happy that I was given the chance to work for a company like Zappos. I want to see Zappos keep growing and making new strides in the industry. With the leadership we have here, I think it will. I am proud to tell people where I work and about all the cool things that my company offers its employees and customers.

In a nutshell, Zappos WOWs me!

Chanele H.

employee since 2007

Zappos Culture means I still love working here, even after four years. I don't think a lot of people can say that about their job. Also, I have fun and funny co-workers who accept me and my creepy obsession with unicorns.

Chelsea P.

employee since 2008

Culture is a set of traditions, Core Values or goals that one or many people embrace in their day-to-day life. Zappos is truly blessed with amazing people that embrace others with similar and different cultures and make work actually feel like a home filled with family. I can't imagine ever leaving my family, Zappos or its Culture.

Chris G.

employee since 2010

I filed my application electronically on a Wednesday and waited. No way Zappos would hire me as a content editing assistant. No way! So I waited, and fretted, and read up on the 'net, as much "Zappos"-iana as my Google-Fu could find. Fun. Weird. Growth and Learning. Creative and open-minded.

Creative? CREATIVE! So that Saturday, I emailed them a poem on the Zappos Ten Core Values.

#1. You should Wow the customers every day.
#2. And say, "Change is coming again? Hooray!"
#3. Be fun and happy and a little odd.
#4. Be unique and creative and we'll applaud.
#5. Keep learning and stretching in all that you know.
#6. Interaction with others will help friendships grow.
#7. Fun camaraderie, that's what we're taught.
#8. You have what you need; don't waste what you've got!
#9. Have a fire in your belly! Be ambitious and zealous!
#10. (But don't brag about it. We all might get jealous.)

(Not my best work.)

Kicked myself all Saturday afternoon. Too much. Too cute. Bad idea. They ARE a multi-million dollar company, after all. You'll come off as some kinda goofball. Fretting, yeah. Until I got this email back from HR ... on a SUNDAY. Message: Thanks, Chris! Very clever poem! In return, I have a haiku for you:

We are still screening Resumes.

But have no fear! We'll be in touch soon.

Best regards ... .

I guess I'm their kind of goofball. That's Zappos.

Christina M.

employee since 2006

It's almost my fifth year here at Zappos. Here is how I still feel: I love my job, I love my team. I love my life. Working here has made me a better person. I believe we all deserve Zappos Culture in our lives! I wish everyone could have this. I am looking forward to another wonderful year here. :)

Clay D.

employee since 2006

Our Zappos Culture allows us to be more than just employees. It lets us bring our unique perspective, interests and personalities to work with us. Together, we are the Zappos family. We're one of the most diverse families you'll ever find. For me, the most exciting part of being part of this family is discovering just how much we can accomplish.

Courtney M.

employee since 2009

Working at Zappos has been one of the greatest experiences of my life. I love coming to work every day, and knowing that I have become a part of such an amazing family. I think it is awesome that Zappos encourages individuality because that is something that I truly value in the workplace.

At Zappos we work hard and we play hard. From the picnics, to the FUX river outings, beer Fridays, innings, the other, nerf wars, and happy hours. You would find it hard to believe that there was ever any time for work. I cannot believe how lucky I am to work with the exceptional individuals that I do, because at the end of the day they are the ones that make Zappos what it is, and they have made my experience here so amazing.

I have learned so much since I started here at Zappos, and I look forward to many more years of happiness together.

Crystal B.

employee since 2010

The Zappos Culture is amazing! When I started here, I did not realize the awesomeness that I was about to walk into. I found out quickly that people with whom I will forever feel connected surrounded me. For the fist time in my adult working life I felt that I had found others with whom I can truly be myself. What a wonderful feeling that was.

Today, almost a year later, I feel exactly the same. Yes, exactly the same as my first week. My department has a team and family spirit like no other. While still remaining humble, I have a sense of pride when I see and work with them.

Crystal R.

employee since 2010

The Zappos Culture is about fun and possibility – a winning combination! I love coming to work each day because, besides the job I'm here to do, there's so much more to it than that ... and that's so rare in the working world. The "fun" is the work environment I encounter each day: The cool Zappos team names and themes, the wacky decorations adorning desk after desk, the zany dress-up days and fun contests. (The Peeps dioramas are outstanding!) And so much more. (Oh, I can't forget our Happy Hours and the parades!) And regardless of anyone's rank, tenure, seniority ... whatever ... the enjoyment of this type of fun is encouraged and is intrinsic to who we are as Zapponians. It's really special.

Secondly, the "possibility" is the company's support of personal/professional growth. There are internships, shadow sessions and classes I can take to continuously learn, grow and improve. I feel an unlimited amount of opportunity is available. At times, it almost seems too much! But hey! I consider that a good thing. LOL.

Crystal W.

employee since 2011

The Zappos Culture is what makes working here amazing. I look forward to coming to work for the first time in my life. I absolutely love my job and everyone I work with. I love the quirkiness of this company and appreciate everything they do for me, and I feel as if Zappos appreciates me, too.

Dan B.

employee since 2010

To me, Zappos is all about being me while supporting the team. And that is something worth working for.

Dan C.

employee since 2005

Given the amount of growth I have seen since I have been with the company, the Zappos Culture is more important than ever now. Currently, the Kentucky content department is half the size of what the entire warehouse was when I began, and where it was once possible to know everyone on a personal level I now find myself struggling to keep up with the influx of new hires. This isn't a complaint, mind you, but a reminder of the values that this company was founded on.

In order for Zappos to stand out among the rest, the Culture must find its way into the heart and mind of every individual. Sounds preachy, huh? I don't say that because I'm drunk on the Kool-Aid. I say it because there are some days even I have to remind myself why I came to this company and, more importantly, why I've stayed. The Zappos Culture means being a part of something bigger, taking pride in what you do, and passing that knowledge and experience along so that others can have the same feeling I have when I tell people about my workplace. That Culture isn't located in one man or one building, or one state. It is the collective experience of every individual who has had anything to do with this company.

Danielle T.

employee since 2007

This is my fourth (fourth!) Culture Book entry. Zappos isn't perfect by any means, but the important thing is that the Zappos family strives every day to do better by their employees and customers in order to provide the absolute best experience. I work very hard and try to go above and beyond every day, not because there is a financial reward (apart from my hourly wage), but because I care about the success and well-being of each individual in the Zappos family and about Zappos as a whole. I feel pride in being a Zappos employee and I never tire of telling people about our Culture. I never wake up in the morning and dread coming to work. I am still excited to come to Zappos each and every day, even when the work pile never seems to lessen. I thoroughly enjoy the company of my co-workers and love to spend time with them in and out of the office. I have worked for companies in the past where everyone made nice, but secretly hated each other. Fortunately, this is not the case at Zappos. People have affection for one another here. It truly is a family.

Danika J.

employee since 2008

I can sum up our Zappos Culture in one word – change. I believe it's not only the most important Core Value of all, we embrace it every day. We reach out for ideas and give each one a chance, and feel proud when it becomes reality and affects our future. Change allows us to live up to the implicit "work hard and play hard" motto that all Zapponians live by. With our impending move to downtown Vegas, the sky's the limit for how our Culture will grow. Our influence is catching on, and our Culture is gradually becoming a number one priority for those who strive toward the Zappos standard. I'm excited to see what other changes will take place.

Darren F.

employee since 2009

My time here at Zappos has been one of the best experiences of my life. I consider everyone I work with here to be family, and I think that is the true heart of our Zappos Culture. Working on the A/V team, I get to experience and capture this first hand on a day-to-day basis. Every day is a new adventure for me. Not only do I get to capture and magnify our Culture through the lens of a camera, I get to share it with the world. :) Thanks, Zappos!

Darrin S.

employee since 2004

One of the questions I am most frequently asked by eager potential hires is "What do you enjoy most about working at Zappos?" I have a variety of answers that I rotate through, but most include some element of:

– Talented yet humble coworkers,
– Fun/quirky working environment,
– Belief that successes are built on top of failures,
– Transparency with all stakeholders,
– Autonomy.

The Zappos Culture is made up of all of these elements and that is why I look forward to coming into the office each morning.

Delana S.

employee since 2009

When I think of the word "culture," I think of a way of life … whatever you are brought up doing that may be different or unique and sets you apart from others. Whether it's the type of food you eat, the clothes you wear, or the language you speak, culture embodies it.

Here at Zappos, our Culture sets us apart from other companies and we're proud of it … I know I am. We get free food; we proudly wear our Zappos T-shirts, and speak the language of WOW. After working here for almost two years, I have seen the Zappos Culture mold me into a person that would make my mother proud. (Except at Merchandising Happy Hours. Sorry, Ma.) Some say we are a cult, some say we are crazy, but I say it's our Culture that makes us who we are. It's our Culture that makes us unique and makes others want to take a little bit of Zappos back with them and form their own company culture.

In closing, Zappos is the happiest place on earth for adults and I couldn't image working at any other place. Many have said it, but this WILL be the last place I ever work at. P.S.: Shout out to Krista from HR for giving me a chance.

Diana R.

employee since 2009

Zappos Culture means that you can come to work and feel at home. Co-workers become family, and knowing that you can come to place every day where people genuinely care about you is priceless. Not a day goes by that I don't laugh and smile at work. Zappos Culture rocks!

Eddielynn T.

employee since 2007

I LOVE, LOVE ZAPPOS!!!! I love telling people that I work for one of the best companies ever! I love coming to work every day, I love our unique Zappos Culture, I love my friends here (well, actually, they are my family), I love being a content coordinator for PRIVATE LABEL! Go CONTENT!!!! Gosh … What else can I say? I just LOVE it here so much and I'm so very happy and thankful to be a part of such a wonderful journey and company!!!

Eileen S.

employee since 2010

This is my first year at Zappos and if it's up to me it will be one of many such years. The Core Values here are something I have always tried to live by, but now I have thousands of people that share them and I see them every day. I am so happy I have the opportunity to work at Zappos and look forward to my future here.

Erica S.

employee since 2009

Zappos lets me be myself, goofy humor and all. I work with amazing people that make the workday fly and make hard days bearable. I learn from everyone I work with. I run into people outside of the office and feel a sense of community. Everything from seeing a stripper in the office to hearing a tour member play Britney Spears on the accordion proves to me that Zappos is a crazy Bermuda Triangle of the work world that has drawn people in to create an environment unlike any other. I think Willow Smith says it best: "I like to eat cheese out of a bowl every day."

Erin B.

employee since 2008

Working here at Zappos feels like one long college class that you enjoy.

Erin J.

employee since 2010

The Zappos Culture is neon shoes. It's putting on your neon shoes on in the morning and coming to work at Zappos. It's arriving at work and holding the door open for someone 15 feet behind you. There's never any hesitation to greet a new face with a smile and a warm greeting before the sun is out. It's working until the job is finished for the whole team, not just when your pile is complete. Culture is coming home, taking off your neon shoes, and getting prepared to do it all again tomorrow. It's something simple that makes a statement without saying anything at all. Anyone can have a simple job or an ordinary pair of shoes. But it's the neon shoes that give you a reason to get out and enjoy what you do.

Erin R.

employee since 2004

This is my sixth year working for Zappos and it has been the most amazing six years of my life. A long time ago, a lovely gal named Jamie took a chance on me and sent me to see another lovely gal named Jessica. After that day, my life changed as I heard the words, "You are hired!" I was actually getting my first job out of college and my major (graphic design) was helping me get it. I was thrilled! From my very first day at Zappos in Las Vegas, I knew I was a perfect fit for this company and I knew I was truly lucky to be part of this amazing team. I have always come to work as myself, from back when I was an image coordinator in Vegas to now, as an imaging department supervisor in Shepherdsville. I know the Zappos Culture is the reason I can come to work and be myself. Without it, I would probably be wearing a skirt, heels and … pantyhose … every day. (Barf!) I can't wait to be here for another six years … and beyond.

Geoff C.

employee since 2011

The Zappos Culture is unique among all the places I have ever worked. It's not something that just happens on the first day of work, but rather evolves as you become more comfortable with your co-workers and work flow. It's learning to trust those around you and letting those around you know they can trust and lean on you as well.

Gonzo

employee since 2010

The Zappos Culture means so many things to me! If I had to wrap it all up into one word, I would probably go with my favorite word, GNARLY! Since we don't all know what that means to me, I will go with the more user-friendly word, happiness! My entire life, all I really ever wanted in the work industry was to find a job that would make me happy! I was lucky enough to transfer from CLT to the audiovisual department, and since filming has always been my passion, I couldn't be happier. Also, there is no greater feeling than doing what you love in the environment that you love. I can honestly say that from the moment I set foot in CLT training, happiness is exactly what I felt. Whether it is WOWing customers with my CLT family, or filming and editing videos with the AV team, I truly believe that I am happiest when I am with my Zappos family.

Graham K.

employee since 2009

Welcome to Las Vegas where the Zapponians play and we rock customer service our own way. The Zappos Culture is a lifestyle. It's a part of who you are. Even after the work is done, you don't clock out of being a Zapponian. Our Culture isn't one color or one emotion. We are a blend of backgrounds, personalities, big thinkers, hard players and community enthusiasts. We create a strong internal community that blurs into our personal lives and makes us who we are. Our dedication to the customer never stops. We are never closed, never shut off, never up for letting you down and always up for making you happy. The individual empowerment that our Culture is keen on breeds community growth and enables us to thrive in an open business space. Think about how happy a Zappos box on your doorstep makes you and know that we are just as happy to get it there for you. You have to experience it for yourself. Come take a tour. We would love to have you!

Hannah E.

employee since 2006

I feel very fortunate to have been part of the Zappos family for five years now and for having met so many amazing people along the way. The longer I'm here, the more tangible our Culture becomes to me. You can't go a day around here without seeing genuine examples of our Core Values being executed so effortlessly by people all over the company, not only towards one another, but also towards our vendors, visitors and the overall community. To me, one of the most striking examples of Zappos Culture is something we see daily: Zappos tours. We see hundreds of people take tours of our offices day in and day out, and when you actually stop and take a look at their reactions, their genuine amazement towards our work environment, it's the best validation of just how special our company Culture really is. It's definitely something worth defending and something worth working towards every single day.

Heather T.

employee since 2005

The Zappos Culture to me means not living for the weekends. Not staring at the clock waiting for it to hit 5 pm. It means that my co-workers are also my friends. It blurs the line between work time and playtime. But I think the best thing is that after five-plus years I still go home and say, "Guess what happened at work today?!"

Jackie M.

employee since 2007

To me, Zappos Culture is what makes this company so great and sets it apart from every other one that's out there. From the wacky parades that come down the hallways to the crazy parties we have twice a year, there is never a dull moment here. I am truly blessed to have found Zappos and look forward to continue growing with the family.

Janel M.

employee since 2010

Zappos is a very exciting place to work! The company is filled with passionate people who go above and beyond every day. Fun is woven into everything we do!

Jason C.

employee since 2007

Our Zappos Culture is something you have to live every day in order to maintain it. Many companies have started out with a good culture, only to see it slowly erode during times of change as a by-product of things like growth, cutbacks, leadership changes, etc. In the three years I have been here, we have gone through many changes and the thing I have been most impressed with is how well we've been able to maintain our Culture and our Core Values. There is a true feeling of community and looking out for others in our interactions with our customers, vendors or each other.

Jason L.

employee since 2008

Dear Zappos, thank you for hiring me and for giving me a free pair of corporate ladder climbing shoes (SKU 7138230). Three years ago I was hired on to write product descriptions in Las Vegas and now I manage a video team of over 20 people and a $1,000,000+ budget in Kentucky. Thanks for trusting me and allowing me to take ownership of my career. I feel like I've been pretty lucky here at Zappos and that I wouldn't have been able to advance this quickly at any other company. Both professionally and personally, I believe I have grown a lot in the past three years. I have been exposed to the ins and outs of what it takes to run a successful e-commerce business and made some lifelong friends while doing so. I can honestly say that this is the most stressful job I've ever had, but the people and the Culture here at Zappos make it all worthwhile.

Love, Jason Lee

P.S.: I know you have excellent customer service and a 365-day return policy, but I think I am going to hold onto these shoes for a while.

P.P.S.: Thanks for all of the amazing parties!

Jay de G.

employee since 2007

The Zappos Culture is a lifestyle. For me, it's a certain attitude, a heightened sense of awareness of happily putting someone else's needs and wants above my own. It's a thought process that I've subconsciously extended far beyond the walls of this office. A state of mind where respect, humility and kindness are the focal point in my day-to-day interactions with my peers, co-workers, vendors and guests alike. I feel a great deal of responsibility to preserve and cultivate our Culture because it's who Zappos is. It's who I am! I don't define Culture; Culture defines me!

Jenn F.

employee since 2009

For me, personally, the Zappos Culture has everything to do with family. I love coming to work every day because I'm surrounded by people who make working here a joy. Zappos has opened so many doors for me to meet great people who are always here for encouragement and support. The Zappos family culture and environment really mean the world to me and I wouldn't trade it for anything!

Jennie W.

employee since 2009

I heart my job. I heart my job real hard. Not only do I enjoy the work, I love all of the stuff that goes with it. Think of working at Zappos as the best ice-cream sundae. The actual work you do – the list that's in the job description – is the ice cream. Pretty awesome already, right? But then you add the hot fudge, the whipped cream, the chopped nuts and a cherry. Now you've got the work you already love plus team bonding, happy hours, pinewood derby, Peep shows, picnics, and just general hilarity. Who wouldn't want this delicious sundae/job every day?!

Jessica L.

employee since 2006

The Culture at Zappos is unique. A large part of it is based on Core Value #1: Deliver WOW Through Service. In everything we do, we want to deliver the very best service. Whether it's the interactions with our customers on the phone, the interactions with our vendors or the interactions with each other at the office or in the warehouse, providing the best service should be top-of-mind. The other nine Core Values help complete the full circle of culture that we desire. Our Ten Core Values are more than just ideas; they're a way of life. It's really cool to work for a company where everyone is on the same page as far as how they desire to work and live.

Jimmy M.

employee since 2008

On the clock, beer I did drink.

Jo C.

employee since 2008

Wow ... ! The Zappos Culture means so much to me and it is a difficult thing to put my finger on. There are so many aspects to this wonderful place that I love. The Zappos Culture is a place where I am free to be myself. Working for Zappos has opened so many doors to worlds that I had no idea about. Zappos has a unique way of putting folks where they fit best.

I started at the front desk and two years ago moved to fashion content. I get to look at cute shoes and write about them!! I get to come to work and instead of anyone trying to stifle my personality, I'm encouraged to be myself. I love it here. I love everything about it. I love the nicknames, the rapport with people, the relationships I've built and the lessons I've learned. Zappos is more than just a job to me. Working here was NEVER just a job for me. Zappos is a way of life!

Joe G.

employee since 2011

There have only been two times in my life when I felt I was in the right place at the right time. The first was when I met my wife and the second was being here at Zappos. I am a recent hire and have been nothing short of awestruck at the bonds and camaraderie between everyone here. I feel fortunate to come to work each day and absolutely love what I do. For the first time in my life, I don't dread waking up on Monday morning; I can't wait to get to work every day.

Jonathan B.

employee since 2006

In the time I'm been at Zappos, I have been able to experience the workings of several departments. I love that it is so easy to make connections with all these different people and find out what they do. Whether it's sitting down to shadow them or sharing a drink at a happy hour, it's incredible to have such open access to what everyone does. I'm incredibly happy to be working here and love what I'm doing!

Jonathan B.

employee since 2008

From my first day here at Zappos I knew this company was different from any I had worked at previously. It was also my first real professional job and it has proved to be an excellent opportunity. It makes me feel spectacular to tell the outside world where I work and the type of people I work with/for. It will soon be my fifth anniversary at Zappos and it's unbelievable all I have experienced in my time here. A truly remarkable life experience!

Jonathan H.

employee since 2011

Zappos is magical. Once I step out of my car and into Zappos to go to work, I am happier. No matter what hour of the day it is, co-workers are saying hi, having fun, and there is a positive spirit that is catching. I love being a content coordinator. It is the best career I have ever had. I feel extremely blessed to have a fun and interesting job and to work with people who try to stay positive, have fun and truly care about others. I LOVE Zappos!

Joon K.

employee since 2006

The most important piece of advice I can give is this: Zappos is what YOU make of it! It's that simple, folks.

Jordan S.

employee since 2008

The Zappos Culture is about everyone coming together for a single purpose. That purpose is to create a work environment that we can all look forward to every day. We don't all come from the same backgrounds or have the same ideas. We don't all enjoy the same things. But all of us here are free to be ourselves. We all collectively decide what our Culture is now, and what it is going to be in the future. The only thing that stays constant is our Core Values, which, to us, are our Constitution.

Joshua P.

employee since 2005

Another great year at Zappos! I have been able to enjoy many activities provided by Zappos over the years! Not only do I like to come to work daily, I love to come. The atmosphere is very peaceful with the great orientation of a family culture. Anyone looking into this atmosphere would be envious on how creative and weird we keep it. I have been on the B shift now for about six years and I have ventured into most all departments and have been welcomed by all. So keep on rocking!!!

Kaitlyn Z.

employee since 2010

I enjoy my job because I can be productive in my work but be myself in the way I dress, act and talk. I love that individuality is not only allowed at Zappos, it's encouraged. That's something I've never experienced in the workplace, and something that I know makes Zappos unique. The benefits of the job are also fantastic – free lunches and vending machines, an AWESOME discount both in the outlet store and online, and the full-time benefits.

Karen S.

employee since 2010

The Zappos Culture is so unique and exciting that when I get to work, I feel like I've just arrived at a party! It's great to always look forward to the work week!

Katie B.

employee since 2006

Two of my favorite Core Values are: "Create Fun and a Little Weirdness" (#3) and "Build a Positive Team and Family Spirit" (#7). The Culture at Zappos is like a family. In my department we have baby showers, birthdays and team outings or pretty much anything that involves cake. We also have a big family dinner for the holidays. I have learned at Zappos that we also have the ability, individually, to create and mold the Culture. They encourage the family atmosphere and want you to feel at home. Where else can you wear your PJs to work or come in dressed like a leprechaun and still feel normal because you know other people are dressed the same way? I have been here for about four and a half years now and I have seen quite a bit of change and growth. Zappos has given me the opportunity to be myself and to learn what I am capable of. There have been people here to help me achieve my goals or to just listen when I need to talk. I hope to be able to do the same for the next generation of team members. Thank you, Zappos, for the wonderful opportunity you have given me.

Kaya F.

employee since 2008

This is my third year with Zappos, and it just keeps getting better and better. I love coming to work every day because of the Culture and the amazing people I am surrounded by. I can't imagine working anywhere else! I love you, Zappos!

Kaycee C.

employee since 2005

This will be my sixth year at this amazing company and I cannot believe that time has flown by so quickly. I love watching all the newbies who roll into our fantastic FC and look amazed at everything our company has to offer: free lunch, snacks, drinks, T-shirts, computer time (plenty of Facebook and Twitter people to friend or follow), and most of all, a chance to meet new and exciting people who will no doubt become great friends/team members!!

The family atmosphere here in the Kentucky Development part of the company is unbelievable. My teammates are just awesome when it comes to needing a friend to talk to, somebody to have a great night out with or just a body with a truck to help move something. You can always count on having a few people step up to the plate and say "Hey, let me help ya, okay?" I have yet to wake up in the morning and dread going to work. The fact of the matter is, I LOVE MY JOB!! I look forward to Monday mornings and seeing what the week has in store for me. The busier I am, I think, the happier I am when it comes to work.

Kelly M.

employee since 2011

The Zappos Culture makes the job more than just a normal, "run of the mill" job. Not every employer lets workers come to work dressed as their favorite superhero. And even if they did, most people would look at you like you were a weirdo. Not here. (And yes, I AM speaking from experience.) But it's more than the ability to dress up; it's also the sense of family. Working here is like having a family. You have your grandpas that say the strangest things, the caring grandma, the crazy uncle, and tons of brothers and sisters. From the get-go, I felt at home here and I didn't need to try to fit in; I am just being myself. I love waking up in the morning and knowing that I work at a place that accepts me for who I am. Zappos truly is one of a kind.

Kelly T.

employee since 2010

The Zappos Culture means that I wake up every day excited to go to work. Curious to learn how my co-workers' evenings were. Anxious to share stories and inside jokes. Eager to sit down and start knocking out my work. Striving to shine, both personally and professionally. Bringing the Zappos message of happiness to new and existing customers. It means that I get to be an individual. It means that my leaders recognize my strengths and encourage me to challenge myself and continue to grow. It means that work is an integrated part of my life and one that I cherish. I feel incredibly lucky to have had the privilege of working with my team and see the growth we have had in four short months. Zappos Culture truly maximizes my sense of happiness.

Kenny L.

employee since 2007

I've been staring a blank screen for a while, trying to summarize what the Zappos Culture is and why it's so important to me. But really, it's not a complicated thing. A lot of people associate the Zappos Culture with parades, cowbells, and a shot or two of Grey Goose – and they aren't necessarily wrong.

I love the fact that every day is a new adventure at the office. One day, I walked outside and saw a petting zoo in full swing, and on another day, I walked into the lunch room and people were doing the Thriller dance for an upcoming skit. But as fun as those things are, they're just by-products of our Culture. Really, our Culture is all about the people.

I feel lucky to work with such passionate, friendly and driven individuals, many of whom I'd easily call friends. You could take away the parades, the cowbells, and the Grey Goose (well, maybe we should keep that) and I'd still love working here.

Kevin M.

employee since 2006

It has been a great ride so far and it just keeps getting better! Being a member of the Zappos family means so much to me, and it has been a blessing to share the experiences I've had at Zappos with such a great group of people.   •

You might ask what Zappos means to me? Well, the first thing that comes to mind is creating growth and opportunity. Over this last year, I have witnessed so much growth first hand, and as this company continues to grow, more and more opportunities become available. Sometimes I sit and think about how much this company has grown in the five years that I have been here and all I can say is WOW! Each new day brings more growth and with each new day comes another opportunity anxiously waiting to spring up.

Zappos also means building great relationships and lifelong friendships with the people I work with. Throughout this past year, many of my work relationships have easily turned into great friendships. I feel closer and more engaged with my co-workers on a daily basis. We talk, we laugh, and we share all of these amazing Zappos experiences together. The work we do brings us closer together and in the process, great friendships have been born. I feel blessed to have the opportunity to work for a company that truly cares about its employees.

Zappos is by far the best company that I've ever worked for. Zappos instills greatness in its employees and with greatness we can achieve anything!

Ki M.

employee since 2006

The Zappos Culture pretty much means the ability to be yourself while doing your job. You have the ability to express yourself and not be judged in a negative manner, which creates a much more trusting, open environment. Everyone is more obsessed with their jobs and company goals than trying to worry about what they look like. True story.

Krista A.

employee since 2007

Living here in Las Vegas wouldn't be the same if I hadn't met the people that make up Zappos. There are so many opportunities to meet and interact with others here that it is impossible to be a homebody. The answer is always "yes" here, too, something of an unusual three-letter word in the world. You want more blue drink? YES! You want fat-free ice cream? YES! You asked for Fridays off? OK, YES! I find myself trying many new things because the attitude is so infectious, plus I can spend time moving forward instead of explaining a "no." I love it here and wish everyone in the world could work for Zappos!

Dear Dictionary, the definition for co-worker is completely wrong. Please fix this immediately. Not this, too boring! co•work•er; – noun, Definition: fellow worker; colleague.

This is much better!

co•work•er; – noun, Definition: friend, buddy, associate, chum, co-mate, companion, comrade, confidant, crony, mate, pal, peer, sidekick, partner in crime, shopping partner.

Thank you.

Krista S.

employee since 2011

I totally love Zappos and everything it stands for! I'm truly happy to be a part of the best company ever!

Kristen W.

employee since 2010

To me, the Zappos Culture means to wake up, come to work and perform my job with a seamless transition between my beliefs at home with my family and at work.

Even though I have only been at Zappos a few months, I am constantly in awe at the strong base and core that everyone believes in at Zappos and how this flexibility transforms into unbelievable creativity and results. To be yourself and surrounded by team members with the same beliefs is outstanding. I am so fortunate to be a part of our amazing Zappos family!

Kurra M.

employee since 2010

How does one describe the Zappos Culture? I can only describe how it makes me feel: motivated, energized, weird, empowered, refreshed and, most importantly, HAPPY. :)

Kyle "K-Bone" M.

employee since 2010

I entered the job market when I was 24, fresh out of college. The working world was pretty unfamiliar to me and you can imagine my surprise, when I started interviewing and getting a taste of really being on my own.

Finding a job is difficult. Finding a job where you are truly enjoying what you do is even harder. Zappos came into my life when I started to wonder if there were any people in the world like me. I was beginning to think that I was just going to have to accept an awkward, detached social life at work, and keep my REAL social life completely separate. Why couldn't people have fun at work? Why were most people unhappy in their professional lives? None of this made sense to me.

Finding Zappos was like finding this amazing community of vibrant, healthy, living people in the midst of a zombie apocalypse. Normally I'm the type that abuses hyperbole to amuse myself, but the Zappos Culture really has affected my life, and I honestly wasn't sure that it would. At this point, there's no going back, even if I end up working somewhere else before I retire.

Two huge things jump to my attention: intentionality and effort. It's in the details. The willingness to change is paramount. Clearly, tradition doesn't have much of a place in the Zappos Culture because tradition is what got us into a situation that needed to be fixed as working human beings. Let's be real: a job is a job. There are always things that will annoy us, exhaust us, and make us not want to come in and do anything, much less contribute to the culture.

Zappos is not perfect. The difference is that we realize it, embrace it and do everything we can to make things better. I can buy into that.

Kyle S.

employee since 2007

As a Zappos team member of four years, I've witnessed the growth and change of our company. Through the slow times, the not-so-good times, the growing times and the "this-company-WOWs-the-hell-out-of-me" times, witnessing Zappos grow and prosper as a community has been an experience I'll never forget. A positive experience. Our unique Culture is the backbone of this growth. Where would we be without it?

Lacy G.

employee since 2007

The Zappos Culture is all the small things. Friendships with co-workers, fun projects, volunteer opportunities. Knowing that there is a warehouse full of people to call your family. Speaking freely and being asked my opinion in surveys. Knowing that this is the last place I ever want to work.

Larissa M.

employee since 2010

What I love about my job at Zappos includes several things. First, I would have to say that everyone here feels like family. This is our home away from home. Our co-workers and supervisors actually care about how we feel and how our personal lives are going. They listen and are always willing to help through rough times, either job-related or otherwise. That means a lot to me. We cheer each other up and there is always a lot of laughter to be had. We work hard and know how to play hard too!!

As for the company, I can't say enough about how well we are treated. The benefits are awesome!!! The lunches catered in each day sure help us use our money for other things we might like to purchase like ... Oh ... say a good pair of shoes at a fantastic price!!!! Anyway, it's the most enjoyable job I have ever had, which makes me determined to do the best job I can for the great company I work for! WOW!!!!!!!!

Laura S.

employee since 2005

The Zappos Culture is something I think about often. Over the past few months, I've settled into a general idea or perception about what it means to me. Zappos Culture ... IS me. Zappos Culture ... IS you. Zappos Culture ... IS you and me working together. Zappos Culture ... IS me becoming a better person because of you. Zappos Culture ... IS you becoming a better person (hopefully in part) because of me. Zappos Culture ... IS us building something great without focusing on what we will get back in return. Zappos Culture ... IS us challenging ourselves and one another to do something even greater thing than before, then afterwards telling one another "you're awesome because ... " Zappos Culture ... IS me changing and growing every day, becoming something stronger than I was when I started. Zappos Culture ... IS never standing still, only moving forward, outwards and upward. Zappos Culture ... IS alive because you and I live it, in small ways and in big ways.

Zappos Culture ... WE are the Zappos Culture.

Lauren D.

employee since 2010

I love that every morning I wake up and am excited to get to work!

Lauren R.

employee since 2011

Working at Zappos is b-a-n-a-n-a-s in the best possible way. After a mere two months of working here, I cannot imagine working anywhere else. From my first day I was immediately embraced by strangers, whom I now genuinely consider friends. That is a large part of what makes the Zappos Culture so great and well known. We are all encouraged to be ourselves and accept others for exactly who they are. I've always felt like a little weirdo and now I have found the fellow weirdoes I have been looking for all my life! :)

Another great part of the Zappos Culture is the focus on helping others in any capacity possible. Whether it's being witnessed here amongst our fellow employees or when we go out into the community, we're a happy team that loves to help out. I enjoy all of the community service opportunities that are presented to us and how many people are sincerely interested in being a part of them.

To be able to work and play every day is a privilege that I am extremely grateful to be able to enjoy. I'm so happy I made it in! As a side note, my number one rule for work has always been to love what I do. Consider that done and done!

Laurie W.

employee since 2005

Zappos continues to be a part of my family. There isn't a day that goes by that I don't feel lucky and grateful to be a part of something so amazing.

Lianna S.

employee since 2010

WOW Haiku: How to Survive Zappos (Tech)
When nerf darts fly, duck.
Order water between shots.
When in doubt: cupcakes.

Linda H.

employee since 2005

Zappos is like my second home. It's a place where I can be myself and a place where I can have fun and work at the same time. Zappos is a company that truly cares about its employees, and this shines through daily in the friendly smiles and all of the awesome benefits that we get. Zappos has helped me to grow both personally and professionally!!!

Lisa M.

employee since 2007

Love working here. Challenging and fulfilling. I work with some GREAT people and I have been given the opportunity to meet some amazing individuals. I look forward to the years to come!

Lisa N.

employee since 2009

The Zappos Culture is so important to me. This is truly the happiest I've ever been at a job and that's because it's so much more than a job. It's a place where you work side by side with your best friends ... where people cheer you on and accept you as you are and encourage you along the way. Zappos is not just my workplace, it's where I come to see my family and try to give back even a portion of what I've received.

Luke H.

employee since 2011

I've only been at Zappos for one week and I can't believe how stinking awesome it is here. I am still in a bit of culture shock. After being chewed up by the corporate machine at my previous job, I almost don't know how to react when I am treated like a human being who has ideas, feelings and dreams. I feel like I won the lottery to be a part of the Zappos family ... and it really feels like a family. At the end of my first work week, I wasn't ready to leave and I don't think I've ever felt that way before about a job.

Lynn E.

employee since 2005

The Zappos Culture is unlike any other I've ever encountered. I've worked at several different places in my lifetime and no other company even begins to compare. I mean really, nowhere else that I've ever heard about offers the perks we have here at the KYFC: free lunches, free vending machines, free insurance to a single person, an outrageous holiday party, great annual summer picnics, etc. I could go on and on. Everyone here is like family and I appreciate each one of them. Zappos has been "WOWing" me for over six years now and it still continues to amaze me!

M Weezy

employee since 2010

I've worked in several different warehouse environments and never had the gracious service that Zappos provides. From free massages, parties, food, insurance and much more, there's not much room for complaining. Hoping the employees feel comfortable and happy are qualities Zappos strives for and I believe it truly boosts morale in the company. Finding a place to fit in isn't hard at Zappos. I'm content in the company and only hope to grow more with it. Until next year... Deuces!!!

Maggie M.

employee since 2008

More than anything else, Zappos Culture means coming to work and feeling like I am surrounded by my family – not just my co-workers. When I am down they bring me up, and when I need help they are always there to lend a hand.

Manon B.

employee since 2009

It's a funny thing, working somewhere you're truly happy. I've worked in two different departments here and loved them both. While I'm currently very happy where I am, I'm sure this won't be the last stop on my Zappos journey. And you know what's great? That's totally okay. This amazing company encourages growth, learning, change and individuality.

In many ways though, great as it is, Zappos has ruined the rest of the "real world" for me. I go to the store and if someone doesn't hold the door (or say "thank you" when I hold it) I'm disappointed. Two years ago, I wouldn't have even noticed. But maybe that's what it's all about – heightened awareness, politeness, courtesy, and just plain being good to one another. This place has made me a better version of myself. Perhaps this version would have emerged at some point, because it genuinely lived inside me, but it's almost as if I was reserving it for the life I was going to have one day. A life where all my hopes and dreams had come to fruition and were surrounded by a proverbial white picket fence. I don't need to be wearing a seersucker printed dress or holding a freshly-baked cherry pie, but I suppose I've always had my own version of a Utopian society ... and this version included everyone being their most genuine. Because in this world, most genuine = best behavior, and best behavior = the norm.

So re-enter reality: Crimes are still committed every day, people still lie to each other, and the world is not always a kind place. And yet, Zappos exists. Zappos is a daily reality for me and about 2,000 other employees. Zappos has touched our lives and the lives of many customers in ways that we can't all express eloquently. So I'll leave you with this: I <3 Zappos and Zappos spreads <3. Seems to me there's a pretty good start on that Utopian society after all. Now if we could just start our own airline ...

Marco B.

employee since 2010

There's nothing more exciting than that first kiss with someone. All the awkward nervousness, anticipation and butterflies that cause your heart to leap into your throat; it truly is an incredible rush of emotions.

The weird thing is after that first kiss, inevitably, you experience diminishing returns. Sure, you still enjoy the act of kissing this person, but that endorphin rush is gone. You find yourself chasing it and the more you do, the quicker it slips through your fingers and dissipates. The Zappos Culture embodies the thrill of the unknown like that first kiss. Somehow, the more immersed one becomes with the Culture, the more one is rewarded. The anticipation of what each day holds never fades. Every single day at Zappos is like the anticipation of a first kiss.

Marie K.

employee since 2010

To me, the Zappos Culture is like no other. If you had asked me one year ago where I would be today, my answer would not have been "Living in Las Vegas!" But moving here to work at Zappos has been the most humbling, exciting and unique experience of my life. I feel so privileged to work for a company where my co-workers are my family and my job is my passion. Yay Zappos!!

Marie M.

employee since 2010

As an employee, Zappos Culture means that I have the right to enjoy coming to work and spending time with my co-workers. To me, Zappos Culture means that I have the freedom to be myself and have fun while still doing all I can to help make Zappos better every day. It means I love my job, my workplace, my work-family and look forward to spending time here. In short, Zappos Culture means a better life, a better product and, of course, better customer service :)

Marjorie L.

employee since 2007

Working at Zappos means coming in every day to see friendly faces and hear encouraging words. We pull together as a team to ensure customer satisfaction. Even after three years, it continues to be a very rewarding place to work.

Marlene M.

employee since 2010

What I have gotten from Zappos is that I have made some good friends! And one truly awesome friend!!!!!!! Zappos is open for opportunities to excel. Something or someone always puts a smile in your heart!!

Matt B.

employee since 1999

As hard as we try to define it, the Zappos Culture really means a lot of different things to many people. This year's Culture Book will no doubt demonstrate this once again. No matter how hard you try, I defy you to find one, stand-alone, distinct theme about day-to-day life at Zappos that emerges from all these entries. You'll notice that employees love the Core Values, they love what Zappos stands for (both as a business and employer), they love all the opportunities (both professional and personal) that the company provides. These observations and thoughts, while they all combine to make this place what it is, vary as much as the people and personalities that work here, and therein lies the beauty of our Culture. Not any one specific idea, vision, or service defines Zappos, but rather the freedom everyone has to pursue all the different things that make them happy. On second thought, the general freedom to pursue happiness does qualify as a theme. I stand corrected.

Matt W.

employee since 2009

I am at a loss for words right now so I will quote a person who inspires me ... Mr. Walt Disney. "All the adversity I've had in my life, all my troubles and obstacles, have strengthened me ... You may not realize it when it happens, but a kick in the teeth may be the best thing in the world for you." KEEP ON TRUCKING!

Matthew S.

employee since 2009

I've heard some people liken the Zappos Culture to a cult. That's fine with me. If that's what it means to enjoy an incredible work environment, to be surrounded by a great group of co-workers, and to actually have fun at work every day, you can call it whatever you want!

Meredith M.

employee since 2011

After only three months of being with Zappos, I feel like I have found a home. I love how much the company cares for its employees. I know that I can come in and receive a smile from virtually everyone. And within my department alone, I have formed a core group of friends in a short time. The Core Values that are implemented at Zappos can definitely be seen every day. When I was asked in my interview, "On a scale from 1-10, how weird are you?" I never realized that it would actually come into play. I went from being the quirky friend in all of my other groups of co-workers and friends to being someone who fit right in at Zappos. I hope to be here for a long time to come.

Michael F.

employee since 2010

It has been a little over a year since I made Vegas and Zappos my home, and while you might expect that working here has become habit and routine, it hasn't. Coming to work is still exciting, constantly changing...and that is a good thing. Oh yes, and I armed myself. I am now the proud owner of an automatic nerf gun. Bring it on!

Michael J.

employee since 2007

I have been at Zappos for four years and it is still like day one!!! The Zappos Culture plays a big part in this. Each day I can depend on the smiling faces of every team. The happy family of Zappos is what makes us the best.

Michele K.

employee since 2008

The Zappos Culture makes me smile and tear up sometimes. I have been here almost three years and I'm still amazed and WOWed every day. The people here are like my family. I enjoy spending time with my co-workers both here and outside of work.

It is really nice that we are encouraged to have team builds and other activities inside and outside of work. It helps bring our teams and individuals closer together. Every day here is a rewarding challenge. We work hard and play hard!

Michelle T.

employee since 2007

Imagine an intricate, yet delicate web of intrigue, inspiration and opportunity. An ecosystem in and of itself that is fueled by interaction, engagement and shared beliefs, amplified only by unconventional behaviors, everyday leaders, and a vision to create and be part of something bigger. Welcome to my Zappos Culture.

Miranda W.

employee since 2005

Being at Zappos for six years now, I can definitely say there is no Culture like Zappos'. Friendly and smiling faces, hard work, accomplishments and a family are just a few words that come to mind when I think of the Zappos Culture. Never did I think I would stay at a company for longer than two years as I tend to get bored and am ready to try something completely new around that time. At Zappos, not only am I able to work in a department that I love, but also I'm able to explore the endless possibilities of my own passionate ideas and can make them become a reality.

Monfred M.

employee since 2007

Zappos is not only a place to work; it's a place to have fun. I've been here for four years now and each year gets better and better. This place surprises me every day. Everyone is so friendly and approachable. You can't find a better place to work.

Najum A.

employee since 2009

I have been with Zappos since October 2009 and I must say, my co-workers never cease to WOW me! Being able to work in such a casual, fun environment is a dream come true! Everyone instantly makes you feel as if you are part of the family. From potlucks, birthdays, happy hours, and any crazy event going on, I know I will never have a dull moment with my Zappos family. Thanks, Zappos, for being so amazing!!!

NaKia T.

employee since 2010

The difference between the Culture here at Zappos and the culture of previous companies that I have worked for is that this one is real. It's tangible. It's completely visible. At most places, culture is just a word, a staple, like "thinking outside the box" or "do the right thing." The Zappos Culture is evident in everything we do here, from the interview process, to CLT training, to company/department meetings, to the way we interact with visitors and those we do business with. Zappos Culture IS Zappos and that is why I love being in this place!!

Natashna S.

employee since 2007

Let's see. Where to start ... ? I am sure you've heard that one of the best things about Zappos is our Culture, and that is 100% true! I started here at Zappos on April 17th of 2007. I was hired as a picker in the Kentucky Fulfillment Center. Over the past four years, I worked my way up in the company and am now an online visual merchandiser, working at the headquarters in Vegas!! Exciting, huh? The point of my little history: no matter who you are, as long as you stay passionate and determined you can go anywhere, do anything and become what you've always dreamt of, all with the support of your friends and family. In my case, it was the people I work with who helped me get this far. They are what I consider family, supportive, honest, genuine and sometimes as annoying as a kid brother. I would never give them up! I am who I am today because of them. My Zappos family has always encouraged me to pursue my dreams no matter how big or small they might be. I know that no matter what, they will always be there for me, and me for them. For that, I dedicate this to my family. Thank you for being my rock and never giving up on me! Love you! <3

Nate L.

employee since 2009

Our Zappos Culture is why our Facebook fan page has ~1/5 as many fans as some of these other pages, yet we have significantly more customer posts, shout-outs, and overall interactions happening on our wall. Our customers love interacting with real people. We keep it real. Heh heh heh. Zing Zong!

Nedwardo

employee since 2001

To me, the Zappos Culture means walking with my beautiful and I might add strappy mandals to the break room for Taco Tuesday. It means that I never have to worry about dessert. I only need to walk around to a few different departments to find my basic dessert food groups: ice cream cake and non-ice-cream cake entities. Zappos Culture is about having multiple 'after work' social engagements to choose from on any given day. Actually, Zappos Culture is about having multiple 'during work' social engagements to choose from on any day. It's about walking to the neighboring building and picking up a cup of homemade lemonade from a stand where we can donate money to a current charity. To me, Zappos Culture is about people ... and hard shellfish tacos with that squeeze bottle cream sauce and a sprinkle of cilantro.

Nick M.

employee since 2010

The Zappos Culture is a lot like the message in Bill and Ted's Excellent Adventure. Those two great gentlemen were dedicated to a proposition which was true in their time, and just as it's true today: Be excellent to each other. And party on, dudes.

Pat W.

employee since 2003

I've never felt so busy and behind in my work as I do now, but I have also never felt more accomplished or proud of what I do. In the past year, our department has nearly tripled in size, the quality of our work has been noticed by more people than ever, both inside and outside of the company, and that's just what goes on while I'm at work. Living two miles away from the office in a great neighborhood with my amazing girlfriend (who also works at Zappos) makes life easy and gives us time to hang out with our co-workers, who we also consider to be very good friends. I'm also fortunate enough to live a block away from three of my very best friends (two of whom also work at Zappos), and I really feel like things couldn't get any better. Although I've been with the company for quite some time, every day feels as exciting and new as the first day I walked into the ZFC over eight years ago. Zappos and Tony Hsieh have made my life happier and more exciting than I would have ever thought realistically possible. I am forever grateful and look forward to many more years as a member of the Zappos family.

Patrice Lorene

employee since 2009

On a daily basis I am blessed to wake up, thank God for another day, smile, come to a job that I love, and smile some more! Being a part of the Zappos family is the most phenomenal work experience anyone could ever hope for! I get to laugh for most of the day, socialize, eat cereal whenever I want and (of course) work hard! And once I get off work I still have enough energy for my unstoppable MJ dance moves. Did I hear somebody mention 5 Stars?!!!

Philip S.

employee since 2006

I'm already going on half a decade at Zappos and there's not a day that I am not WOWed by my Zappos family. There's no way to put our Zappos Culture in words. It is something you have to experience for yourself. From the people to the work environment, every aspect of Zappos is filled with a unique passion that I have never witnessed before and it is truly inspiring and motivating to know that I am surrounded by such creativity.

Rachael P.

employee since 2008

The Zappos Culture, to me, means everything. I live and breathe it every day. As a result, it has shaped me into the person I am today. I look forward to coming to work and seeing people whom I consider family.

People here genuinely care about what you're going through, not only professionally, but personally as well. I don't say this because it's something I have been programmed to say. I say this because it's true and I have experienced it first-hand. Zappos Culture has allowed me to be who I am and pursue what I'm truly passionate about. I wouldn't have it any other way.

Raina A.

employee since 2007

Zappos is an amazing place to work! I've been here for over three years now, and I still LOVE coming to work every day. I've found lifelong friends in many of my co-workers and teammates, and I hope to make even more connections and meet new friends with each new year.

Zappos has really given me the opportunity to be myself while allowing me to contribute and grow within the company. It's amazing just how much the company has grown since I started in 2007. There are a lot of fresh, new and friendly faces that walk through the doors with every new training class. It's always super refreshing to see them get so pumped about working here. I remember that feeling when I went through my training class. It's cool because I STILL feel that way today. :)

Randy D.

employee since 2011

I have only been with Zappos for just over three months and there isn't enough time (or space) for me to talk about all the great things that Zappos is! I have never been anywhere that embraces the sense of family and takes care of its employees like peers! The idea that with happy employees comes happy customers really makes a difference in my life and my well being outside of work. Since moving into the Zappos lifestyle, my family and friends can really see a change in my outlook and attitude! Really ... I know it's cheesy, but I love this place!!!

Robert A.

employee since 2005

To paraphrase Mohandas Gandhi, culture resides in the hearts and soul of its people. Zappos as a company and the Zappos Culture have developed to our present iteration due in no small part to every single employee, both past and present, and it is through our people that we will continue to learn, grow, and evolve to the next level.

Robert A.

employee since 2007

Zappos Culture is all about looking at business in an entirely different way. Who would have ever imagined that creating a fun environment, treating customers and co-workers with respect, encouraging creativity, helping employees set goals and focusing on Delivering Happiness would be a recipe for Success? Duh, winning!!

When people are excited about going to work, have a feeling of being part of something great and enjoy spending time with co-workers it really shows the power of our Core Values. Our Core Values are really just a mindset or guide showing us how to treat people and a strategy for living a happy, fulfilling life. When everyone is on this same page, the result is the Zappos Culture. Once someone's mindset is open to living by our Core Values, everything else seems to fall in place! Zappos Culture = Zappos Core Values.

Ruben R.

employee since 2009

I'm half way through my second year at Zappos and I still have the same awesome feeling that I had on day one. Everyone here bleeds the company Culture and it shows in the daily life of Zapponians. The Zappos family is not just a tag line. We truly are a family.

Samantha S.

employee since 2009

The Zappos Culture means genuinely having a great relationship with your co-workers. This is one of the first jobs I've had that I consider a career. This is also one of the first jobs I've had where I don't dread going to work every day. It's fun to see how the company has changed and grown in such a short time and I feel lucky to be a part of it!

Sandra H.

employee since 2005

Hi all! Another year has come and gone, and it is time once again to let other people know just how awesome Zappos is to work for. I encountered something new this year at Zappos. After six years of employment, I finally was able to go to the Las Vegas encounter. Not only was this my first time flying (which was awesome), the four-day stay was too.

On Monday we arrived at the Vegas main headquarters, and all of the people met us at the door with smiles and hugs. (Not really a surprise.) Through the days ahead I was able to do some one-on-one with several people to get a feel of what they do and how their jobs coordinate with the things that I do back in Kentucky. The department that WOWed me was customer service. I worked with Eric on several calls and he was amazing. Before I left him for the day he gave me his corporate challenge shirt. (The challenge was going on while I was in Vegas.)

For entertainment in the evenings, our group did some major pigging out, and went to the strips, and did (some) casinos. Would I want to live in Vegas? Probably not, but I sure am happy that these wonderful people here in Vegas do. It was an awesome, once-in-a-lifetime experience for me. To top it off, the cost of this was on the best company in the world to work for. Thanks, Zappos!

Sara M.

employee since 2011

Email tag, darts fly. Work hard, party harder. Shots! Meeting now, break down walls. Push the lines, research new methods, design, create, write. Search for the happy code place. Eat, talk, zing-zong, tours, popcorn, coffee – that's all in one Zapponian's full day. PS – I'm Swiss!

Sara W.

employee since 2010

I guess a piece of me, no matter how small, always believed that my destiny with Zappos would follow the path of any other relationship. After a year, the rosy glasses would come off, the honeymoon period would be over, and things would get real. The nice, friendly company I had met in January 2010, would become the nagging, clingy, needy employer who turns out to drink a little more than I thought and constantly "forgets" its wallet when we go out to eat. I thought the magic would be gone.

I have been pleasantly surprised to discover that the spark is still there. The Zappos that I met on my first day through the warehouse doors has continued to be the most supportive, unique, and exciting company I have ever worked for. Although nothing and nobody is perfect, I have matured and grown in my time here, and learned important things, both about myself and my relationships with others. I have learned that, not only do I have a voice (even though my face gets red when I use it), but that it matters. Other companies treat you as one of a million, a set of hands. Zappos treats you as one IN a million. And I'm not sure I will ever love another company as much as I love Zappos ... warts and all.

Seth L.
employee since 2010

Cul·ture [kúlcher] – shared beliefs and values of a group: the beliefs, customs, practices and social behavior of a particular nation or people. When I first began, I didn't really understand what the Zappos Culture was all about. I thought that employees here just liked to find excuses to slack off while they were at work! Now that I've been here for a while, though, I see that Zappos isn't made up of a bunch of slackers. Zappos is made of up hard-working people who really care about WOWing others, whether they are customers or other Zappos employees, and who have fun while doing it. The Zappos Culture is built partly around these two things: WOWing others, and having fun. It's a Culture that encourages you to make someone's day, to be yourself, to make friends, to grow and learn and to believe that the word "no" isn't in the dictionary. I love the Zappos Culture because it has allowed me to enjoy what I do and have fun with my "co-workers" (read: friends).

Shanda F.
employee since 2007

My feelings about Zappos Culture might be best expressed in a monologue from the made-for-TV movie, "Sybil," starring a young Miss Sally Field. "Oh, look at you painted up in your little halter top."

Sharon K.
employee since 2007

Zappos is a unique company. Management constantly wants to know employees' opinions, ideas, needs, and wants. Policies and benefits are constantly changing to reflect what the employees need and want. The Culture and family spirit are visible in every activity and department. Teams are encouraged to have outings to get to know one another personally. Zappos wants its employees to be cared for and happy.

This is a great place to work, make friends, and be part of a very large family. Who could ask for anything more?

Sonnet T.
employee since 2010

A three-legged dog walks into a bar and says, "I'm looking for the man that shot my paw." LOL :)

Stephanie H.
employee since 2010

Each time I try to describe the Zappos Culture to friends or family that are not employed here, I have to say, "You cannot understand it until you are in it or part of it!" To me, the culture here is the environment ... the whole atmosphere and attitude of the workforce. It's being able to show my crazy, goofy side without fear of being judged because the people watching are just as crazy or goofy! We are a family and my team in the studio makes my job what it is: FANTASTIC. I never imagined having a position in such a place.

Stormey
employee since 2009

The Zappos Culture is a phenomenon and I hope that it is the beginning of a continuing revolution in customer service! I feel that my company loves me. I hoped I would be able to say this at one point in my life, but when I thought about it, it was always a vision of my own company loving me. Never in my wildest dreams did I think I could work for someone else and still feel like it was my own and like I was loved because of it. I take ownership for everything I do every day because what I do directly affects the company and the customers and I so want to make them happy. I love the way it makes me feel loved back. The Zappos Culture has given me this. How amazing is that? Pretty frillin' amazing!

The Culture, to me, is love. When you create something with so much passion behind it and it not only survives, it thrives, you know you have a gem. We are all gems because of our customers. Who would have thought treating people with kindness, honesty and compassion could create such a wave? And we are making waves. It's awesome to work for Zappos and be a part of something so important. I am grateful.

"Enjoy your achievements as well as your plans. Keep interested in your own career, however humble; it is a real possession in the changing fortunes of time."

– Max Ehrmann's "Desiderata"

Sunshine J.
employee since 2010

I love that my family can feel like a part of this company as well. It's become a great mixture of career and fun for me. I've made some great friends!

Surbhi M.

employee since 2011

I was hesitant to come into work late after a vacation weekend because I thought my manager would consider me a slacker. Instead, he asked if he could help me with reporting. Another morning, I was ready to fork up $50 to cab my way to work because I forgot to request a shuttle ride on time. Instead, the "kan-du" team made special arrangements to pick me up from the airport at 8 a.m.

Every day, I come into the office trying to find ways to impress my team with new ideas and projects. Instead, my teammates impress me by encouraging each other to take more leadership responsibilities.

It seems that every time I expect my work environment to be that of a typical company, where the burden lies on the new-hire to be perfect and have a tireless work ethic, the Zappos family reminds me of the opposite: Having a work-life balance is important, making mistakes is OK, and my co-workers' contributions are just as important as my own to overall success. Because of this, the Zappos Culture means supporting one another, encouraging both personal and career growth, and working as a team. I'm still a newbie, but I'm sure I'll feel the same way next year!

Susan D.

employee since 2005

WOW! Over six years with this great company! It has been a great learning experience. I started when there were 100 team members and now there are over 1500. The things I loved when I started here are still the things I love. There are no boundaries here; you can achieve anything you set your mind to. All this, plus the mindset that you're going to have fun. I think the best part of Zappos is the people. There are always smiles and laughter, and we want to be here. Nowhere else can compete with our Culture. It is what gives us the edge. It is what makes us Zappos. Thank you for giving me the best job I have ever had!!!

Tara J.

employee since 2007

I love that all the people I work with genuinely care about one another. My team eats lunch together regularly and just chats often throughout the day. I recently had a baby and everyone was excited for my husband and me and really stepped up while I was on maternity leave to make sure I didn't come back completely slammed with work. Everyone I work with is truly part of my extended family.

Teralane S.

employee since 2007

Let's see, I have been at Zappos going on four years now. Zappos is big on family and has always stressed that our co-workers are our family. I used to say that my home family is my only family. It wasn't until recently, when I started having major issues at home that my Zappos family kicked in and showed me that I can have both. They had always been there for me and I didn't realize it till recently. I'm sooo grateful for that. It is a strong bond that we create here at our home away from home that you won't find anywhere else.

It feels good to have togetherness, camaraderie and good spirit, especially for someone who has been involved with cheerleading and dance team all my life. The team spirit that we have here is like being in high school all over again, in a positive way. :-)

Of course, you have your bad days, but it's up to you to change the next day. Come in feeling happy and positive and things will always work out the way they are supposed to. Even if you have to fake it till you make it!!! Power over mind. I always treat others the way I want to be treated – with respect, honesty and with sincerity. If you only hope for the same but don't necessarily expect it, you won't get let down. I've always tried to make people smile or laugh and if it doesn't work the first time, I'll keep trying till I crack a smile out of ya.

Tessa H.

employee since 2010

To my dearest Zappos: Thank you so much for showing me wild, free-flowing, productive creativity. I finally feel like I can be myself and be appreciated for simply that. If I have dreams and aspirations in the company, I truly believe that I can do it! Thank you so much for being the great company that you are. :)

Thomas T.

employee since 2007

I love Zappos!!!! I am blessed to have an opportunity to work in a place that promotes growth, individuality, and happiness. I have been here almost five years and I am still a very happy employee. I love the people I work with and the job that I am doing. Zappos is definitely more than just a job. I love this place.

Tiffany G.

employee since 2008

Zappos is fun, hard work, laughter, "your mom" jokes, friendship, camaraderie, noise, clutter, happiness, silliness, openness, kindness, cookies, muffins, birthday cakes, teamwork and so much more.

Tim S.
employee since 2009

It has been an awesome year. Seeing Zappos evolve over the last year has been amazing; there have been so many changes for the better. Getting the chance to build out a complete team with the best and smartest guys truly blows my mind and shows what can be done when the right people are focused on the same vision.

Getting to meet new faces from other departments that have a little interaction with the department I am in is very cool. These bonds formed from corporate challenge, happy hours, company events and KY Hero Academy are moments I will be able to keep with me forever. Everyone contributes to the overall Zappos experience, which creates one big WOW! I look forward to seeing what happens over the next year and what new friendships form.

Tom C.
employee since 2009

Each of us knows why we're here around this campfire tonight. We're all of us chasing a good scare, trying to find a truly bone-chilling fright. Every Saturday night, we come together and spin a horrifying yarn about impossibly twisted monsters or wicked magic and curses that never once touched the world. We imagine a life upon which the supernatural encroaches, wreaking unspeakable terror that irrevocably alters our lives for the worse.

Imagine, just for a moment, a world even more terrifying than the ones we've dreamt up. In this world, the merest chuckle, the barest whisper of laughter, fills a room with silence instead of smiles. In this world, concepts like imagination, satisfaction, and hope are anathemas, replaced instead by mediocrity, complacence, and dissatisfaction. The downtrodden trudge through their daily lives with heads down, never meeting one another's gaze or aspiring to achieve their abandoned childhood dreams. In a world that's been cut off from its own desires, how can its inhabitants even begin to imagine a different life? Who can rekindle the light of personal optimism against the crushing darkness of the corporate machine? Submitted for the approval of the Midnight Society, I call this story, The Tale of Laughing in the Dark.

Tricia Ann D.
employee since 2009

Since the first day I walked through Zappos' doors, its Culture has had a huge impact on my life. It instilled the "Don't worry, be happy" outlook on everything in my life more so than before! Everyone cares so deeply about everyone else, like a true family that if one is hurting, we all hurt.

I couldn't imagine life without my Zappos family. Being able to come to work and be my goofy self to the max is fantastic. We embrace one another to help each of us reach his or her goals, both at work and outside. The Zappos Culture and its effects never stop once we clock out for the day, and I wouldn't have it any other way. Hopefully our happiness and passion will pass along to everyone we come across and it'll spread across families and companies. It brings a whole new light and life to one's perspective.

I know no matter where I go in life, the Zappos Culture I've experienced will live on with me. Zangsta pride!

William B.

employee since 2010

When I filled out the application for Zappos, I could tell this would be a place I liked ... I mean, with questions about my favorite superheroes (Mermaid Man, by the way) or what my theme song would be, how could I not?

The people that I work for are amazing, always willing to help out. The people I work with, side by side, are just as fun and wonderful. This has definitely been my favorite job of all, and I hope to stick around for a nice long while.

Yhaira Y.

employee since 2008

One of the things I remember from training is that several of the speakers who visited our class spoke about how working for Zappos started out as a job, but then slowly became more to them. Never having experienced that before, it was hard for me to fathom that at the time. Sure, I'd had "fun" jobs, but they were mostly in my early college years, so you can imagine the overall environment two and a half years later. I now understand what they felt about this company.

Working here is a lifestyle. Not only does my daily life revolve around Zappos, but a majority of the people in my life outside of work are also Zapponians. I've met so many awesome people here and even some of my closest friends. Honestly, the reason I'm still in Vegas is Zappos and what it has brought to my life.

Zach W.

employee since 2010

Starting a new job is hard. After four years with a San Francisco company, I joined Zappos and made the move to Las Vegas to join the Zappos family. Having moved four times in my career, I had become somewhat of an expert in starting over in a new place and making new friends. But it's never easy.

What I appreciate most about the Zappos Culture is the people. Within weeks of joining the Zappos family, I felt at home. Not because of company events or weird team-building exercises, but because at Zappos we don't see a line between work and home. The people we work with are friends – genuine friends. Our friendships and comfort with being able to be ourselves makes us more productive when we're at work and happier when we're not. There isn't any one Core Value or cultural phenomenon that makes this possible; it's the whole package. Being humble, creating fun and weirdness, building a positive team and family spirit and so on. Living by these Values brings us together. I'm grateful for the warmth my new co-workers have shown me. I'm humbled by the friendship they've offered me. Being comfortable in my new home is what the Zappos Culture means to me.

Zelia Lee K.

employee since 2007

Zappos is one of the best jobs I've ever had because they accept me for who I am. This job has made me a better person and helped me be a better team member. I've learned a lot from this job and had a lot of fun doing it. My team members are like my family; I really enjoy that about my job. I have a great boss and that is a rare thing to have. Thanks for everything, Tony and the Zappos family.

Zappos Core Value #8

Do
More
with
Less

(Or do more when little)

Andi R.
employee since 2009

I am constantly able to live in that "OMG, guess what?!" moment. I've always loved to talk about myself and amaze people with the adventures of my life. Now I am able to brag about the wonderful work we do here and how lucky I am to be a part of it. I seriously love my Zappos family.

Anonymous.
employee since 2009

I realized the full potential of culture to deliver happiness when I heard from a Zappos Insights client. He created a culture change at his company and the results were outstanding. But here is where it got really interesting. He said, "The positive changes didn't stay at the office alone. My wife immediately noticed the change in me. Instead of coming home, exhausted from the day and needing some 'me time,' I'm energized from the successes of the day and eager to see my family." Can you imagine what the world would be like if this was everyone's workday? I love experiencing it on my own team. When we interview a potential new team member, the candidate often asks what we love about working here. I love hearing that everyone considers this team their family and that they're growing and learning every day, and loving the process.

Augusta S.
employee since 2007

Every time I think about what Zappos Culture means to me, it takes a moment to describe it. Then I think about my journey. Everything about my journey has been about the Zappos Culture. Growth, learning, freedom, passion, determination, remaining humble, feedback, fun, challenges, strength, communication (open and honest), building relationships, discovery, alignment and most of all, being a part of an amazing family.

I've said it all along. I am the Zappos Culture. Every family member at Zappos is the culture. It is up to us to continue to grow it as we grow as a company. What does that mean, "grow it?" It means to make absolutely sure we continue to do the things we have done in the past to make us unique, different and special. To step up to the challenge of us growing so fast, but remembering to take time for the important stuff, like holding the doors open and saying "Good morning," to each other. Assisting when asked and assisting even when you haven't been asked. Being there for each other in the good times and the rough times. Spending time together outside of the office so we get to know each other. Being able to ask for help when you need it, and no one looks at you like you're an idiot, but rather that you want to learn and grow. It's simple really. Continue to be who we are and remain humble as we grow as a company and a family. That's how we got here. To make sure we are in a state of gratitude and not a state of entitlement. So, culture to me is my life inside and outside of Zappos. It's what drives me every day!

Elia L.
employee since 2009

Culture is defined as the behaviors and beliefs characteristic of a particular social, ethnic, or age group (e.g.: the youth culture). The Zappos Culture is unique in every sense of the word. We are more than just a business that believes in taking care of our customers, both internal and external. Our culture drives the way we treat each other, our vendors and our awesome customers. The Zappos Culture allows us to interact with open and honest communication. We encourage everyone to continue to build a positive team and family spirit. I am humbled each day by the choices that we make around here. We want to make choices that will WOW our customers through service. We strive to make the Zappos customer service experience the best that it can be. I really enjoy working in an environment that supports each person's uniqueness. Our differences make us stronger and also give us a greater appreciation for one another. I learn something new every day. What a great feeling to know that the company and culture is set up for success. Our culture is not perfect. We understand that it is a constant effort to further our culture. Every person has a responsibility to himself or herself and to each other. By working together, we can make the world a happier place.

Emaile H.
employee since 2006

What is the Zappos Culture? It is a bunch of different adjectives like: fun, exciting, weird, playful and family-oriented. But my absolute favorite is innovative! Over the years, I have seen this company change and grow in ways I never thought possible. The goals that were set have been broken and far surpassed, and we continue to be refreshed and renewed. In all honesty, it's been scary at times, but I've watched this company pull together as a family on every challenge we've encountered. We have celebrated the good and endured the bad. (Very few were bad.) And we've come out unified as an even stronger family. When I think about how this company is changing the world through customer service, selection, and personal emotional connections, it makes me proud to be a Zapponian!!

Jenna T.

employee since 2008

For me, the Zappos Culture is all about increasing the quality of life! Not just at work, but at home too! Being a part of the Zappos family for the last three years has changed my entire outlook on life. It has made me realize that life really is what you make it. Enjoy the good times and cherish the precious moments. Don't sweat the small stuff and don't take life too seriously. No one makes it out alive! Is what you're living for worth dying for?

Jon W.

employee since 2008

As I sit here in the middle of an all-out team finger rocket/stress-ball battle, I can't help but wonder what life is like for most office workers. I get to work in a place that lets me be me from the moment I walk through the door until the moment I go home. I have a fantastic team that is more like a family than I have ever experienced, and our goal is to spread the word that work can be a fun place while boosting overall happiness and productivity. Although I am going into my fourth year here, my father still uses quotation marks (") when he mentions my "job" on Facebook. I know that he is only doing it in jest, but it's actually kind of great in my opinion. I talk about the Zappos family and what I get to do in Insights with such enthusiasm and excitement that he jokes that it can't really be a job. I can't wait to see the future of the Zappos family and I look forward to the exciting journey ahead! Now I think it's time to collect a stray finger rocket or two and fire back at my team ====>   ====> ====>

Marie M.

employee since 2009

Culture defines a company's DNA. Our values were in each one of us before we came together as Zappos family members. I have the amazing gift of being in a position where I am tasked to share the amazing things we do with the outside world. The best part of my job is knowing what we are doing here every day is making businesses (and the world) a better place!

Marissa J.

employee since 2009

Enough said ...

Mig P.

employee since 2008

The Zappos Culture has evolved over the three years that I've been here. There are a lot of new faces, since we are growing quickly, but we're always actively looking for new ways to connect and bring people together, both inside and outside of the office. Since there is a conscious effort and emphasis on culture, it has strengthened over the years. Nothing is ever constant. Everything changes. It is a work in progress to enrich the culture for years to come and make it better than yesterday.

Pamela C.

employee since 2006

The Zappos Culture has meant continued growth and becoming a better person each year. With the Core Values we live and breathe each day, you can't help but apply them to your daily life, either at home, at work or both. It is a culture that becomes an infectioon that you wouldn't mind getting every day!

Renea W.

employee since 2007

Core Value #2 ("Embrace and Drive Change") has really resonated with me this past year. After four years, I'm still amazed to be working with incredible people and continuing to grow (and learn) in the various positions I have held within Zappos. The opportunities are endless and I plan on embracing every moment!

Rocco D.

employee since 2010

Make magic!!! (Make the font as big as you can, and very very bold. We need boldness to convey the importance of making magic)

Trish B.

employee since 2009

The Zappos Culture is about making a difference. In business, in the community, within each other and in the world.

FEBRUARY 10, 2011
Silverton Casino
LAS VEGAS, NV

MONSTER
ENERGY
ENERGIZES
Kentucky

OCTOBER 2010
Graduation

LIVE! WITH REGIS AND KELLY
High Heel-a-Thon

LIVE! WITH REGIS AND KELLY

High Heel-a-thon

Zappos.com

VW Das Auto.

IN SUPPORT OF THE heart TRUTH

Zappos.com
"Best Dressed Award"
High Heel-a-thon
2010

FUN IN
Fulfillment Center

DIRECTOR Rated R-Desk
PRODUCTION "SNAPS"
SCENE 2 TAKE 7305
ROLL

Having Fun
WITH ZCLT

TLC

DEAN MARTIN DR

I-15

Zappos Core Value #1

Deliver WOW
Through Service

**(Even if it involves pulling a rickshaw with
three women while running in golf shoes)**

Allison K.

employee since 2010

To me, the Zappos Culture means being able to be myself and express my thoughts and ideas in an open environment. I love Zappos!

Ashley M.

employee since 2007

It's funny, there are the very visible elements of Zappos Culture that we all love: parades, goofy costumes, happy hours, amazing parties, and slightly disturbing costumes ... the list goes on and on. But there is also so much that happens behind the scenes that makes this is a company I love to work for. When I think of our Culture, I think of a working environment where your boss will say, "You believe in your idea, make it happen, you have my support." Where you work as hard as you can, not just for the paycheck, but because you're excited about the work and how you can make an impact. Even though I spend so many hours a week working with my team, they are also some of my closest friends. I love hanging out with them outside of work, shopping, dinner, 5k runs, or even taking vacations together. I am so happy that I found Zappos, that they were willing to take a chance on me, and that I've had the opportunity to learn so much and make such great friends.

Caron O.

employee since 2007

I <3 Zappos! I truly appreciate that I am able to work in an environment that inspires me to be a better person. I am inspired professionally by the people I work with and truly appreciate the opportunity to learn and create new systems and processes. More importantly, I am inspired to improve my community and myself.

I was excited and humbled when we were asked to be part of our new downtown community. I think that says so much about Zappos ... that we want to be good neighbors and that we want to help build a community. I am proud to be part of the Zappos family.

Erin G.

employee since 2011

The Zappos Culture creates an environment where you're accepted for who you are and where you have the freedom to be what you want to be!!

Mayra M.

employee since 2010

Zappos. What can be said that hasn't already been said? This company as a whole doesn't preach Core Values; we live, breathe, eat and sleep them. Our company's set of values allows me to aspire to be a better person. They allow me to wake up every morning happy to go to work because I get to hang out with some of the most awesome people I've ever met. I love this place!

Michelle F.

employee since 2007

Most of the candidates that come through our doors to interview for a position at Zappos ask us what we love most about working here and our answer is always how great the Culture is and that it actually means something to everyone. I love that we truly build a positive team and family spirit. I love coming to work on Monday and getting to see everyone and find out how their weekends were. And I enjoy spending time with my teams and co-workers outside of the office. Because of this, it never truly feels like work. And for the great Culture that we live and breathe every day, I am grateful.

Nicole G.

employee since 2010

I have been at Zappos for one year now and I am happy to say that the Culture, the happiness and the joy that overwhelm you when you walk into the office never gets old and never goes away. I am so lucky to wake up every morning and be excited to go to work, not only because I love what I do, but also because I love everyone I work with.

Paul K.

employee since 2010

The Zappos Culture means being part of something bigger and grander than just "being at work." For me, it has meant working with great friends, and loving coming into the office to do my job. It means not only working hard to maximize profits for the business every day, but being encouraged to seek out ways to make a difference in the community and the world around.

Rowena D.

employee since 2006

The Zappos Culture means having a place to work and build a career while having fun and enjoying life! It's a place of learning with some of your closest friends and family. Zappos becomes a part of your life in a good way. A place that is truly work-life balanced, where your whole family – kids and all – become part of the Zappos family.

Ryan S.

employee since 2010

To understand the amazing Culture we have here at Zappos, I think one has to begin with bad culture – almost like looking at good and evil from a theological perspective. Because to understand how incredible our Culture is here, you have to have been subjected to "open" door policies, ambiguous performance evaluations, mandatory "fun" events and mission statements that require both a thesaurus and the willingness to suspend disbelief to understand. You would have to be tired of treating customers and vendors like the enemy – like outsiders, really – and of going to work every day not knowing anything about the people with whom you spend most of your waking hours. You would have had to suffer under the tyrannical rule of a micro-managing boss who couldn't care less about you or your career, who toils under a CEO who is both omnipresent and never present, who answers only to the shareholders and the bottom line. You would have to have experienced that Sunday night dread of knowing that in a few short hours, it's back to the drudgery of toiling away anonymously and unrecognized.

If this all sounds familiar, then it's easy to appreciate just how special the Zappos Culture is. It's not perfect, but it truly and honestly strives to be perfect. Outside of my actual family, I don't think I've ever felt more like a part of a family. My co-workers are my friends, and we work towards a common goal – one that we can believe in and one that governs everything we do: to Deliver Happiness. And if I

had to point to one thing that makes this company special, I would say that Zappos gets all the small things that make people happy right: free and good coffee and drinks in the break rooms; a vendor extranet that allows vendors to access information; flexible dress codes and work schedules; continual feedback (good and bad) between everyone (up and down); lots of events, few of which are mandatory so you don't feel bad about missing one; training, both to make you better at your job and to make you a better person in general; executives that are down to earth, accessible and friendly. By themselves, these things are small, but their amalgamation makes customers, employees and vendors feel special, happy and engenders a productive workplace.

So what does the Zappos Culture mean to me? I guess it means all the things that bad culture doesn't. It means all the little things that matter are important to those who can decide to change them. It means that everyone has the ability to change anything, if they are passionate about it. It means that everyone from the top down in the company cares about one another (and not just about what you do for the company). In addition to the company, it is the vendors, customers and the bottom line.

Sarah Z.

employee since 2009

Zappos Culture is unique, fun and crazy! You should never expect to have a "normal" day here!

Stephanie S.

employee since 2006

What's your passion? After working at Zappos for five years, I've forgotten what it's like to work in "the real world," so it's a little hard for me to compare it to others. However, when I see tours coming through the office or people talking about Zappos on blogs, I get a glimpse of how lucky we really are. The CEO, CFO, COO and other "higher ups" all sit in cubicles right next to us. We all share the same free food and we all are thought of as equals. This hasn't changed in the five years I've been here. Passion – After finding out we were relocating, Zappos reached out to each employee and asked "What is your passion?" (For me it was Education/ Day Care for my two kids.) Then they tried to figure out how my/our passions can improve the company, no matter the cost, resources or time! I'm amazed at Zappos, including Tony, the employees, my teams, the vendors ... the Zappos Culture! It has changed my life in so many ways, helped me get on my feet, to become a passionate person and be involved in my life and in the lives of others. I'm not just a bystander anymore. The Zappos Culture is ... passion!

Zappos Core Value #10

Be
Humble

(Even when you know you're
looking snazzy in your sleepwear)

Alyxandria D.
employee since 2010

(Cheers theme song.) Making your way in the world today takes everything you've got. Taking a break from all your worries sure would help a lot. Wouldn't you like to get away? Sometimes you want to go where everybody knows your name, and they're always glad you came. You wanna be where you can see our troubles are all the same. You wanna be where everybody knows your name.

Charlette P.

employee since 2010

As a member of the baby boomer generation, I never expected to find such an awesome place to work at my age. It is the absolute BEST place I've ever worked and my Zappos and 6pm.com outlet family is the greatest! WOW, WOW and WOW again!

Claude M.

employee since 2008

I love God. I love my wife. I love Zappos. I love my dog. As you can see, Zappos came before my dog. :)

Connie B.
employee since 2010

I started working for Zappos in Sept 2010 in W2 as a "seasonal" and then was asked to join the 6pm.com Outlet Team in January of 2011. I am now a permanent employee. I have worked many places before (because I'm an old lady, HA-HA!) and I have NEVER, EVER worked at a place that is more fun! I actually look forward to going to work each day and working with so many awesome people.

1) I love delivering "WOW" to our customers!
2) Changes occur every day!
3) It's fun to create weirdness!
4) Being adventurous, creative and open-minded is what it's all about!
5) I want to grow with the company as it succeeds because I always want to learn new things!
6) It's important to be able to communicate with each other to build strong relationships!
7) The people I work with are not only my team; I consider them family!
8) Doing more with less is awesome!
9) I am passionate about my job and I'm determined to succeed!
10) You've got to be humble and have a good state of mind!

Gregory B.
employee since 2008

Even after the acquisition, it is great to know that our individualities are still accepted and valued. I know of no other company that has a leader who is as involved in the lives of their employees as Tony is of Zappos and 6pm.com. This may explain the many offers he has to speak to audiences on happiness. We are truly blessed to be a valued part of his vision.

Jordan E.

employee since 2010

What is the Zappos Culture to me? It's helping a co-worker push their car that is stuck in the mud out in the pouring rain, while getting filthy dirty and not thinking twice about it. It's taking time to sit and listen to problems another person is having outside of work because you truly care. It's writing "I appreciate you" notes letting them know that they're the coolest person on the planet. The Zappos Culture is a lot of things, but knowing that you're making lifelong friends is the best part of all! And for that, I am so very thankful. :)

Katherine H.

employee since 2009

The Zappos Culture is Like no other: awesome. We are treated very well. No one is judged by others. Team members are great and we all accept one another! This company Is by far "the best I have ever worked at"! The Zappos Culture is so positive and we are among friends and family. I can talk to any one of my leads and management at any time. I love Zappos for a lot reasons, mostly because of the way they really care about all of us! Zappos provides all lunches and drinks and snacks. The company also pays for our insurance. That's part of why Zappos keeps delivering "WOW" to our customers!

Leigh Ann R.

employee since 2010

I have an old-school ideal of what the Zappos Culture means to me. I am a single mother and it is so similar to what I've tried to teach my children all these years: Be a good person, work hard and have fun while you're doing it, treat people the way you would want them to treat your mother, and always have time for an adventure!

Sarah H.

employee since 2010

When I hear "Zappos," I think of an amazing shopping experience! I was a loyal Zappos customer long before becoming an employee. Now, many years later (thanks to Claude), I am living my dream in a shoppers' paradise! I love being surrounded by Alexander McQueen, Marc Jacobs and Vivienne Westwood every day! Some of my favorite Zappos items are: Alexander McQueen Skull clutches and scarves, Marc Jacobs handbags, Vivienne Westwood Pirate boots, Frye boots, and Minnetonka boots! I am obsessed with BOOTS! I LOVE ZAPPOS! My fellow team members are more than co-workers; they are family! My favorite Core Value is #3: Create Fun And A Little Weirdness!

Sue M.

employee since 2008

In my opinion, the intent of the Zappos Culture is our greatest resource! When I first heard of Zappos and did some research to see what this company was all about, the Culture and the Core Values that embody it excited me and drew me in even more strongly than the specific job opportunity did. In the Zappos Culture and Core Values, I saw my own core values, and I knew this was a match made in heaven! At that moment, I knew that I would do whatever work Zappos wanted me to do, as long as I could be a part of a company guided by these Core Values. I came from a company that operated purely by the numbers, and the experience was very frustrating. The evolution of our Culture to include Delivering Happiness made me even happier! What a great business to be in! It is what I have always wanted and sought to do! I am happy every day to be a part of this growing family whose daily work it is to deliver happiness to each other, to our customers and to everyone with whom we interact! :)

Tenicia S.

employee since 2007

Zappos is truly a great company to work for. Everyone makes you welcome with open arms. The company encourages both personal and professional growth, which is awesome. I recently re-enrolled in school because I was inspired by my coworkers' focus and drive to find a career related to their degree and by my manager, who encouraged me to take risks and be proactive! I knew I had to find my passion and began that journey. With the support of my Zappos family and friends, I am on my way to accomplishing another goal and dream that will prepare me for my future.

Terri O.

employee since 2011

To me, the Zappos Culture means being comfortable in my own skin. I love being a name and not a number! I am new to Zappos, and have recently been battling Hodgkin's Lymphoma for two years. I was very nervous about going back to work with a bunch of scars and being a bald female, especially somewhere new. Since starting here at Zappos, I have been accepted just like a normal person and I am so thankful for the Culture of people here. Coming to work here has been a personal motivator. I know now that I can accomplish anything and Zappos is the greatest job – one that lets me do just that. I plan on being here a long time, ready to WOW whoever needs it! Thanks to everyone in the Zappos family for accepting me for who I am and welcoming me into the workplace with open arms. I love shoes, therefore, I love Zappos! YEAH for Zappos!

Valineshia F.

employee since 2007

To me, Zappos is more than just our Culture. It reminds me of a big happy family. I couldn't be more honored to work for such a company. Being here is like a gift; you get to learn, and have fun and just be yourself. I have been working here for over three years now and I have never seen a company that cares so much about making employees and customers happy! I'm so thankful!

Bubble Trouble
AT 2011 NEW HIRE
GRADUTATIONS

DELIVERING **Happiness**

DELIVERING HAPPINESS *Pre-Launch Party*

JUNE 1, 2010
Jet Nightclub
LAS VEGAS, NV

FIRST CLT *All Hands* **MEETING**

DANCING TO
Michael Jackson

COLD *Chillin'*

Create Fun
and a
Little Weirdness

(But remember that the only game of craps
happening in the pool should be of the dice kind)

ZiP™

Alec F.

employee since 2009

I find myself recalling the opening lines of a Tale of Two Cities.

Alex C.

employee since 2010

Fun, creative, accepting, evolving ... a few keywords that define the Zappos Culture. I've only worked and lived here for half a year, but feel like I've accomplished so much. Working at Zappos really made the transition extremely easy, and I have the inviting and friendly individuals here to thank for that. I'm extremely happy to be part of the family!

Amara S.

employee since 2005

2011 marks my sixth year at Zappos. It is amazing to look back at all we accomplished while looking forward to the many exciting opportunities that lie ahead. No other work environment has given me the freedom to truly impact change. It is refreshing to know so many people believe in me and challenge and inspire me constantly. I am surrounded by people I will continue to call my friends for many years to come. We are all a part of something special.

Amelia S.

employee since 2009

This place is amazing. Nowhere else would I have had the opportunities I've had here, and I will certainly never be able to work for any other company ever again. Can't wait to see where we're going next.

Andi E.

employee since 2010

The Zappos Culture is pretty much the opposite of the culture anywhere else I've worked. The customer's experience is first and foremost and this applies equally to internal and external customers. Great ideas can come from anyone. Nothing is impossible. Get it done. Stop and celebrate (even small) successes, but then quickly move on to the next goal.

Anonymous

employee since 2002

The more things change, the more they stay the same. That's not an easy thing to do for a company that has grown so much in the span of over a decade. It is fascinating to see that despite all the growth that we have experienced and all the changes we have gone through, Zappos' core component ... its culture...remains the same. One big difference, however, is the number of people who have embraced that culture. Aside from the fact that Zappos employs a lot more people now than it did back in 1999, it seems that the Zappos Culture is being embraced by people outside of Zappos, including companies we work with, Zappos customers and business owners that have picked up "Delivering Happiness — A Path To Profits, Passion, and Purpose." It is astonishing to see the impact a company that is passionate about customer service can have.

Anonymous

employee since 2005

To me, the amazing part of the Zappos Culture is that while the company is significantly larger than it was when I first started and its culture has evolved, the important parts of the culture have remained the same. I see many of my co-workers as life-long friends and the family environment is still present.

Anonymous

employee since 2007

This year, for me, the Zappos Culture means friends, family, fun, perseverance, sweat, and tears (of joy, of course!). Friends and family come to mind first because I've always felt at home working with my Zappos peeps. Regardless of how crazy things get, they are here to support me and vice versa. When things get tough, everyone pulls together to meet our goals. In the end, all the late nights and hard work mean so much more when you work with great peeps like this. I love Zappos and there's no place like it!

Anonymous

employee since 2008

Corporate individuality (or how to be "me" in the "we").

Anonymous

employee since 2010

So another year has passed. Things are fast and furious right now and I am actually at a loss. All that jumps into my head at this moment is "It is what it is" and " Pushing a bunch of buttons."

Anonymous

employee since 2010

Zappos means never having to say you are sorry. There are no rules and you won't be filtered in what you say, wear, etc.

Anonymous

employee since 2010

To me, the Zappos Culture is ordered chaos. It is a collection of everyone's ideas and opinions, which can make it chaotic. And yet, there is a force that guides everyone towards a goal, and which brings order from all the chaos. It is very rare to see such a phenomenon at a workplace. There is usually so much order that things get stale and stifling, or there is so much chaos that nothing is achieved and all goes to oblivion. However, the Zappos Culture is balanced. People can form their own ideas and implement them. There is so much activity that it seems like chaos at all times. Yet for some reason, things actually get done. I eventually realized from all these different ideas, everyone just wants to help one another improve and achieve goals.

Anonymous

employee since 2010

What is Zappos? I was SO happy when I only had a chance to interview with them, and it was so fortunate for me to be able to join them right out of college. I was one of those who think thought everything you heard on the outside was just for attention, so people would know about Zappos. NOPE. Not so. Everything you hear on in the media is true. I <3 this company! Now we add Z in front of everything. The culture is just Zawesome! It is LITERALLY my Zecond family here. 1337 <3 (Yep, so nerd of me)! And where else can you have nerfNerf - guns wars at work?

Anonymous

employee since 2010

The Zappos Culture means a diverse group of people can work well together. Not easy to accomplish and it doesn't always work, but when it does, it's the greatest place. I think the Zappos Culture is continually evolving and I'm interested to see what it will be like in a few years.

Arsi bABA

employee since 2011

WOW! I've been here for only a month or so and it feels as if I've found a family away from home. The Zappos Culture, to me, is finding people who make it hard for you to remember what you used to do and how you lived before you came here. Having traveled a few thousand miles here, I already feel at home.

Aye T.

employee since 2010

The Zappos Culture means leaving a home, moving to a new city, getting a new job and still feeling like it was the best decision I've made in a while.

Zappos is dynamic and fun; barriers that would normally be there are missing. Change seems to be the norm. I don't know what the future holds and yet it doesn't bother me. I always thought making new friends in a new city would be much harder, but Zappos has proven me wrong. There's also that intangible glow telling me that, even though it's just work and I'm digging in the trenches, there's a bigger picture out there and I can be making a difference to the life around me.

Barrinator V.

employee since 2009

The Zappos Culture allows me to think outside of the box, present my ideas to listening ears and pursue the betterment of our organization as a whole. It is a feeling of empowerment and freedom of thought and logic. This is unique within the context of my career and I'll always appreciate and hold true to this philosophy. :)

Bill W.

employee since 2007

Without fail, when someone finds out that I work for Zappos, the first thing I'm asked is: "Is it as great a place to work there as I've heard?" It's awesome to be able to honestly say that it is. It's also great to work for a company with such a genuinely positive image – not simply a corporate hype machine.

Bob S.

employee since 2010

I've only been here a short time, but I can say without a doubt that the Zappos Culture is something that must be experienced. Words cannot do it justice.

The Zappos Culture allows people to be themselves, both in terms of behavior and attire. It empowers each individual to grow. Each day is a new adventure filled with fun, excitement, and awesome events that are shared among a group of amazing people!

Bobby M.

employee since 2010

The Zappos Culture, to me, means bringing all kinds of different people, with different personalities and religious backgrounds, together to form one family.

Brent C.

employee since 2007

It is easiest for me to define the Zappos Culture by looking at other words for culture, including sophistication, refinement, urbanity, civilization, cultivation, polish, taste, discernment, discrimination, society, mores, background, traditions, ethnicity, customs, ways of life, ethos, philosophy, values, principles and beliefs.

Brian E.

employee since 2011

Las Vegas is a great city, but it's a tough city as well. It's hard to find a place where you really fit in. For me, Zappos has been that place. Take hiking, for example. I used to hike most weekends by myself, unable to coax my friends to join me. Now I have a family of hiking buddies, and they've shown me some of the coolest routes I've seen around Vegas. That's what the Zappos Culture means to me: Finding a good group of friends who care about you and want to share their passions in a really fun way. It's been amazing.

Brian K.

employee since 2010

The Zappos Culture means having a work family that is genuinely interested in your personal success. It means leadership as an opportunity to serve. It means a continual pursuit of happiness by helping others pursue happiness.

Bryce M.

employee since 2009

Work hard. Play harder.

Christopher W.

employee since 2008

This is a modified "book cipher"... I have downloaded a book (the plain text version) from Project Gutenberg to encode my entry this year. Each number is the character-offset into that file. That means the first character is 0, the second is 1, etc (yeah, it's C-style indexing. Live in the now!) Find one of my favorite books out there, and use it to see my message! Let me know if you managed it - by then you'll know how. Oh, and one hint, although you shouldn't need it: revenge. 2412774 1751120 2570563 2185379 1305544 1687451 1990316 2212533 1492060 1029507 383722 1584024 1350502 2092764 387711 1767754 1047021 1960211 2140752 360659 1092852 772287 2547153 1473893 1251140 776610 377265 758666 2394593 1522393 385880 1540362 2137351 1876247 30675 1738887 33825 2599595 140530 235928 1600953 295146 1772235 574024 644840 500906 2626720 1768499 1330357 2170941 439835 2241762 1511170 2006556 2129815 1011839 2344678 279082 1643645 403721 289992 1138541 387346 1685753 1230418 44069 2641407 2153833 1763201 1634158 136965 1769281 300831 748261 842214 1861449 422660 951361 639742 134173 1090273 2467079 2455620 1206012 2627404 447978 308340 1224574 1359877 1944354 1489324 2104908 2004627 169279 2583678 587566 1290040

1039835 1738335 1691671 1043886 421392 2376199 2337382 873245 362098 235762 1674304 589697 451400 2130785 789889 961844 2194993 495997 298266 2150527 1194630 153370 1834589 1610997 341556 963065 834833 1512777 1939964 687751 1644269 1892983 1335736 2504962 946001 1594811 439068 1821401 802336 1740254 1605685 534400 1106866 2567274 844405 2156444 642149 1525992 334697 2646194 923405 1509422 284903 2103061 418816 542112 1475049 348376 325803 2445644 2645572 1626893 2006402 1137266 2558032 197483 2186062 36527 254616 908856 555294 2030821 2577158 574853 334971 2653028 2288663 604012 1858330 1030160 1366163 2448806 890533 167345 2307435 1070034 1799150 2324668 2191204 1843135 2212179 2113149 126049 2487302 747384 286654 1443027 335769 1386900 1164412 402177 1389633 1382300 1347587 101938 2103177 1108831 540314 2013595 494225 271328 2645781 407483 2589622 49198 2254530 1960081 1720277 1379054 140531 1085499 458044 2669535 535290 245125 1015573 2201279 476645 530249 2607570 939504 532334 2490308 439095 2151147 1580078 219204 2132110 654439 329259 1619352 1192378 1647992 1876447 1715168 2422363 1229672 1360801 1881731 2233365 2327892 454200 536940 194989 897192 1333727 1878328 668719 335627 1349523 743 39334 1983945 1234953 279720 1477558 454733 545216 2178796 1308250 1116003 738683 2486438 1389914 1836920 1967068 1136300 1186170 613643 2341131 219991 2013096 1781002 1979578 637871 2366699 1136966 1184294 1531457 1750780 1591065 593317 1127540 2359568 521222 1619260 2406633 382766 1302067 1381140 196196 2062550 1429373 1795918 1950125 1022223 1167238 2048080 1327943 105517 1967730 2552229 1594376 809014 1466379 893575 2379505 1164565 1710488 904652 1647307 1821681 127515 1778452 725785 805111 53507 1042053 2390867 1438604 200682 1327826 219837 661373 2260423 28728 1076046 1672392 1548003 1627714 354679 284438 2544915 2543241 2340860 1293518 367683 754875 2360021 1621549 1695620 1839057 2569364 1457534 21225 2097827 2567445 2105106 989238 2555476 2363270 1910865 1606153 1974564 247754 2320758 1796185 221089 1817471 1634834 1679080 378425 1120111 1878119 176295 495419 512199 404348 1339497 1279668 645752 1753253 2347980 432453 993728 2682937 1111334 2582241 1950969 733758 361195 131705 1816995 1451523 1758783   1503056

Corey B.

employee since 2011

In one word ... fulfillment! I came to Zappos at the beginning of 2011 and I can't express enough how much I love being here. Making the transition from a very structured environment to Zappos has been an interesting experience. I had been looking to join a forward-thinking company like this for a very long time. When I first came to Zappos, I was worried everything might be too good to be true. Now that I've been here for a few months, every day I see how genuine people are, how hard everyone works to keep Zappos amazing and to move the company to the next level. It's inspiring, and I'm glad I'm a part of it!

Crystal C.

employee since 2008

Zappos makes me wanna ... DANCE!
http://www.spiritdancerz.com

Danielle C.

employee since 2010

The Zappos Culture means "Come as you are." There is no need to pretend to be something you aren't or try to fit into a certain personality group. We can be open, honest, and ourselves here!

Danny S.

employee since 2010

The Zappos Culture is what drives this company forward. The force behind that? Our Ten Core Values. The force behind them? The employees that are living the Core Values on a daily basis. I wish more companies shared our values because working in such a fun environment (with parades and random after-work activities) has made me happier. I can tell people that I am really happy and look forward to coming in to work at 7:30 on a Monday after a long weekend. (Honestly!)

Dave F.

employee since 2010

Each person has a unique value system based on his or her experiences. But the collection of values shared among individuals is what makes a group's culture. That is how we identify ourselves as all belonging to something bigger than just a single individual. I go to work to be with my friends who also want to be part of something bigger. Along the way I happen to help Zappos make a buck. When it's the 11th hour, a decimal increase in some stock price doesn't motivate me as much as making sure my friends are taken care of. Even if that means taking another shot, breaking an old ping pong table, or having to reinforce the disabled parking rules.

Dave S.

employee since 2010

I don't like to think of myself as a skeptical person, but I must admit that there are many occasions where I am quick to doubt public images of companies and pass them off as well-spun PR. Prior to joining Zappos, I had heard stories of how everyone here is so happy and that colleagues were more like friends and family than just people you work with. And while I didn't doubt that this would be true in some cases, I was a little hesitant to believe that everyone got on so well. But it took a grand total of about two hours of working here for that idea to turn around. I asked for a recommendation for a moving service to help me move into my new apartment and within minutes, two of my new team had volunteered their Saturday to help me move. They even stayed for hours as we struggled to reassemble the most strangely built bed in the history of the world. Now, almost a year later, I could fill this entire book with stories of those around me who made me feel at home (and I'm a long way from what I would traditionally call "home"). Now I genuinely look forward to coming in to work, with no feeling of dread. There's plenty of hard work done here and the stories coming out about the Zappos Culture may hide that fact from casual observers, but it's not a burden. We have an amazing team around us to help us complete the work and learn on a daily basis. I came to Zappos after a tough run of some of the hardest months I had to contend with in the past 27 years, and I am genuinely grateful that the tough run ended here. I couldn't tell you one specific thing that makes the Zappos Culture what it is, but the net result is something unique.

David R.

employee since 2008

Working at Zappos reminds me of the expression "We are all kids at heart." It is interesting, because at Zappos we work extremely hard and always strive to provide great products and services for our customers. We do all of this while keeping in mind that we and our co-workers and ourselves are kids at heart. The opportunity to be ourselves in a fun atmosphere creates optimal working conditions!

Dean C.

employee since 2009

It's a dart flying by your face randomly. It's an intense afternoon game of Zing Zong. It's a beer with friends. It's a castle that surrounds your cube. It's a place you want to be. It's the place to be.

DJ B.

employee since 2010

Zappos is a place where people hold doors open for you. Not just the door to the building, but metaphorical doors too. If you have a dream, Zappos will do whatever it can to help make that happen. You can create your own opportunities and have support from every direction. Free ice cream is great too!

Dylan B.

employee since 2008

```
//Open your web browser console, type
this in and enjoy! var head = document.
getElementsByTagName('head')[0], script =
document.createElement('script'), jsonp = 'jsonp'
+ (new Date).getTime(), url = 'http://api.zappos.
com/CoreValue'; window[jsonp] = function(data)
{ var buffer = '<ul>', inc = 15; for (var i =
0; i < data.values.length; i++) { buffer += '<li
style="font-size:' + inc + ';">' + data.values[i].
name + '</li>'; inc = inc + 5; } buffer += '</
ul><a href="' + data.jobsUrl + '" style="font-
size:' + inc + ';">Sign Me Up!</a>'; document.
getElementsByTagName('body')[0].innerHTML =
buffer; head.removeChild(script); }; url = url +
'?callback=' + jsonp; script.setAttribute('src', url);
head.appendChild(script );
```

Ed L.

employee since 2005

```
Another year has passed and it's time for another
Culture Book entry. #!/usr/local/bin/perl use strict;
my $ed; my $zappos = 1; while ($zappos) { \t$ed-
>{happiness}++; \t$ed->{age}++; }
```

Emmanuel M.

employee since 2010

At this writing, I've been working at Zappos exactly one year and six days. It has been an incredible learning experience, both professionally and personally. Like all journeys, my journey to Zappos started because of my mom. She saw a segment on Oprah one day about Zappos and its culture, and told me I should apply. I looked into it online and I was sold. Long story short, I made it into Zappos and made the move from San Francisco to Las Vegas. I've never been happier coming into work. I love what I do, the people I work for and the people I work with.

Evgueni N.

employee since 2011

What strikes you the most when you start working at Zappos is how much autonomy and trust you get. This helps you take the responsibility and ownership for what you are doing, which results in awesome satisfaction for our clients and ourselves. Yes, help is provided upon request, of course, but there is no hand-holding. It's great!

Hina J.

employee since 2008

It is a great experience working with friends and aiming for the best customer service every day!

Ian Christian M.

employee since 2008

Though it has many facets and influences, I've always found that the Zappos Culture could best be described through the lens of the upstairs men's restroom of the 2290 building. There's a social atmosphere about the men's restroom. The long line to use the toilet leads to idle chatter, and quick updates are given while comers and goers wash and dry their hands. On the wall above the toilet, a clever Zapponian has provided a conflict resolution device for quarrels that happen even in a place with a "... Positive Team and Family Spirit..."(Core Value #7). A 12" ruler dangles from a sign that reads, "This ruler is for resolving arguments." We see in the men's room a space where people, "Embrace and Drive Change." (Core Value #2). In the corner near the entrance you can find a relatively recent innovation – a sturdily stacked cubby for dropping off laptops while making a quick bathroom stop between meetings. The floor is dry one day, wet the next. (Not even a billion dollar company is above a leaky pipe.) A true testament to "Being Humble" (Core Value #10). And what could be more "...Fun and a Little Weird..." (Core Value #3) than a plumbing anomaly that causes a toilet to bubble when an adjacent toilet is flushed? Unfortunately, we will soon be parting ways with this amazing restroom and moving downtown, where we can only hope that the restrooms will represent the Zappos Culture and uphold our Core Values in the same way.

Irene V.

employee since 2007

The Zappos Culture is like no other. Working here, I've realized that there is such a thing as loving where you work. It's great walking through the buildings and seeing friendly faces. It's also great to run into Zapponians outside of work. Even if you've never met before, you tend to gravitate toward each other and say hello. Our culture is something hard to put into words but wonderful to experience.

James C.

employee since 2010

The Zappos Culture involves more than just being crazy at the office with co-workers. ... It's about making our community a better place. Revitalizing old downtown Las Vegas into a community-oriented, creative environment is a goal a lot of us have now. I'm happy a lot of us are thinking bigger than just ourselves, our families and friends We are trying to make the world around us a better place and share that helpful, friendly Zappos attitude far and wide.

Jamie W.

employee since 2007

The main goal of the Zappos Culture has always been happiness. It started with, "How can we make Zappos a fun place to work for our employees?" Then Zappos took it one step farther and focused on, "How we can provide our customers with the best shopping experience online?" And now that vision has expanded to our community and "How can we share our culture with others?"

Jason H.

employee since 2010

One time we were playing Zing Zong, and my friend hit the ball so hard it went off the fridge ... and then off the water cooler ... and then off the window ... and then we all laughed. Then this other time, we were on a road trip and a hippie guy on our team kept trying to spoon with people and it was a barrel of laughs. Another time, we went to this laser tag place and I shot my friends with lasers and it was cool. Then one time we went to a meeting and the projector wouldn't turn on so we made funny jokes about that.

Jeffery N.

employee since 2008

The Zappos Culture is about making a difference in the company and for our customers. It is the freedom to try new things and take risks in hope of making a better experience for all involved. Zappos accepts everyone just as they are and lets them be themselves to contribute to an overall culture.

Jeffrey S.

employee since 2010

What does Zappos Culture means to me? Well, that is easy! It's about being awesome! At most companies, work is all about coming in, doing your eight hours a day and then leaving. Where's the fun in that? That's not being awesome. Here, I feel like people work hard and play harder. They are awesome because we all enjoy working here; we want to succeed, which makes us work hard. But then we also love hanging out with each other and doing fun stuff at work. Yeah, not every day is glorious, but we all try to make it as fun as we can. It works. In part, we strive to be awesome to our customers! We try our best to do a great job, no matter what. We go out of our way to help those who need it. That is pretty awesome to me. Not to mention that I honestly think we are about more than money here. There are lots of things that we do to try to help out. Aside from the numerous charity events we sponsor, we are also trying to make our community a lot better. There are groups working into building up the downtown community to be ... well ... awesome like us. It's all about being awesome and striving to be more awesome!

Jen W.

employee since 2009

To me, the Zappos Culture means amazing friends and providing lots of opportunities to learn. Working with people I respect, admire, and have fun with outside of work has made a huge difference in my life and is something I'll never take for granted. Being encouraged to learn new things – whether it be through conferences, "Hack-a-Thons," or from the countless people who are smarter than me – is something other companies don't value as highly as Zappos does. I've become a much better person, both personally and professionally, just from being surrounded by people who are hungry to learn and willing to teach.

Jennifer V.

employee since 2009

To me, the Zappos Culture means being able to have some serious fun while doing some serious work! We all work hard and well together, but there's not a day that goes by that there isn't some sort of shenanigans going on that makes the workday more enjoyable and just funny! There has not been one day in my almost two years here that I haven't LOL'd at least once!

Rock on, Dev!

Jesse C.

employee since 2005

I've said a lot about the Zappos Culture over the years, but this year I've learned something new and amazing. Our culture is not one thing or one idea. It's many rolled into one, and visiting the different departments of our company will really give you a sense that we truly are a large family. It's exciting to see that we are able to shape our culture based on our own traits, and that sub-cultures spring up as a result. Changing departments has been an interesting and enjoyable experience for me. It's like we're all singing the same tune, but we don't all sing it the same way. In the end, we all know the lyrics, and we can't wait to hear how others sing the song.

Jia T.

employee since 2010

The Zappos Culture is by far the thing I enjoy the most about this job. I enjoy everyone's friendliness and enthusiasm on a daily basis. It makes coming to work each day a very enjoyable experience. I love all the activities that go on here, from the haunted house to the peep shows. Things like this relieve stress and make the day that much more enjoyable. After coming to Zappos, I noticed that I have become a much happier person. I am more outgoing and more social. I enjoy the friends I make here. We do a lot of things outside of work, such as hiking and running. It's very easy to find a group with similar interests. The culture here is so great that it makes it fun to be here. Everyone is respectful and open with each other. It's definitely the place to be.

Jimmy J.

employee since 2010

 rt @therealkatzer curl http://api.zappos.com/
CoreValue?excludes=description | python -mjson.tool

Joel J.

employee since 2010

In the time I have been here, I have learned that I get out of the Zappos Culture what I put into it. By being active in the culture, I gain a sense of community. Those who complain they don't get what everyone is talking about are those who sit on the side when the team is decorating a workspace, doing a parade, or any of the other things that strengthen bonds. In addition, the culture isn't just about what I get out of it, but what my team and the organization gets out of me and everyone here from living the culture. Having a strong understanding of the culture is the backbone of our success, and that is what allows us to quickly work through any issues and towards success.

John B.

employee since 2009

It all starts with http://api.zappos.com/CoreValue. Our Core Values really drive our culture. Below are some of my experiences with the Core Values.
1) Deliver WOW Through Service: Our Holiday Helper Program where every Zappos Employee hops on the phone to help customers in our busiest time of the year.
2) Embrace and Drive Change: ZFrogs . Have a great idea but don't have the means to get it done. Pitch it to our internal venture capital group.
3) Create Fun and A Little Weirdness: Tech Doughnut Eating Contest.
4) Be Adventurous, Creative, and Open-Minded: "Hack-a-thons" give us time to try some off-the-wall project that may never see the light of day.
5) Pursue Growth and Learning: Coding Challenge Fridays allows us to learn from each other and have some fun at the same time.
6) Build Open and Honest Relationships With Communication: This Core Value allows us to communicate to our co-workers when we feel like something was not properly handled. It makes putting things out in the open a lot easier.
7) Build a Positive Team and Family Spirit: My Zappos co-workers have become some of my best friends. I think this says it all.
8) Do More With Less: Sometimes we do Less with More – our Rube Goldberg Machine competition.
9) Be Passionate and Determined: Work isn't all fun and games. When things get tough, it helps that everybody has your back. Providing late night dinners when you are putting in overtime always helps.
10) Be Humble: Usually the response when somebody takes on a Herculean task for you is "Oh, it was no big deal." The truth is that it was a big deal, and we have different employee recognition programs to really let somebody know that they rock!

John P.

employee since 2008

Like all good things, there are highs and lows. "Don't cry because it's over, smile because it happened." – Dr. Seuss "Sometimes you're flush and sometimes you're bust, and when you're up, it's never as good as it seems, and when you're down, you never think you'll be up again, but life goes on." Just remember that we <3 you no matter what. That's what family is all about.

Johnny P.

employee since 2007

The Zappos Culture means saying no to brilliant candidates because they fail the culture aspect of the interview. Most companies would find a way to make an exception. Not Zappos. You can be the world's best developer, manager, or merchandiser, but if you are not humble, passionate, and (fill in the other eight core values) you will not have the privilege of being part of the Zappos family. Tony, Fred and the rest of the leadership team worked too hard for too long to make exceptions now. There are brilliant folks out there who are amazing culture fits. Finding them can be needle/haystack hard, but it is a wonderful experience when that candidate walks in the room.

Jon W.

employee since 2010

I started work in the Zappos office this year and it has been the most welcoming environment I've ever experienced. People go out of their way to introduce themselves to you – even people you may not be working with directly. I've been invited to lunches, dinners and a large number of social activities organized by people at Zappos. It's amazing how friendly everyone has been. In the office, people are very receptive to ideas and suggestions and will take time to explore them with you no matter how big or small they may be. Innovation and just trying things are encouraged to see what works. The effort and enthusiasm that people put in each day rubs off on you, from people on reception to senior management. The all-hands meetings have been a real eye opener to see what happens in other areas of the company; the videos and performances are really entertaining and make you realize how creative people are throughout the company.

KAAAAANG!

employee since 2008

The Zappos Culture means that when I want to discuss zombie survival strategies, I can approach and debate with the people I work with about this legitimate apocalypse scenario.

Keith T.

employee since 2011

The most amazing aspect of the Zappos Culture is the way everyone joins together into a family. A quote from Richard Bach I read over 30 years ago has proven true without exception in my personal life, but I've not experienced the same truth professionally: "The bond that links your true family is not one of blood, but of respect and joy in each other's life. Rarely do members of one family grow up under the same roof." Zappos has proven to me this truth not only exists in a professional setting, but it can thrive! Having your family's back – and knowing they have yours – removes failure as a possible outcome of taking risks, leaving only learning or success. As I said ... Amazing!

Kevin C.

employee since 2008

Zappos is everything a modern, progressive, thinking company should be and is. Our culture drives everything we do – our fantastic interaction with our customers and how we operate. Lots of companies claim they have a culture, but few live and breathe the culture in reality. Knowing that I have the Zappos Culture behind me really makes a difference, in both my work and home life. The Zappos Culture, to me, means I have real friends and I am part of a thriving community here at Zappos.

Lauren A.

employee since 2007

A Kind of Embarrassing Quote From My 2001 High School Journal That is Relevant, I Promise
Age 16: "I keep talking about that, don't I? 'I want to be a part of something.' Makes it sound like I want to join a cult or a secret society or some other crazy group, but really, the 'part of something' I'm referring to is friends. I want to be a part of another person, or people ... "
This is my fourth Zappos Culture Book entry since becoming a part of the cult/secret society/crazy group known as Zappos. WOW! I believe it and I don't. I mean, I believe that I've been with Zappos for over three years now, but I feel like I've grown and learned and changed enough for ten lifetimes. If you're one of the multitudes of executives or managers or recruiters from other companies who have requested a Culture Book in order to learn more about the Zappos Culture, read this next sentence. Zappos allowed me, a kid with no degree and no experience, to go from call center employee to technical business analyst in three years. Let me repeat that and give it its own offset paragraph, maybe in bold if our Culture Book designer is cool with it:
Zappos allowed me, a kid with no degree and no experience, to go from call center employee to technical business analyst in three years.
If you're looking for the best way to integrate aspects of Zappos Culture into your own business, don't look at the fun stuff. Don't get me wrong – I love fun! (I put the fun in functional requirements!) But what sets Zappos apart is that we've created an environment where we identify and recognize internal talent – where even entry-level employees feel as though they're being set up for success and not failure, where you're able to build a career with a company that you love and pursue bigger dreams than your experience might allow.

And this happened organically, because Zappos Culture is about building relationships – Why wouldn't you want your friends to go on to great things? As a result, it's a place where people genuinely care for you and want you to succeed. And where they want you around for the fun stuff. Because you're a part of it.

Lenny B.

employee since 2011

I think the word "fate" has the wrong connotation, but here's the set of circumstances that led me here, in a remarkably straightforward manner:
* I've had a long friendship with one Ian M., legendary developer of Mappos, although I had only met him in person a handful of times.
* Several rounds of layoffs left me the lone developer in my office, which wasn't a bad situation, but in hindsight, not the best place for me to be.
* Former coworkers encouraged me to explore new options, which let me practice interviewing and learn to recognize a good thing when comes up, and then go after it with all I have. I had no idea how soon I would put this lesson to use.
* My boss finally set up a long-overdue trip to our Costa Rican office, probably more as an effort to placate the remaining developers at the company.
* Only on the flight I had a middle seat between an impossible-to-understand tico and Melanie BallecerB ., contract recruiter for Zappos. They were the first of many wonderfully friendly people I would meet over the next several months.
* A week later, Zappos announced the plans for a new San Francisco office. Melanie called me a few days later and the rest is history. I'm so fortunate that, of all the places this path could have taken me, I ended up here. It isn't hard to understand why many people consider Zappos a "calling."
I've told this story a million times in the last four months and have yet to tire of it. But I'm telling it less frequently these days because I'm more excited about our amazing new office, my beautiful life in this new city, and all the bigger and better things I'll have to talk about in the next Culture Book after a year of hard work and a lot of fun.

Lynn W.

employee since 2008

The Zappos Culture extends my family exponentially! (And I had a big one to begin with!) There are always folks who can help and/or amuse you. I love working here because we are a big family that works hard and plays hard. The passion that folks show here inspires me to "raise the bar" and be passionate myself.

Mark M.

employee since 2008

The Zappos Culture is awesome! We must make sure it is protected at all costs. I personally recommend protecting it via a rax/factory wall-in, although on shorter rush distance maps you may want to wall in with a depot/rax to prevent a 6 pool or other early cheese. After scouting on 10 or 11, if you anticipate early pressure you can throw up a bunker to further fortify the culture. After that, it's totally up to you. Cloaked banshee harass, m3 ball, mech doom push, there are lots of routes you can go to ensure our culture is protected and the game is won.

Mark J.

employee since 2011

The Zappos Culture, to me, means embracing who you are and who everyone else is and welcoming everybody's unique outlook. The collection of backgrounds and personalities makes this place something special – something that can't be duplicated because no two people are alike. Everyone is dedicated to the same goal, to deliver WOW, and together we shape the way we do that.

Maureen S.

employee since 2010

Last December I left my friends, family and work in Chicago for life with Zappos. I wasn't looking for a new job or a major move, but after learning about the Zappos Culture, I was immediately taken. This is quite a special place and I already feel like a family member here after four short months. I also have an abundant supply of Zappos T-shirts and fabulous prizes.

Mauricio J.

employee since 2010

My first impressions of the Zappos Culture were, "This is too good to be true." Then that thinking morphed into, "There must be a catch." Then it went into, "Be careful, don't lay your defenses down just yet, just remember your past work experience." And then it moved to, "It is pretty much impossible that so many people can be nice all the time." All this in a period of three months. Finally, I got to the point that, some random day, all my worries were gone. Then my 12-year old daughter told me in a casual conversation that, even though she was missing her friends from her previous school in another state, she was happy that I was not the "sad" Dad that she had been living with during the past four years. Thanks to Zappos, I am now playing Ping-Pong after a 25-year lapse, I am improving in my Zing-Zong skills, kidnapped Amara's pet llama and made her pay a penance that consisted of wearing a chicken hat for one whole day! I performed my first keg stand, I still suck big time at Beer-Pong, but I have dressed as King Tut, Chicken, Flying Pig, Medieval Knight and (best of all) I ate 11.75 KK doughnuts in 20 minutes with the support of all my teammates at Retail Systems. So now my life can be described in two important periods BZ (Before Zappos) and AZ (at Zappos). :-)

Meg M.

employee since 2007

I am four years old in Zappos yearz, and it just keeps getting better! I am amazed at how we all pull together to constantly improve what goes on inside and outside the walls of Zappos. That sometimes means moving the walls, climbing over the walls, smashing down the walls – or – installing windows. Ahh ... the kind of windows that allow views, not the software.

Michael M.

employee since 2010

Have I died and gone to work heaven? I am doing the work I have a passion for. I am working with the most amazing people I have ever met. I always look forward to coming to work where I can always be myself. Pinch me! My first year at Zappos is completed. I am so glad I made this lifestyle change, because Zappos is a better way of life, not just another job. Really!

Michael O.

employee since 2010

As a relatively new employee, I'm most impressed with how everyone really lives the cultural values here. From the smiling faces to the open attitudes, to transparency and "Ask Anything," there is a continual striving to embody the Core Values everywhere you turn. I've worked for a number of start-up companies because they are exciting, interesting and fun. It blows me away that Zappos has been able to scale up and keep the start-up feel. This is truly the last company I intend to work for.

Mike J.

employee since 2010

Zappos has a unique blend of outrageous and caring individuals without whom you just can't imagine working. They make your day brighter and awesome in every way, and the culture here is so amazing that I actually want to go to work for the first time in my life! Whatever I want to do or achieve, I get the feeling that I can do it here ... "In off the red!"

Nick G.

employee since 2010

Zappos means working with the sort of people you'd want to work and play with: People who are kind, caring, and who want to do cool stuff!

Nick P.

employee since 2006

What does the Zappos Culture mean to me? I think the thing that stands out the most is how it's very hard for me to draw the line between my friends and co-workers. I've never made so many good friends in one place as I have at Zappos. College comes close, but Zappos wins in overall count. I can't really think of any of my friends (outside of Zappos) that can say they are friends with more than one or two of their co-workers. I'm truly lucky to be surrounded by amazing people.

Pawel S.

employee since 2007

Testing ... 1, 2. Testing.
Diane, it's 1:00 PM. Henderson, Nevada. I'm working at Zappos and have been doing so for the last four and a half years. The people here are strange, but I've warmed to them and their zany ways. There's still never a boring day, and always plenty of new things to learn. I see a lot of Amazons in the hallways, but as far as I know, nobody has yet been sentenced to death by snu-snu (a truly horrible and wonderful fate). I've recently shifted teams from the Henderson-based development team to the San Francisco-based development team. In my haste and excitement, I seem to have forgotten to move to San Francisco (where the Giants roam, future home of Starfleet Academy). At any rate, I kind of like those guys, despite their propensity to be 600 miles away, so I really hope we can make this long-distance relationship work. I'm also pretty excited about the future, with our impending move to downtown Vegas. I've seen a lot of cool things already happen here in recent years and we have a boat-load of talented and awesome people brainstorming new ideas. It's going to be righteous. It also probably helps that I wasn't one of the people who just barely bought a house in Green Valley. Don't worry, guys – I've been driving 25 miles each way every single weekday since starting at Zappos. Get a subscription to Audible.com and pass the time awesomely. Pawel, Out.

Rachel M.

employee since 2010

The Zappos Culture allows me to do what I love to do in an environment that wants me to do it. What does that mean? Well, basically I get to use my brain in ways that other companies wouldn't (and haven't) allowed me to. I get to think outside the box. No mold to fit in, no red tape, and nobody saying, "But that's not how we do it here." I am given the freedom to do my job in the best way I know. I work with great people who are smart and forward thinking. There are lots of places to work, but not a lot of places like this. Thank you, Zappos, for that.

Ray M.

employee since 2007

The best part of Zappos isn't the free drinks, food, or even all the happy hours. While those are all (very) awesome, what makes Zappos such a great place to work is the people.

Rebecca N.

employee since 2010

What the Zappos Culture means to me is a chance to bond with my co-workers on a deeper level than I could in other companies. They say it is like a family here, but I would say it's more like what you wish your family were like. You can't choose your family, but here we have a group of people working together towards a common goal and building relationships along the way. It is so much better than most families.

Richard E.

employee since 2008

The Zappos Culture allows me to grow both personally and professionally. I am really happy here and I look forward to accomplishing our goals each and every day. The Zappos Culture allows us to work with people who are friendly, knowledgeable, and always willing to help. My managers and peers are supportive and involved in my career development. They challenge me each day because they truly want to see me grow ... and I have! Looking back on the three years I have been here, I am humbled by how much I have learned and how wonderful the people I have met truly are, both personally and professionally. Some folks here at Zappos have become close friends with whom I spend time with outside of the office. Zappos is a place that I feel honored and privileged to participate in each day.

Richard H.

employee since 2011

I have been at Zappos for about two months, and I am simply amazed that a job can be so much fun. The work hard/play hard philosophy is unlike any I have experienced in the past, and I wouldn't have it any other way. Just when things start to get a little too serious, a Nerf dart whizzes by, or a parade marches across the office. Crazy, right? While the fun is great, I am even more amazed by the people I work with. My co-workers are some of the most intelligent and genuine people I have ever known. I feel so lucky to work here.

Rick D.

employee since 2011

A breath of fresh air. An oasis in the desert. My most comfortable pair of shoes. Zappos feels like all of those and more – a great place to work, a fabulous place to have fun, and a source of new friends. Standing apart from (current) corporate America, the Zappos Culture creates teamwork, yet celebrates individuality. And while many of these things are not common in other companies, Zappos is willing to share this with anyone who asks. In short, the Zappos Culture – to me – means sharing. Sharing knowledge, sharing good times, sharing hard times and sharing help. From great support of charities to a great support system for each other, the Zappos family is a family of givers.

Rigo

employee since 2010

I often want to make use of various writing styles to eloquently describe a feeling, but felt that raw fit best for this one. I feel at home every day when I get here. I am surrounded by brothers and sisters whom I love and admire, and I am often challenged with obstacles that make me stronger. As such, I can't think of a better place to spend my life.

Robin C.

employee since 2007

Zappos allows you to work in an environment where there are always surprises happening and you can be yourself. There is never a dull moment here! I love it! I would also like to say that I think of my co-workers as extended family. They make me absolutely love coming to work every day.

Ryan A.

employee since 2007

Chancho. When you are a man, sometimes you wear stretchy pants in your room. It's for fun.

Ryan Q.

employee since 2008

This is my third Culture Book submission and things at Zappos are just beginning to cook. There is tremendous growth all around and big changes are coming, as all eyes point downtown. I think sometimes the work we do here should take second place to the "culture work" we need to do to prepare Vegas for us. Here's to another year!

Salvador S.

employee since 2010

I work here and all I do is break things! :P

Sara M.

employee since 2008

Yep, I am still me. That's what Zappos lets me be. Always know what's real.

Sean M.

employee since 2005

I asked you first.

Shannon G.

employee since 2010

To me, the Zappos Culture means being part of a company that is changing the way people think about work and community. Traditional rules of corporate behavior don't always apply and ... guess what ... it works!!!! It means having the freedom to learn, to take risks, and to act without fear of reprisal or admonishment. It means being with people who are respectful, kind, professional, and are not afraid of being a little weird! At the core, the Zappos Culture promotes diversity and uniqueness on every level, supporting individuality and creativity. At most companies, these are traits that people have to leave at the office door. The Zappos Culture is organic. None of it is forced. People are here because they want to be, and they have an acute appreciation for the blend of work and real life. Why does fun have to stop when you get to work??? Well, here it doesn't stop!

Shaun H.

employee since 2011

It's refreshing to be part of an environment where everyone shares a clear vision. Productivity comes effortlessly. Friendships are easily formed. I'm slowly taking it all in. But an environment like this is also intimidating. I've been given a unique opportunity, and I don't want to screw it up. Deep down, I know I'll be fine. All I need to do is stay true to myself, and that's the easiest thing to do!

Shawn L.

employee since 2010

I love Zappos because people here actually listen to one another. It's great seeing brilliant ideas that non-managers come up with get implemented. It's a nice change from a lot of other companies I've worked for. This is by far my favorite place to work.

Sheldon S.

employee since 2007

Recently I was thinking how much Zappos has changed as a company since 2007. I'm coming up on my fourth anniversary. I can still remember getting up at 5:30 am to go to my CLT training class. Our class was held close to the "Bald and Blue Hair Day" and just about everyone in the class volunteered to get shaved or dye their hair blue. A few people thought the whole thing was a bit too bizarre. One person in particular did not show up the next day, and they were done. If they had lasted two days longer they would have qualified for the "quit bonus." (LOL.)

I think events like this show that Zappos hires the right people, since it creates a family spirit by having weird or different types of events. I remember my remaining classmates to this day, and still say "Hi" to them in the hallways. Most of them are doing different things within the company than they were doing when they started out. I think it's important that Zappos promotes people from within the company. Some of the bigger changes I've gone through are: the development team doubling in size a few times, the 2008 layoffs (a low point), the Amazon acquisition (a high point). Based on how well we have come out of these situations, I don't think other companies deal with change as well as Zappos does. Our culture has basically remained the same during the past four years, which speaks well to the design of the Core Values, and our HR department hiring the right people. I look forward to Zappos continuing to grow and reach the top of the "Best Places to Work" list.

Siddharth P.

employee since 2010

The culture at Zappos is what really sets this place apart from the rest. Imagine a place where people are super helpful, a place where you can be weird and actually have fun while working, a place where every single day is special ... and where you are guaranteed to be WOWed by someone! Zappos is really awesome!!

Sotheavy O.

employee since 2007

A haiku:
The Zappos Culture forgives
Even a major mishap
Refrigerator

Steven A.

employee since 2011

"Work hard, play hard." Yes, it's a cliché, but that statement is probably the most succinct way of summing up the Zappos Culture for me. There is an amazing amount of dedication from the employees here. They are truly committed to doing their best work. Sometimes that means early mornings and late evenings, but that's OK because we all want to see Zappos continue to succeed. That being said, we also love to play. The word "play" has a broad definition here at Zappos. It can include impromptu parades, company happy hours, team outings, throwing pies at company management, Nerf gun wars ... the list goes on and on. There is actually too much fun stuff to get involved with! Zappos is easily the best company that I've worked for. There isn't any one thing that makes it the best. It's the combination of all of the great things that Zappos has to offer: the people, culture, opportunities, free food, unbelievable benefits, events, etc. all make Zappos the great company that it is. I still can't believe I work here!

Steven L.

employee since 2009

The Zappos Culture has created the biggest family I've ever been lucky enough to be a part of.

Stevo (Stephen H.)

employee since 2005

The Zappos Culture means a lot to me. I don't really even consider it Zappos Culture anymore. That's just the label I use when I have to explain what someone may perceive as extraordinary kindness or service in everyday interactions outside of the office. If they've heard of us, then they understand why I am the way I am, as if Zappos turned me into some WOWing machine. I don't think that's the case. I think Zappos has just done a good job of finding and hiring that kind of person, and I couldn't be happier working with so many like-minded people.

Summer D.

employee since 2010

I have never worked at a place quite like Zappos. I love the atmosphere of having fun while working, and that I can be myself without any worries. I've even caught myself calling this home!

Susan A.

employee since 2007

WOWza!!! Another year has passed and I am still truly enjoying my life here at Zappos. It is exciting to see how fast the company is growing and changing, but what is even more exciting is all of the ways that the company is staying the same. At other companies you would tend to see the culture and camaraderie slip away as the company grows, but in the case of Zappos, it stays just as fun and lively and close as Day One, just with more people. My direct team has grown too. We have a ton of new people and I have enjoyed getting to know the new folks a lot. It has been a big year in my personal life too, with the addition of my second child. What is cool is how important and supportive the team has been for me in my life, even outside of work! Thank you, PM Team and Zappos for making my career at Zappos fun and meaningful.

Sweatervest

employee since 2010

Zappos Culture Recipe
Ingredients: 1 cup working hard; 1 cup playing hard; 3/4 cup personality; 1/2 cup innovation; 1 tbsp. naughty; 1 tsp. nice; 1 cup FACT; 1/2 tbsp. Nerf; 1/4 cup party; 1/4 cup dancing.
Mix all ingredients in a company for a while. Put mix in the desert and heat up to anything over 100 degrees. Cool until Louisville humidity is reached and a small amount of San Francisco fog settles on top. Cut into 2000+ pieces and serve. Add alcohol to taste.

Ujwala B.

employee since 2010

A day full of smiles and cheer; lots of soda and an occasional beer; work is fun and not mundane; tasks here happy hours, picnics and parties all year 'round. Nerf darts are always flying around; stay clear or shoot back some with your Nerf gear; Core Values that keep us near and dear a place where mind is without fear.

Zappos is the place to be, for sure!

Vincent C.

employee since 2010

The cool thing about the Zappos Culture is that there is always an opportunity to be part of the culture and to participate in your own way. It's about staying true to who you are, recognizing individuality and bringing individuality into your work. It also means creating a positive connection with others and supporting each other for success. And... having fun!

Vincent S.

employee since 2010

I had no idea what was in store for me when I decided to apply for a job at Zappos about seven months ago. I had heard about the wacky environment, the parties, and fun atmosphere. I figured the stories were exaggerated or maybe just the result of having a random fun event here and there. You know, the usual corporate-type events like "Funny Hat Friday." Regardless, it was exciting for me, never having worked for such a large company before, let alone a company that prided itself on its culture and how it treats its employees. So I thought, "Bring on the funny hats!"

There were no funny hats.

(Well, sorta.)

From my first interview to this very minute as I am writing this at my new desk in a new department, I've been blown away. The wackiness and fun atmosphere is actually quite understated because it's not linked to any one person or event or thing. It is a natural attitude that is the collective result of our separate personalities that we are encouraged to express and share. The parties and fun events are just bonuses we all look forward to. With all the work to do and goals to accomplish, just like any other company, the Zappos Culture is the driving force behind the passion for what could have easily turned out to be just another place to work. Instead, it's an environment I enjoy working in, one where I want to give my best to my team – a group I have come to feel is my weird and lovable extended family. Every day I feel like I'm going to my second home, comfortable and secure in knowing I have somewhere I can work and have a great time doing so. But all of what is Zappos and what makes it special is not that it's some perfect place where all this awesomeness just happens. It's through everybody's effort and dedication to keeping the culture alive. It really is a living, breathing entity that would disappear quickly if it weren't constantly supported, not just by big company events, but (even more importantly) by all of us in how we work and have fun with each other on a daily basis. It is what we make it. That is truly the key to the Zappos Culture. And cupcakes! =)

Virginia V.

employee since 2010

To me, the Zappos Culture means being the same person at work as I am outside of work. I value having a distinction between work and home as far as my time and my priorities are concerned, but not when it comes to who I am. The Zappos Culture means that I no longer need to decompress when I get home, because work doesn't compress me in the first place! And an added bonus is not having to maintain a separate work wardrobe! ;)

Vitaliy K.

employee since 2010

Intense, undying fascination with the letter 'Z'. Zorro is a mere zlug under our feet when it comes to worshipping the elegance and simple beauty of this extraordinary letter. Almost everything invented and propagated at Zappos has to start with 'Z', like homage to a temperamental deity. Even the most zublime and intense zport of Zing Zong pays its respect to the best letter of the alphabet. Let the Z's continue to prosper, along with Zappos and this awezome company! All hail Z!!!

Will Y.

employee since 2010

If I had to pick one of our Core Values that best represented the Zappos Culture, it would be "Deliver WOW Through Service" (Core Value #1). It wasn't until my fourth week of CLT training, when I talked with customers all day, that it really sank in what WOW meant. WOW meant writing a thank you note to the customer who just got back from Egypt during the 2011 revolution. She took over 30 minutes to tell me stories of what it was like and how she felt lucky to be home safe. WOW meant surprising myself at how vested I felt in every problem a customer had. WOW meant helping a customer and literally have them end the call saying, "I really love you. You all should win the Nobel Peace Prize or something. Seriously, I love you!" People ask me "How does CLT training help you with your real job?" CLT reminded me that in everything we do, we should be able to WOW the people around us. If we are building a website, people should use it and tell their friends "WOW, that was awesome!" If we are working with the community, the folks we worked with should say, "WOW, those Zappos people are amazing!" When I'm working with my team, I want to help them leave the office and think, "WOW, today was an amazing day at work!" So that's my goal at Zappos: To WOW you till it hurts.

Yoandy T.

employee since 2010

The Zappos Culture gives me the freedom to be myself at work, not just outside of it!

CHRISTOPHE
Salon Night

CUSTOMER
Service Week

CHUCKWAGON
• Brats
• Burgers
• Chicken
• Slaw
• Baked Beans

2010 ZFC
Holiday Party

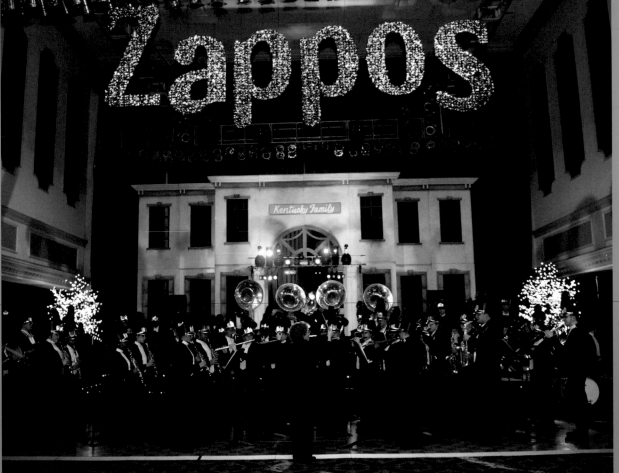

JANUARY 7, 2011
Horseshoe Casino
ELIZABETH, IN

ZAPPOS...
POWERED BY
People
(AND ANIMALS)

Zappos
.com
POWERED by SERVICE

Happy

Holidays

ZFC™

Build Open
and Honest
Relationships
with Communication

(With or without a microphone, it works wonders)

Aaron F.

employee since 2007

My, oh, my, how things change ... All in the spirit of Core Value #2 ("Embrace and Drive Change")! Although one thing has stayed the same – the way that Zappos continues to WOW me! I can still say that this is the best job I've ever had. I've had the opportunity to grow professionally and personally, and met many new friends in the process. I'm still here, with no plans to go anywhere! Zappos, you rock!

Aaron H.

employee since 2010

There are multiple reasons why I love Zappos. For starters, I love the free food because the money I don't have to spend on food I can put towards gas . I also love the other great benefits. Zappos has a great work environment and the nicest people to work with. I've probably worked in almost every department here, with a few exceptions, and I can't think of any complaints about any of them. Basically, Zappos is one of the all-around best places to work.

Abdullahi A.

employee since 2010

Zappos is the best place I have ever worked in my life. There's always so much fun and you make a lot of friends. One of the things I like most about Zappos is the Core Values!!!! I keep on reading them and I even tried to memorize them. Surely they mean it!

Adam H. aka big poppa

employee since 2010

Zappos is a good place to work. They take care of you, and that's all I have.

Adam M.

employee since 2011

A place to work where you can actually be yourself! If you want to die your hair blue, you can! And you won't be looked down on, because the people that you work with probably dyed their hair that color too!

Overall, Zappos is a great place to work, even if you're a little weird and crazy!! Just be yourself, and have fun with it ...

Adrian M.

employee since 2010

The Zappos Culture is more than simply having fun at work. Our Culture leads us to make meaningful connections with those who are sharing the Zappos experience with us, whether they are our peers, vendors or customers. Not a day goes by that I'm not WOWed by our Zappos family..

Al B.

employee since 2010

What sets Zappos apart from many of the other companies I have worked for is that the Zappos family takes our Core Values to heart. The Core Values aren't just some gimmick, spoon-fed to the public for the sake of promoting a positive public image. They are exactly what they are: The values that are the heart of the organization, and it doesn't take long for the new folks coming into the family to see how that the Core Values actually are part of the fabric of the company, from those of us at the ground level all the way up. Take, for example, Core Value #7: "Build a Positive Team and Family Spirit." I had moved to Kentucky from Chicago a few months before starting with Zappos, so when my birthday rolled around, I didn't know anybody locally. All of my friends were back in Chicago, and I was pretty homesick. While a lot of people take their birthday off to celebrate, I went to work like any other day, and didn't mention my birthday to anyone outside of a few of my closer comrades. My manager mentioned it at the startup meeting, and then I just went about my day. Some time after lunch, I was working at my packing station, and when I turned around, my entire team was standing there and started singing "Happy Birthday." Such a small, simple gesture really made going to work on my birthday the best thing I could have done that day. Never before have I worked for a company like Zappos. I didn't know such a positive company Culture existed. The support shown by those around us, the camaraderie, and the general familial vibe make the warehouse a microcosm of awesome rather than a mere workplace. The day I received my letter informing me that I had been hired full time, I was ecstatic. I didn't just want a job. I wanted to be a part of the Zappos family. Now here I am, and I couldn't be happier about it.

Albert D.

employee since 2010

What does the Zappos Culture means to me? Zappos is like a home away from home. It has a family atmosphere. Each day I come in I learn something new about myself and about the people around me. I have made Zappos a huge part of my life. I can't see myself working anywhere else after being here. This is the only place that allows us to have a fun experience at work. Another plus about Zappos is the free vending machines and insurance. But the most important thing I like about being here is the friendships that I have built with others and the understanding with my supervisors and leads. Any time I have an issue, I am able to sit down and to talk about it with any of them.

And on another note, the B-shifts rock here in Kentucky.

Albert R.

employee since 2009

The Zappos Culture means you are able to express yourself and not feel like you are left out. This is the best job I have ever had.

Alex C.

employee since 2011

Zappos is great! I have worked at many other warehouses before, and this one blows them away! I encourage everyone to try and work here at least once in your life.

Alex G.

employee since 2011

Working at Zappos is fun and crazy! It's like working in Wonderland, but without the nonsense, or like being at a carnival, but with not so many pony rides.

Alex L.

employee since 2011

I haven't been working at Zappos for very long but I can tell I'm going to be working here for a while. The Zappos Culture is unlike any other place I have ever worked. It is a very upbeat place, which is one of the things I like the most. I don't dread going into work everyday, which is nice.

Alex S.

employee since 2011

Zappos isn't your normal work place. Getting ready for work isn't something I dread anymore. Coming from fast food to a factory job was a big change but, trust me, it was worth it. There's nothing better than a fun work environment and that's what Zappos is. This is one of the greatest jobs on the planet, period.

Alex T.

employee since 2010

What I like about Zappos is that we get free lunches, and the people here are easy to get along with, and the shipping department is the best department in the whole place!

Alexis S.

employee since 2010

The Zappos Culture is a party! A party where the family all comes together and works to make sure the process stays up and running. I feel this way because at a party, you have a good time, and as an employee I have a great time working here with the other team members and leads. We all look out for each other and make sure we are happy and satisfied with what we do here. Zappos makes this job fun and bumping. Even though i haven't worked here for long, I already know I will never find a boring year at Zappos. Each day that goes by, something new and funny happens. Here's to all us weird peeps at Zappos who make that happen. Thanks, Zappos!!

Alfonzo C.

employee since 2010

The Zappos Culture, to me, is a gift from the gods. It's the enjoyment of learning about one another, as well as loving one another. The power of the Zappos Culture has been a new beginning for my life! :)

Alfred R.

employee since 2010

I like to work here because it's a nice place to work. You don't have anyone on your back. You are assigned a zone to work and you make your rate. I have no problems with working here.

Alice H.

employee since 2011

The Zappos Culture means the ultimate to me. Where else can you find a work atmosphere so pleasant that you look forward to coming to work the next day? Working together and being family-oriented brings out the best in everyone, which, in turn, makes Zappos a successful place of business. In the short time I have been here, I can truly say that I have had a WOW experience (With Out Worry). Thanks for the opportunity to be part of such a great establishment!!!!!

Alisa R.

employee since 2011

I have only been here for a week, but Zappos takes care of its people better than anywhere I have ever worked.

Allen H.

employee since 2009

Zappos is truly the best job I have ever had. Even with all the changes we have endured in the past year, Zappos still manages to keep the family-like atmosphere. Plus, we were ranked #12 of the Best Places To Work in Kentucky. Who wouldn't love this job?

Alyson M.

employee since 2010

Important! Important! Important! The Zappos Culture is important. I believe that it is a strong foundation that truly helps Zappos employees. Having ten simple sayings (Core Values) to refer to and remind co-workers of if a person needs a little encouragement during the workday is a great tool! Be passionate and determined, Zappos employees, current and future!

Amanda G.

employee since 2010

I may have only been here for a few months but this is the happiest place on earth. Disney does not have anything on Zappos!!!! We all rock.

Amanda H.

employee since 2011

Starting here was a scary thing. I was nervous that I wouldn't make friends or know anyone. Being here is awesome. One of the best jobs I've ever had.

Amanda J.

employee since 2010

The Zappos Culture means a lot of things, in my opinion! It's about friends, family and understanding. Every person you meet is dealing with something, and we should all be understanding and sympathetic. A smile can go a long way on a long day!

Amanda M.

employee since 2008

Zappos is a wonderful place to work. It has great benefits, including wonderful insurance. Zappos really helped my husband and me out when he went through a serious surgery. They were there for me when I just needed to talk. Zappos makes the FC a fun place to work. I think that Zappos is the best place that I have ever worked. Zappos is like a family; we are here for one another. The fun things that Zappos does for employees include employees' families. I think that is very cool.

Amanda T.

employee since 2010

Zappos is a wonderful and fun place to work. I am proud to be part of the family here. I honestly believe that the friendships I have made here will last a very long time.

Amanda T.

employee since 2010

The Zappos Culture, to me, means an awesome workplace. When you work with people who care about their work performance, your day goes by so much faster and you're having fun at the same time. Not only is Zappos totally rockin' for having free vending machines, but free lunch as well. I have come in on my off day and worked, just for some potato bar. De-lish! ;) Really, though, I love coming in to work and eating free food, having awesome managers and having a great time. Yes, we do have crunch times when we are running around like chickens with our heads cut off, trying to get that last order on the truck, but we still have fun doing it. I love working at Zappos because I feel like ever since I started working here I have just moved up, and I never want to quit!!!

Amber B.

employee since 2011

The Zappos Culture is the energy of your fellow employees and teammates at Zappos. The energy level is always high. Everyone is excited about the workday at Zappos and we strive to make it as fun and productive as we can.

Amber C.

employee since 2010

The Zappos Culture, to me, means a big family! Everyone here is like an extension of my home! There is so much diversity and everyone can be comfortable just as they are. No matter if you are covered in tattoos from head to toe, covered in piercings, or are just as happy as you came on this earth, everyone accepts you. If the world could be more like Zappos, we would have much more peace. Thank you, Zappos, for making my dream of having a job I can look forward to every day! :-)

Amber L.

employee since 2003

I say the same thing every year... I love my job!!! Enough said. :)

Amber N.

employee since 2011

I really like my experience at Zappos. It is one of the best jobs I have ever had. I have worked many jobs and this is the most laid-back place that I have worked in a long time. It's a great place and I really enjoy the job.

Amino I.

employee since 2010

I like Zappos!

Amro S.

employee since 2011

The Zappos Culture ... I left my job at KFC to look for a job that would make me happy and make some money at the same time. With the Zappos Culture, I can't wait to come in to work because of the culture that greets me here. This is the way that we need to work. It means a new life for me.

Amy E.

employee since 2010

Zappos is the greatest place to work. I am thankful they took a chance on a ten-year, stay-at-home mom and made me part of the Zappos family. A-2 receiving is awesome! I have the greatest managers, leads and team I could ever ask for.

Amy M.

employee since 2011

Zappos is my home away from home.

Andrea H.

employee since 2010

Zappos has grown at a phenomenal pace since I started here almost a year ago. The focus and pride that leaders keep on the Zappos Culture and the roots that the company was built on during our massive, fast-paced growth is amazing. Being part of a company that continues to grow and allows crazy fun during the workday, day in and day out, is something I hope I am a part of for many years to come.

Having the opportunity to work with the Las Vegas and Kentucky teams every day makes me realize how true and committed this company is to its culture. The ability to sustain the Core Values that Zappos is known for during all of the change and growth going on is a major success and a win for the employees and our customers. Zappos sets a great example to other companies. You really can grow at a fast pace and maintain the culture, while so many other companies feel they have to throw that away when they start growing quickly.

Andrea S.

employee since 2011

I am very new to the Zappos family, but I love the relationship between the supervisors and employees. I also enjoyed returning to my childhood when one of my supervisors asked me to hula-hoop. LOL! Too fun. I felt ten years old again! Gotta love Zappos!

Andrew H.

employee since 2004

Zappos has continued to experience phenomenal growth and yet has maintained its focus on the company culture. We have known for years that this will be the most challenging thing to maintain. However, through creative methods, a dedicated staff has been able to continue doing activities and team-building events while maintaining industry-leading service commitments to our customers! It is awesome to know that when you come to work, everyone around you will work together to accomplish anything!

Andrew H.

employee since 2007

Doughnuts on light sabers.

Andrew K.

employee since 2011

Zappos is the best place on the planet to work Need I say more?

Andrew M.

employee since 2010

AC Slater ("Saved by the Bell") once told a love interest, "Let's face it, you're caviar and I'm hot dogs." I think if AC and his love interest had met at Zappos instead of at the Malibu Sands Beach Club, their story would have turned out differently. At Zappos, everyone is equal. More then that, everyone participates in creating our culture – a work environment that is friendly, enjoyable, exciting, a little zany and always comfortable. I have noticed that this unique vibe and energy is manifest even outside of work. Not only do we plan activities and get together after hours as a team, but I am even more surprised by the amount of knowledge my family and friends have of my work experience. As if after a long ten-hour shift all I do is enumerate every last detail and funny story that had occurred at work that day. It's crazy how much I enjoy this job. Almost a little unhealthy!

Andrew N.

employee since 2011

To me, The Zappos Culture represents a way of life in a work environment that is rare. It is the reason why I wanted to be a part of the Zappos family! It is amazing how pretty much everybody that works at Zappos has a friendly face and is willing to WOW me, no matter what. There isn't a better place to work in the world and that's why Zappos is more than just a job. It is a way of life that, no matter how strange it may seem in the beginning, infects everyone privileged to experience it.

Angela C.

employee since 2010

I have been at Zappos for six months and it has been a really fun ride. The people here are the best! And who doesn't like free lunch? Having a job that you actually like waking up and coming to every day says a lot.

Angela H.

employee since 2005

Zappos is a great company. It's my home away from home and the people here are my family. Never have I ever worked for a company that works so hard for the team members. Zappos rocks!

Angela P.

employee since 2010

I love my job!!!! When I first started at Zappos, everyone invited me in with open arms and treated me like I was already a part of their family. Zappos is more than just a job!!!!

Anitra E.

employee since 2004

The Zappos Culture, to me, means coming into work every day and being able to have fun. We get free food, free insurance, and awesome holiday parties. Every spring and fall, we have festivals where we can bring our families. Since I started at Zappos, the culture has gone from nothing to something more than a job. I can never imagine leaving this place because Zappos rocks!

Ann R.

employee since 2010

The people here are great, for the most part. They are very patient with newbies. Great Christmas parties.

Anna B.

employee since 2007

I don't know where to start. I love my job at Zappos because it is the greatest job I ever had! When I tell people about it, they can't believe all the great things my company does for me. They pay all my insurance, feed me lunch every day and let us do fun and silly projects all the time. They give me $50 every month to give to one of my fellow employees. How awesome is that? This is not all they do, but I don't have the time to list the rest! Maybe next year?

Annette G.

employee since 2010

I joined Zappos over a year ago and I have to say it has changed my life. I enjoy coming to work now. I look forward to seeing all the different people that over time have become my friends. Every day there is something new and interesting to look forward to.

I try to incorporate The Zappos Culture in my daily living and that makes the way I look at things a whole lot different than the views of most of the people who don't work for Zappos. I hope that I will be here for a very long time to come!! Thanks, Zappos!!!

Annette S.

employee since 2006

Hey, the Zappos Culture! Well, where do I start? It is unlike anything I have experienced before. The feeling you get when you enter the building is amazing. Everyone is happy and friendly every day and all day. There is never negativity; always a positive energy. It is like everyone is family here. We get together after work sometimes and have happy hour and enjoy everyone's company. Zappos is always looking for ways to WOW us – karaoke, wii dance-offs, cornhole and free lunches. Where else can you work and have that much fun and get paid to do it?! It is amazing to work at Zappos and I intend to be here until I retire.

Anonymous

employee since 2008

Live every day like it's your last!

Anonymous

employee since 2010

The Zappos Culture means we can be one of the fastest shipping companies in the world with the stress level of a much slower company. When things get rough, people really pull together, making any job easier.

Anonymous

employee since 2005

It's great!

Anonymous

employee since 2006

The Zappos Culture shows me that the company thinks of its employees as more than just employees. Zappos makes coming to work exciting and more than just a job. The Zappos Culture also makes me believe that I can achieve my goals in anything I really wish to do as long as I focus on it and work hard. This company does more for its employees than any other company I have ever known. That's what makes the Zappos Culture so awesome!!!!

Anonymous

employee since 2010

Zappos is a great place to work. We have a lot of fun and do a lot of activities designed to help us get to know others who work within the Zappos family. There are also a lot of great benefits as far as moving up in the company and a lot of classes that are useful to each individual.

Anonymous

employee since 2010

The Zappos Culture, to me, is a home away from home. A place where there are a lot of new faces and personalities. No matter what kind of day you're having, there's always someone around to help you through it, whether it's the silly person who always makes you laugh or that one person you can always go to that makes you feel better and helps you realize you're not alone. Zappos has created a truly inspiring culture and organization that I believe is beneficial to each of us in our day-to-day lives and as citizens of the world. Where else could you be working and see a giant penguin running around snapping pictures? It's an all-around fun and caring place to work. Two thumbs up, Zapponians, for being totally awesome!

Anonymous

employee since 2010

The Zappos Culture means being able to express myself and be myself at work, as well as having fun. It is a completely different work environment from any other place I have been. It is focused on work as well as having fun and keeping employees happy. I love my Zappos family!

Anonymous

employee since 2010

The Zappos Culture is something unique and very special. It's what makes Zappos stand out from other companies. Instead of going through the steps of an average day at work like you would at any other job, Zappos has a surprise waiting for you at every turn.

Although a lot of our shifts are scheduled for holidays, Zappos never leaves you feeling like you missed out on the fun. They prepare wholesome meals for you to enjoy and encourage fun and friendly competitions ... Easter egg hunts on Easter along with an adorable Peep show competition that comes in April, candy-grams from your manager on Valentines day to let you know you're loved, and all sorts of other holiday fun. They don't need a holiday to have a friendly competition. For example, I've seen competitions for the person who can bin and verify the most items, with gift cards as a prize. But the Zappos Culture is more than winning prizes. It's about having fun and being able to say you feel as though you're working with your family.

Anonymous

employee since 2010

I have friends here, which is uncommon for me!

Anonymous

employee since 2010

Since I started at Zappos, I have come to see just how dedicated our company is to its employees. We dedicate ourselves every day to making our customers happy and, in return, Zappos makes us happy. I am awed everyday about how Zappos participates in a lot of charity events and I am proud to say I did the "Polar Plunge" for Special Olympics this year. I am so proud to have done it! It was so COLD, but that is what Zappos does . Whatever needs to be done, we find a way to do it. Thanks, Zappos. I am proud to work for you!!!

Anonymous

employee since 2010

I have no idea what it means to me, but I think that we could have more Culture-related activities to help make such a large place seem more of a family than a work place. That might improve our numbers and all our state of minds.

Anonymous

employee since 2007

I would sum up the Zappos Culture in one word: revolutionary! I'm not talking about some marketing buzzword. This is the only place I have ever worked where my ideas and opinions are truly valued.

I feel that anyone in the world can have the next great big idea, and it seems Zappos shares that same thought, because every person in this warehouse has a voice, from the person unloading the trucks to the person planning our yearly forecast. Everyone has the same opportunity to be heard. It's not just "Yeah, we'll look into it." I have seen ideas go from "Hey, have we tried to do ..." to "We are now doing it this way."

I don't see Zappos as a business; I see it as a force, and if we do it right, it could change the world. And that's what I mean by revolutionary.

Anonymous

employee since 2011

The one thing that I really like about Zappos is the fact that the environment at work is very fun, relaxed and there are many people who are into the same activities and music as I am.

Anonymous

employee since 2007

The Zappos Culture is a one of a kind!

Anonymous

employee since 2009

The Zappos Culture is unique. It's unlike any place I've ever worked. We have fun and still can WOW our customers!

Anonymous

employee since 2007

Zappos is a great place to work because you feel like family here. We have fun as we work. Zappos also knows how to throw a party, because it is less like a company party and more like a family reunion. All in all, Zappos is one big, wonderful family, and I love working here.

Anonymous

employee since 2009

The Zappos Culture is what keeps me coming to work every day. The people I work with are more like family to me than they are co-workers. I come to work knowing that I will smile and have a good time 99% of the time!

Anonymous

employee since 2010

When I come to Zappos I'm coming home here with all my family and friends.

Anonymous

employee since 2010

Even though I don't have ear gauges , tattoos and piercings, I still feel at home here. The team leaders are always in a good mood. You can change your job area and learn from the pipeline classes. The food and free snacks are a plus. I like the positive attitudes; it makes me feel better when I'm in a down mood.

Anonymous

employee since 2005

Getting up in the morning and coming into "work" has not been a horrible thing for me for over six years now. I have met some amazing people over the years and many have become lasting friends who have played a part in my happiness, both inside and outside of work.

Anonymous

employee since 2008

Zappos is a fun, interesting place to work. You get to meet a lot of new people and things are always changing. Zappos is always trying to incorporate fun activities throughout each year for its employees and their families. Zappos allows people to be themselves without any judgment. Everyone is treated the same as everyone else. I enjoy my job and working with all my co-workers. The benefits are great; I love the insurance, the free vending and the free catering, which helps out a lot, since we don't have to spend money every day for lunch.

Anonymous

employee since 2010

To me, the Zappos Culture is all about having fun while working. Whenever I run into somebody, they are always willing to spare a moment to talk. It really goes a long way for overall morale even in the toughest of times for the business. There's never a bad day here!

Anonymous

employee since 2011

Zappos is a very different place to work. It is a fun environment that lets you be yourself.

Anonymous

employee since 2011

The Zappos Culture is a free and fun environment. I have met so many new friends just coming to work. I love being able to work and have fun at the same time.

Anonymous

employee since 2010

I believe Zappos employees go out of their way to make things happen. It amazes me every day what we accomplish as a team. I was hired during peak season and I now hate boots. (LOL!) Obviously I work in Putaway. :o) Since my very first day I have felt welcome and at home. I have made some of the greatest friends that I wouldn't trade for anything. I look forward to the upcoming seasons working here with my new family. Bring on the boots! Thanks, Zappos!

Anonymous

employee since 2010

I have learned many new things working for Zappos. I have been given a wonderful chance to become part of a huge family. I have met some of the most wonderful people. The Zappos Culture helps people open up and find their inner selves. Being able to work in an environment that allows people to have fun and be wacky makes people feel at home. I could not ask to work for a better company!

Anonymous

employee since 2010

Very fun and great place to work.

Anonymous

employee since 2011

I have only been here about three weeks, but I'm really liking it. The work isn't very difficult and my co-workers are some of the most amazing people I know. When I do come to work, I pretty much just look forward to seeing the people I work with and my leads. They try to make things more enjoyable for us, which supervisors in other places don't.

Anonymous

employee since 2010

It's nice working at a place that doesn't require shaving on a regular basis. And the managers and leads (the ones I've had dealings with) are all awesome.

Anonymous

employee since 2010

The Zappos Culture is a good environment and people here work really well as a team.

Anonymous

employee since 2011

I have never worked in such a friendly, helpful environment. From the supervisors, to the leads, to the rest of the crew, everyone is willing to lend a helping hand and that has truly WOWed me! Thanks to all.

Anonymous

employee since 2009

It took me about half an hour just to find the link to write what I wanted to say. With the assistance of my friends here at Zappos, I finally figured out where to go and start writing what I am saying right now. As for what to say about the Zappos Culture, well, even doing something like this, I had so much fun. I love my job and I will tell people this every day.

Anonymous

employee since 2010

Culture is one of those words that describe who and what we are all about. It really defines us (Zapponians). Zappos is one of those fabulous places to work because of its Culture. I've never worked for a company where you felt like you could completely act as yourself, as you would with your own family. This is the first company that seems to really WOW their customers and their employees. This is a place of family and friends that work together to set and break records. This place really keeps people on their toes by making constant changes, as needed, and I can look forward to the future.

Anonymous

employee since 2011

Zappos is fun place and everybody here is fantastic. That's why I like Zappos more than my former company. I have never seen anything like this company. The Zappos Culture creates a wonderful environment. One of the reasons why I like Zappos is the free food, which other work places don't have. Zappos, you are the best.

Anonymous

employee since 2011

The Zappos Culture is beautiful for many different reasons. When you walk in, you see the drawings on the walls and how fabulously the HR office is decorated. Employees are offered free food and free health insurance when they get hired, which is really awesome. The other social services, like computer access, make you feel like you really aren't at work, not to mention the pipeline where you can learn about career advancement. All these things and more make this company look like a beautiful, small community. I call it the Zapposville community.

Anonymous

employee since 2011

The Zappos Culture keeps the work environment fun. Most companies tend to portray their work environment as overly professional. Zappos has shown me it is very much possible to keep a work environment professional while allowing for a little weirdness. I feel at home here.

Anonymous

employee since 2011

The Zappos Culture is very family oriented and we all work together as part of a team, and that is what our Culture is all about. Friends, family, fun and...oh yeah...work!!!!!!!!!

Anonymous

employee since 2009

I like my job.

Anonymous

employee since 2010

Zappos has such a friendly environment that I'm always excited about coming to work!!! I love the fact that they care about my well-being and allow me to have free insurance. Fun, friends, food and free insurance. "Yeah, Zappos!" Who can beat that?!!!

Anonymous

employee since 2010

The Zappos Culture means a diversity of people in a place having fun. It's a fun place to work and has sweet benefits.

Anonymous

employee since 2010

Zappos is a place to be original. It's a place to be yourself and know that everyone around you is cool with it.

Anonymous

employee since 2010

Wow, what can I say? This company has a Culture unlike any I have ever experienced. The sense of family, togetherness and teamwork here is something light years beyond most companies and it honestly took a little getting used to, after spending so many years in a different kind of environment where it was always numbers, numbers, numbers. It is refreshing to be a part of a company that really does care about its people, and goes above and beyond to try and ensure employee happiness. I am very proud to be a part of the Zappos family, and I will not ever leave here willingly. I will have to be dragged out kicking and screaming, hollering bloody murder all the whole way out the door! Thank you Tony and the rest of the Zappos family. For the first time in my life I can truly say that I love my job and look forward to coming in every day. (Well, almost every day!)

Anonymous
employee since 2010

My time here at Zappos has been amazing. I love the people I work with and I wouldn't trade this job for any other job in the world. Here we are family and my family is the most important part of me. We might all be different and weird here, but that is what makes this place amazing. I am proud to say that I work for Zappos.

Anonymous
employee since 2011

The Zappos Fulfillment Center is truly like a family. No matter what position you hold at Zappos, whether you are starting day one at the bottom or if you are a seven-year veteran at the top, people hang out, talk and get along. I have worked several places and never has upper management been so open and available. They truly have an open door policy! They enjoy talking to all the team members and encourage them to contact them to ask any questions. It is a fun place to work.

Anonymous
employee since 2010

I think the Zappos Culture is all about friendliness. Although not everyone at Zappos is friendly all the time, I think for the most part it's a fun and exciting place to work. It's not like most of my other jobs, where I dreaded coming to work and couldn't wait for the weekend. I really like coming to work now. I feel like all of my friends are here.

Anonymous
employee since 2006

I love that the Zappos Culture is like no other. Family spirit and kindness are hard to come by these days. But somehow here at Zappos ya'll bring it out in people. The past five years have been great. The long-term friends I've made here are priceless, and I would not change it for the world. Keep up the culture activities. To me it brings us team members closer together. A lot of companies do not push for fun at work but they ain't Zappos. Keep rockin' out!

Anonymous
employee since 2010

To me, the Zappos Culture means family and fun. I have met so many people while working here, and each one of them cares about you as if they were part of your family. Any time you have issues or just need someone to talk to they are there for you. If you're really feeling down, you can always count on your Zappos family to bring your spirits back up with fun and happiness. Zappos is the best place to work. You will always be recognized for your hard work here.

Anonymous
employee since 2010

Zappos is a great place to work. I love working for a company that does so much for you and encourages you to be yourself. I have actually got to put up a few pieces of art, which I love, around the ZFC and hope to put up more! Maybe in Vegas????? We all know how to have a good time around here, especially at work. :o) I have worked here for a year now and I hope to be here for many more years to come! I love all my Zappos family!!! Stay weird and classy, Zappos!

Anonymous
employee since 2005

I have worked for Zappos for quite some time. This is by far the best job I have ever had. Working here, you are part of one big family – a family that supports you in good times and bad.

Anonymous
employee since 2010

Since being hired here at Zappos, I have met a lot of awesome people. I haven't been employed at Zappos for very long, but I feel that some of my co-workers are like family. I enjoy all the culture events and the free lunches. I plan on retiring from Zappos, which is hopefully not far off. This is one of the best jobs I've ever had.

Anonymous
employee since 2010

Working at Zappos is amazing. There are so many benefits you get working here, like free insurance, free vending machines, free lunches, discounts when you buy items from Zappos online or in the outlet store. You even get to have fun working here because you get to go to the holiday party during Christmas and then there's the Spring Fling, where you can have fun and hang out with your Zappos friends, and the list goes on.

Working at Zappos is not like any other job for many reasons, a few of them being what I just mentioned. As for me, I gotta have my music, so I just like the fact you can bring in and listen to your iPod while you work.

Anonymous

employee since 2007

The Zappos Culture means family to me. A place to go and be yourself while doing a job. Coming into the building is like entering a picnic ground and all your family has gathered for a reunion. I have never enjoyed a job more. Since joining my family here at Zappos, I can't think of one day when I woke and said I do not want to go to work today. Every day is a new adventure here in Zappos-land and that what keeps it exciting. Love my Zappos Kentucky family! They show happiness all day long. We have Zappos Kentucky family spirit!!

Anonymous

employee since 2010

The Zappos Culture, to me, is the Core Values that Zappos lives by on a daily basis. I live by the same values on a daily basis at my house, raising my children. I have a made great friends here that I truly care about. Zappos treats its employees so well it makes me want to work hard for all the extras that Zappos provides – things that other companies do not even consider. Zappos has opened a new happiness door in my life. Thanks, Zappos, for letting me be part of such a great culture and company.

Anonymous

employee since 2011

All of the managers and leads I have worked with at Zappos are all helpful and fun to be around. They are a part of what makes this a great place to work!

Anonymous

employee since 2006

I've been with Zappos for almost five years and have enjoyed every minute of it. I recently visited another company and it made me realize how great Zappos truly is to it employees. I am blessed to work here and with such a wonderful group of people.

Anonymous

employee since 2011

Zappos is a really fun place to work. I love the free food, the happy atmosphere, and the benefits aren't too shabby either! :)

Anonymous

employee since 2006

I have been at Zappos for a while and I still really like it here. Everyone is so nice!

Anonymous

employee since 2006

Zappos is by far the best company I have ever worked for. When I tell my friends and family about the Zappos Culture and the fun things we do, they just can't believe it. This is the first job I've had where I don't dread going to work. It's very refreshing and I feel blessed to have this job. Thanks, Zappos!!!!!

Anonymous

employee since 2010

I'm new to the Zappos family, but I think it's an awesome place to work! Everyone here is so friendly and helpful. I've never worked for a better company! Thanks, Zappos, for hiring me.

Anonymous

employee since 2007

I will always cherish the experience that I have gathered here at Zappos because of the culture, the people and the vast system that is Zappos. The Core Values have made this job complete. The business part makes you more professional in the business world. I would encourage anyone to join this fine establishment.

Anonymous

employee since 2010

I like working here at Zappos because we can have fun while working – lots of teamwork, and great people. Everyone is always so eager to help or answer any questions you might have.

Anonymous

employee since 2010
Benefits.

Anonymous
employee since 2008

Go, Zappos! WOOOOOOOOOOOOOOOOOOOOOOO OOOOOOOOOOOOOO!

Anonymous
employee since 2010

What does the Zappos Culture mean to me? Well, it doesn't mean all that to me yet because I haven't been here long enough to truly like it. But for the most part, stuff is OK. What I like about Zappos Is that you can wear what you want and there are some fun times.

Anonymous
employee since 2010

Zappos is amazing. I meet new people every day and it really does feel like a family. Plus, free food is amazingly awesome!!!

Anonymous
employee since 2010

It does not matter how overwhelming a building makes you feel, it is the close feeling of family that keeps me coming to work everyday. My first impression was that this is a huge place and I am only going to feel like a number. To my surprise, after the new feelings wore off, it is amazing that I am cared for as well as I care for others. Thanks, Zappos for making this more than just a job.

Anonymous
employee since 2006

When I think of the Zappos Culture I think of how great it all sounds and how great it all used to be. But lately they have been falling short of following through with all the promises. A lot of departments seen to have time to participate in all the activities, but other departments are so busy that they aren't given the time to participate .

Anonymous
employee since 2011

I just started working at Zappos, but first impressions are good. Seems like a very relaxed place to work. Most all the folks I have run across are very friendly.

Anonymous
employee since 2011

Working at Zappos is a unique experience that I hope everyone can enjoy. From the game of hot potato at the end of the shirt, or Jeff dressing up as a penguin while sporting a wig, and all the other activities that we have done, Zappos stands out from the rest.

Anonymous
employee since 2009

Hard work to make the time pass quickly.

Anonymous
employee since 2006

Being a part of the Zappos family is truly a blessing. When I go to work each day, I truly believe we are all working together towards one common goal and that is unlike any other place I have worked. Everyone is treated with respect and dignity and that goes a long way!

Anonymous
employee since 2009

Zappos is more than just a job to me because it keeps lights on in my house, a roof over my head and food on the table. Zappos helps me keep on. So as I said, Zappos is more than a job to me. It means life.

Anonymous
employee since 2011

You meet new people and it's a fun environment!

Anonymous
employee since 2007

Zappos is a good place to work. I have worked for a few other companies and none of them give you free lunches. When I went to my first orientation, I could not believe what I was hearing. It was like a dream: free lunches and all the family outings they have. What more could you ask for? People are so caring of one another. I enjoy my job and my co-workers.

Anonymous

employee since 2010

There's a lot of culture here at Zappos. I like to think it's like a cake mix, and at the end of every day we have birthday parties.

Anonymous

employee since 2010

As of this writing, I have been with Zappos for approximately five months. Coming from the New England area to Kentucky was a culture shock in itself. Family brought me here and I was hired at Zappos one week after my wife and I arrived. Now I know that my family will be keeping me here ... my Zappos family. A high-stress white collar job is what I left behind and I joined a group of people who share my work ethic, my love of creativity and "coloring outside of the lines" when it comes to customer service. Nothing is too good for our customers. And to my new company, Zappos, nothing is too good for me. Can you believe that? Totally incredible.

One thing is for sure, if our country were run and managed like Zappos, we would have no homelessness, no hungry children, a cleaner and greener planet, no wars and no deficit. I am looking forward to my future at Zappos and am eager to move up as I learn.

Anonymous

employee since 2010

At Zappos, you can be having a day from hell one day and you come in the next day and find out overtime was cancelled for the week. Then you quickly forget about the day you had before and walk around with a smile on your face like you just won the lottery and you have the best job in the world!!!

They always try to find ways to keep it interesting, upbeat, and fun. It is so hard explaining to someone on the outside what our environment is like here. People just don't understand our quirky ways of making our days go by more easily. I would love to bring everybody I know here on a field trip for one day, just so they can relate and understand when I get excited about something different or quirky we had done that day.

Anonymous

employee since 2010

I absolutely love coming to work at Zappos. The people here are like my second family. We are a tight group that tries to be there for everyone, whether it be a good laugh, a hug or just a simple hi. Everyone is unique and different and Zappos embraces that. Here it is OK to be a little bit weird.

Anonymous

employee since 2007

The way Zappos cares for, welcomes and appreciates its employees is and continues to be like no other place I've worked. In a warehouse environment, it is easy for many to lose sight of this and set their focus on a single task (rate, etc.) But at Zappos, remember not to lose sight of the big picture. As long as you get the fact that a work place can be a happy place, you will thrive at Zappos, and you will find yourself surrounded by wonderful people. Overly negative people don't seem to stick around too long. It's amazing how that works.

Anonymous

employee since 2008

Co-workers are like your family here. I have truly made some amazing friends here. I am thankful for that!!

Anonymous

employee since 2011

I am amazed at how everybody here at Zappos treats one another. People from all walks of life work together. I've never worked with so many people of all ages and from different backgrounds willing to work together and get along.

Anonymous
employee since 2006

Great benefits, parties and even better co-workers, or can I say ... Zappos family. Yeah, Zappos!

Anonymous
employee since 2011

For someone who is relatively new to the Zappos Culture, the thing that stands out to me is that personal expression is not only tolerated (not so in many organizations), it is strongly encouraged. Going from a traditional environment where the expectation is that you minimize "non-work" conversations/contact and go about your business, to the Zappos environment where you are expected to open up and socialize is a change. You are not confined to a water cooler. The whole office is a water cooler.

Anonymous
employee since 2003

The Zappos Culture is about taking care of everyone you are working with. It is making sure everyone knows that they are special and that they have a purpose. Zappos goes above and beyond to show us that we are more than just team members ... we are also appreciated and part of a family. To some, the "work family" is the only real family they have. If you are going to spend 8, 10, or 12 hours a day somewhere, you want to be able to enjoy yourself and your company, and Zappos tries to make sure that is possible.

Anonymous
employee since 2010

The Zappos Culture means freedom. Freedom to share ideas. Freedom to express yourself. Freedom to have fun and enjoy yourself in a place most people dread coming to.

Anonymous
employee since 2011

Glad to be here and happy to be part of the Zappos teams. Zappos is a lot more fun and hard work than most people think.

Anonymous
employee since 2008

I have worked in places before that paid for your insurance, but never provided free vending machines, catered lunches or had employee appreciation days. This is by far the best company I have ever worked for in my life. I would recommend that anyone work here if given the chance. It's a once in a lifetime opportunity. I can't see myself going anywhere else any time soon. I have never loved coming to work as much as I do here.

Anonymous
employee since 2009

Simply amazing. The Zappos Culture is crazy, complex and yet, so simple. Get the right people together and amazing things happen. I love being part of a company that is full of positive people who work hard and play hard. This is my first job out of school and I could not be happier. I am surrounded by intelligent mentors who challenge me to become better. Thank you to everyone who makes Zappos what it is! This place is awesome!

Anonymous
employee since 2007

The Zappos Culture is awesome!! Where else can you go to work and be your true self?

Anonymous
employee since 2011

Zappos is the most laid back, fun environment I have ever worked in.

Anonymous
employee since 2007

Zappos truly is the best place to work! I am 40 years old and this is the easiest job I have ever had. The Culture is what makes us one big, happy extended family. The company itself does so much for its employees – from the benefits, catered lunches, free vending machines, free Zappos shirts, etc. I could go on and on. Thanks, Zappos!!!!

Anthony B.
employee since 2011

I've only worked at Zappos a short time and I can already tell it's a place I will want to stay with for as long as possible. It is by far the best and most fun place I have ever worked. Everyone and everything has been great so far, and I hope things only get better from here. Hopefully this is just my first of many entries into the Culture Book. Thanks for everything.

Anthony H.
employee since 2011

An environment that you can feel comfortable in no matter how you decided to represent yourself, whether you want to come to work in a black suit or wearing black make-up all over your face. Little things like this are what make this company an example other companies should follow, unlike the norm that makes you act like a person that you're really not or a person that nobody really is.

Anthony R.
employee since 2010

The Zappos Culture, to me, means ... the way things go around Zappos, how to carry yourself at work and what the company expects of you.

Anthony V.
employee since 2010

What does the Zappos Culture mean to me? It's a life-changing experience that makes you re-evaluate the way you've been taught to work by other organizations. It's the difference between being a contributor vs. just punching a clock.

Ashley C.
employee since 2009

After working in the medical field for eight years, I needed a break so I gave Zappos a try. I love my job!! I left all the stress behind with my old job, but not the craziness!! Zappos is crazy about craziness and that's what makes coming to work each day a new experience. You're never bored! Everyone is like one big family and we always have each others' backs!!

Ashley H.
employee since 2011

Working at Zappos is not just working; it is getting the job done and having a great time while you do it! I have worked with a couple of other companies and their main goal was money, money, and money. While we all agree money is nice, it's not everything. With Zappos, the goal is not only to keep the customer happy, but to keep the employees happy as well! What other company does that??? None. I not only work by the Zappos Culture, I live by it too!

Ashley M.
employee since 2010

When I come into work, I feel almost at home. I love the people I work with and I love my leadership! Who can say they honestly love what they do? I can. The reason I can say that is because of the people I spend my shifts with. During peak season, I was with these people more than my own family. And you know what? That is OK with me. Because if I can't be with my family, I want to be with my Zappos family.

Ashley M.
employee since 2010

The Zappos Culture, to me, is to be able to express myself freely. I love being able to come to work each day and not be afraid to be myself.

Ashley M.
employee since 2011

The Zappos Culture, to me, refers to the way Zappos differs from other companies. This is definitely a one-of-a-kind company; they try to make their employees feel like family, doing activities with employees and making us compete for prizes. They do such things as having company parties, like a holiday party for Christmas and a Spring Fling to bring employees closer together and make us feel appreciated for our time at Zappos. To me, Zappos is an amazing place to work, and the Zappos Culture is based on what Zappos does for their employees to elicit comments like mine.

Ashley S. AKA A.J.
employee since 2011

The Zappos Culture is about as friendly as you can get. The staff makes you feel welcome. It's a great place to work. You feel like you're at home here, but with a whole lot of walking to do.

Audrea H.

employee since 2007

The Zappos Culture, to me, is a complex mix of unity, family, goals, fun, trust, kindness, individuality, friendships, and values. It's the ultimate sense of unity to know my fellow Zapponian is as passionate about the Culture and company as I am. Some divine work is going on here and I feel blessed to be a part of it! Zappos is the first company that I've loved to work with and the last company that I want to work for.

Baby J.

employee since 2010

Three words that come to mind when I think of the Zappos Culture are fun, goofiness, and freedom. This is a place where you feel free ... Free to be yourself, free to remove the batteries from the robot that you used to be. We joke, we play pranks, we play games, but we still work super-hard. There are not many companies where you get to play basketball in the office while rolling around at high speeds in office chairs. That is what I love about Zappos; playing hard is as encouraged as working hard is. In under a year, my co-workers have become some of the best friends that I have and I truly enjoy coming to work every day. I laugh more at work than I do on the weekend. I love Zappos!!!

Barbara T.

employee since 2007

I love working at Zappos. I have worked other jobs, but none can compare to Zappos. I have made many friends. I love the challenge of picking, picnics and T-shirts.

Barry P.

employee since 2011

The Zappos Culture is about being a little weird. Now, don't get me wrong. A lot of us are weird, but some, more than others. That's what keeps Zappos unique.

Ben V.

employee since 2006

Zappos Culture: (n) 1. A way of life. 2. Communication without boundaries. 3. Pride.

Synonyms: 1. Having fun at work. 2. Coworkers are your family.

Beth L.

employee since 2010

When I first started at Zappos, I was looking for work to fill my time during my Christmas break. Zappos was hiring for a few weeks so it worked out perfectly. Then I realized that this place is more than just a job; it's like a family.

I decided that I wanted to stay at Zappos while in school. Bob P. (AKA "Pickle") was the first boss I ever had that I considered a friend. I've had a few managers since then (Tracy B. and Duane E.) and they have made me (and others) feel so welcome. They're amazing! Even when you're going to different departments to help out, those team members and managers make you feel right at home. I don't dread coming into work the way I used to in the past. Everyone is so willing to help, especially Josh B., my favorite lead. All my girls on singles QC always went out of their way for each other; but then again, everyone here does. It's also a FUN environment. Easter egg hunts, wii bowling tournaments, the holiday party and different outdoor activities. I may only be part-time because of my intense school schedule and I may spend my breaks studying and doing homework, but I'm thrilled that I am part of the Zappos family. I now know why Zappos is always ranked as one of the best places to work because it really is.

Beverly B.
employee since 2009

I love working at Zappos because it actually doesn't seem like work at all. The people here make it seem more like a gathering of friends and family than work. I have worked for many different companies and none can compare to Zappos. The benefits you get are outstanding and management isn't bad either. Zappos truly knows how to treat an employee as family and not just as a number on a time clock.

Bill K.
employee since 2010

The Zappos Culture means a lot to my family and me because they get to be involved in the fun things that Zappos offers. This past weekend, Zappos had their annual Spring Fling. We brought the kids and grandkids and they had a blast. When it was time to leave, the grandkids didn't want to go. Last fall was fun, when the Delivering Happiness tour came by here in Sheperdsville, KY. They had a live band, food and drinks. And this was all during work!!!!!

Billie D.
employee since 2010

Zappos means security for my family and it is a very friendly and exciting place to work. Everyone that I have met has been very helpful to me while I learned my job. They all seem to go out of their way to treat co-workers like family. I love it here!

Blake D.
employee since 2006

Zappos has managed to retain its Culture, which is impressive, considering the amount it has grown over the years. You will not find another company that truly cares about its employees the way that Zappos does, and I personally appreciate that. Also, I find it very comforting that Zappos continues to uphold our Culture, which is a crucial part of what makes Zappos so special!

Blake J.
employee since 2010

When thinking about what The Zappos Culture means to me, a lot comes to my mind. First off, everyone is treated like family and the environment where we work is absolutely amazing. The free food and the games we play to get know the new employees and the old are always fun.
It's also great that we are allowed to work in groups of two. I really enjoy working with people with different personalities and people with all kinds of weirdness. Everyone is weird in some way and at Zappos it makes everyone feel welcome and it brings everyone even closer. I really enjoy working here; everyone should be able to work at a company like Zappos!!

Bob P.
employee since 2010

WOW! My first ever Culture Book submission. What a great place to be! A place where helping others grow in order to reach their goals and potential is a cool thing to do. A place where telling someone they are awesome is totally normal. A place where getting a hug from a team member isn't weird. A place where there is so much to learn and so many opportunities to do so. A place where it is OK not to use spell check. Pretty freakin' cool!!

Bobbi K.
employee since 2008

The Zappos Culture, to me, is simply awesome! Work is fun, exciting and you never know what to expect! There's always something wonderful going on and we are ourselves – tattoos, piercings and even blue hair! We love the Zappos Culture!

Bobby W.
employee since 2009

I like the Culture here because of all the great people I work with.

Brad A.

employee since 2010

Zappos! What can I say? Free food, great benefits, free Zappos T-shirts, and really great people! We work hard, but it's balanced out by the fun we have. Our managers encourage us to think outside the box for ways to get the job done while having fun doing it. Company-sponsored events are always entertaining ... you never know what will happen or what surprises are in store.

I have met many people I am proud to call friends and as we continue to grow I am sure many more are on the way. Having a job where we are encouraged to learn has allowed me to get a broader understanding of how Zappos is run and that will allow me to rise in the company, making it a career, not just a job. It is wonderful to work for a company that is more than work; it is like a second family! Oh yeah! Did I mention free T-shirts! Here's looking forward to many decades of serving our customers the Zappos way!

Brad R.

employee since 2010

I had a great time at the Spring Fling this year. I came out a couple hours before my shift. It was kind of nice to get a couple hours off work in the sunshine. My parents came along to check it out. We got some hot dogs and cotton candy. It was pretty fun. We all enjoyed watching the millions of kids running around and playing on the bouncies. We had a good time and I'll be back again next year.

Bradly H.

employee since 2010

The Zappos Culture is the unique ability all Zapponians have to keep a fun, up-beat attitude through anything while maintaining a steady workflow. It's being open minded and fun loving, accepting anyone for who they are while being yourself, and having an enjoyable time while working.

Brandon A.

employee since 2010

I am a devout Zapponian. I love this place. I love the free food, especially as I am a large man. I eat, like, eight ice creams a day.

I love the people here. They know how to hire the right people. Everyone is easy to get along with and all the managers are really cool. This is easily the best job I've ever had. With every other job I've had I dreaded coming into work. Because of the work environment and people at Zappos, I actually look forward to coming to work here. I love this place!

Brandon C.

employee since 2011

Zappos is a great environment to work in and the people you work around are awesome! I have shared many good experiences here at Zappos so far, and have met many great people. The food is good and the grape juice is even better!!! (As long as you can find it; it's in the refrigerator!) Not only is the food good but, I mean, come on, who doesn't want to have a killer discount on new shoes and clothing. Also, the benefits here are great. All around, the company is good and the people you work for are even better. That's really all I have to say but I hope to see you!!

Brandon C.

employee since 2010

Well, what the Zappos Culture means to me is having a good time and a family-type environment as you work with others to WOW our clients with our service, treating everyone with respect and just making the work we do enjoyable.

Brandon C.

employee since 2009

The Zappos Culture: Delivering WOW!!!

Brandon K.

employee since 2011

I have only been at Zappos for three weeks, but the difference between the Culture here and the culture at other companies I have worked for is amazing! Here at Zappos, they want you to be yourself. They don't want you to be stamped from a mold and pretend to be someone else. This place is so different I don't refer to it as coming to work; I refer to it as coming to fun!

Brandyn M.

employee since 2010

Zappos is sooo awesome that I actually enjoy getting up to come to work. And the people here are great!!! Yeah, Zappos!!!

Brenda A.

employee since 2010

I try to be an inspiration to the younger people at Zappos. I love working here even at my age. I am retired after 32 years, but it is a fun place and keeps me young at heart and the walking gives me a lot of good exercise. WOW!!!!!!!

Brenda B.

employee since 2008

As the years have passed, Zappos has become many different things to me. My first year, Zappos was promise and opportunity because, as we all know, when you first arrive it's like Disneyland and you can't wait to get started on your adventure! My second year at Zappos was family and fun ... and we have LOTS of that!! Now I am on my third year and the meaning has changed yet again for me. Now, Zappos means personal growth and diversity. Zappos has given me an environment that encourages self-discovery and personal growth. I have learned in the last year that, even though you don't need that to help you look within, working at a company that has an environment like this makes it much easier – not only to look within, but also to grow and develop what you find! Zappos in my third year is the best yet, because I have looked within and found some more wonderful things about myself. Thanks, Zappos!! ?

Brian A.

employee since 2010

The Zappos Culture means that I get to come in everyday and work with really cool people that I have a lot in common with. We are all different in many ways, but that's the Zappos type of Culture. There's every type of person here, each with his or her own culture.

Brian C.

employee since 2011

The Zappos Culture has created probably one of the most interesting and (amazingly enough) successful businesses I've ever worked for. The spirit of actually taking care of your employees is what means the most to me. The simple things are the most important: no dress code, which allows you to be the person you want to be on an everyday basis; a free meal every day that you work, because I can almost guarantee that for some employees this may be their only meal of the day; and last but not least, the ability to actually advance in this business. Everyone, no matter how different, has a "true" equal opportunity here. The simple fact of not judging and taking care of employees will always make Zappos one of the top companies to work for in the United States. The Culture of this business will always keep the company successful and everyone satisfied to work here. :)

Brian F.

employee since 2010

Ten years ago I wasn't looking for a wife. However, the instant I met her I knew I had found one. Last year, I was just looking for a job. I wasn't looking for a change of culture and/or lifestyle. However, in the same way I met my wife, when I was introduced to Zappos I knew that I had found the community I wanted to live, work and play in for the foreseeable future, if not longer

In the past year, thanks to Zappos, I have met friends I consider family. I have been inspired to set and accomplish goals. I have taken a pride in the company for which I work that goes beyond anything I have ever felt before. I have had happiness delivered to me while Delivering Happiness to others. Wow!

Brian F.

employee since 2007

Zappos is great because they care about their employees and they're always helping out the community. I left the company once and came back, I will never leave again because this place is the best job I ever had the food and benefits are the best!!! The Christmas party is also off the hook!!!!

Brian J.

employee since 2010

The Culture here at Zappos is like nothing I have ever experienced before. What I really like about this job is that, although I have had jobs where my fellow employees were my friends, it was not like the friends that I have here. I can talk to anybody about anything and they listen. Plus, I also try to make time to chill with these guys after work. This company does not want you to come to work and not like anybody or not know anyone. They want you to come to work and know everyone in your department and just feel comfortable working here.

Brian K.

employee since

Ode to my job ... or, why I dig my career ... (Title still in the works)
I am a recruiter – a talent scout – and what better company to recruit for than Zappos?! I love my job for many reasons: the benefits, the environment and the culture. But the biggest reason is the people. I work with some of the goofiest, most eccentric, strangest, craziest, unique individuals I've ever met ... and I wouldn't have it any other way. The most enjoyable part of my day is seeing the candidates' eyes widen as I discuss Zappos and what it means to me; it's like watching a light bulb turn on as their smile gets bigger and bigger. I feel the majority of people working today have had jobs where they were miserable; jobs where they were unappreciated, unrewarded and unfulfilled. As if to add insult to injury, they are required spend the majority of their time away from their friends, families and loved ones. To truly appreciate what Zappos is you have to have had those negative experiences. Without life's sour patches, the sweet isn't as sweet

"The New Colossus" is a sonnet mounted inside the Statue of Liberty and to me it is very fitting with regards to my role in the ZFC Recruiting Department. "Give me your tired, your poor, your huddled masses yearning to breathe free/The wretched refuse of your teeming shore/Send these, the homeless, tempest-tossed to me/I lift my lamp beside the golden door!" It is extremely rewarding to be able to offer someone an opportunity for happiness. Rather than welcoming swarms of displaced refugees, we welcome the people who have had miserable job experiences. We ask employees to be themselves, to get involved, to be part of something bigger and to create fun and a little weirdness. We should be selling tickets! I don't offer jobs; I offer opportunities and experiences ...

Brittany R.

employee since 2009

The Zappos Culture is one of kind! This company really strives to let all employees be themselves and have fun! With all the events, from picnics to parties, there is always something fun to do, and your team really does become your family. Everyone is willing to help. And the benefits are out of this world. Change keeps you motivated to do your best. Moving up the ladder is always a possibility. I plan to stay with Zappos for a long time.

Brittany S.

employee since 2009

What is a Zapponian? In the years I've been here I've asked myself that several times, each year with a new answer. So this is my 2011 version of what a Zapponian is to me. It's someone who values a genuine connection between strangers; a person who values family. A Zapponian never dreads going into work, but approaches the day knowing that our fellow Zapponians have our backs. We work, laugh and even sometimes fight like a family. It is an individual who embraces a purpose greater than the 9-5 grinds and who strives to better himself or herself.

Brittney M.

employee since 2009

Let me just say that Zappos is awesome because of the Culture. The Culture, beliefs and rituals at Zappos are different than at any other place. "Work hard and play hard!" I Love It!! We work great as a team and we have so much fun during our culture activities. I always look forward to coming to work to see my fellow Zapponians. We are a breed all our own, and proud of it. FYI, you have to be a little goofy to work here and enjoy it!

Bryan I.

employee since 2009

In my opinion, the Zappos Culture is just like a family culture, and just like in a family, you have to adapt to the changes. At work there are co-workers that you work well with just like a very close relative. On the other hand, some are like your crazy uncle that no one wants to spend time around. In the end, no matter how you view each other, you are all working towards a common goal, whether that be building family ties or working to make sure that orders go out when they are supposed to. I love my family and am very appreciative to have them, just like I am very thankful to have my job at Zappos.

Bryan P.

employee since 2007

I've been working here for almost three and a half years now and I see something new about the company every time I come in. It's never dull.

Bryan P.

employee since 2011

The Culture at Zappos is fun and adventurous. A good team and family spirit keeps the culture strong. I think Zappos is a great place to work. I love working here and look forward to coming to work every day. I like that we will get together outside of work as friends. I think Zappos is more than just a job. It is all about daily experiences, through community involvement, charity work, pipeline training classes, traveling and speaking with people within our Zappos family.

Bryan S.

employee since 2010

The Zappos Culture, to me, is the foundation of what has made me the happy person I am today. I have grown close to my fellow team members in a way that I never have at another place of employment. Each person I work with I consider family and I enjoy coming to work every day. Zappos is a place like no other and I look forward to spending many more years working side-by-side with my favorite people.

Byron S.

employee since 2005

The Zappos Culture is what sets Zappos apart from any other company or organization. Our Culture is and always has been exciting and consuming. Many have tried and failed to mimic our Culture and will continue to do so. That is what makes the Zappos Culture so great yet so complicated to explain. We have no culture guidelines or requirements. We understand that culture is not something that is checked off of a list. We understand the value and worth of knowing that the next generation of great culture ideas can come from anyone at any level of our organization at any time. The reason that we are unique and have held to our Culture is the fact that it is always changing and evolving. Most organizations take a step-by-step approach to their culture and do not have the courage or intelligence to change or evolve it within their organization. We have never struggled with this concept and can continue to grow and expand our Culture without any self-imposed limitations or delusions of what our Culture "should be." Culture, in most organizations, is stagnant at best. Within Zappos, our Culture is living, growing, and continually evolving. At Zappos, we understand that in order to move into the future you must leave the past behind. In other words, Culture is cool.

Candace H.

employee since 2009

Zappos has been – and I'm sure will somehow stay – a never-ending adventure. It has been fun from the beginning, as well as fulfilling as far as a job. I hope to take in as much WOW here as I can happily return. Every day proceeds to offer and show me more in one way or another. Thanks to all in this Culture adventure.

Candi B.

employee since 2009

I love my job and all the benefits that come with it. Any time someone asks me where I work and I say Zappos, they usually respond by saying "I heard that was a great place to work." Then I tell them it's true!

Candis B.

employee since 2011

I would have to say it is a unique job experience! Not like anywhere else, that's for sure!

Capria C.

employee since 2010

The Zappos Culture is by far the absolute best of any company, anywhere. The most important thing to run a successful business is truly caring about the employees. Tony Hsieh knows how to do it right. We have a crazy, amazing Culture and an extremely strong sense of family here. I don't dread going to work the way I have with other jobs. I love coming here because I know that no matter what, I'm going to have fun while I'm working hard. Culture is everything to Zappos. The picnics, the parties, the karaoke, and the people are what make us who we are. Nothing, and I really mean nothing, compares to the awesome things we have going on at Zappos.

Cara H.

employee since 2008

Zestfulness, Awesome, Privileged, Pro-party, Out of this world, Successful. All of these words represent Zappos in more ways than one. I have been with Zappos for three years now, ever since I turned 18. I remember the day I turned 18 I told my father that Zappos is where I wanted to be! I already knew that I would be given the chance to become successful here. And three years down the road, look where I am! That's what I mean when I say the word successful.

Zappos has given us all the opportunity to become successful and to make our jobs what we want them to be. How many companies can you say that about? Everyone who works here or has ever worked here knows that this place is out of this world! As soon as you start that long walk from the gravel you are greeted with friendly faces. All the way through security to the break room were you don't need cash for anything! It's almost like we are on our own little cruise ship were everything is provided for you and the only thing you have to worry about is how long the lunch line is going to be! Man, everyone here works our booties off! But we also know how to partaayyy our booties off! We are so lucky to work for a company that lets us play as hard as we work. Not only at the holiday parties, but also at Spring fling, Fall Festival, peep shows, Zappos Olympics, and much more! I party a little bit every day at Zappos! We are also privileged and lucky to work at such an A-W-E-Some place. How many people can write in their own Culture Book and brag about their job? Not many! Come to think of it I've never heard anyone else brag about their job ... well unless they were a celebrity! We are lucky that we work at a place were everyone knows our name instead of treating us like Employee #891. And last but not least, Zappos is full of life and zestfulness! We are Zappy, Zun, Zrazy, Znpredictable, Zetermined, Zrowing, Zearning, Zare, Zucky, and the one thing I love to show off ... we are Zapponians! Thank you to everyone who keeps our Culture alive!

Carol C.

employee since 2010

I like working for Zappos. I've met a lot of good people. The lead managers are very nice and very helpful when you need them. I love getting 40 percent off shoes. I can't believe that Zappos gives us free food. And getting hired at 60 years of age makes me feel good. Life doesn't stop when you get to that age because some places won't hire people that age. I want to thank you, Zappos, for hiring me. And I will give my all to you. Thanks again!

Carol H.

employee since 2010

I have been here for more than a year now and Zappos means a lot to me. I feel like we are all family and I have a bond with my team members and my manager that I have never had at any other job before. I hope I am here for many years to come.

Carrie L.

employee since 2010

The Zappos Culture, to me, is coming to work and always being able to be myself. I have never worked for a company that encouraged me to be the individual that I am. The atmosphere is always fun and it never feels like work. I consider Zappos my home away from home, full of friends and amazing people.

Carrie P.

employee since 2010

One thing I've learned from Zappos is that change is good. Embrace change, as Zappos is always changing for the better.

Carter L.

employee since 2010

The Zappos Culture? It's the fabric that is used to knit together my superhero cape! It empowers me to make a difference, motivates me to succeed, and gives me an opportunity to care.

Cassy D.

employee since 2010

The Zappos Culture is mostly about family to me. I have had some awesome people come into my life through Zappos, people I will always remember and keep close to me. I met my "bestie" at Zappos. She is the greatest. "She took the fork right out of my plastic." So many thanks to you, Zappos, and your family Culture!!

CeeJay A.

employee since 2011

To me, Zappos is an awesome place to work. You can be yourself and have fun while you're at work. How many jobs have you had like that? This is honestly the best job I've ever had, and I hope to expand my career further. My fellow Zapponians, have fun!

Chad B.

employee since 2010

Culture is the feeling I get when I walk in the door here. It's working with the best group of people in the world. It's high fives in the hallway, water gun fights in 100-degree weather and potluck dinners shared as a family. The Zappos Culture is what makes me want to wake up in the morning regardless of the challenges ahead. Culture is dressing up like a gnome and embarrassing myself because I know it will make my team laugh. Our company defines Culture and it's the only place I want to be.

Chad B.

employee since 2010

My employment with Zappos has been quite different from anywhere else. The company is strong and continues to grow daily. I have enjoyed meeting so many different kinds of new people, and what I mean by that is there are a lot of unique people within the factory. I started as a temp associate in October of 2010 and became full-time in January of 2011. The qualities of the job here and benefits are really great also, but we work a whole lot of overtime. The company provides and caters lunches and the vending machines are free, which I really like. I have never worked for a company that provides this. My manager is a great person too, along with our leads. Very understanding and respectful ladies. However, I'm sure we drive them crazy. This company can change really quickly on a day-to-day basis, so you have to be flexible, but I'm sure it will be worth it in the long run. I'm very pleased to be employed here and feel this is a good start and a new beginning for me in my life and career. Zappos will truly WOW you.

Chad T.

employee since 2007

There is one constant at Zappos and that's change. It embraces and drives everyone!

Charles D.

employee since 2010

From the time I was 16 until I was 24, I had 11 different jobs. Nothing made me happy for long enough that I wanted to make a career out of it. I'm proud to say I celebrated my 25th birthday at Zappos. They gave me a free T-shirt to commemorate it! And I'm actually hoping for many more.

In this company, the managers are more interested in your success than in your mistakes. I've shaken hands with the CEO. The higher-ups I've met have all been humble and friendly. I've been here almost nine months at this writing and no manager has ever raised his or her voice to me. That's nine months and the bubble hasn't burst yet. But what sticks out the most for me is that the amazing attitude you gain at Zappos tends to bleed over into your home life. The Core Values aren't just for work. You can be that honest, fun, approachable person anywhere. Why stop being weird and different just because you're at the grocery store or the bank? And the health coverage here is like nothing I've ever seen before. I had a wisdom tooth removed for $14. I got new glasses with transition lenses for $30. I don't even have a co-payment. That's so rare that receptionists have tried to argue with me when I told them that. Zappos is the best workplace I've ever been.

Charles M.

employee since 2011

This is one of the only organizations where I've worked where I truly enjoy coming to work to see what bizarre thing is going to happen next. People you come across have a smile on their faces and will go out of their way to help you. This place is truly one of a kind.

Charles S.

employee since 2010

I wish I could tell you what the Zappos Culture was all about, but honestly, I don't think anybody can. It just means different things to different people.

Charles W.

employee since 2010

WOW, what year it has been, delivering WOW in leaps and bounds. Along with all the growth we have experienced we have not lost focus on the heartbeat of Zappos, which is its Culture! Free lunch, health insurance, T-shirts ... what more could you ask for? Oh, yeah! And they let me dress up as a penguin for the heck of it!!!!

Cherie G.

employee since 2010

I love working for Zappos and all the crazy leads here.

Cheryl R.

employee since 2010

The people I work with always seem to help me when I have trouble keeping up the pace, or if I'm unable to lift or pull materials with the hand jack. When I have a special project to do, my friends help with ideas to better solve the issue and how to find an easier way.

Chris E.

employee since 2010

Zappos is the best place to work because of the free food! Zappos lets you be yourself and always creates a fun but "Zafe" workplace.

Chris F.

employee since 2005

I would have to say that this is the best place to work ever. I have been here for six years now and I could not even imagine ever working anywhere else. I have so many friends here that most of the time it doesn't even seem like work. Thanks, Tony! You're the best.

Chris O.

employee since 2011

This job has, seriously, been the greatest opportunity I have had in a long time. I love my co-workers and my managers. They are all a tight family of awesomeness. This place is amazing ... sometimes too amazing, I think. So amazing, in fact, that I cannot use regular words to describe it, but I shall try. "Yipty nipbut qwandala darbu. Blizzle gitten gittengar, haryoofersh ... derzzzz ..."!!! I hope that has helped to explain how awesome it is to work here. I love this place and wouldn't trade it for anything.

Chris W.

employee since 2007

I started at Zappos a little over four years ago and I loved it right away, mainly because they fed me and gave me T-shirts. (Lol!) But, joking aside, it's become a second home to me. The picnics, the obstacle course they brought in ... this place is like working in a playground most of the time. My co-workers and I all have a great bond, we work hard and play harder, as close as any family can be. I'm not sure how I got by before I met my Zappos family, but I can't imagine life with out them. The Zappos Culture is life the way we want it to be: free, creative, fun and accepting.

Christian R.

employee since 2010

The Zappos Culture is what keeps the company from focusing only on earning money, focusing instead on the employee who is on the front lines, working hard for the company's success. It also provides for a friendly environment among employees by giving them good values that can be applied at work and at home. If these values are ever taken away, that will be the day the mighty Zappos empire will fall.

Christie C.

employee since 2011

I have been part of the Zappos family for only a few short months! This is a wonderful place to work and wonderful people to work with. I look forward to what's yet to come with my career at Zappos, and the life-long friendships I am sure to make!!!!!

Christina J.

employee since 2010

I have given much thought to what I would share about my experience with The Zappos Culture. There is really only one word that sums it up ... "fantabulous!" Being a recruiting assistant allows me to witness the excitement first hand when I share what our culture is with a potential new hire. They initially have the look of an older child whose parents are insisting that Santa is, indeed, real. However, as I share how we truly embrace who people are and that we believe fun is a requirement at work, that look of disbelief is replaced by one of hopeful belief. When I see them out on the floor a couple of weeks into their new job, I often get hugs, thank yous, and ear-to-ear grins. The feeling I get from that is indescribable! I sincerely believe this is the best company in the world, and I am proud to play even a small part in bringing others into the Zappos Family.

Christine S.

employee since 2010

It is like one big happy family on a vacation with no booze, and/or a field day. I wear a size medium.

Christopher B.

employee since 2009

Zappos is a good place to work and everyone is just like family.

Christopher N.

employee since 2010

The Zappos Culture means craziness, but in a good way. Never have I worked at a place where I can be myself. I'm not a lifeless zombie. I am me and those people over there are them. I know it sounds crazy, but it's true. Zappos is not a job, it's a huge family making people happy with cool new products.

Christopher S.

employee since 2009

To me, the Zappos Culture means having a sense of community. When we are here, we are more than just co-workers. Every day at Zappos, new friendships are formed and people are brought closer together.

Christopher T.

employee since 2011

I'm new to Zappos but the people around here make it feel like I've been here a while. This is an awesome place to work. Although I am by no means a morning person, I do not mind waking up at 5 A.M to come in to work. It's by far the most enjoyable place I have ever been part of.

Cindy P.

employee since 2006

Zappos is a great place to work. I really like the fact that they are all about family. There are not many companies that really care about their employees, let alone their families.

Clarence D.

employee since 2009

What I like about the Zappos Culture here in Kentucky is that we can be open-minded, work hard, have fun and enjoy coming to work.

Claudette M.

employee since 2009

As an older worker, Zappos has exposed me to a different way and different atmosphere in the workplace than I have known before. I find it interesting and confusing. To leave so much of the responsibility of getting the work done to the individual is a good concept, but there are an awful lot of people who still need constant supervision. Eventually, I suppose it will catch on.

Claudia H.

employee since 2008

I love working at Zappos. The Culture here makes work feel a little less like work. We can listen to music while we work, which makes the ten hours feel more like nine hours. (OK, just kidding ... more like eight and a half hours!) :) I work in the returns department, so I'm glad to see that some of our customers have a sense of humor also. Now if we could just do something about that weather! :)

Clayton P.

employee since 2010

Zappos is unlike any company I've ever worked for. I have yet to be talked down to here, whereas at most workplaces, that would be a common occurrence. There is a strong feeling of unity amongst the employees. Even though you have not met some people before, you are still given a warm greeting and a welcoming smile as if y'all see each other every day. It seems that every week you are given something, like a prize or T-shirt, or asked to come to a company event where you are given even more things and there are even more good times to be had.

Cody I.

employee since 2011

Zappos to me is like a box of chocolates. It's always entertaining and always different. It's not just a job to me. I love coming in to work every day and laughing about something. Zappos has actually made me enjoy working. It's the greatest job I've ever had and I look forward to a long future in the company.

Cody T.K. "Box Maker"

employee since 2010

This is probably the best job in the world ... Zappos, that is. I love everyone here that I've met so far. That, and the Culture is so rich. I doubt that you could find these factors anywhere else. I've enjoyed a lot of things so far, even though I only started back in October. One of the most amazing things that I've experienced here is the potential for growth within the company. With the short amount of time that I've been here, I have been given the opportunity to learn almost everything in my department. Box-making may be my favorite because I can be a little creative in my work. I could explain that but I'd ruin the surprises. I especially love the fact that we also get some good free food. Yeah for the Culture and the Core Values. These are what separate this company from others. I'm sorry to be writing such a large submission. Could we get an index of where our entries are posted? That might be fun. We could learn about our friends' experiences here. It's going to be kinda hard to find a specific person in such a large book. Well, that's all I've got.

Coleman M.

employee since 2011

I'm writing this on my second day of work, and I've never felt more welcome when starting a new job than here at Zappos. Instead of just stares, people are coming up to me and introducing themselves. While I certainly won't remember their names yet, I really appreciate the gesture and it makes me feel welcome. That type of thing has never happened to me before at a workplace and I can already see the difference the Zappos Culture has made. I can't wait to see what the future holds for me at this company. It will be hard to go work anywhere else after experiencing this!

Colton H.

employee since 2010

I love Zappos. It's amazing how that becomes truer every day because no matter what happened the day or week before, we always come in here as a family and work our tails off to deliver WOW to customers. So the reason I love Zappos is because of how close we all are! Long live Zappos!!!

Corey D.

employee since 2009

Zappos is the icing on the cake. As our Culture is the cake, that's sweet little fluff! So go ahead, and try a piece!!!

Corey F.

employee since 2010

Zappos is more than work; it's a place to get away, and everyone here is your extended family. When you come to work it's not like any other job. You get to express your personality through clothes, tattoos, etc. You get to be yourself. I like that if you have a problem you can walk up to anyone and they will be more than happy to help you out. They also have awesome cookouts and events planned throughout the summer where you can go and hang out at no cost to you.

Cory H.

employee since 2010

To me, the Zappos Culture means that every day when I arrive at work I have someone to talk to. Actually, sometimes I literally have someone to talk to from the second I walk in the door to the second I walk out. It's good to have friends, and it's fantastic to have a job working with them. Hopefully next year I'll have something more profound to say.

Cory K.

employee since 2010

The Zappos Culture has actually helped me grow as a person. I left $50,000 a year on the table to come to Zappos as a warehouse team member in 2010. I struggled with my bills, I piled up debt and I've never been happier! Obviously I'm not thrilled about the financial issues, but the fact that I finally forced myself to leave a company where I was unhappy to come to Zappos really helped me grow as a person. I have met some awesome people since I've started here, and this is honestly the friendliest overall group of people I've ever been around. The Culture and the general atmosphere at Zappos have helped me to come out of my shell a little more, and I've built stronger relationships with people, for which I'm grateful. I have loved my time here at Zappos and look forward to being here for the long haul.

Cory M.

employee since 2010

The Zappos Culture, to me, is a way of life. Before starting at Zappos, I had not heard much about the company, so I had no idea what I was getting myself into. Now that I am here, I have been encouraging my friends to apply for a job here. This place is amazing! The people are great to work with and I consider many of them more family than co-workers. Every day I wake up looking forward to coming to work because I know it is going to be yet another great day! Everything is exciting about my job, from the culture events, to team-building exercises, to the parties that Zappos hosts for us. I even get together with several of my co-workers frequently outside of work so we can have a good time there as well. I love my job here at Zappos and wouldn't trade it for anything. There is a reason Zappos is #6 on the list of Best Companies to Work For. Thankfully, I am able to be a part of that! Thanks, Zappos and my fellow Zapponians. You all are the best!

Courtney H.

employee since 2010

Culture is a huge aspect of Zappos. I often sit back and think about what exactly this Culture is. We have amazing benefits that blow my socks off. Woozah! We have awesome free lunches! However, to me our Culture is not about these benefits. It's about Core Value #7: "Build a Positive Team and Family Spirit." Zappos is different than most companies in that my co-workers are my friends. The people I am surrounded by are truly genuine in their character and motivation. This is not a place where you "clock-in" and "clock-out." This is a place where you discover yourself, not only professionally, but also personally. I am grateful every day to go to work and be surrounded by the amazing, awesome, Zappalicious people that are my co-workers!

Cristina T.

employee since 2011

Zappos is awesome!!!!

Crystal B.

employee since 2007

"The mind is its own place, and in itself can make a heaven of hell, a hell of heaven." – John Milton, Paradise Lost

The Zappos Culture is not made or developed in a mission statement. It is grown in the heart and shared with others.

Crystal E.

employee since 2011

Zappos is a great place to work! We are like a family. I have never been treated better at any other job I have ever had. Zappos cares about its employees and they treat us all like family. It is a fun, down-to-earth environment every day. No matter what kind of mood I'm in when I arrive at work, things always seem better here.

Crystal G.

employee since 2006

This is the best company I have ever worked for. I enjoy working with my team in a family-like environment with great relationships. This company has helped me to grow personally and professionally, and to take the initiative for my accomplishments.

Crystal M.

employee since 2008

Zappos is a great place to work. They do so much for employees, and the people that we work with are awesome.

D.W.D.H.

employee since 2008

Zappos reminds me of "the melting pot" I'd read about in history class at school. The Zappos Culture, at its most basic level, is diversity, and learning. It is really just learning to accept others, no matter who/what they are.

Dahir N.

employee since 2010

I like Zappos because it's a good company.

Dan C.

employee since 2011

It doesn't take long to realize that the Zappos Culture is the real deal. In the brief time I've been here I have come to realize that the Culture influences everything at Zappos. Having looked in as an outsider for a long time, I saw all the perks and benefits that Zappos had to offer and I was excited at the prospect of actually getting the chance to work here. Once inside, I realized that the perks and fun stuff mean little to nothing without the underlying, all-inclusive Culture. Free snacks are just free snacks, but a workplace where caring about one another and encouraging one another is real and active – that's golden! In my career I've never come across a place that put so much emphasis on personal development, not just as an employee, but also as a human being. Our Culture has bred in me a desire to be better and to make my peers better, not just for the sake of profit and growing the business, but also for growing relationships. This place has become more than work. It is home and I honestly feel that Zappos offers the opportunity for everyone who works here to leave at the end of the day a better human being – all born out of an honest spurring-on that only genuine family can provide. I'm proud to be here and I look forward to what the future holds for our great family.

Daniel L.

employee since 2010

The Zappos Culture is a way for me to provide for my family, supplying finances, insurance and clothing. I am thankful for a company like Zappos that gives me this incredible opportunity to own my responsibility as a husband and father by working hard and making a life for my family.

Daniel W.

employee since 2010

The Zappos Culture is a unique experience because it includes more than just going to work every day.

Darci S.

employee since 2011

Zappos means a ton to me. This is the first real job I've ever had and it's so amazing. They provide free food for their employees and they really show they care. That's one thing I love – that and the fact that I'm given a chance to work here where I can prove myself! Thank you, Zappos!

Darrin V.

employee since 2010

Zappos has a lot of different personalities that keep things interesting. The people who work at Zappos make it very easy to get up and come to work every day.

Daryl S.

employee since 2007

I have worked in many different departments at Zappos and I now know that picking is for me. May 2011 marks my fourth anniversary and a few months ago this became the longest job I've ever held. There have been several changes in the last couple of years ... some good and some not so good. But to quote Core Value #2,"Embrace and Drive Change." We all have to go trough changes, even when we don't want to. Overall, Zappos is a great place to work and the work itself is not bad, most of the time. It's nice to be able to walk all day and find shoes/apparel and eat free food on breaks. I also love the insurance and the holiday parties!

Dave G.

employee since 2007

This will be my fourth year at Zappos and I am amazed at all the changes that have taken place. When I started we were a small, energetic company that wanted to make the best of what we had. And we did. The culture was like nothing I had never experienced before at a place of business and I was sure that, as the company grew, it would not last. The company grew and things changed, but the culture stayed the same. Then the economy went into a tailspin and businesses all over the country were suffering and bowing out and changing. Zappos also had to change to guard itself through those tough times but, once again, our culture never changed.

Then came Amazon. Many of us felt that our Culture, as we knew it, would come to an end. The rumor mill was something to behold. Many of us felt as though we had sold out. Many thought that we would get lost in corporate America. We thought that we had seen the end of the light that shined on us so brightly and made us different, and better than our competitors. We all loved Zappos and loved what it was all about. WOWing not only the people that work here, but also our customers and competitors was very important to us all. We didn't know what to expect. Tony assured us that Culture would not change and our Core Values were still intact. He assured us that the light would not go out, but grow brighter. He begged us to remember our Core Values and to "Embrace and Drive Change" (Core Value #2). He assured us that this was all for the best. So we believed in Tony and put our nose to the grindstone and worked harder than ever to ensure that we were all doing our part. It turns out that Tony was right. Zappos has grown and our Culture has too. I have seen the changes and am amazed that we are still the small, energetic company that we were when I started, albeit in a large company's body. I am proud to say that I work for Zappos. I am proud of our Culture and that it has proven to be an unbreakable force. I am excited to see where we will go from here and how I can do my part in strengthening our culture even more.

David B.

employee since 2006

I like working at Zappos because of free lunches and insurance.

David B.

employee since 2011

All the people I've met here are awesome and every day I can't wait to see what will happen next. Zappos is the only company I've worked for where I never want to miss a day.

David C.

employee since 2006

Zappos can be a fun place to work. There are a lot of interesting people here.

David D.

employee since 2011

The Zappos Culture, to me, means having fun and enjoying being around the people you work with. It's having an overall sense of family.

David D.

employee since 2010

The Zappos Culture means each employee is an integral part of the company. Each of us provides something to this company. We are one. We are Zappos and the Zappos Culture has no boundaries.

David H.

employee since 2011

I really like the fact that we are allowed to dress the way we like. The free food is nice also. Everyone seems to get along like family, and if you need any help there is always someone willing to help. You are always learning new things. And where else would you get paid to play games or improve your education?

David P.

employee since 2009

I like to work hard, but I don't hear about the good things I do. I hear about one a month. I would like to hear a lot more.

Dawn B.

employee since 2005

I have been at Zappos for going on six years now and I love this place. I have never, in all my years of working (27 of them), worked in a place that treats their employees the way Zappos does. From the great pay, benefits, free vending, catered lunches to all the gatherings that they do, including the spring fling, summer picnic, fall festival, holiday party, spirit week, and let's not forget employee appreciation day, we are all treated like a family. They regard our outside families as much a part of the Zappos family as they do employees. This company is the best place I have ever worked. They make it fun to come to work, which makes us want to work harder for them. Who can truly say that they actually look forward to coming to work every day? Zappos employees, that's who!!!!

Dawn F.

employee since 2009

I love working for Zappos. They make you feel like family and this is your home away from home. The Culture here is better than that at any of the other places I have worked. I have never worked for a company where you are allowed to have as much fun as you do here while you are at work. Zappos rocks!!!

Dawn L.

employee since 2008

The Zappos Culture means that I can always go to work enjoying my job and my work family, that I always feel welcome and accepted as myself and having fun. I truly love what I do here (work) and the people I do it with.

DeAndra R.

employee since 2007

I have been with the company going on four years now and it continues to WOW me. The culture here is unlike that of any other company. Most of the people I work with are more like family than co-workers. No matter what, you always have someone to lean on in times of need. All the activities and special gatherings allow us to get to know one another more personally. Everyone is so nice and welcoming, and from my very first week I felt like I belonged here. It is hard to find a company that is so welcoming and encourages you to be yourself. It is very refreshing to work for such a diverse company and I look forward to working here for many years to come.

Debbie C.

employee since 2010

Working at Zappos has been an interesting experience because I am a nurse. Working here has shown me more about what teamwork means. Teamwork in my department is great. No one expects you to know everything and it doesn't matter how many times you ask a question, they answer it or show you how to do it. I like the activities we do and I am impressed with the Core Values this company has. I have made a lot of friends since I started and I go home and tell my family what is going on. If I know of someone who needs a job, I tell him or her to apply to Zappos. I really like the way this place makes me feel – like Zappos is my second family, not just a job..

Deborah L.

employee since 2004

I love Zappos because of all the things they do for us and the good people I have met here. They are really like my family. Where else can I go and have a good time and get paid for it? Zappos rocks!!

Deborah S.

employee since 2007

The Zappos Culture is about living life now. Working is a big part of life and Zappos lets us live it with happy vibes.:) Our Culture is goodness.

Debra J.

employee since 2010

I came to work at Zappos in August 2010, attracted by the wonderful and wacky Culture I had read about. Changing jobs was a big leap of faith for me, as I was in a higher-level position at a large organization. What led me to take that leap was that I wanted to work somewhere that treated people well ... all people. Zappos treats everyone the same regardless of his or her position within the company. Every person is valued. Every person is important. When people find out where I work, I get all types of questions, but the most often asked question is about how Zappos became so successful. I always respond that our business model is based on common sense: treat people well, be sincere and people will respond positively. Crazy concept, huh? My leap of faith paid off immeasurably. I have never been happier.

Debra J.

employee since 2010

Oh, how happy I am to be a Zapponian!!! I had heard through the "grapevine" for several years that Zappos was a great place, so I had to apply for a job. I'm the type of person who is shy and quiet at first, but then once you get to know me I'm wide open. I worked first during peak season, and oh my, what a crazy time that was. Through all the blisters and tiredness, I still went home and talked about how much I enjoyed working at Zappos. What other employer offers a spring fling and a summer picnic, and a great place to work? In this Zapponian place you see and meet all kinds of people, but I absolutely love working here. My co-workers are awesome. Even though the days are long and tiring, we all somehow are still able to smile and laugh at the end of the day. And at home in the evening while relaxing in bed, what do I see? LPN'S, different-colored barcodes, shipping tape and boxes ... and a lot of smiling faces.

Debra W.

employee since 2011

Zappos! OMG! It's so hard to explain. In the short time that I've been here I have seen so much. For example, the people really act like they care; they make sure you are always safe, and even if you're working hard, they manage to add a little fun. You can expect the unexpected. It's unlike any place I've ever worked! Truly awesome!

Denise L.

employee since 2010

The Zappos Culture is unique. There's no way to fully describe it, you just have to be part of it to feel it. At most companies there are cliques or groups and you have to fit into one group. Not at Zappos. You are who you are and that's it. Everyone fits in and there are no misfits; weirdness is a thing to admire. You are accepted as a person. Tattoos, piercings, extreme hair color or style … none of that matters here. There is a strong team spirit and a family bond that has to be felt to be understood. This helps create an awesome working environment that makes everyone more relaxed. I didn't believe until I felt it myself and now I am glad I did. Zappos rocks, hard core!!!

Denise R.

employee since 2007

In the four years I have been at Zappos, I have seen a lot of change. But the one thing that has not changed is the way Zapponians treat one another. We are like a family. I have landed my dream job. I have met some of the most outstanding people. It is great to be part of this awesome family.

Derek K.

employee since 2010

When I arrive at Zappos, it doesn't feel like I'm going to work; It feels like I am going to see family. Everyone knows one another and is supportive and helpful. Zappos is an environment unlike any I've worked in. The best thing about Zappos is getting to see Jeremy and his beard on the days I work.

Derek L.

employee since 2008

Monotony … every employee's worst nightmare. To work for a place that strives to change things and break the mold of every other company is refreshing. The emphasis on having fun while delivering awesome service to the customers makes a big difference.

Derik S.

employee since 2010

To me, Zappos is a great place to work because of the people. I've made a lot of friends in the seven months that I've been here. The benefits at Zappos are a huge part of why I came here. Just to know that my seven-month old child, my wife and I are well taken care of is a big deal for me and I appreciate Zappos making that a priority. Thank you.

Derrick D.

employee since 2011

The Zappos Culture is better than the culture at any company I've ever experienced thus far. I can't imagine any better!

Devin P.

employee since 2011

Zappos is a great job because the food is free and the people are great to work with. It is a wonderful job!

Devon S.

employee since 2011

Zappos rocks my socks.

Diana R.

employee since 2005

WOW! I can't believe it's been almost seven years since I started at Zappos. I feel truly blessed to work here. It is an awesome place to work. Sometimes (most of the time) I wonder if I am cool enough to work here! Maybe all the coolness will rub off someday! I hope to be part of the Zappos family for many more years.

Diane H.

employee since 2005

The Zappos Culture makes this a fun place to work. It has a lot of benefits. I tell all my friends and family to come here and get a job, because you can be yourself, wear whatever you want, and you are still treated well and thanked for a job well done.

Diane P.

employee since 2007

The Zappos Culture is a pyramid – a solid foundation of amazing values, a layer of dedication and determination, a layer of smiles and laughter, a layer of helping others whenever you can! At the end of your day, without our Culture, Zappos would be just another place to work!

Dillon M.

employee since 2011

I love the way people at Zappos care about other people and I like the free lunches.

Dina M.

employee since 2010

Zappos is a fantabulous place to work!! What other company gives employees free lunches, free benefits, free T-shirts and many other great things? I felt welcome and appreciated the minute I walked in the door. I have never truly loved a job until I started working at Zappos! I liked my previous jobs, but I love Zappos! I want to spend the rest of my life working here! If you don't work for Zappos ... I truly feel sorry for you!

Donald W.

employee since 2008

In the 40-plus years that I have been earning a paycheck, I have never worked for a place like Zappos. The company actually encourages you to have fun and even sets aside some time every once in a while for you to do just that. And you cannot beat the benefits anywhere. The only time I ever ate for free was when I was in the Army, but here I don't have to dodge bullets. I have worked for other places that paid the employees' insurance, but each one finally gave up on that and made us pay. Not Zappos. The insurance just keeps getting better each year. I'm sure there will come a time when Zappos can no longer pay for our insurance, but I hope that doesn't happen until after I retire. And Zappos really knows how to throw a party. It is a really great place to work.

Donna B.

employee since 2011

I joined Zappos after 30 years of preparing mortgages. A nice desk job. My son had already been working here for several months and got hired on permanently, so I decided to give it a try, since mortgages aren't doing so well these days. Talk about culture shock! But I love the atmosphere here and the non-stressful work environment. I am competitive, so I'm already striving to meet quotas. As I've worked (right now I'm in packing and shipping) I've been discovering what Zappos' Ten Core Values are and I'm impressed with a company that wishes to instill all of those concepts in its employees. I'm a temporary Zapponian right now, but not for long.

Dorothy P.

employee since 2010

WOW! What a great place to work! Great benefits and a company that shows how much it cares about its employees by doing all they do for us. Makes you feel like family instead of just an employee. Thanks, Zappos, for all you do for us!!!

Dortha G.

employee since 2011

I have never worked at a job that I loved as much as Zappos! I love arriving at work every day and leaving with a smile on my face, no matter how tired I am. I love the family environment and the fact that, no matter what, I will always have someone I can turn to, whether it is something serious or just about the newest improvements on a sparkly, purple charger. Nothing can compete with Zappos Fulfillment Center.

Doug A.

employee since 2011

After working the daily grind of construction for the last 15 years, the Zappos Culture is a breath of fresh air that actually makes me look forward to coming to work for the first time in a long time.

Douglas H.

employee since 2010

Working at Zappos enabled me to have a Christmas that was not going to exist. The Culture here means that everyone is willing to help and explain how to do what needs to be done. We work hard and we play hard. Free meals and vending machines are great. I defy you to find that anywhere else. I hope to stay here for some time.

Douglas H.

employee since 2010

It's been very refreshing for me to work in a place where people are happy and nice and considerate of one another. Thank you.

"Dr. Rock"

employee since 2010

The Zappos Culture, to me, means having a good time at work, which is not something I was used to. I come from a construction background and a lot of the time, work was no fun at all. Now I don't dread going to work; I look forward to it!

Drew H.

employee since 2009

Zappos is a fun place to work. We are people with spirit. It's not just a job!

Dustin A.

employee since 2010

To me, the Zappos Culture creates an environment in which anyone with a positive work ethic, good attitude and a little personality may succeed. If the Ten Core Values that make up our Culture transcend the workplace, they can lead to a happier, more fulfilling life. Openness to new ideas is something sorely needed in our society today. Doing more with less maximizes the "utils" (units of happiness) one may gain from a finite amount of resources. A little weirdness helps create a barrier between enough and excess when it comes to efficiency. When someone is humble yet confidant, they are easy to be around and often exhibit a sense of natural leadership. In the end, the Zappos Culture is about how one treats one's co-workers and (to a greater extent) all mankind. Living the Zappos Culture will lead to better relationships, a more positive attitude and greater success in and out of the workplace.

Dustin S.
employee since 2005

The Zappos Culture is what separates Zappos from other companies. Team members at Zappos are exactly that ... parts of a team. We all really feel like parts of a family. We can depend on one another when we need help. Zappos is like a land of opportunity for a lot of people. We can be ourselves and still feel comfortable pursuing growth and learning with the company, both professionally and personally. I have been with Zappos for six years and the opportunities that have been presented to me are amazing. Zappos does a great job of making sure none of us forgets how much we are appreciated. Examples of this are the holiday party, picnics, team building, free lunch/vending, free insurance, karaoke, etc. We all work together to get the job done no matter what it is and there is always a great reward, whether it is something tangible or just the feeling of accomplishing something and being successful. The Zappos Culture is our main focus and I believe it will continue to pay off. I could write so much more, but I don't want to take up the whole book! :) Thanks for the opportunity to be a part of The Zappos Culture!

Dwayne P.
employee since 2006

I have been with Zappos for about five and a half years and have loved every minute. I started the year I graduated from high school and didn't really know what I wanted to do with my life. After about two and one-half to three years of being with the company, I realized that business management was interesting. I have been a lead for about two years now and plan on going to college for business management. I am currently working on a few tasks before I take the next level. Zappos offers everything I need to move up and I love that we have the pipeline. Zappos isn't just about pursuing growth and learning (Core Value #9). We also have fun. We participate in activities for different holidays, like decorating our departments, dress up for Halloween, and who can forget the Peep Show once a year. Then there are the benefits; we have the best. I don't plan on leaving anytime soon. We are family here.

Dyan E-M.
employee since 2011

To me, the Zappos Culture means the freedom to be exactly who I am without worrying about being judged. The Culture here at Zappos is one in a million. I am encouraged to express both my creative side and my intellect. I wouldn't trade it for the world. Thanks for letting me be a part of this awesome Culture.

Eddie P.
employee since 2010

At first, the Zappos Culture was a shock to me. We went through orientation and they told us all these great things and most of us were like ... yeah ... right it's too good to be true. Then I went through my first week out on the floor and everybody made me feel so welcome. In no time at all, the team I was working with was like my second family and I had tons of friends in other areas. Zappos is definitely more than another job or a career for me. For the first time in my work history, I actually look forward to coming here in the morning ... I never refer to it as work. It is my second family!!

Edward B.
employee since 2007

I love my job and the people I work with. My co-workers are like friends and family. I've been with Zappos for four years now and hope to be with the company for another 40.

Elizabeth B.
employee since 2011

Zappos is a great place to work. Free food, free drinks and great people. What else could you ask for? There is never a dull moment. Definitely my home away from home.

Elizabeth T.

employee since 2011

I have been at Zappos for one week now. I have exactly WOW to say about the company thus far. Everyone from the supervisors on down has been nothing but great. I have already learned many different things and feel really good about it all. I am eager to continue to learn as much as I can at Zappos. This is the most employee-friendly company I have ever worked for and I cannot wait to be a full-time Zappos employee. Thank you.

Elizabeth W.

employee since 2007

I am really enjoying working for Zappos. It's unlike any job I've had before. I love the people here and I really do feel like I'm surrounded by family and friends. This is a cool place to be!

Emily N.

employee since 2010

The Zappos Culture is all about having fun and learning something new! Zappos offers helpful classes (that you get paid to take) and encourages everyone to "Create Fun and a Little Weirdness" (Core Value #3)! The Zappos Culture is crazy, fun and inspiring! Zappos is so much more than just a job – it's a great big family of weirdos! :)

Eric G.

employee since 2010

Zappos is a great place to work, with wonderful people. If you don't like the job or the people you work with, it makes it harder for you to go to work every day – an expression I believe in because I find myself looking forward to going to work. Zappos is one of the bright spots in my day.

Eric K.

employee since 2011

I just started at Zappos and it's already the best job I've had. Great people to work with and everyone is in a good mood here.

Eric M.

employee since 2010

The Zappos Culture means working with awesome people who care about each other. It's about the relationships. It's about the people.

Eric M.

employee since 2010

I am only a part-time employee, but this is a great job. I am able to do my job to the best of my ability without much oversight, I get free meals and snacks, and great discounts on shoes!

Eric T.

employee since 2010

The Zappos Culture means a lot to me, because without it the company and the people wouldn't be the way it is today. Culture is what makes this company so successful and the people so much fun to be around. This is more than just a job, it's a lifestyle, baby!!!

Erick H.

employee since 2007

I love working here. Every day when I come in, I'm looking forward to whatever new crazy thing is going on. Zappos has helped me get through some rough patches in my life and now that things are going great it has helped me to stay motivated and become an even happier person.

Erin S.

employee since 2007

When I think about our Culture, I think about family. I love the people I work with. Most people dread getting out of bed and going into work every day, but not me. I know when I go to work, I'm going to be surrounded by friends.

Frank P.

employee since 2010

Zappos gave me a different outlook on life. Thanks, Zappos.

Gary W.

employee since 2010

A great family environment and an awesome place to work!

Ethan A.

employee since 2011

One of my favorite things about Zappos is the money I save because of the good, free food and all the discounts.

Fred S.

employee since 2010

My main purpose here at Zappos is to make the next person's job easier.

Gayla G.

employee since 2007

Four years ago I was looking for a job, hoping for something to open in my field. (I was a press operator.) I stumbled upon Zappos and in the last four years I have met some truly amazing people. The job has become more than a job. Life takes some funny turns, and this is one detour that really paid off.

Eva G.

employee since 2010

The Zappos Culture means to be a family and to love one another. :)

Fuad P.

employee since 2007

To me, the Zappos Culture means sharing ideas, feelings and habits. I look forward to coming here every day and having so much fun.

Geoffrey N.

employee since 2010

The working environment that the Zappos Culture creates is very fun to be part of. The success of this company, in my opinion, is dependent upon its unique culture and the Core Values that everyone lives by.

Frank N.

employee since 2009

The Zappos Culture means that we work as family, sharing ideas to help one another; and I love the way our safety issues are taken seriously. I also love the shoes and the money, and I am very happy that i work for such a company.

Gary J.

employee since 2010

Zappos is more about a family atmosphere than a work place. Plus, we have games to pull everyone together as a team. The parties are awesome! Zappos goes all out for its employees. You go to work and they encourage you to take classes to help you to improve yourself.

George R.

employee since 2006

It is fun to work at Zappos because the people are outstanding .

George S.

employee since 2010

One of the reasons I like Zappos is that our hard work is acknowledged in so many ways and that everyone is willing to help others when needed.

Geovanni C.

employee since 2010

Zappos is the best job I have ever had. I love coming to work and having a fun time.

Glenn A.

employee since 2010

The Zappos Culture means that if I had Ninjin Skills, I wouldn't go ninjin nobody that didn't need ninjin and no Jewdee Choppen neither. It means that if I were to step out onto the plane of cognitive perception and admit to the projected dynamics of our internal structure, the "R"ealization of what if would prove that this grid is composed of geometrical shapes made out of love.

Gordon R.

employee since 2010

The Zappos Culture was something I seemed to fit into fairly easily. It was a little strange at first, but I managed to understand and fully embrace it. To me, the Culture has come to mean family and a lot of fun. I came in that first day to orientation not knowing anyone and I barely knew anything at all about Zappos. After being in orientation for one day, I realized that this was the place for me. After that first week, I had made 32 new friends who became 32 new family members. We jelled together immediately. It was the neatest thing! We have all become so close that we can finish each other's sentences, and when one of us has a problem we all help out. We get together as a group after work and do great activities. I've come to trust and love my co-workers. And how many people can say they have a work relationship like ours? Not many. And now lets talk about fun! It's great when my alarm clock goes off in the morning and I don't mind getting up to go to work. On my way in, I often wonder what kind of adventure is awaiting me. For instance, in the dead of summer, when you're so hot and your energy has been zapped, nothing beats a good old-fashioned water gun fight! Even more fun is when you're working and have no idea it has even begun till you walk around a corner and you're suddenly surprised by cool blasts of water from several of your friends, while on the clock. It's the greatest! I've worked for some good companies in the past, but Zappos is by far the best. We are cared for daily and are held to a high standard. We function by WOWing customers. Zappos has WOWed me! Thanks, Zappos, and thank you to all my friends here.

Grace H.

employee since 2007

To me, the Zappos Culture is about being myself. We live by the Ten Core Values every day. One of the best parts of my job is talking to new hires about our Culture, the Core Values and everything that is great about Zappos. I love seeing the enthusiasm in the faces of the people that really appreciate what Zappos is all about.

Greg B.

employee since 2010

The first day I walked through the door at Zappos, the unease and uncertainty of a new job vanished. I was a member of the family from day one. During my time here, I've been through one of the roughest times of life and my Zappos family stood by my side the whole way. And they still do!

Greg D.

employee since 2008

The Zappos Culture is great. It allows people to have a good time, inside or outside of work. I believe it brings everyone together to make Zappos more than just a job.

Greg K.

employee since 2010

More than just a free lunch! More than just a free T-shirt (and glasses and key-chains and cowbells!) More than just a free haircut! More than just a free benefit package (cost for prescriptions, zero)! The Zappos Culture is more than just a sum of its parts and people. (Thanks to everyone who makes Zappos what it is ... and what it isn't.) Because of the WOW I have here, I am excited about coming to work for the first time. What more can I say?

Gregory P.

employee since 2007

It's going on four years and I'm still amazed at the things that I discover about Zappos – some good, some that I just don't understand, but it's always a pleasure to come to work. I'm going to retire at the end of December. (It's time. I'll be 63.) I will miss the people and the job, but not the 70-mile drive from Lexington. Thank you for four years of memories, from the grump in maintenance.

Gregory S.

employee since 2011

Lots of great things are great at Zappos. First off, all the free stuff, food, drinks and candy. Even though I haven't been here long, working at Zappos is the first job I've had where I didn't dread coming to work. The people are great and the environment is awesome. What could be better?

Guy O.

employee since 2011

The Zappos Culture is like nothing I have seen before. Many companies talk about treating their employees well, but Zappos does more than talk.

Happy Helen

employee since 2008

I was welcomed into the Zappos family almost three years ago. I love coming to work. Our Culture is unlike any other. We are a unique, diverse company. I feel that you impact every person you come in contact with, positively or negatively. I have been nicknamed Happy Helen – a name I wear proudly. Zappos allows me to be me. I am able to be more outspoken and do silly things that I would not normally do. I am so grateful to be part of a company that treats others as they would like to be treated, and the front-runner in changing the way business is done for customers as well as for employees. I am proud to be a Zapponian. I believe in our Core Values and the Zappos way of life. Thank you for being a unique and wonderful company.

Harold B.

employee since 2008

After three years at Zappos, I still enjoy going to work every morning.

Heather H.

employee since 2010

Zappos is unlike any other job I have known or heard of. I love my job!!! I drive about an hour to get here, if that is any indication. Benefits are awesome, free food and the people vary so greatly, yet it just works out so freakin' well. I also think the shifts are a great part of what makes the wheels turn so well!!! What a great company!!!

Heather W.

employee since 2010

The Zappos Culture, to me, is about being part of something bigger than myself. I love working at Zappos. The best part about my job is my co-workers. We all get together outside of work, so it isn't just a professional relationship. We enjoy one another's company and we are part of what makes each day great! Thank you Zappos for all the wonderful compassion you have for your employees. Deliver the WOW!!! :)

Holly E.

employee since 2011

I moved to Kentucky just to work at Zappos. I left the beautiful Litchfield County Connecticut Hills just to see what Zappos was all about. In the past, I worked for two giant companies, so, I knew a lot about corporate culture. Here in Shepherdsville, it is a lot like family. I like most of the people here and I can honestly say I have been treated well here in comparison to other places. Each person is a noble visitor in this life. Zappos lets us be who we are.

Hugh G.

employee since 2010

The Zappos Culture is unlike that of any company I have ever worked for. Meals provided, great benefits and neat people. It is always good to see a bunch of hillbilly, hootenanny Kentucky folks working together but having fun at the same time. God bless Zappos, the Commonwealth of Kentucky and the United States of America!

Irma C.

employee since 2005

I think the atmosphere here at Zappos is awesome. People are happy and they love what they do. I have never had a job like this one that empowers employees to change for the better. They always are there to WOW us.

Jack D.

employee since 2011

Zappos has awesome classes in Excel, personal finance, and Zappos Culture.

Jack S.

employee since 2010

The Zappos Culture is a huge part of what makes this place successful. I'm an engineering graduate, and right now I'm not really sure where I want to be or what I want to be doing, career-wise. I've come to appreciate the people that I've worked with here because, no matter how monotonous things can be or what you're making hourly, the people and the environment make the difference. Although I am currently trying to discover a career path, I'm enjoying my time here and the chances I have to advance. I love working with people, and listening to them and I have the chance to do that now!

Jackie G.

employee since 2011

Of all the jobs I've ever had, this is the best. The people are wonderful. Everyone is ready to help you out any time you need it. It's just like one big family. I love it here!!

Jacob Devin C.

employee since 2011

The Zappos Culture is all about making the workplace as comfortable as home. It's easy to feel happy and lose yourself in your work when you surround yourself with such a level of comfort as Zappos provides. The people are very much like family; no one is ever too busy or upset to talk, even if only for a moment! When the people are so warm, it really makes it easy to blend in and feel comfortable. The tolerance for music devices allows an even more fun and social environment. Although the Culture allows a great variety of friendships to flourish, it also creates a pleasant individual experience. There are plenty of opportunities for "me time" while you work, and having music really enhances the pleasure of it all. Put simply, it's easy to get wrapped up in Zappos! I'd give this job two thumbs up, but that doesn't quite seem enough, so I'll rate it with a massive two tanks up!!!! And the tanks are on top of skyscrapers!!! THAT ARE ON FIRE!!!!

Jacob K.

employee since 2006

The Zappos Culture is its people – the ones we work with on a daily basis, and even the ones we rarely see. It's the friends we make and the fun we have. It's being here, this place.

Jacquelyn D.

employee since 2011

I am proud to be a Zapponian! I love coming to work and being part of the Zappos Culture! My team members are great and we all like working together! Laughing and having fun are part of our daily plan! When I was making a career change, I was sure that Zappos was the place for me! Why wouldn't a girl want to work in the biggest shoe closet in the world (LOL!)

Jaime M.

employee since 2010

There are no words to describe my first year at Zappos. I have already seen many changes and have enjoyed embracing every one. The people are amazing and for the first time in my working life, I actually enjoy to coming to work. Thank you, Zappos, for taking a chance on me and letting me find myself and a career!

Jaime W.

employee since 2011

The environment here at Zappos is great. From the day I started here, I have been treated with respect. I like that when I come in every day, we are asked if anyone has anything to add about life or work. When someone does a good job, they are praised for it. I have always felt comfortable here. I think it is a great place to work and to have a second family.

Jaimes M.

employee since 2011

I think the Zappos Culture is about working in an a place that you can feel comfortable and relaxed around the people you work with and have a great time while delivering WOW through service to customers.

Jama D.

employee since 2010

I like Zappos because it is the best company to work for in the world.

James P.

employee since 2007

With the company's standards for ensuring that Zappos is a fun place to work, it makes those of us who put in our best effort shine that much brighter. Then you know that you have someone with excellent character as a co-worker and friend.

James B.

employee since 2010

The Zappos Culture is what keeps me here. I live quite a bit further away from the fulfillment center than many other employees but decided to continue working here even though I was offered a position elsewhere that paid several dollars more. I wasn't sure what kind of company culture I would land in if I took the other job. Staying with Zappos, I knew I'd work hard and enjoy each day.

James C.

employee since 2010

Weirdness and fun all wrapped into one!

James C.

employee since 2010

I have been here three months and it is the best place I have ever worked. I love the people and everything they have to offer. Zappos is a one-of-a-kind place. It is everything a person looks for in a workplace.

James H.

employee since 2010

The Zappos Culture allows me to be me! In turn, that allows me to bring a smile in with me every day!

James N.

employee since 2010

One of the things I like most about Zappos is that it's a laid-back place where everybody gets along. And how can you beat free lunches? The work in shipping is really easy and the managers and leads are great.

James P.

employee since 2011

What I like most about Zappos is the wonderful work environment!

James Q.

employee since 2008

Three years of good friends, good food and good times. Yeah, Zappos!

James R.

employee since 2011

Room for growth, meeting new people every day and creating long-term friendships.

James R.

employee since 2010

I enjoy working here at Zappos because of the free lunches and the free vending machines. I can listen to my music and the work environment isn't as serious as other places. I don't have to cut off my ponytail. The workplace is friendly. You can ask anyone for help and they're happy to assist you.

James R.

employee since 2008

Zappos changed my life. My last career ended with a big crash. When I was ready to re-enter the workforce, I applied at Zappos not knowing what to expect. What I found was a new career, a new outlook on life, and a bunch of great people to work with who also became my friends.

Now, after being here for three years, I only feel stronger about Zappos. I have only worked at one other place that actively encouraged co-workers to be friends outside of work. Companies that do not do this have no idea what they are missing.

James S.

employee since 2009

The Zappos Culture means everything to me. It has let me grow in all areas of my life – at work and at home. I want to thank Tony and all of Zappos for a great job and a great learning experience. There is no place in the world like Zappos!!!!

James S.

employee since 2005

The Zappos Culture, to me, is living and breathing the Zappos Core Values. Everyone at Zappos lives by those Values and Zappos makes a huge commitment to keep them alive and well. The Culture is everyone being dedicated to Zappos and Zappos being dedicated to everyone. It doesn't come easily. It takes everyone coming together to create this wonderful, fun-filled environment. The Zappos Culture is what makes me want to stay here until I retire.

Jamie H.

employee since 2009

The Zappos Culture means a lot to me. Who wouldn't want to come to work and build a scene out of marshmallow peeps or compete in a hula-hoop contest? It definitely helps to break up the day and it makes waking up before dawn that much easier.

Jamie H.

employee since 2010

Culture is very important at Zappos. I feel as if everyone I work with is part of my extended family. I love Zappos and really enjoy working here. Zappos is awesome!!!!!

Jamie L.

employee since 2010

To me, the Zappos Culture is a feeling. It gives me the freedom to be who I am. I am proud to be a Zapponian!!!

Jamie S.

employee since 2010

The Zappos Culture means having an awesome job, surrounded by awesome people ... and knowing that we're delivering WOW to awesome customers!

Jan M.

employee since 2010

When I started with Zappos last year as a seasonal, I thought the company was unusual to have a lounge area to play ping pong, air hockey, and even a Wii system ... to say nothing of free food and drinks from the vending machines and catered meals on certain days. Now it's more than just games and food, it's about wanting to work together to accomplish a mission: providing the best possible service to our customers and to our fellow employees. It's knowing that by working together we can do anything..

Jane S.

employee since 2011

I just started at Zappos three days ago. Everyone is very friendly and helpful. I'm going to like the four-day schedule when I get used to it!!! It's great not to worry about lunch. The food here is great! Stop by for a visit!

Janell S.

employee since 2011

Even though I have only been here a short time, I have discovered that the Zappos Culture is unique and different. It embraces who you are as a person and builds your character and your commitment to your job. Everyone is helpful and a little wacky at the same time! I am very glad to be a member of the Zappos family now and for years to come!

Janet M.

employee since 2007

I have been at Zappos for over four years now and I have really enjoyed working here. It is by far the best place I have ever worked at. That is saying a lot because I have worked at my family's business in the past. Zappos does so many things to keep our jobs fun and it offers the greatest benefits ever!

Janice M.

employee since 2011

Since I have been at Zappos for three weeks now, I have met many new friends. We all work well together as a team. I have been exposed to several jobs here already, and I especially am looking forward to taking advantage of the training classes that Zappos offers to all employees. We have already had a group Italian food day and there are a couple of company events coming up soon. It truly is a family atmosphere here, and you are praised when you make or exceed your goals.

Jared M.

employee since 2011

Overall, an awesome experience. I never expected to like work, but the people I work with here are just great. This is the best job I have ever had.

Jason C.

employee since 2011

In the short time I have been a part of the Zappos family I have encountered many friendly people. The work environment makes me love coming to work. If I'm in a bad mood, seeing my Zappos family instantly puts me in a good mood. I really do look forward to coming to work every day!

Jason H.

employee since 2009

To me, the Zappos Culture means that I am part of a big family that is always there for me. It is a big group of friends that I get the opportunity to work with every day. I have never had so much fun at work before. Often I find myself working late because I am enjoying my day so much that I don't even realize what time it is. I feel very fortunate that I am part of the Zappos team and look forward to many more years of fun and growth.

Jason R.

employee since 2010

The Zappos Culture is what I always dreamed of at other jobs. I've always looked for a company that treats its employees well and understands and lives by the "work hard, play hard" mantra. In the past I complained about all the things that employers should do to convey that they have at least a little respect for the people that make them their millions. Zappos has put an end to my search. I honestly could not imagine going back to the mundane depths that characterize other companies. I love Zappos!

Jason T.

employee since 2010

I really love that people at Zappos are not judged based on outward appearance but by what is in their hearts. I hope we never lose that. It is refreshing to work with people who love to have fun, embrace humor and model humility.

Jason W.

employee since 2004

I feel that the Zappos Culture is the willingness of everyone to pull together to get the job done. People are not just willing to help one another; they want to help one another. It's not about cheers or crazy decorations. Those things are not really Culture. The employees are the real Zappos Culture and how they work hard every day to make our customers happy. It's also how those same people are made to feel like family. A family helps one another out, trying to make life better for each member.

Jason W.

employee since 2010

What the Zappos Culture means to me is having a workplace that is a step above the ordinary. When you come to work every day you expect the unexpected.

Javon P.

employee since 2011

Seasons change because of the laws of nature. People change because of the laws of life.

"JDiddy"

employee since 2011

I can't believe I get paid to do this. Love me some Zappos!!!

Jeff G.

employee since 2006

I have been at Zappos for about four and a half years. Every year I have been here, the company has grown. In most businesses, the larger it gets, the less "mom and pop" culture you have. Not at Zappos. This place grows and grows and I think that the more it grows the more the company does for us. The parties grow bigger with each passing year. The benefits get better with each passing year. I feel that as long as I believe in Core Value #2 ("Embrace and Drive Change") and #4 ("Be Adventurous, Creative and Open-Minded") the company will continue to Deliver Happiness!

Jeff R.

employee since 2010

It's a fun yet weird place to work. A place filled with people from all different walks of life.

Jeffery A.

employee since 2011

Zappos is a place of hope. In my short time here, I have met an array of people, from a grandmother working to keep things afloat to the son of a wealthy family trying to make it on his own. Zappos is much more than just a job; it's a place where you find an extended family and maybe some true friends. I come in every day wondering what new stories I will have to tell when I get home. The days are long, but I would not want to spend them anywhere else.

Jeffrey A.

employee since 2010

To me, The Zappos Culture means being reliable and efficient, and having fun!

Jeffry D.

employee since 2009

The Zappos Culture is the reason I love my job. The friendships I have gained and the fun that I have while working can't be compared. Sometimes I catch myself in awe that so many people with such diverse backgrounds come together and work so well together. I love working for this company and with the people around me. Thank you, Zappos, and shout out to all the amazing people I work with in the ZFC!

Jen D.

employee since 2009

The Zappos Culture blows me away every day. There are so many layers and facets that can only truly be uncovered and appreciated with time. It's amazing how a company that acts like Zappos does and treats its employees so well can grow and thrive each year. The Zappos Culture is truly unique!

Jennie L.

employee since 2005

This is the first job I've ever had that offers employees so many benefits, not to mention our bonus for the past two years, which has amazed me and helped me buy Christmas presents for my kids and grandkids. Besides all the benefits, it's like home because of all my friends, who are a great group of people. I'm proud to call them my friends. Our holiday parties are over the top! Our picnics rock! We get together outside of work to hang out, go bowling or for karaoke – whatever everyone chooses. It's nice to just relax with our Zappos family instead of just working together. I could go on, but I'm just so happy I have this job!

Jennifer E.

employee since 2010

The Zappos Culture makes every day fun and exciting. For example, different shifts often play jokes on one another. I look forward to coming into work each day, not just because I have to be here.

Jennifer F.

employee since 2011

Zappos is definitely the best job I've ever had. It's not like other places I've worked. Here I actually have fun.

Jennifer G.

employee since 2011

I have never worked in such a relaxed, crazy, atmosphere. It is fine to be yourself. You are able to talk with the people around you. The people here at Shepherdsville rock! Where else can you work and have so much fun?

Jennifer H.

employee since 2010

I started at Zappos as a seasonal employee during the Christmas of 2010. Then I worked in the Special Project unit during the transition period when Amazon got involved with Zappos. I am now a full-time employee and I am so proud to be at Zappos. I have made some extremely good friends who have impacted my life and I can see having them as friends forever. My bosses are upbeat and supportive, as well as understanding in times of need.

In general, the people at Zappos are positive and make the work environment fun. I laugh at least once a day at Zappos and I cannot say that about any other place where I have worked. We get free lunches every day, free Coca-Cola and free vending machines, and best of all, our benefits are free. It all makes you feel cared about. I would recommend Zappos to anyone.

Jennifer L.

employee since 2010

"WOW" about sums Zappos up. We get lots of extras, including bonuses and lots of little things that make this a company unlike any other. There are get-togethers, T-shirts, free food, crazy days when we dress up as characters, and so on. When people ask me why I like my job I mention these things, but it goes deeper than that. On workdays I am here with my team members more than I am with my family. They have become my other family by lending an ear or making me smile bigger than I have done in a while. It is a support system that was never part of any other company I worked for in the past. That, to me, is what makes Zappos a place I am happy to come to every day. Zappos has become part of me and I have become a Zappos hero of Culture. The good thing about the Zappos Core Values is that I seem to carry them with me elsewhere. I find myself realizing that it's OK to be a little weird and open to new ideas and people. I guess you could say Zappos gets into your soul.

Jennifer Sue S.

employee since 2009

The Zappos Culture, to me, means working at a place where everyone gets along and has fun while they are working. My favorite of the Ten Core Values is #3 "Create Fun and a Little Weirdness"! I am definitely one for weirdness and fun! :) I think it's great how Zappos is considered one big family.

Jeremy A.

employee since 2010

To me, The Zappos Culture is going beyond being passionate, becoming obsessed.

Jeremy B.

employee since 2007

Zappos is cool. I've been here for four years and I can't imagine working anywhere else. W1 rules! I can't wait to get back over across the street ... ha-ha ... much luv and go, big blue coach! Cal is the Man !!!!!!!!!

Jeremy E.

employee since 2011

I like working here because the job is pretty easy to learn and to do. Zappos has the coolest atmosphere that a job could have. My co-workers, leads and managers are all really cool. I get to wear anything I want to work, which makes things a lot more comfortable. Lunch is free and so is anything in the vending machines. I have never heard of anything like that anywhere else. Most of all, I like this job because there is nothing not to like about it!

Jeremy H.

employee since 2010

Zappos means a lot to me because it makes me happy working here.

Jeremy R.

employee since 2007

I have been working for Zappos for over four years now and love it more each day. It's amazing what Zappos does for its employees. The average laid-back person can come work here and if they have an open mind, they will be transformed into an all-out Zapponian. This was the case with me.

Jerry H.

employee since 2010

I was hired in March of 2010 after long career working for another company. What a culture shift! Zappos has been a breath of fresh air. The Ten Core Values actually have a purpose other than just looking good on paper. I can't help but feel the Zappos Culture is alive among us, and that, through our interactions with others, we maintain and nurture it.

My fondest memory is of my first year when I saw how everybody rallied and chipped in during peak season to meet all of the delivery challenges. I remember being amazed with the buzz and energy each day as I walked through security. You could just feel it. Job titles became meaningless as temporary processing stations and conveyors needed to be installed and set up at a moment's notice. It was crazy, but somehow we all worked together to make it happen. It really felt good to be a small part of this effort to get products shipped to our waiting customers.

Jerry M.

employee since 2009

I like Zappos because, even with my tattoos and piercings, I am not frowned upon. I fit right in!! I love it at Zappos.

Jesse V.

employee since 2011

I have only been a part of the Zappos team for three weeks and already I really enjoy work. Everyone here at Zappos is friendly and they do not mind helping. This company is unlike any other you could think of. Something crazy and unexpected happens every time you turn around. You make friends faster than you can think, and the bosses aren't half bad either. It's a great job and a fun place to be.

Jessica B.

employee since 2010

I am really happy here. I've never had a job where I had so much fun while working. All of the people are really nice and helpful. It's also a plus that so many things are free. I wouldn't want to work anywhere else! :)

Jessica C.

employee since 2011

Zappos has a wonderful work atmosphere. When everyone is excited to be at work, it makes the time fly!! The free vending and catered lunches rock!

Jessica G.

employee since 2009

The Zappos Culture is a huge part of what keeps me coming to work each day. You hear about how Zappos is OK with piercings and tattoos, but it's much more than that. Zappos encourages you to be who you are, to express the unique aspects of your personality and to share your personal oddities with the rest of the company. We strive to expose that spark in people – that little voice in your head that says, "Don't conform!" Zappos is super-original and no other company can copy that. It's refreshing to get so much sincerity from such a big corporation. You get a feeling that you (as an individual) are important and not replicable or expendable. Everyone has a niche, and when we all work together, we're unstoppable. We're a family.

Jessica L.

employee since 2011

Zappos is a good company.

Jessie C.

employee since 2010

I love Zappos, because it has revolutionized the way people buy shoes by having the largest variety available. We are a diverse group of individuals that knows how to deliver WOW! I couldn't ask for a better group of people to work with! Zappos is also one of the few places that I can actually get my weight down while getting paid. Also, I love food, and Zappos always keeps my tummy happy by making sure I'm well fed each day.

Jessie V.

employee since 2010

The things I like about the Zappos Culture include the fact that you can bring your personality in to work and not have to take it off at the door. Also, the people I work with are amazing and fun to be around. I have worked at many places where, when you walk in the door, you feel like the company owns you. They tell you how to act, dress and even think, sometimes. The fact that Zappos is willing to accept you for who you are and not for what they want you to be is awesome!!!!! Go Zappos! WOOOOOOHOOOOOO!!!!!

"JimmyJam"

employee since 2010

My first day at Zappos was a tad overwhelming. I had never done warehouse or factory work before, and I had never worked with such a great mass of people. But as soon as I walked through the front door and saw a mural of everyone's drawings and signatures decorating every wall throughout the front lobby, I knew that this was the place for me. When I finally made it into the warehouse and saw young and old, tattoos and piercings, purple and green hair, and even a few pair of bright yellow UFO pants, I knew immediately that this was where I belong. As it turns out, there aren't many places where you can just show up and be yourself. Thankfully, Zappos actually encourages it. How many companies in the world sport "Create Fun and a Little Weirdness" as one of their Core Values? So, to me, the Zappos Culture means that the unique personalities and ideas of thousands of team members come together to form the fantastic organization that is Zappos.

Joanna H.

employee since 2007

Zappos has been a challenging way of developing a career path. No company I have worked for offered anything near the kinds of benefits that we have at Zappos. To be a team member and shown respect and gratitude is rewarding in and of itself. My management team trusts me to make decisions without questioning me over each point. I've learned things here I can apply both at work and in my everyday life. I don't have to second-guess myself. Zappos has made me a stronger, more confident person.

Joe C.

employee since 2011

I just started here at Zappos and I'm surprised at the community every day. Everyone is nice and, as an employer, Zappos goes far beyond all other companies.

Joe H.

employee since

Although I have been here only three weeks, I find Zappos is a very interesting place to work. There is a great vibe among all the employees I have met, even in such a short period of time. Everyone is quick to offer help if you are unsure about what to do or where to go, and willing to do what it takes to make sure you can be successful here. It is a very laid-back environment, although it's also fast-paced and things get done quickly. The management and other employees have made me feel welcome and taken extra steps to make me feel comfortable.

Joe L.

employee since 2010

I have been with Zappos for just over a year now and I have been on the maintenance team for about two months. I did not have any previous experience in warehouse maintenance but they gave me a shot and I am truly grateful. I intend to make the best of it and continue learning and moving up. I love my job!!!!

Joe W.

employee since 2010

If I were to describe the Zappos Culture in one word, it would be "awesome!" There is no other place like Zappos, and that feeling starts from the top and works all the way down. Working for a company that allows you to be exactly who you are, dress the way you want and have fun at the same time ... who does that??? From the benefits, to the free lunches, free vending machines, free Zappos T-shirts, holiday gifts, etc ... it's incredible! On top of all that, if you want to move up in a company, this is the place. The pipeline is phenomenal; they give you the tools and knowledge you need to advance. I could go on and on about how much I love working here, but I have to get back to work. Thank you, Zappos!!

John A.

employee since 2010

Zappos is a great place to work! I like the company and the people who work here.

275

John L.

employee since 2011

What to say about my time at Zappos? Never had a job where I was so happy. All my supervisors are so cool and not too good to get their hands dirty. That is pretty cool. I am so glad I joined the Zappos family.

John O.

employee since 2010

The Zappos Culture means a lot to me. The parties are awesome. The people and surroundings are fun – from drawing super-heroes for culture events to the awesome lunches.

John P.

employee since 2011

Zappos is a fun, friendly environment. Everybody is so nice and willing to help you when you need it. The supervisors and leads are always there. The place is laid-back and always geared toward customer satisfaction! The biggest plus is that you make a lot of friends!

John W.

employee since 2010

The Zappos Culture makes for a fun and safe place to work. There are numerous opportunities for advancement.

John-Marvin D.

employee since 2011

I've only been at Zappos for a few days, but it's already my favorite job. I've never been anywhere with a better atmosphere. The people are amazing and everyone is different. I have not yet run into any talking cardboard cutouts, nor do I expect to. I haven't felt at home like this in a very long time. I love Zappos.

Jon F.

employee since 2010

Zappos is way more than a job. It's a lifestyle. It will get you out of your shell. Bottom line, Zappos rocks the socks and jams the clams!

Jonathan D.

employee since 2010

In these hard economic times, the Zappos Culture still provides free healthcare and insurance. I also enjoy the picnics and parties that Zappos gives its employees.

Jonathan F.

employee since 2010

I love the atmosphere at Zappos. It is fun to come to work and create a little weirdness!

Jonathan N.

employee since 2011

I have worked at Zappos for a month and already it's the best job I've had. Everyone is helpful and willing to lend a hand when I need it. It's like one big family. I would recommend Zappos to anyone.

Jonathan R.

employee since 2010

When I think of Zappos, I think of a fun, stable job. Before I joined Zappos I worked in the fast-food restaurant business. I got few hours, a low pay rate and the job was both stressful and messy. Now I get better hours and a higher rate, as well as overtime. So this job helped out my financial situation. I'd rather be working than sitting at home with nothing to do.

The work environment here is comfortable; everyone is pleasant and we help out one another. I probably have two of the coolest, nicest leads and my manager is very easy going too. I don't feel like I'm constantly being watched. Also, one of my leads looks like a big teddy bear. Zappos actually cares about its employees and someone always helps me out when I don't know what to do. I am very happy with my job.

Jordan M.

employee since 2011

It's fun. It's an awesome place to work, and everyone here is great!!!!

Jordan P.

employee since 2011

I haven't been here long, but I do like it. I love being able to see all my favorite name brands and I love seeing what I might buy next. Let's just say my boyfriend isn't too happy because I keep buying new shoes every week, but it's all good. When you start, the people here are sweet. They help you out when you need it. It's great to finally be in a work place where almost everyone is in a good mood! I like it so much I plan on being here for a while and buying about 100 more pairs of shoes! :)

Josefina R.

employee since 2007

Trabajar en Zappos es lo mejor que me a pasado. Es el mejor lugar de trabajo.

Joseph B.

employee since 2010

The Zappos Culture means making work fun. You never know what excitement awaits you each day.

Joseph N.

employee since 2009

The Zappos Culture rocks! The Ten Core Values are part of everything we do! Great people, great attitudes, and great service! Go, Zappos!!!!!

Joseph W.

employee since 2011

High five!

Josh B.

employee since 2010

Personal and professional growth!!!

Josh H.

employee since 2010

Family. Zappos is one of the few companies that actually cares about its employees. Without this atmosphere, the company would be just like any other money-hungry corporation.

Josh H.

employee since 2010

I like that Zappos tries to get us to interact with one another.

Josh L.

employee since 2011

The Zappos Culture, to me, is based on maintaining a positive outlook mixed with fun and adventure. It's a culture that anyone can be a part of. It's much like a melting pot – all kinds of things are thrown in and the outcome is a not-so-orthodox culture where books are not judged by their covers.

Josh M.

employee since 2010

The Zappos Culture is truly a life-changing experience. The Ten Core Values, if lived out on a daily basis, will not only make you a better person, they will also make your life more enjoyable! I have found myself creating friendships with people that I probably would have never approached outside of Zappos. The culture allows you to be heard, recognized, and respected for who you are, not just for what you look like! We truly are one big family! The culture also inspires you to be more than just an employee. My favorite Core Value is #5, "Pursue Growth and Learning." Most companies limit the amount of involvement you have with their operations. Zappos encourages you to be more involved, and because of this, I am inspired to want to take my career here as far as I can. I am passionate about my job. I look forward to coming to work. I try my best to explain what the Zappos Culture is to people who do not work here or who have never heard of Zappos. You cannot get a complete understanding until you have experienced it for yourself!

What does the Zappos Culture mean to me? Everything!!!!

Josh W.

employee since 2010

I can't imagine working for a better company. Thank you, Zappos, for the opportunity.

Joshua "Thor" D.

employee since 2007

Zappos is people. We may be famous for our shoes, but none of that would be possible without the men and women who work here. We are all different and we embrace it. Different ages, religions, races and creeds – we all work together to get the job done.

Joshua B.

employee since 2011

I think the Zappos Culture is about learning how to work with people that are introverted or new to work relationships. It's about how to respect one another, listen and learn new stuff every day. I haven't been here long, but it is a great work environment and all kinds of people teach you stuff you need to know. I really like working here because of the people and the crazy, fun environment. Culture is also about different ways of living, different people and what they believe in. I think this is really great because people need to know about how other people are. I love our culture.

Joshua G.

employee since 2011

I've worked for a lot of companies in a lot of different places, and I have met a large number of people in those years, but oddly I do not remember 25% of their names. I remember a specific job I had (names and information have been changed to protect the innocent) where I didn't even know my manager's name for the first three weeks! I haven't been at Zappos very long and I already know everyone in my department. The Zappos Culture is extremely important to me because I believe that is how humans are supposed to act. We are supposed to be social, to have friends, laugh and have fun. The Zappos Culture is how workplaces should function.

Joshua M.

employee since 2010

The Zappos Culture defines the work we do. Every day there is something different going on. It could be an Easter egg hunt, a random "just because" party, or some kind of game created to build up a sense of family. The culture breaks up the normal grind of the work we do. It encourages teamwork and a sense of ownership. We wouldn't be who we are today without our culture. Thanks, Zappos!

Joshua M.

employee since 2010

The Zappos Culture, to me, is a fun and eventful day at work! The Zappos Culture is a way of life!! The culture not only affects my life at work, it has transformed my life outside of the warehouse. Zappos cares about each person's past, present and future. That is why Zappos is the best place I have ever worked!

Joshua S.

employee since 2008

You couldn't find a better company to work for. Zappos is a company that will thrive for a really long time.

JR W.

employee since 2008

The Zappos Culture, to me, is a fun, family environment where everyone is open and honest – something I was pleased to join when I started at Zappos back in 2008. :-)

Ju K.

employee since 2009

I love working for Zappos. Every day is a challenging new experience. There is always some strange, fun or hilarious things happening. We are always meeting new people and building our family workforce. I look forward to being here every day! I wish everyone could experience one day here at Zappos. Our family here is awesome!

Judith R.

employee since 2010

Working at Zappos has been a great experience. I love the way Zappos can get so many different people together and have them bond and really work together.

Judy D.

employee since 2006

I have been working for Zappos for the past five years and this is the one company I've worked for that gives so much and asks for so little. I really appreciate all the free lunches, the T- shirts, parties and all the wonderful picnics they arrange for us. You not only make good money, but Zappos saves you a lot of money. Just think what it would cost if you had to buy your own lunch, your own T-shirts and all other benefits. Also, I love the way Zappos is so open-minded. There is never a dull moment here. You have a second family here that will support you in anything you try to accomplish. I love Zappos and truly appreciate everything they have given me.

Julia J.

employee since 2011

To me, the Zappos Culture means looking forward to coming to work every day with great, fun people. I've only been with Zappos for a short while and I love it. The leadership teams get involved and get to know the employees and they make it a fun place to work. Go Zappos!!

Julie E.

employee since 2008

I would like to say that Zappos is the best place I have ever worked. They really care about their people. I love my job and all the team members I work with. Tony is the best person! He takes care of his employees very well. All of the Ten Core Values are practiced at Zappos. It should be number one on the list of best companies in the world to work for, not just number six. We have fun and still get the job done. We also have the best bosses to work for. Thanks for giving me the best job I have ever had. And thank you, Tony, for caring so much about your employees. Zappos rocks!!!

Julie M.

employee since 2010

I love the fact that I work for a company that encourages "Creating Fun and a Little Weirdness" (Core Value #3). I can come to work wearing my favorite skunk hat or cat ears and no one has a problem with it. Co-workers that embrace these Core Values make this a wonderful place to work. I am free to be myself and I can honestly say that this is the best job ever!

Julie T.
employee since 2010

I have been employed at Zappos in the pack-ship department since September 2010. I came in during the Christmas season – a very busy time in the life of a Zapponian. However, no matter how busy it became, everyone still had time to help one another. The greatest thing about working here is the way people seem to care about one another. No one is ever too busy to help or have a kind word of encouragement. Our management in pack-ship is wonderful. They aren't just supervisors and leads; they are friends. This feeling also crosses the boundaries into different departments. I have had the opportunity to work in several other areas and wherever I am, I feel welcomed by management as well as peers. Zappos offers great fringe benefits also, including free lunches and vending machines, pipeline classes to help us grow within the company, and many extras for employees and their families. I am truly blessed to be employed here and to have such great friends. Thanks, everyone. You are great!!!

Julie V.
employee since 2007

I have no idea who said it, but I have loved this quote from the first time I heard it. "Happiness is like peeing in your pants. Everyone can see it, but only you can feel its warmth." I think this quote represents what the Zappos Culture means to me. We are a company that is all about happiness. We Deliver Happiness to our customers and we get the happiness that comes from making someone's day. So, we send out happiness that comes from being happy, so we pee in our pants and everyone knows we are happy because we peed in our pants, and then we are happy, not because our pants are wet, but because other people are happy because we are happy. It's kind of like the circle of life.

Justin D.
employee since 2010

Zappos has many great benefits, even for part-time employees. Having games and parties during the workday is unheard of to me. I don't know of any workplace that does these crazy, fun things. Free food and satellite television is another great benefit. The 40% off employee coupon is amazing as well. I don't think I've owned so many shoes in my life! The environment here is very family-like. Everyone is friendly with little negative attitude.

Justin F.
employee since 2010

I started at Zappos last year thinking this was just going to be another job where I would have a hard time trying to fit in with the people I work with. After getting to know the people and the workplace, I realized that Zappos is a great place to work. Everyone is expected to ask questions. I enjoy waking up every morning, coming to work and having fun because that is what this place is about. It's not just about free insurance, free lunches and free T-shirts. It's about a family that works together and is always there for one another, with no questions asked. We're all a family here and that is how every company should be, no questions asked.

Justin L.
employee since 2010

My life at Zappos is the most exciting and beautiful life in the world. This is more than just a job; this is my whole life. I love putting shoes away on these l-o-n-g shoe racks filled with static electricity. My friends at the Zappos "FC Bario" are even more loving and caring than the homes in my neighborhood. They are more than just friends … they are family. Giving y'all my "Gangsta Hillbilly" handshake! Peace and harmony!

Justin S.
employee since 2011

The Zappos Culture means family to me – open, honest and dependable!

Justin W.
employee since 2010

"Culture" is a word that I have often overused and/or used incorrectly. The definition of culture at Zappos is more alive than in any dictionary published because here, culture lives, breathes, and evolves on a daily basis. I enjoy this evolution because with a living culture I also evolve as a human being. Wow! How many jobs in the world make you think about evolving as a human? Not many. The Zappos Culture and its Core Values apply to my life in general. It's more than just a job, it's an understatement.

Justin W.

employee since 2007

Our Zappos Culture is about inspiring people to find what they are passionate about and pursuing that passion. It is about surrounding ourselves with positive, motivated and creative people who continuously drive the company forward. It is about playing hard and working harder, with a smile!

Justyn N.

employee since 2011

Since I started working here at Zappos, I have enjoyed myself very much. This is the best job I have ever had. And since I started working at the age of 14 and am now 27, I have had many jobs. The people here are very nice and the managers are great at teaching me everything I need to know about my job. It's easy to make friends here also. The atmosphere is very laid-back and I love the fact that there is always something to do, whether I have to find work to keep myself busy or if shipments are ready to be put away. I plan on being here for a very long time, and I hope I can prove myself more and more every day. I was the most excited I have been in a very long time when I received a letter saying that I am a full-time employee. Thank you so much for this opportunity and I know I will prove that I am an asset to my co-workers and to this enormous, fast-growing, adventurous company.

Kalee S.

employee since 2007

The perfect job isn't hard to define. The perfect job is an environment that provides you with happiness. Zappos makes me truly happy. I love the Core Values, the people, the benefits, and the ... everything! Most of all, I just love what we do. We provide the best customer service, which is what I'd want as a customer. We do our absolute best to make everyone – customers and employees alike – happy. I know that I wouldn't be this happy anywhere else or doing anything else. If I had one million dollars in the bank, I wouldn't leave Zappos. People think I'm lying when I say this, but I'm not. If you think I'm lying, give me a million dollars and watch what I do! =)

Kara P.

employee since 2011

What can I say? Working for Zappos is awesome!!!! The benefits are amazing; management is wonderful; and I love how you don't have to be so serious at work. I am so grateful to work for such a great company!!! How many people do you know who could say the same thing?

Karen D.

employee since 2005

I just want to let everyone know that Zappos is the greatest. I have never worked for a company that gives so much to the people that work for it. And best of all, we are treated like we are family. They even sent me to Las Vegas to see how that part of Zappos works. They're an awesome group. I've been here at Zappos for six years and loving every minute of it. I plan on being here forever and ever. I love all my Zappos BFFs!!!

Karen G.

employee since 2005

Zappos is a great place to work. They view us as equals. People are workplaces and this is the best place, with a little fun and weirdness every day. Zappos shows us how much they care about us all the time, and the Ten Core Values are very important to us. They are the company; they keep it going and make it a great place. Zappos, you rock!!!

Karen M.
employee since 2010

Over the last 30 years, I've worked for eight companies in seven different industries. While these were good companies with a lot of great people, they struggled with motivating and keeping good employees. Morale was usually low and they couldn't figure out why. Now I know why! Zappos figured out that culture is not a list of ideals on the wall; it has to be part of the company's DNA. It's why our customers love us. It's why I'm proud to be here. And it's why I'll stay.

Kari H.
employee since 2009

At first glance, someone might think, "Oh, the Zappos Culture means you are fun and weird," and of course, they're right. But what is amazing to me about our unique culture is that it is so much more than that. When I come to work, I feel like I am coming home and working with my family. I know that on any given day, not only will I see people being goofy and crazy, but I will also experience true friendship, teamwork, and a "realness" that I have never found in any other work environment. I am so lucky to work with a stellar team. When I feel like I can't provide another ounce of energy to my job, they remind me of what I can accomplish. Even on the hard days, the Zappos Culture still proves strong. So a big shout out to the amazing Kentucky family for being just that, a family. I know that the reason I love Zappos is because of you all. You are the Zappos Culture.

Kasey M.
employee since 2011

I think Zappos is a great place to work! I am new and everyone has been nice and very helpful to me. I like that we get free lunch and free health insurance. This is a place where I could work forever! I love it here!

Kate F.
employee since 2011

The Zappos Culture is extremely new to me, since this is my second day on the job, but I already feel like part of a team. Possibly a quirky, crazy team, but that's how I like it. The people are kind and helpful and, although my first day was stressful, I still left with a smile on my face. I woke up sore the next day, but I was ecstatic to go to work again! I hope I grow and blossom in the culture of Zappos. I have so much to learn and there is nowhere but up in this company. Friendships will form, education will occur, and a life I have only heard about will soon shine through. This is the perfect place for a kooky person like me!!

Katherine B.
employee since 2010

To me, the Zappos Culture means great friends and an extended family!! I have made some life-long friends here who are family. We even have a monthly BBQ and bonfire! Zappos wouldn't be such a great place to work if the people didn't make it that way!!

Kathleen H.
employee since 2006

The Zappos Culture is a way of life. No other company has it! We are a group of people who call this place "our home away from home." We are a family! I've never worked in a place where everyone loved being around each other. Everyone is willing to help out one another. Everyone does his or her job without having to be told what to do so, while having fun doing it! There's always something fun going on inside the warehouse and outside of work too! I'd like to give a "shout out" to my peeps that make work fun. Thanks! There is only one culture, and that's the Zappos Culture.

Kathy D.
employee since 2006

Zappos is the best place to work! I've been here for five wonderful years And you are treated like family. It's a great feeling to come in and like your job. Zappos gives so much to its employees. When I started it was a small company, but now it has grown so much! And it keeps on growing. I love Zappos and I'll be here forever. Thanks, Zappos. :)

Katie F.
employee since 2008

I have worked for Zappos for almost three years now and my co-workers are like my extended family!!! I have fun with them not only at work, but outside of it as well. Some of my best friends are my co-workers. Even though we are going through a lot of changes, Zappos still keeps the family atmosphere alive. I have enjoyed working for Zappos. =)

Katrinia J.
employee since 2010

The Zappos Culture is unique. I love coming to work and being around my Zapponian family. I love the fact that, when I mention where I work, people get all excited and start sharing stories about their experiences with us.

Kayla C.

employee since 2007

I love my job and the people I work with. This is my second home and family. What I love most is the unexpected things that happen. I come in every day asking myself "What's going to happen next?" It can vary from Pipeline dressing up and playing games with each department to bringing in a mock chow wagon. You never know what they have up their sleeves.

Keith S.

employee since 2010

An honest workplace full of very interesting characters who make you feel good about having a job and who you are. Family and friends is what this place is about and you can see it in the faces of those you see while simply walking into the building.

Kelly B.

employee since 2010

Zappos is a fun place to work. I went from working with 90% grumpy people to working with 90% happy people. As long as you get your job done you can goof around. Perks are a bonus too! There aren't many places that pay for healthcare, feed you and allow you to play WII, Karaoke, or surf the web on your break, just to name a few. This job has its challenges, but why not have fun doing it? Zappos is an awesome place to work!

Kelly M.

employee since 2010

I really love it here! I have only worked at a few places before Zappos, but they didn't have such a warm atmosphere. I feel great coming to work. Zappos is the greatest. The end.

Kelly P.

employee since 2011

What the Zappos Culture means to me is being able to come to work and enjoy it every day.

Kelly P.

employee since 2011

I love Zappos! You get free vending machines and free lunch. There are great people here; I haven't met one person I haven't gotten along with. I have even told a few of my friends about Zappos and they have applied and are now working here. Zappos is one of the best jobs I have had!!! Zappos, Zappos, Zappos!

Ken B.

employee since 2010

Great place to work. It's a family here. Jeff is a great manger to work for.

Kendell W.

employee since 2011

It's a place where many different types of people can come together and work in a safe, fun environment, while making new friends.

Kerry M.

employee since 2011

I have only been here for a few weeks and I absolutely love my job and the people I work with!! I love that Zappos lets you show the real you and doesn't take your personality away just to do your job. And my manager and leads are always there for me.

I also love the fact that you never know what you might come to work and see, like managers dressed like penguins, which was totally awesome. That's all I have to say for now!! :)

Kevin T.

employee since 2008

I am the happiest I've ever been in my whole working life! It's not just a job, it's an adventure. It means that I'm going to retire a happy man, someday, and look back and miss this job. Enough of that! For now I will enjoy every second of my time with Zappos.

Kim H.

employee since 2009

When I go to work at Zappos I don't have to worry about fitting in or what other people think of me. After you work here a few weeks, your fellow Zapponians start to feel like family members and there is a sense of pride in the air.

Kim C.

employee since 2007

The Zappos Culture means being able to come to work and be myself. This is the only company that I have ever worked for that tries to make a difference in everyone's life. The atmosphere within the company follows us throughout our daily lives at home as well as at work. I love working for such a great company. Zappos rocks!!!!

Kim F.

employee since 2010

Culture, to me, means being able to bring your personality to work, whether it is weird and crazy or goofy and loud, and no one will judge you. I believe that the Zappos Culture (and hard work) is what makes this company what it is. The culture here is what makes me want to get up and come in every day with a smile on my face and ready to work. To me, without our culture, Zappos would be just another warehouse in Louisville with unhappy workers who hate their jobs. I feel that I am blessed to have such a great job with the most amazing people. Thank you to all the Zappos peeps who make work fun!!

Kimberly D.

employee since 2011

I've only been a team member for about a month now and it's been the best working experience I've ever had. Zappos welcomed me like no other employer in my past had . Everyone has been super-nice to me. They helped me through training and treated me with complete respect. I can definitely see why Forbes Magazine calls Zappos one of top places to work. I don't go to work sad every day or dreading the day. Working here isn't just a job; it's being part of something more. Zappos makes it fun by creating culture – something fun, new and exciting. And it's not just someone creating things for you to do. You actually have a say in the fun activities. I would love to become full time. I'm actually praying for it. I don't see being happy with any other company after experiencing Zappos!!

Kimberly S.

employee since 2007

I have been working at Zappos for almost four years now and I love it. The people here are great! I have made many new friends that I consider my family. This is the best company to work for. They treat their employees well – benefits parties and all!!!!!

Kira H.

employee since 2008

The word "family" comes to mind when I think of the Zappos Culture. Zappos is my home away from home. I have friends and co-workers that treat me as if I were part of their family. There is always someone to talk to you if you don't feel like yourself. Another thing that comes to mind when I think of the Zappos Culture is fun! With all the Zappos outings and events, this company knows how to have a good time. I wouldn't want to work for any other company!

Krissy R.

employee since 2010

The Zappos Culture is a way of life. It's our combination of working hard, playing hard, forming wonderful relationships, and having the freedom to be ourselves that makes the difference. Here I've found my escape, my home away from home. Now I bet that took the fork right outta your plastic!!

Kristen K.

employee since 2010

The Zappos Culture through my eyeballs includes (but is not limited to) wearing a tutu to work, hanging with co-workers on weekends, celebrating every holiday in costume with style, laughing until you cry, working hard and sometimes wicked-long hours, playing hard and recovering from wicked-long hours, being respected, sharing ideas, napping in the Zen Den when you've had 'that kind of day,' wearing safety goggles because of the Nerf Gun War that surrounds you, "The Dougie" on repeat, being serenaded on your birthday by 50 cent, having the freedom to do big things, party bus rides to awards banquets, the KY+LV Love for one another, constantly documenting the crazy at work through photography and tagging the evidence immediately on Facebook, 3:00 lunges, loving the people around me, and feeling so incredibly blessed to call Zappos my home for eight hours a day. Blessed am I. Loved I feel. High five!

Kristen M.

employee since 2011

I like that everyone is very friendly and makes you feel welcome, learning new things. It's a very stress-free company.

Kristi H.

employee since 2010

When I started working here, I thought "This place is crazy!" :) I would wake up and be excited, wondering what was going to happen at Zappos today. This company's culture truly defines the word "culture." Here at Zappos, we work hard so we can play harder. Putting all of our Ten Core Values into place each day is something that impresses me most about this company. I learn something new every day, and I am guaranteed to laugh out loud ... maybe even to the point of crying ... because we have so much fun! I feel honored to work for this company and I am grateful for everything that Zappos has to offer. :) Oh, and don't forget ... CareBears Rock!!!

Kristie R.

employee since 2007

The Zappos Culture is incomparable! It's the best place I have ever worked! It's a company where you're encouraged to come to work and be yourself, have a little fun :) and are embraced for who you really are. I'm fortunate to have an opportunity to work with such amazing people, and to view my co-workers as family. Work hard, play hard! I love Zappos!

Kristina W.

employee since 2010

I like the fun and weirdness of working here. I have never worked at a company more fun than this one. Zappos is more than just a job.

Kyle K.

employee since 2007

A day at Zappos Haiku:
A free Mountain Dew
An enjoyable day with my friends
Sandwiches again

Kym H.

employee since 2010

Zappos is the first place I have worked where I don't dread coming into work. I have made the most awesome group of friends who would do anything for me and I would do anything for them. I love being a part of the Zappos Culture Crew and helping to promote our culture in our workplace and in my own home. My kids even walk around saying "Be Passionate and Humble." I love all my Zappos Girls!!!!!

Lacee Y.

employee since 2010

Family! The Zappos Culture, to me, means that I can be myself and have a good time with my job. You can make life-long friends here, and maybe one day all jobs can emulate the Zappos work environment.

LaDonna W.

employee since 2010

It's great to come to work knowing you're coming to a happy place. It's the best! Yeah, Zappos!

Lakisha R.
employee since 2010

What does the Zappos Culture mean to me? If I had to use one word it would be appreciative. There's no other company, large or small, that would ever take the time to get to know their employees the way Zappos has. From the application process on, Zappos makes sure they get to know us. That's why at this company, everyone's job feels equally important. No one feels like the little man. And that's why the culture at Zappos is like no other.

Latetcia P.
employee since 2011

My experience with Zappos is awesome!!!! When they say we have a culture here, we really do! From the diversity of the people to the hot potato while dancing to Michael Jackson's "Beat it." The people are friendly and made me feel welcome from Day One. They pulled me out of my quiet little shell. I am changing and growing here, becoming more outgoing and loud, still being me, but with more courage. Zappos employees take pride in helping others. Want an example? A new employee ran off the road the other day and got stuck in the mud. The only people who stopped to see if he was OK and to help push the car out of the mud were Zappos employees!!!!

Laura A.
employee since 2008

This is the best job I have ever had. Not knowing what to except when I first came here, and this being my first warehouse job ever, I could not have come to a better place to learn, because of the way I was taught and who taught me, the people I work with every day and the values we strive to work and live by. They are what makes this place number #1 with me and proud to have a Zapponian family to call my own. And all I had to do get this was get the work out and really want to be on the team. The rewards and benefits are like no other because, when it comes to Zappos, there is no better place.

Laura C.
employee since 2006

I have been lucky enough to work at Zappos for over four years now, and the company has never let me down. Even though we are going through some very big changes and some fears may be spreading, I have faith that our culture will stay strong. As long as we have the passion to lift one another up and always treat this job as "more than just a job" we cannot fail! We are very blessed to have all the benefits that we get, but without our culture we are nothing. Our love for "Creating Fun and a Little Weirdness" (Core Value #3) is what attracts people to Zappos and keeps them here. It's not just about great health benefits, free food, and awesome parties. It's about being able to be comfortable being yourself and having a family atmosphere when you come to work. I love the people I work with and I love this company, and I am very grateful to be a part of it! Thank you, Zappos!!

Laura S.
employee since 2011

I think Zappos is a great place to work. It has great benefits along with free lunches every day. I believe that Zappos really takes care of its employees, which makes me happy to be part of the Zappos family.

Laura Y.
employee since 2011

To me, the Zappos Culture means learning different cultures at work and learning new things. It means being in a family environment, working with others and helping everyone.

Lawrence H.
employee since 2011

The Zappos Culture is an employee-friendly, fun and exciting work atmosphere that allows employees to be individuals.

Leah M.
employee since 2005

Every day when I go to work, Core Value #1 pops into my mind ("Deliver Wow Through Service"). I am blessed to work for a company that puts the safety of its team members first. I personally strive to carry that "Wow" on to all of the team members, empowering them to make safety fun. My Safety Team is not just the six wonderful peeps who call safety their home, but also every team member who is on board!

Leah S.
employee since 2010

The Zappos Culture is about everyone creating a great atmosphere. I love the attitudes, and diverse backgrounds of people here. Everyone gets along, and that makes the workplace much more enjoyable and positive. Keep the values going! I feel Zappos really cares about its customers and its employees, and that means everything!

Leo H.

employee since 2010

Zappos isn't just a job to me; it's so much more. It's home, family, fun and a career. What I like most is the opportunities that Zappos offers, including the ability to move up with hard work and turn this job into a career.

Lerlaine C.

employee since 2010

The Zappos Culture, to me, means family; it's my home away from home. The creative minds we have here are spectacular. Every day, we grow closer to one another! Yesterday we were strangers; today, co-workers; and tomorrow, lifetime friends.

Leslee L.

employee since 2010

When you feel lost and confused, there's always someone around to help you get back on track.

Linda B.

employee since 2010

To me, The Zappos Culture means acceptance of others, regardless of diversity. I love Zappos!

Linda C.

employee since 2006

Coming to work at Zappos was the best thing I have ever done. I have a new, wonderful family here, and I couldn't ask for better people to work with or for.

Lindsay K.

employee since 2011

The Zappos Culture means more to me than I can put into words. For starters, I have never worked somewhere that I loved so much. It's more like an awesome family than an awesome job. It is very important to me to show my leads, managers, and other team members that they mean a lot to me. I do whatever I can to be a great worker, a safe person and to be as inviting as I can to my peers. I have experienced being away from Zappos for six months. It was possibly the hardest six months of my life. Not because I didn't have a job (I had one), but because there is no place like Zappos. I was amazed at the safety violations I witnessed. They would never happen at Zappos. I also realized very quickly that I was just a number to them. It wasn't something they tried to hide. It was a truth that was out in the open. I was in disbelief. Now I'm more than grateful to be back here where I belong. I hope to be able to grow with the company and my family, and maybe even move up in the company as well. I recommend Zappos to anyone. It will change your view of what a great place to work is. I love Zappos now and will love it forever!!! <3

Lisa C.

employee since 2010

I am a new member of the Zappos family and I have been truly amazed at how similar this culture is to that of a company where I worked 20 years ago. I truly feel at home in this environment. I feel very blessed and thankful for this opportunity.

Lisa G.

employee since 20009

I like the Zappos Culture because the company does not discriminate against anyone they hire. It doesn't matter what your age is or what you look like. We are all given an opportunity to work and prove ourselves. Thanks, Zappos!

Lisanna L.

employee since 2010

The Zappos Culture is a feeling of family – a home away from home. You can find me smiling every day because I know that I am supported by positive people who work together to make a difference. I now have a deeper appreciation of the small things in life. I believe in The Zappos Culture because it guided me back to my happiness track when I was lost. I am excited to continue my Zappos journey!

Liz K.
employee since 2011

Although I just recently started with Zappos, I already know that this will be my home for years and years to come! I had always followed Zappos and read about its culture, but nothing can describe the actual feeling when you get here. I immediately felt like part of the family, and instantly a huge weight was lifted off of my shoulders: I can be 100% myself here. I have enjoyed waking up these past few weeks, not dreading having to go to work, but excited to get here! I can't thank Zappos enough for letting me be a part of the family. I'm so excited to see what is to come. Zappos rocks!

Logan R.
employee since 2007

Free food and awesome benefits. Enough said.

Luis C.
employee since 2010

The Zappos Culture, to me, means to be a hard worker, be safe and aware of your surroundings and not breaking the safety rules.

Luis M.
employee since 2009

I think Zappos is very important for me because it gives me time to see my co-workers, enjoy their company and learn. The pipeline class is very important for our culture. The teachers are very good and, in general, Zappos is different because of its culture. We enjoy life here. We help one another to work and be happy, and we are always waiting for something new.

Luke D.
employee since 2005

What does the Zappos Culture mean to me? It is the reason why we work here. The culture is evident in how we deal with our customers and the people around us. Everyone is family!! When you wake up in the morning, you're excited about coming to work and helping anyone you meet. We hold doors open for other people, even if they're 100 yards away.

What I love most about the Zappos Culture is that I am not the only one who experiences it. Everyone around me has the same ideals and feelings, and it shows daily. When it comes do resolving any issue that arises, we jump all over it. It's great being surrounded by this way of thinking and also being "part of if all." I hope that I can continue to grow right along with Zappos. It's been a pleasure and a privilege. Thanks for reading my post.

Luseni M.
employee since 2006

I have been with Zappos for a few years now, and it is strange to think of a company as a culture. But just as with any human endeavor, eventually culture is what defines you and your tribe. I know, because my grandfathers had a kingdom that still exists today. It has a language, rules, traditions, values, practices, taboos and clothes that separate us from any one else. The test is through the generations. If you show up, can people tell who you are? I see Zappos as a young culture in the making because it takes much more than values to make a culture and it can survive through generations. If you put 10,000 people in a room, can the Zapponian(s) be identifiable? It is even harder if you send only one out. Are you unique, special, or memorable enough that people will either know you are a Zapponian or say who that person is? I am fortunate enough to see a few generations here at Zappos – grandparents, parents, sons and daughters, which is a good sign. It encourages everyone to know our Values as the first step, but do not be fooled. Just because you can rattle them off in three months does not mean that you are cultured. We have great summer and holiday parties, but how about the Zappos birthday, the one day that we are all off to celebrate who we are. I look forward to when you can be identified as a Zapponian and it stands for something you earned and what people aspire to be.

M.A. S.

employee since 2010

The Zappos Culture here means everything to me. Not only is this the best place I have ever worked in my life, but also the fact that this place saved me and kept me strong through the most trying period in my life. It might seem like a job from the outside, but inside it is a strong, spirited group of people who welcome you and make every day here worth it! This isn't about culture, but family. My family away from home. Thank you for everything Zappos!

Madonna F.

employee since 2010

I really want to share with anyone who truly cares how thrilled I am about being here at Zappos. To me, this is not just a job. Since my arrival here at the end of 2010, I have met the greatest, kindest and most inspiring people I have ever had the pleasure of working with. There is always someone with a smile, or someone asking you how you are, and they really mean it. The leads seem to genuinely care about you as a person. My managers have been the "knock 'em out of the universe" types. Did they come from super fantastic? I am very glad to be here. Thanks, Justin.

Malcolm L.

employee since 2011

The first time I walked through the doors at Zappos, I was thinking that this place reminds me of high school. But it's kinda better then high school. People are really happy to be here and there's free food ... a great deal of it. I hope to be full some time soon .

Mandy R.

employee since 2006

Once again, Zappos has proven to be my true family. I love you all sooo much! :)

Manecia P.

employee since 2007

Zappos is all about being a family and I love the people here. They're not only my friends, they're my family. I have never worked anywhere like this before. It doesn't get any better.

Margarita R.

employee since 2011

Working hard while still having fun! :) <3 Zappos.

Mariah W.

employee since 2010

We are one big family that works together to get things done. We need to WOW the customers. We can have fun and be ourselves, never having to worry what we are going to eat for lunch or drink all day. It's a relief.

Mark E.

employee since 2010

Culture is one of the best things that Zappos offers its employees. It helps make this a fun and enjoyable place to work.

Mark M.

employee since 2005

Being a member of the Zappos family has generated a sense of pride within my family and me. When someone asks where you're employed and you say Zappos, watch them light up. Always questions, always positive feedback about our family. My wife and children share in the pride of being associated with Zappos. Family, friends and pride: sounds like a recipe for success.

Martika B.

employee since 2010

Zappos rocks my socks!!!

Marty M.

employee since 2011

Although I just recently started working at Zappos, I've already learned that the people here are friendly and willing to help me learn the best and most efficient way to do my job. I believe this is really a good place to work and have fun at the same time. As my old buddy Forrest Gump would say, "That's all I've got to say about that!"

Mary D.

employee since 2008

I have been with the Zappos Fulfillment Center since 2008. This is the best job I have ever had. Zappos takes very good care of its team members and we take care of Zappos. The culture here is all about family and having fun while we rock it out with our customer service 24/7. Zappos gives us great benefits, great parties, free vending machines and outstanding discounts. In turn, the team members give Zappos 110% every day at work. I love working here. It's not just a job!!!

Mary G.

employee since 2010

I believe that Zappos is a very good place to be because the company seems to care a lot about keeping spirits up and tensions down. Some of the ways they do this are through the variety of activities that they sponsor. They try to establish a good rapport with all employees and allow us to feel like we can openly discuss any situation that may help us do our job better. They offer great incentives to work with them and plenty of opportunities for advancement within the company.

Mary H.

employee since 2010

The Zappos Culture is the set of rules we live by every day. People here WOW you every day. There is always something to learn and someone to teach you how to do it. When something breaks down (like the sorter), everyone works hard together to make sure our customers are taken care of and the orders are shipped. Our culture makes teamwork easy and makes it fun to go to work.

Mary J.

employee since 2007

Zappos is my family away from home. The support I got throughout this year from my Zappos family kept me sane when I had lots of issues with my "home" family. Thanks to all who WOWed me this year.

Matt B.

employee since 2010

I have never worked anywhere like Zappos. I absolutely love the culture. The managers make work fun every day. They always do fun activities and have fun contests. I plan to stay at this place until I retire!

Matt H.

employee since 2011

The Zappos Culture is having your cake and eating it too!!!!

Matt H.

employee since 2010

The Zappos Culture, to me, comes down to one simple word: Pride. Pride in doing what is right for the customer and for your co-workers. I believe our culture is one of excellence that resonates throughout every group in the company. Doing a job halfway is not acceptable to anyone I have worked with, which lets me know that I can depend on anyone for help. It also lets me know that people are depending on me to hold up my end as well. I have only been with the company a few months, but this by far has been one of the more unique and rewarding experiences of my life.

Matt M.

employee since 2010

The Zappos Culture is pretty crazy for a warehouse job, which isn't a bad thing!

Matthew C.

employee since 2010

The Zappos Culture makes this a fun place to work. I believe the culture is the backbone of Zappos. It brings everyone together to work hard plus have a good time!!!!

Matthew C.

employee since 2010

During these tough economic times, the people of central Kentucky and southern Indiana are very fortunate to have an opportunity as unique as Zappos as an employer. Unlike many other companies, we are continually growing and opening up new doors for employees. It's a great job to have and be a part of something much bigger than just a warehouse. The culture is great as well. There are not too many jobs around that can boast of a set of Core Values like we have. The people here are like family to me and I plan to continue to further my career here at Zappos and help out our cause in any way I can. Keep up the WOW!

Matthew C.

employee since 2010

The Zappos Culture is similar to that of the order of the Jedi and the Sith, combined with great teachings, such as passion, determination, teamwork and leadership.

Matthew F.

employee since 2010

The Zappos Culture, to me, is the incentive we get for being creative at work and, through that creativity, being more productive in daily tasks. It's also the ability to connect with people at all levels, no matter how high up the ladder they may seem. Lastly, the Zappos Culture means that I can embrace kitty cats openly and freely amongst my co-workers without reproof. :<3

Matthew H.

employee since 2011

Being new to Zappos (I've been here about a month), I still find things every day that shock me about the Zappos Culture. I think the thing that still is hard to grasp sometimes is, who's in charge? Now, that could be taken the wrong way. We're not all running around like chickens with our heads off. Actually, the best way to describe this culture is that there is such a great sense of camaraderie and family that it seems like no one is superior. Only that they happen to be running the show. Nothing is too big or too small for someone to take on here and you have to be ready for that. To look at it on the flip side, everyone is equal in the amount of fun they have. If you don't come to work ready for the possibility that the person managing or training you might be wearing a wig and clown paint, you will have to adjust your outlook on the path to success and satisfaction at Zappos.

Matthew H.

employee since 2010

Zappos offers an excellent opportunity for employees to enjoy their jobs. This place doesn't twist your arm and make you suffer through each day. The Core Values really set a standard that makes Zappos better than any other job.

Matthew M.

employee since 2010

I like my job. I love picking and staying busy.

Matthew S.

employee since 2006

I am here because I am treated well. Zappos cares about its team members. In turn, I show my appreciation by passing it on to customers in the form of WOW, and trying my best to make each customer as happy as possible. I have been at Zappos for four years and plan to be here for many more.

Matthew S.

employee since 2011

I've only been working at Zappos for several weeks now, but already, I can say it is the best job I've ever had. The people I work with are great, the environment is positive, and the free food is a great perk! I think I'll stick around here for a while and see what else goes down.

Matthew Woodrow M.

employee since 2010

Going on my second year now at Zappos and I thought it couldn't get any better than my first year. I was wrong. A lot has changed in the warehouses and it's been the most interesting year ever! Along the way I have met many new friends. This year was the first year that Zappos has had Seasonal Squad Leaders. For me, that meant taking on a challenge that I was looking forward to. We had hundreds of employees come in to work throughout our peak season, and giving the leads the help that was needed was great. The highlight of the year for me at Zappos was the holiday party. I had heard a lot about how big, great, wild and fun they were. Well, those words don't come close to describing the time I had here. Zappos keeps advancing in the 100 best places in the country to work, and it's in the top two for me! I couldn't ask for more than Zappos has given me. It's more than just a job!!!

Maureen D.

employee since 2006

The Zappos Culture! Now, that's a mouthful! The Zappos Culture means making the best of every situation. Being happy and satisfied in your life, work and (most of all) your environment. For a lot of people, Zappos is like getting free therapy. You can let your hair down and be as silly, relaxed and sometimes even goofy as you want to be and it's OK. It's even expected. If you allow yourself, you can't work here a day and not laugh or make someone laugh. Too many of us get caught up in the stress of life and forget to smile and enjoy life. Zappos works very hard at giving us the tools to do just that. Zappos has a support system that I have not found anywhere else. The people here care about you. Whether it is work or home, someone here is always willing to help.

Mayol M.

employee since 2011

To begin with, everyone at Zappos is supportive of each other; especially if you ask for something you don't know about the job you are working on. I really like people here and the Zappos Culture, and I am glad to be a part of the Zappos family.

Meghan B.

employee since 2011

To me, the Zappos Culture means that I no longer cry as I am riding in to work. I no longer feel like I am working. It feels more like hanging out with all of my best friends while completing an enjoyable task. Banana.

Melissa C.

employee since 2010

Zappos is a great place to work! On top of all the benefits, like free lunch, snacks, and insurance, it's also a very friendly environment. Fun activities offer a great way to get through the workday.

Melissa H.

employee since 2011

The Zappos Culture is awesome!! I have been here three weeks and I love coming to work every day. I have never enjoyed a job so much!! The culture is very family-oriented and I love everyone I work with. Everyone is extremely nice and very helpful. :) The benefits are outstanding. I'm excited to be a part of the Zappos family. Whoop Whoop!!!

Melissa L.

employee since 2006

As I sit here trying to think of the best way to summarize what the Zappos Culture means to me, I realize just how hard it is to put it in a simple sentence or two. There are so many things that make our culture what it is. It's everything from co-workers becoming your best friends to having creative control in our jobs and unconditional support to do what we feel is right. I cannot begin to express how thankful I am to be part of a company that values my ideas and truly cares about my growth, personally and professionally!

Melissa L.

employee since 2010

I enjoy working for Zappos. I am having to de-program myself from corporate America. This is a whole new world where you are a person, your age doesn't matter and you're not over-qualified. That is all I kept hearing while I was looking for a job. I am truly blessed and grateful for my position here at Zappos. Thanks.

Melissa S.

employee since 2010

Since I've been here at Zappos, I have met some of the most awesome people in the world. Working here is great!

Micah A.

employee since 2010

As a Culture Crew member, the Zappos Culture, to me, is just having fun and being able to enjoy yourself and your day at work. We have lots of fun here and always deliver an outstanding job. Our co-workers turn into family and, with this company expanding exponentially, it is difficult to keep that feeling. That's what the Zappos Culture is to me.

Michael B.

employee since 2006

Zappos is the best company I have ever had the privilege of working for. Come on, you know it's true!! I wake up every day and look forward to coming to work. Not the, "Oh, man! Do I have to do this again? Go to the same boring old place and not have any fun?" Zappos is all about culture and fun. Just look around and you'll see it every day. Zappos continues to WOW me.

Michael B.

employee since 2007

The Zappos Culture has taken over my life. When I go home, I still try to live by the Zappos Core Values. I try to have a blast while still getting stuff done. Zappos still rocks my socks off, while my socks are still on.

Michael H.

employee since 2010

Zappos is a great place to work. Nobody is ever mad and the culture is great. It's a fun workplace and I really like it here better than any other job I've ever had. I actually like coming to work now, for a change. The supervisors and managers are cool.

Michael L.

employee since 2010

I love Zappos. It's the only place an employee is truly appreciated. The lunches, activities and the open communications with all employees and leads make it a great place to work.

Michael N.

employee since 2010

What I love the most about Zappos is the environment. Of all the jobs I've had, not one has been this laid-back. I enjoy what I do! I don't think I'll ever be able to find another job that compares to this one! I also love the free food they have for lunch. It's awesome, and so are the health benefits. Rock on, Zappos!

Michael P.

employee since 2011

Absolute funki-liciousness!!

Michael S.

employee since 2011

After only one week of working here at Zappos I've discovered it has been everything they told me it would be, and much more.

Michael N.

employee since 2011

The Zappos Culture, to me, is totally different from any job I've ever had. It is very family-oriented. I actually enjoy working here because of the environment. I want to be part of this organization for as long as I can. All the people here are friendly and crazy, but in a good way. I recommend this company for everyone because you can work and have fun at the same time.

Michael W.

employee since 2010

The Zappos Culture is a way of life. Instead of trying to explain myself, I will give a synopsis of Portal. (Portal 2's release date was only a few days ago.) In Portal you awake as a test subject inside a glass room. You are allowed out by stepping through a portal that opens in your room's wall, letting you outside of an adjoining portal that appears immediately outside of that room to your right. Gradually you progress to rooms similar to this, testing your abilities of cognitive reasoning, until finally you acquire a gun that can actually shoot these "Portals" wherever you choose to aim it. The game follows a very short, slightly humorous storyline that ends as abruptly as it began. I give the game a 5 out of 5. Zappos is awesome and you should buy Portal and Portal 2. That is all.

Michelle H.

employee since 2010

Zappos is important to me because it's like my second family. We always have so much fun at work. I love my co-workers and always look forward to coming to work.

Michelle L.

employee since 2010

To keep morale up in the company, I think if someone passes six safety audits in a row they should be given an extra day off! No points or sick or vacation time used! Culture means everything to me and Zappos, so we should find little ways of keeping morale up!

Michelle M.

employee since 2009

To me, the Zappos Culture describes a place where everyone is seen with the same eyes, where people really seem to care. It's unlike any job I've had before, and I've had many. It's easy to see why a lot of people want to work here. I'm very glad I do.

Michelle T.

employee since 2010

As a former medical professional, I thought I was on the right path with my life and career until a series of unfortunate events led me here. Much like the movie "A Series of Unfortunate Events," it turned out to be the most awesome thing that has ever happened to me!! I found a renewed passion for life and work. I found a home away from home, not only at Zappos, but also with the safety team. We truly work together as one to keep our family safe. You really can have both, and thanks to Zappos and Tony for showing us that it's OK to love your job and look forward to coming in every day. I also look forward to continuing my pursuit "of Growth and Learning" (Core Value #5) as I work toward my career goals. :)

Mickey S.

employee since 2010

The Zappos Culture means teamwork, fun, creativity, family, friends, passion, hard work, weirdness and hilarious people, all working together to make this something that most people would call work, although it's way more enjoyable than any other place you've ever worked at.

Mikeala W.

employee since 2010

Zappos. I never really knew about the company until 2010. I may have heard about it a few times, but never thought about it. Now I work for the company and I love it. I love the friendly working environment. I can come to work in a bad mood but I won't stay that way for long because somebody is always saying things to make me smile or laugh. I wish there were more places like Zappos. I hope to continue working here for many years to come.

Mindy H.

employee since 2006

The Zappos Culture is what makes it such a good company. No other workplace offers the things that Zappos offers. The positive vibe is what motivates us to work so hard. People really respond well when they feel appreciated.

Mirzeta S.

employee since 2007

I love my job and the happy people around me! The benefits are good. It's just a very good place to work.

Mohamed H.

employee since 2009

I like Zappos.

"Mouse"

employee since 2010

The Zappos Culture, to me, is a lot like your family at home. Sometimes it can be challenging to grow together in a direction that fits all. Just like home, it can be fun, exciting and sometimes a little weird. I love my family at home and wouldn't trade them for anything. The same goes for Zappos. It's a challenging, fun place to work and to build lasting relationships with people that I like to call my work family. The Zappos Culture is growing together like family. We are all different and weird, but in the end we take care of each other. Love ya!

Mr. Thomason.

employee since 2009

The Zappos Culture is awesome! I <3 Zappos!

Namron B.

employee since 2011

Working at Zappos has been a great experience. Some of the activities we do might make people laugh. But it's those kinds of things that make it one of a kind. Plus the food, mmmmm ...

Naoto I.

employee since 2010

Hello. I have been a Zappos employee for about three months. I enjoy working with the employees here. Everybody is very friendly and helpful. Of all the jobs I have held, I have enjoyed Zappos the most. I am very thankful for the free food and drinks along with being allowed to listen to my mp3 player. I've worked at other warehouse jobs and none of them offers any of that. Another thing I love about Zappos is we have ice cream. If you knew me well you'd know I can't live without ice cream, so amen to that!! HOLLA BACK!

Nathaniel S.

employee since 2010

Zappos is unlike any place I have worked before. This has been the only business to feed my tummy and give me a paycheck as well. I have met some of the most unusual people and it makes for a different experience.

Nelda H.

employee since 2010

I have been with Zappos only a short time and have already seen the great family bonding they speak of. When I worked in the seasonal time, it was awesome. Not only were the people I worked with exciting, the spirit of the company was amazing. I am 52 years young and have never been more excited to work for a company. My husband and I have 9 children and 12 grandchildren, and still counting, so I am well aware of the values and the hard work that go into building a great family. This is what Zappos has done for their extended family of employees; it has involved hard work, good values and a sense that everybody matters. Family values are so very important to me, and that's what makes Zappos such a great company to work for. I will be a Zapponian for a long, long time and I expect to be just as enthusiastic as I am today. Thank you, Zappos, for making me a part of your family.

Nicholas F.

employee since 2010

The Zappos Culture, to me, is like a high school where all the people are friendly.

Nicholas G.

employee since 2011

What does the Zappos Culture mean to me? The first thing is the free food. When you're a big guy like me, you love any place that pays for your meals. Second is the people, including the managers, who are outgoing, funny, and spontaneous. The third and final thing is the hours. I love having three days off every week. That's what the Zappos Culture means to me.

Nicholas M.

employee since 2010

The Zappos Culture creates a different kind of workplace. I have never worked in a place as fun or creative as Zappos is.

Nicholas P.

employee since 2010

I love working at Zappos because the environment is awesome. It is truly a different culture. Zappos has heated smoking areas, free lunch and vending machines. Zappos takes care of its employees and doesn't just care about profits. That's the main reason I love Zappos ... because Zappos loves me.

Nicholas W.

employee since 2010

Zappos has brought me close to some great people.

Nick C.

employee since 2011

Zappos is a wonderful place to work. You have fun while you're working. Leave the drama at the door and do what you need to do with some chill people, old and young. Plus, it's cool when you go into a ditch and people come from work to help you out.

Nick M. (Kidd)

employee since 2010

Zappos is awesome. The women are fun to talk to (the best time is at the holiday party.) Free food and free insurance are pretty cool. The management team isn't bad, although there are a few that take some getting used to. Enjoy.

Nicolas P.

employee since 2010

To me, the Zappos Culture means working at the company for three days and feeling like I've worked here for three years. That's just how friendly and casual the environment is.

Nikki T.

employee since 2007

Zappos = WOW!! This is my second time working for Zappos. I was given the chance to come back after I had to leave under certain circumstances. Zappos is truly a great place to work. You can be yourself and feel good about it. There is so much to learn here and you learn something new every day! It is awesome when you have managers and leads that make it a great place to work!

Noah J.

employee since 2010

For me this year, the Zappos Culture has meant working harder than I ever have before and loving it, and at the same time having more fun at work and with my coworkers than I ever had. Normally those two things would be mutually exclusive, but here, they go hand in hand. The Zappos Culture has meant seeing my co-workers and me being developed and moved into positions and departments where they can excel and grow, both professionally and personally. The Zappos Culture has also meant recommending jobs to friends outside the company, watching them get hired, and knowing they love the company just as much as I do.

Oscar C.

employee since 2010

I am from Puerto Rico and I was still living there when I first heard about Zappos. I needed a job in Kentucky so I could move my family back to the states. After applying for several jobs and getting no interview opportunities I was feeling a little frustrated. Then I heard about Zappos through a friend of my wife who was working here. I sent my application and Zappos responded in less than a week. I told them I was still out of the country and that I was planning to move here soon. They told me that was not a problem at all. They interviewed me by phone and told me to call them as soon as I arrived in Kentucky to schedule a personal interview. I moved from Puerto Rico on July 13th 2010 and on July 27th I was hired full time, with benefits, by this great company. It could not have worked out any better. I was finally able to move my family back to the states. Working for Zappos has changed my life in a very good way. I could not ask for a better welcome from my co-workers and from the people of Kentucky. That's what the Zappos Culture means to me. This is by far the best job I ever had.

Osman S.

employee since 2010

The Zappos Culture, to me, is a blend of many objectives, goals, and traits that stir up like a tornado in front of someone who witnesses it and simply says "WOW!" When you're around it, you know it's special. Objectives include: achieving success by delivering our services to our customers and the bond created through involvement with fellow workers as a family. The goals and courtesy we maintain among one another are to accomplish tasks accurately and then go a step beyond expectations. Traits we cultivate include a humorous attitude and a goofy, silly and fun perspective at work. The perspective we deliver – The Zappos Culture is – an aura and energy that illuminates every individual.

Pam M.

employee since 2011

I was just recently hired, and what a great place to work!!! Everyone is so nice and helpful!

Pam R.

employee since 2010

Zappos? What can I say? This is an awesome place to work. I feel like everyone is family. They really care about one another. Our culture here is wonderful. I love coming to work to be around so many great people. I have made so many friends here. The company makes you feel wanted and they do things to keep you here. The Zappos culture involves everyone, regardless what race you are or how you look. Thanks, Tony, for making everyone happy!!!

Pamela D.

employee since 2007

I have worked for Zappos for three years and I love it!!! Zappos cares about making the workplace somewhere we want to come to. I watched how Zappos cared so much about an employee who became ill at work one day and it touched my heart. A good friend and co-worker was so excited when she e-mailed Tony and he actually e-mailed her back. They even came in one week and shut the place down and threw us a huge party. No one was expecting it. They WOW us and, in return, we want to work really hard for them!

Patrice D.

employee since 2006

Free lunch, free vending machines and awesome benefits. What a great place to work! And to meet such great people!!!

Patricia B.

employee since 2010

I think Zappos is awesome because of their benefits program and the fact that you can continually learn new how to do new jobs and take classes to improve yourself!

Patricia J.

employee since 2006

I don't think there's any other company out there that does the things Zappos does for its employees. We are spoiled. Occasionally people leave the company, only to return saying they didn't know how good they had it until they had gone to work elsewhere. That alone says a lot. Keep spoiling us, Zappos. I like it!

Patricia M.

employee since 2010

When I started working at Zappos, I didn't realize I would love it here. It's not like any other warehouse job I have ever had. Here it's accepted to be a little different. I actually enjoy coming to work and I have met a lot of weird and wonderful people whose company I enjoy every day. Zappos' Core Values are what I want to use as a foundation for my life outside of work.

Patricia S.

employee since 2011

I came here from Sturgis, Kentucky about six weeks ago to apply for a job here at Zappos. As I arrived, I was greeted with smiles and friendly faces from everyone I met. I started on April 6 of this year and I have had a wonderful time since then. The team members are great to work with and we have a lot of fun. On the Saturday before Easter, we even had an Easter egg hunt. Zappos is a great place to work!

Patrick B.

employee since 2009

In a word, the Zappos Culture means family. Not always perfect, but we are a family!

Patrick K.

employee since 2011

I can't really think of too many things that I have seen at Zappos since I've only been here for one week, but the one thing that I have noticed is the way that the majority of Zappos employees treasure the freedoms the company provides. The freedom to express ourselves and to be individuals is amazing. I have been welcomed into the Zappos family and hope to be a member for a very long time.

Patrick M.

employee since 2010

The Zappos Culture is a very fun, relaxed environment, with great employees that are respectful, kind, helpful and fun to be around. Although Zappos has great benefits, what separates it from other companies is its endless demands to WOW customers and employees.

Paul B.

employee since 2010

First and foremost, my new career with Zappos is without a doubt the best job situation i have ever had in all the years I have been working. Zappos' management is fantastic, friendly, helpful and sincerely concerned about the employees' well-being. The work itself is super, as there is always something new to learn and most of the positions are structured so that you challenge yourself to do as much as you possibly can. Personally, I enjoy testing myself to see if I can improve my last rate. I don't always succeed, but that is the neat part because you can always try again. I look forward to many more years a member of the Zappos family.

Paul C.

employee since 2011

Zappos is a place where all kinds of people come together to make up a unique kind of family. The weirder you are, the better! It is one of the only places that I know of that you will see people of all sorts that you're not likely to see together anywhere else, talking like they have always been close friends. Zappos is a start to a better community.

Paul D.

employee since 2010

I have now been working here just a little over seven months and I love every day that I'm here. I came in as a temp and survived long enough to become a success story. I have been sent through many departments and shifts, but one thing has been a constant: the people. We are the Zappos Culture. I am very thankful to be a part of a company that puts such an emphasis on culture. It makes coming to work a pleasure.

Paul D.

employee since 2010

The Zappos Culture, to me, is a combination of all the things we do and say to improve our relationships with our customers and with one another, both as individuals and as a company.

Paul P.

employee since 2010

To me, the Zappos Culture is awesome. The people around you make you feel right at home. You don't have to be shy about anything. If you have any problems you always have someone in the workplace you can turn to for help. It is a very good company to work for and I am proud to be a part of the team.

Paul S.

employee since 2010

Zappos is a wonderful place to work. This is the first place I've ever worked that allows you to be yourself with absolutely no criticism. I have been with Zappos for one year and I truly enjoy my job. I don't recall meeting anybody within the company that I couldn't talk to, and all employees are easy to get along with. I truly hope this is the last job I will ever have. Zappos rocks!!!

Paula H.

employee since 2010

I would like to say that this is one of the friendliest places I have worked at. The people here are encouraged to be themselves. It's nice to know that in a plastic world there is still some individuality. The benefits here are great and the only limits you have here are the ones you put on yourself. If I could change one thing here it's that I would love to have some music piped into the warehouses. What about it, Zappos?

Paula P.

employee since 2006

I love Zappos. I can honestly say that this is the best place I've ever worked. It's not the benefits, although they are wonderful. It's not the pay, although it's pretty terrific also. It's not even the free lunch, although that's a super benefit as well. I love Zappos because it's more than a company ... it's a family. I know that no matter what is going on in my crazy, hectic life, I can always fall back on my Zappos family for encouragement, a helping hand, and sometimes, even someone to just listen to me when I need a friendly face. We are a family. We don't get along 100% of the time, but what family does? There are a few goofballs. (OK, more than a few.) But by and large, everyone here sticks together. Zappos is awesome!!!

Pedro B.

employee since 2010

Success is what an individual dreams and works for, and family is sometimes who we work for.

Peggy G.

employee since 2006

The Zappos Culture means everything. It is the way we live, the way we treat people, the way we laugh and cut up and make the day go by ... the little things that make a big difference. Zappos is awesome ...

Philip D.

employee since 2011

Even though I have been here for just a couple of weeks, it's already clear to me that this company is different from any other place I have worked. It is wonderful being part of an organization in which everyone is pulling in the same direction, and no one is standing around moaning and groaning.

Phillip M.

employee since 2011

In my brief time at Zappos, I've come to realize that this is more than a place to work. My co-workers are all so driven that it's nearly impossible not to follow their lead. I felt accepted and welcomed immediately. I look forward to furthering my career in this creative, yet humble environment that some people call work.

Phillip P.

employee since 2011

The Zappos Culture means being able to express ideas of possible ways to improve quality relations at the workplace. Advancement and openness throughout Zappos is awesome as well. Communication skills can develop here. The family atmosphere here at Zappos helps a long shift fly by and performance runs more smoothly. I'm happy someone told me that Zappos was hiring, but I had no idea of all the benefits of working here. I enjoy it and hope to be here for many years to come. Thank you.

Phillip S.

employee since 2009

It's a great job!

Phillip S.

employee since 2010

The Zappos Culture means getting the job done together with the best people I know.

Priscilla D.

employee since 2009

This has been the best place I have ever worked. Not only do we have free insurance and vending machines, the parties are awesome! Most of the time it feels like I live here, but that's OK because we are all like family. The most exciting thing was when I went to Vegas and got to meet some awesome Zapponians. They were out of this world!

Purple Pete

employee since 2009

When I think about the Zappos Culture, I think of myself. I am the Zappos Culture. I am odd, bright, eclectic and unique. Zappos is the only place I have ever worked that embraces that. It's part of why I love going to work every day.

Rachel D.

employee since 2010

The Zappos Culture means being myself, looking forward to going to work, and loving my job.

Ramona B.

employee since 2011

The Zappos Culture is an opportunity to learn from and work with people from other countries.

Raymond C.

employee since 2009

I like the fun and weirdness of Zappos because I like to make people smile and have fun in the workplace, and I like when people laugh at crazy stuff. I love Zappos!

Rebecca B.

employee since 2009

I think that Zappos is a great place to work. We treat one another like family.

Rebecca B.

employee since 2009

Zappos is, by far, the best place I have ever worked. It has given me opportunities to advance in my future. I would recommend Zappos to anyone. I feel so thankful that I have my job here. You don't just WOW your customers; you WOW your fellow employees too. Thanks, Zappos, for everything!!!!!!!

Rebecca N.

employee since 2010

The culture at Zappos is awesome! I was fortunate enough to stay home with my son when he was younger. Returning to a work atmosphere was an adjustment for me, but I knew from the minute I started filling out my application that this company was going be a good one! No stuffy questions about what you would you do in this situation or that. Instead, you get a question asking what your theme music would be!

I feel that Zappos accepts, welcomes, and appreciates each of us for our individuality, which is a rarity in my experience! I am new to the company, but I feel like this culture is a perfect fit for me. There are so many perks to working here, from the obvious (free lunch) to the not-so-obvious (the ability to come as you are ... piercings, tattoos, and even blue hair). I look forward to the future here and growing with this chock-full-o-culture company.

Rebecca S.

employee since 2010

The Zappos Culture means a lot to me because this is a place I can call home. My co-workers are like family and we share so much together. We hang out at work and outside of work, and have a blast doing it!

Regina B.

employee since 2011

I'm a new hire. I like Zappos' friendly, helpful environment.

Rhonda C.

employee since 2010

What does the Zappos Culture mean to me? "WOW" is part of Zappos' Core Values and WOW is all around. Zappos cares about its employees and, in turn, the employees care about Zappos and each other. It is a fun atmosphere to work in and you are free to be who you are. I am a University of Louisville Cardinal Fan and am glad I can express that and not feel pointed out!!! (GO CARDS!!!) There is a lot of work, but you are providing a service to customers. On the Zappos box it says, "Shipped with Love." It really suggests to the customer that their merchandise was handled with care. Zappos is a fun place to work and hopefully all those who have worked here have the same opinion. Thanks for the opportunity!

Rhonda T.

employee since 2003

Struggle makes me stronger; change makes me wise. My job at Zappos has made me a better person and brought happiness to me and to my family! I love Zappos!

Richard H.

employee since 2011

After 37 years in public work, I found myself at Zappos. It has turned out to be the best thing in my job history that could have happened. The people are fantastic and will bend over backwards to help. The benefits are unheard of in this day and age and I find that folks genuinely want to be here. Feedback I have seen from customers is along the same lines. Zappos has it together and what we do really works. You rock, Zappos, and I only hope I can be a small part in this big, wonderful machine for a long time to come.

Richard R.

employee since 2011

The Zappos Culture means honest people with good morals and attitude. Hard working, with a drive to learn and do more for their company and the people around them.

Richard R.

employee since 2010

The Zappos Culture means working in a friendly environment where people really care about their jobs.

Richard S.

employee since 2007

I like the fact that some of the people I work with are more than just co-workers; they are good friends that I can go to for anything. That's my favorite thing about the Zappos Culture – we are encouraged to build a positive team and family spirit!

Rita B.

employee since 2006

This company has been the best company I have worked for in a number of years. My co-workers have been here for my family and me when we needed someone, and I thank God that I work at a place where there are such great employees. And that is why I work very hard for them every day that I have been here – to show them I care, just like they did. Thank you all for caring!

Robert H.

employee since 2011

The Zappos Culture is unique. There are a variety of people that make up the Zappos family. The leaders like to make work enjoyable. (Who doesn't want to have time fly because you're having fun?) One example was when we had to seek shelter from a tornado and a group of people ended up playing gunfights with foam darts. One guy had a machine gun type, which was funny because it was something unexpected.

Robert K.

employee since 2010

The Zappos Culture means a lot to me because I can come in to work acting a little crazy and go home feeling good about it.

Robert K.

employee since 2011

The Zappos Culture means being able to come to work and be yourself!!! Wear whatever kinds of clothes you want and be around equally cool people. Managers, supervisors and leads are all very friendly and diversified!!! Put simply, Zappos is an amazing job and I wouldn't want to be anywhere else when I can be here!! And another thing, I hear the Zappos parties are epic!

Robert W.

employee since 2009

I started my assignment at Zappos a few months after I turned 18. I was a temp without the slightest knowledge of anything Zappos-related. My parents were a bit reluctant to have me work so much while attending school, but I was adamant that this would be a good decision for my future and I predicted correctly. Zappos is more of a lifestyle; you form bonds with the people you work with and I am truly blessed to have had such a fun job at such a young age. It's truly amazing that Zappos treats its employees so well with so many benefits and incentives. I received my Associate of Arts degree from Elizabethtown Community College and then attended Western Kentucky University, majoring in Film/Corporate Communication. Zappos has definitely given me a whole new outlook on how companies should operate. I am leery of entering the corporate world for fear that no company will live up to the Zappos' standards, but I know I'll have little to fear because I will carry a piece of Zappos with me everywhere; whether in the form of the Core Values or a carrying a Zappos bag for my many tennis racquets!

Robin W.

employee since 2011

I am so happy to be back at Zappos! It is a great place to be. Here, I do not feel like I am just a number. Zappos takes very good care of their "family" and ... hey ... the free lunch doesn't hurt either.

"Rocko"

employee since 2009

This ever-changing world in which we live makes you want to cry, "wait for it!!!" I would never have thought there could be such a place as this. It's my own little world. Old school, new school, black, white. We make it work as one unit to get the job done. Change is good sometimes, but it's nice to know that at Zappos the Core Values and our culture will stay the same.

Roger H.

employee since 2011

I have only been here for one week and I love this job. Everyone is great to work with and the managers seem more like co-workers than bosses.

Ronnie B.

employee since 2010

The Zappos Culture has created a whole different work place. I've never worked for a company like this before. It's been very interesting and I'm glad to be here.

Ronnie D.

employee since 2011

Where can I start? There are so many things about working at Zappos that make it more than just a job. Free vending machines and lunch, free insurance and discounts ... and that's just the monetary part. Then you add things like the supervisors treating you like a human being and not just a number. Don't just take my word for it; ask one of the thousands of Zapponians employed here at "one of the best places to work."

Rory G.

employee since 2010

It's the power of good people that make Zappos different from most work places. It's the attitude of "let me help you" and we want you to have fun while you work. It's the team attitude where you have a sense of being included. We are here to work – let's do it in a way that's upbeat and personally fulfilling. It's the smile attitude. When someone is smiling, it's easy to smile back. It's those good lunches that make you feel like people care!

Rosemary S.

employee since 2011

Zappos is like a huge family! We all act like brothers and sisters! We find ways to keep it interesting and entertaining while our parents (the managers and leads) find new and interesting ways to keep us in line! But we stay on task and on top of everything to make our parents happy and make sure we get awesome new toys and T-shirts! :-) Love It In Zappos World!!

Roxane Z.

employee since 2005

The Zappos Culture has a big influence on me. I love the culture we have here. People are always WOWed and amazed when they hear about the Zappos Culture. I wish to continue to share this culture with my friends and family in hope of hearing more "WOW!"

Roxanne R.

employee since 2007

The Zappos Culture is not like any other. Don't get me wrong; you have to work hard. The customer comes first, but at Zappos you are allowed to be yourself. My favorite thing is when we have massages and our managers and supervisors serve us lunch. The management team and leads are awesome; we never know what they are going to come up with to make sure we have fun. If you work hard you will be rewarded with awesomeness. P.S. Zappos holiday parties are the best. Go Zappos!!!

Roy M.

employee since 2010

The Zappos Culture has impacted my life on both a professional and a personal level. Happiness at work was something that I thought was unattainable until I started working at the fulfillment center. From day one I was treated like family and that continues one year later. I am a better person because Zappos truly lives and promotes their way of life!

Roy P.
employee since 2006

Zappos is the best place I have ever worked. They take care of everyone; we are all like family, and if you want to work for a great company, come join us!!!

Russell H.
employee since 2010

A warehouse full of shoes .

Ruth P.
employee since 2010

I love Zappos!! It's a great place to work.

Ryan K.
employee since 2010

I just started at Zappos last week, but I already know that I enjoy my job. They are good to their employees.

Ryan R.
employee since 2008

I love Zappos. It's a great place to work.

Sabrina A.
employee since 2011

What the Zappos Culture means to me is that Zappos has a plan to keep things fun and organized. It makes the job that I have fun and interesting.

Samantha C.
employee since 2010

When I first started working at Zappos, it was a little weird because I had never worked anywhere that cared so much about its employees and its culture. Zappos thrives on its culture. I love it here and wouldn't want the culture to ever burn out. It seems to me that every person brings their own little spark of culture in with them when they come here and they leave it behind for others to take part in it. I love the benefits and the discounts as well; it is amazing that a company would be so vested in their employees that they are able to do these things for us! There is so much that I love about Zappos, but I am not writing a book!!! In short, Zappos is the best place to work and it is more than just a job to me and to my family!

Samantha D.
employee since 2010

I love Zappos because it's a great work environment. They have awesome benefits, like medical and dental insurance as well as life insurance. It's nice to know your job has your back if any thing ever happens. When things start to get slow, we make it more fun to make the time go by faster. You will always have something to do when the sorter goes down – like once we played Simon Says because it was down for three hours. Zappos offers free food and you can wear whatever you want besides short shorts and tanks that show your bra. Zappos was my first job and I've been here for four months now. I hope to be here a long time. Go, Zappos!!!!

Samantha M.
employee since 2010

The Zappos Culture, to me, is crazy, wacky and fun! It's by far the best warehouse job I have ever worked at. With the free food, benefits and insurance, what's not to like? The employees here at work make the job fun, while being safe and staying on task all at once. =)

Samantha M.
employee since 2010

I have never before worked for a company that allowed employees to be themselves. Zappos really embraces everyone's is uniqueness. They encourage us to let our true colors shine. That opens doors for empowerment within the company as well as in everyday life.

Samantha M.

employee since 2010

To me, the Zappos Culture is being able to be serious enough and still work hard enough to get the job done the right way. It's also about being able to make your work environment fun. It's nice to be able to work and not have to be so serious about everything all the time. Everyone wants to feel comfortable and just be himself or herself, especially at work, where we spend so much of our time.

Samantha S.

employee since 2010

The Zappos Culture means having a place that I can come to and work hard without feeling like I am. I enjoy the work I do and the people I do it with, and that makes the night go by fast. I always want to come back the next night so that I can have fun while I make money!

Sami Sweetheart

employee since 2011

I have never had a job that made me actually like getting up every morning. At Zappos, you can be yourself and no one judges you. It's a pretty amazing family to be part of. I love my job! :)

Samuel R.

employee since 2007

There are several great benefits that come from the Zappos Culture, all of which stem from the Ten Core Values. I can honestly say that the way my co-workers treat me every day WOWs me. We have opportunities to invest in ourselves through education and teamwork. Everyone here brings something to the table for others to learn from and build on.

Sandy S.

employee since 2005

Zappos is a great place to work. I have just recently become a lead and have learned so much. The opportunity to grow is here if you want it. Do you want it?????

Sara M.

employee since 2011

After only being at Zappos for about a month, the culture seems pretty simple to me. Zappos is family. At the end of the day, it's your family that's there for you. It's your family you can count on. It's your family that counts on you. Even on those "craptastic" days when it's pouring with rain and I've gotten zero sleep the night before, I'm happy driving into work because I know I'll be surrounded by a team that genuinely cares about what we're doing, who we're doing it with, and the customers we're doing it for.

Sara S.

employee since 2010

Zappos is one-of-a-kind and an awesome place to meet some cool people. Zappos rocks my socks!!!!!!

Sarah B.

employee since 2010

I have been at Zappos for a little over three years now, and this has been the best job I've ever had. The people I work with are amazing ... very diverse but we all treat one another with the same respect. You can feel free to be yourself. It's like a family. We are a family, which is good when you're at work more than you are at home. It gives you something to look forward to when coming to work. Another good thing about Zappos is the benefits, and it really helps me since I am a college student. To sum up, what makes Zappos so amazing is our Core Values. They make us stronger, wiser, and not ashamed of being ourselves. I love Zappos!!!

Sarah J.

employee since 2005

Zappos is the most amazing job I have ever had! Working here has changed my life. It has taught me how to be a better person. Zappos' Ten Core Values carry over into my personal life. There have been many times that I was faced with a situation that I was unsure about, but then I stopped and applied the Core Values to help me determine what to do. Thank you, Zappos, for all that you do!

Sarah L.
employee since 2010

Zappos has great benefits – free food, a team spirit and pretty good pay.

Sarah O.
employee since 2005

Cinderella is proof that shoes can change a person's life for the better. Couldn't be more proud than to work with such an amazing family of friends as I have here at Zappos.

Sarah T.
employee since 2010

To me, Zappos is different from any job I've ever worked at because everyone seems to have a mutual understanding about how Zappos operates. It's like a hidden curriculum that people pick up on, almost without even realizing it. Everyone, even new hires, go the extra step to make this a fun and safe environment; whether that be picking up trash that's in the walkway, holding a door open for someone, or helping out another department. We all go above and beyond and I think a major part of it has to do with the fact that we are genuinely being taken care of like family with all the amazing benefits. People fit right in starting at day one.

Sarah T.
employee since 2010

To me, the Zappos Culture means being able to be yourself. It's coming in and knowing you're going have an amazing day because your managers and leads are awesome. It's also knowing that you really are one big family! =]

Scott C.
employee since 2010

By definition, "culture" is the behaviors and beliefs characteristic of a particular group. At Zappos, the prevailing behavior and belief system is a unified mindset, where the quality and quantity of production goes hand in hand with workplace happiness and job satisfaction. Everyday job functions seem to be seamlessly intertwined with a real sense of pride, camaraderie and desire to be happy while at work. Team members genuinely feel appreciated for their commitment not only the company, but to this company – one that is striving to be the best in the world.

Scott S.
employee since 2010

I like the Zappos Culture because it helps you to get to know the people you work with and you also get to play fun games as well as get a break from work.

Scott Z.
employee since 2005

Simply put, "story-worthy experiences." Taking the time to talk to someone you normally might not notice. Helping someone achieve a personal goal they have previously set. Creating a moment of joy or humor with someone who was previously down. Building a new, lasting friendship with someone every day. Realizing at the end of the day that someone at Zappos has touched you in the exact same way. This has been and always will be the core meaning of the Zappos Culture, to me.

Scotty C.
employee since 2011

I love the Zappos family feeling and how everyone goes out of their way to help you with work or with private matters.

Sean B.
employee since 2009

The people are friendly here and love to help you when they can. I love my job and box-making can be awesome to work in. Zappos has great parties and we can rock it out every time. I plan on working here for many years to come.

Serena M.

employee since 2010

The Zappos Culture, to me, means a family outside of my own family. My co-workers and I get together outside of work and just hang out with one another and we are all friends online. That's not to say that we don't have disagreements (though they are actually few), but just like a family, we learn to work through our differences. It makes the workday fun because we can laugh and joke around together while we are getting our work done!

Shaina M.

employee since 2008

I have worked at Zappos for almost three years and it has been a wonderful experience. The family spirit constantly creates a wonderful atmosphere and makes every day I work, a joy. Go, Zappos!

Shannon DeLaine A.

employee since 2008

Zappos is an amazing atmosphere to work in. It's the only place I've ever worked where I can be me. I value the company because they treat us fairly; they genuinely care about their people. It's the only place where I've ever looked forward to coming to work. I enjoy being part of the big team effort to make the customer happy. It's fun here at Zappos, because of all the ways we work together to accomplish the same goal: Delivering Happiness. We stand above other companies because of our differences in the most positive way. I'm proud to work for a company that stands for so much.

Shannon S.

employee since 2006

The Zappos Culture, to me, means family, acceptance and lots of fun. <3

Shannon S.

employee since 2010

The Zappos Culture is amazing! I have never worked for a company that genuinely cares about its employees. It's the little things that matter, like surprise breakfasts. How can I forget about the lunch?! They make it seem like it's fun, not work. I love it!

Sharon C.

employee since 2010

Peace of mind is what Zappos means to me – being able to go home and enjoy my family instead of taking my job home, as I did in other jobs where I felt like I worked 24-7. Not here. I love the culture. And my manager is great. I'm proud to tell people I work for Zappos. And Josh is not bad either.

Sharon F.

employee since 2010

11th Core Value: Be Wild!!!

Shawn M.

employee since

The Zappos Culture, to me, means working around, getting to know and getting along with all different types of people. Not stereotyping anyone. Always being helpful and cooperative. Coming to work with an open mind.

Shawn T. ("Link")

employee since 2011

I've only been here a short while, and I can tell you that Zappos is a great place to work. Everyone is "supra" friendly (that's one whole level above super). I feel comfy when I come into work, knowing my peers are here to help out when I need it and provide support. I'm glad I started working here and I, for one, don't plan on ever leaving this fantastic place.

Shawne K.

employee since 2010

What does the Zappos Culture mean to me? It means not having to fear the impossible because we make our own possibilities. Our attitude and everything depends on us, not the task at hand. We love our jobs and embrace the changes around us.

Sheila C.

employee since 2007

I have been with this company for four years now and love it. I have never worked for a place like this before. You can learn so much here ... learn to be a lead or even a manager or just be a team member. We have fun here, we get to party and be ourselves. It's great.

Shelby D.

employee since 2010

The Zappos Culture means having fun at work and making work fun. Making lots of friends and making them your family. The Zappos Culture is a good thing and I hope we continue to use culture a lot more in the future.

Shelby P.

employee since 2010

Zappos has a terrific work environment. We enjoy our work, enjoy our fellow workers and take pride in our productivity. It's a winning combination that makes us feel appreciated, as well as encouraged by the friendly "Zatmosphere."

Shelia J.

employee since 2007

Before I was fortunate enough to get this job, three and a half years ago, I had forgotten who I was. Not only did I forget how to have fun over the years, but also how to be a strong, independent woman. The people here are the best! I am grateful to Zappos for helping me to realize that I can do anything I set my mind to. Our culture here is outstanding; it brings us together as a true family. We all stick together no matter what! Thank you, Zappos. I hope it never changes! :)

Sherry A.

employee since 2010

The culture signs around the buildings say it all! There is so much fun and weirdness that goes around, it's really a fun place to hang your hat and a great place to meet new friends or (sometimes) get reacquainted with some old ones.

Silvia I.

employee since 2010

I learned about Zappos from a friend who works here, and when I was working on my first peak season, I couldn't get enough. I had to come back and show the Zappos family what I'm capable of. This place is like my second home. I'm here more than I'm at home, but I'm not complaining. The people are great ... maybe a little weird ... but aren't we all special in a way? I was so excited to be hired full time. It was the best news I had heard in a long time. I'm exited to be here and I want to move up one day. Even after I graduate from college with a bachelor's degree in business, I want to be the HR specialist for Zappos. I still want to come in and pack a couple boxes. (LOL!) I will be delivering WOW through service and I will enjoy every second of it. I'm a happy Zapponian!

Sonia B.

employee since 2011

God bless me with this Zappos job!`

Stacy C.

employee since 2011

I enjoy the work environment we have here. It's a lot of fun and great people to work with. The free food is a bonus!

Stanly F.

employee since 2010

Before I came to Zappos, I had heard some good things about this job, but until I actually worked here I didn't realize somewhere like this existed. The culture, activities, people, benefits, parties and picnics, as well as free lunch and being part of one big family WOWing the customers ... everything about Zappos is amazing. I have held some good jobs before, working for some good companies, but now I finally work for a great company and I feel like I can go places. Thank you, Zappos, for giving me the WOW!!!!

Stefanie W.

employee since 2008

Every year, the Zappos Culture continues to evolve for me. At first, it was the overall friendliness of my co-workers that impressed me. People seemed to be supportive of one another rather than competitive. Then, I noticed that people genuinely cared for one another. The Core Values weren't just words on banners, but actually practiced. Soon, I was overwhelmed with a sense of empowerment. The good stuff, the ideas, the course of my destiny here at Zappos is truly up to me. I could choose to "ride it out" here or I can make a difference ... be a part of the action. Of course, I've chosen the latter. Thankfully, so have many others and these are the people that will take Zappos to that next level. I want to see the day that our culture will be the norm for other companies. It's already happening!!

Stella K.

employee since 2011

This place is beyond all other work places. Zappos is in a class all its own. A number one class.

Stephanie B.

employee since 2010

I love Zappos. It's an awesome place to work there is no other company as great as Zappos. The people and the benefits are wonderful. I hope to stay here until I retire.

Stephanie L.

employee since 2010

Zappos is a great place to work. Not only do we have a great time, I really enjoy the people. It truly is a home away from home. Everyone here at Zappos is willing to pitch in and help their co-workers out. It's a good feeling to be a part of something that is growing so rapidly and has such a huge effect on people. Zappos is the best! Oh yeah, and care bears rock!!!

Stephen B.

employee since 2010

The family and camaraderie that we have at Zappos is great, and that no matter how long we have been here, we are always willing to help the new people.

Stephen G.

employee since 2010

Working at Zappos as a temp during the peak season was pleasant. Individuals have the potential to excel by meeting their job goals and expectations. Through company training and initiatives, we have the potential to be career-oriented. You can tell how much a company appreciates its employees through such benefits as free meals, the fairness Zappos shows to employees, as well as by the benefits provided to full timers, including various celebrations and different events.

Stephen W.

employee since 2010

Zappos is great! The free lunches and vending machines are awesome. The parties and random activities are also pretty cool. Zappos is definitely the best job I've ever had.

Steve H.

employee since 2010

To me, the Zappos Culture is about embracing diversity, empowering teamwork and bringing different views and thoughts together under one roof.

Steve T.

employee since 2004

I want to say thanks for all the opportunities I have had here. I have learned a lot in my many years at Zappos and have been able to travel to many states and meet a variety of people. It has been an honor to work for such a great company!!!!! Zappos rocks!!!!!

Steven A.

employee since 2007

Zappos has been my home for the past four years. With any job, you are going to have ups and downs, but at Zappos I have had more ups than I have downs. I remember coming in on my first day in 2007, not knowing what this place would be like. Come to find out, it has been the best company I have ever worked for. I love coming to work every day not knowing what to expect, it makes my job interesting. Thank you, Zappos, for giving me a job that I love. :)

Steven G.

employee since 2010

The Zappos Culture is about working in a place where it only takes ten minutes for a job to become routine. That is not a stab at the Zappos Culture. It is a testament to the fine employees at Zappos who are very helpful and willing to educate you about different jobs.

Steven P.

employee since 2011

It's a nice, friendly work environment and it's got great work schedules.

Sue C.

employee since 2006

Zappos is the only place I have worked where your co-workers feel like family. We are always here for one another, good or bad!!

Susan M.

employee since 2007

The Zappos Culture, to me, is having the opportunity to excel in every way I can to make sure the customer receives quality products. I like watching all the growth that is going on at Zappos, and I like all the fun we have. I have learned a lot here and made many great friends. I look forward to coming to work every day. Thank you, Zappos, for giving me this job. I am thankful for all the extra benefits we have!! I love my job!!

Susie A.

employee since 2010

I got hired during peak season in 2010 and fell in love!!! Working here is really not like any job I have ever had before and, to be honest, I don't think of coming to work as just "my job." The people I work with are like an extended family!!! Not only can I WOW customers in a "single bound," this place WOWs me every day!! And that's something to talk about!!!

Susie C.

employee since 2010

I get to make new friends and work with them every day. Part-time picking is the greatest, with great co-workers and bosses.

T.C.N.

employee since 2011

The Zappos Culture means having another family away from home. Also, the benefits and free vending machines help make the days here better because it shows the company cares for its employees, and this means everyone works harder and is happier doing their jobs.

Tabetha J.

employee since 2011

I have only been at Zappos a couple of weeks now, and I have met a lot of cool people. All the leads and managers are very helpful. I have worked a lot of places in my past and I never want to work anywhere else. Zappos has made me part of the family and that's hard to do. I love coming to work every day. Thank you for your time.

Tadesse A.

employee since 2010

Zappos is not just a job for me. I get a lot of good things. I love Zappos. God bless you.

Tammy B.

employee since 2009

WOW! Wonderful, Outlandish, Weird. A very close-knit family of team members with a lot of personality, spunk and competitiveness. Competitive on who's going to come up with the next best thing to bring us together, share a smile, or make sure all of us feel appreciated for all our hard work! Nothing or no one is ever too weird. A feeling of acceptance.

Tammy H.

employee since 2008

I truly love my job and the peeps I work with. 2010 was not such a good year for me, in terms of my health and other things in my personal life! I had a hard time dealing with it. But as soon as I walked through the doors at Zappos, I felt a calmness about me!!! The peeps I work with every day did not realize it, but they were what got me through 2010! The positive energy from all of my co-workers was amazing. In turn, I was as positive as I could be! I guess what I'm trying to say is that I love my family here at Zappos! They made me smile, and when they cried, I cried. For any new peeps out there, Zappos is the place you want to be. Stay positive, open and remember to have fun doing it!!! Life is too short and Zappos is here to try and lengthen your life!!!! Thank you, Zappos! I truly love you from the bottom of my heart!!!

Tammy J.

employee since 2010

Zappos is the coolest!!! Where else in the world can you have so much fun and at the end of the day still feel like you were able to accomplish things?

Tammy M.

employee since 2010

The Zappos Culture means waking up in the mornings excited to be on my way to work, looking forward to seeing my co-workers who are like family to me, and enjoying working for a company that actually cares about me, being comfortable in my work environment and being allowed to be my odd self, without anyone passing judgment on me. I think I have more fun, more laughter, and work harder here at Zappos than I ever have at any other job.

Tammy M.

employee since 2010

I have enjoyed working here in Kentucky for about a month now. The size of this place WOWs me; I have never seen such a clever way to store so much great stuff in one place. I am beginning to connect with different folks here and they are feeling like my second family. At times it doesn't feel like I'm at work, the atmosphere is so amazing. We are here for a common purpose – to WOW the customer. This is a great place to work.

Tammy R.

employee since 2009

First and foremost, the Zappos Culture means family to me. We share a special bond that has gotten us through the craziness of peak season and sorter crashes and loads of overtime. The other major thing that comes to mind is our Core Value system, especially Core Value #3 ("Create Fun and a Little Weirdness"). Maybe we just have a special group of people; maybe it's a night-shift thing. Who knows? Regardless, our shift really knows how to bring the fun and the weird with all of our pranks (done out of love, I promise :D) and nicknames and general silliness. Our shift (B2) has really come together over the past few months and I have to say that I've never once dreaded coming in to work. The benefits and free food are pretty flippin' sweet, too. :D

Tangie J.

employee since 2010

Zappos is the ultimate place to work. It's not only the employment, the benefits, and all the other wacky stuff here at Zappos. It's the people. They are the most wonderful people to work with. Everyone is always helpful, even when they could be having a bad day. The management is great. The HR team is always helpful, no matter how many times you need them to help you log into your ADP. They just smile and say, "You're welcome. Have a good day and come back if you need to." This is the best job in the world and I am not just saying that because I work here. Everyone should have a job like this. It's great!!!!!

Tanya P.

employee since 2010

What I like about the Zappos Culture is that it's fun, exciting and you never know what's next.

Tasha F.

employee since 2010

The Zappos Culture, to me, is unlike any I've ever witnessed and it has grown and improved over the years. We are co-workers, friends and family. If one of us is in need, none of us hesitate to jump in and see how we can help. We come in to do our jobs, but we also have fun. Zappos gives us free health insurance, free food and a comfortable working environment. I feel Zappos cares about each of us as people, not just as numbers. I can never imagine working anywhere else! Zappos rocks!

Tasha L.

employee since 2007

I have been with Zappos for three and a half years. I had never before worked for a company where I enjoyed getting up to come to work. I consider my team members as family. We can have fun and do our work at the same time.

Teresa B.

employee since 2010

I love this job better than any other job I have ever had! I love the people. It's the coolest, most fun job in the world!!! I plan to retire from here! Go Big Blue!!!!

Teresa K.

employee since 2010

Zappos = the best job ever!!! I am so happy to be a part of the Zappos team. I have never heard of a company that cares so much about its customers and its employees!! I was previously a temporary team member, but now that I am here, I'm here to stay!

Teri W.

employee since 2011

The Zappos Culture, to me, means acceptance. I've never before worked anywhere that felt as much like a family as Zappos does. They make you feel like you and your opinion matter, and that means a lot.

Terrance S.

employee since 2010

Zappos is a fun place to work and I like the computer we use. I also like the ten-hour days we work with three days off every month.

Terry F.

employee since 2008

I love my job! I love the atmosphere we have here at Zappos! I love hanging out with friends and having a good time inside and outside of work. I look forward to many more years working for Zappos!

Terry T.

employee since 2010

A fun place to work with great perks.

Thomas B.

employee since 2011

The Zappos Culture is a multi-ethnic workplace that brings together people with a wide variety of lifestyles, backgrounds, values, ideals and nationalities. It strives to find a common ground by offering a wide range of benefits, a fun working environment and mutual respect. This is what sets it apart from other companies and that's why its success is so hard to duplicate.

Thomas W.

employee since 2010

I am a recent full-time hire at Zappos. I look forward to many years of being part of the team. Zappos has treated me great during the three months I worked here as a temp employee and I am excited to share the future with such an excellent company.

Thomas W.

employee since 2011

Zappos, to me, is like a dream job, without the six-figure picture on my check! (HA! HA!) Where else can you wake up in what you slept in and slide into work with your P-jammers on?! I love what I do here for Zappos and my supervisor and leads! They are great individuals who get down and dirty with you. I hope to be here for a long time, and possibly retire along side of my wife, who works here with me. That is so awesome too, because I love her bunches!!!

Tiffany J.

employee since 2010

The Zappos Culture means I have a good time while at work, but I also work hard. You can enjoy the time that you're at work and stay busy. There is never a boring moment.

Tiffany M.

employee since 2010

The Zappos Culture, to me, means a few things. Family, for one, because everyone here treats everyone else like part of their family. This is like our "home away from home." We have smiles on our faces and enjoy one another's company. The Zappos Culture also means learning and interacting with others. When you learn, it gives you a chance to grow in the company and get to know more about Zappos. Also, when you learn, it gives you more of an idea of what is going on. Interacting with others makes your whole experience at Zappos memorable because in this "family," no one is singled out. You come here as you are and you are accepted.

Tiffany M.

employee since 2010

What's not to like about this environment? Employees are treated as equals. You can be yourself without fear of someone judging you. One of the things I love most is Core Value #3, "Create Fun and a Little Weirdness." Not all jobs will allow you to do that. Zappos makes me feel right at home. They really know how to keep employees happy. I consider myself lucky to have a job that I actually like. I appreciate Zappos for all they do for us to keep us smiling. So in return, I work harder to make Zappos happy.

Tiffany N.

employee since 2010

My time at Zappos has been short but amazing. My co-workers are like my family. There isn't a day that goes by where I don't laugh. Even when it seems like the work will never get done, we always come together and make it happen. There are no winners or losers, just a group of people aiming for the same goal. There is nowhere else on earth quite like this place.

Tim C.

employee since 2010

To me, the Zappos Culture means having a good attitude, treating others with consideration and doing something out of the ordinary, like wearing a big funny wig for no reason other than to make someone laugh.

Timmy H.
employee since 2010

To me, the Zappos Culture is events and get-togethers with your fellow team members outside of work, developing work relationships, friendships and family-type relationships.

Timothy E.
employee since 2011

The Zappos way of life is so cool. Friendly people to work with, always happy to come to work. It's good to know that Zappos has always got your back.

Timothy Q.
employee since 2010

The Zappos Culture is a wonderful thing. It allows me to be my true self and not get shunned for it. It makes for a fantastic work environment, in my opinion.

Tina M.
employee since 2010

I like working here because it is fun. The leads are nice.

Todd S.
employee since 2010

The Zappos Culture means having fun and doing the right thing. Co-workers become family/friends. It means looking forward to coming to work. I come from a crazy corporate environment and Zappos has really changed my life. I do not want to be anywhere else.

Tom Y.
employee since 2011

Zappos has tiger blood. Not even Charlie Sheen is "winning" as much as Zappos is and (in fact) he is extremely jealous that he's a F-14 and Zappos is a Space Shuttle. WINNING.

Tony K.
employee since 2011

Wow! Culture shock! I had never been excited about going to work until I became a Zappos team/family member. Now, I look forward to it every day. I am part of something special and take pride in my work because everyone here takes pride in his or her work!

Zappos cares of its employees as much as they value their customers. I love the freedom I have to be myself and work at my own pace. I am truly blessed to be part of the Zappos family and look forward to many years of service. I am also grateful for the company's Core Values, which really have helped me in both my career and my family life. Thank you, Zappos.

Tori K.

employee since 2010

The Zappos Culture means being yourself at work – meeting new people and learning about them. I like all the fun things they do for our Zappos family.

Tracy C.

employee since 2010

I have been at Zappos for six months and this is by far the best place I have ever worked. Not only are the benefits great, but the people I work with are awesome and I couldn't ask for a better place to work. I enjoy coming to work every day, which means a lot to me because at my last job it took all I had to make myself go in. At Zappos the people I work with all get along, do our jobs and help each other out whenever we can. I couldn't ask for a better place to work!!!

Tracy F.

employee since 2007

Everyone here at Zappos makes me feel appreciated. I love everybody, from my fellow team members to my managers.

Tracy M.

employee since 2011

As I finish my third week at Zappos, I can honestly say it is an amazing place to work. The atmosphere is awesome and everyone is eager to assist new people. I think one of the best things about the company is the philosophy of making the work atmosphere fun but still a business. It's also nice to know that I work for a company that is very big on promoting from within. I now believe the HR representative who said, "Once you start working here, you will never want to work anyplace else." Thanks to Zappos for making this a wonderful company and (hopefully) a very long relationship!!!!!

Tracy O.

employee since 2010

Someone please come find me! I'm lost in quad 3!

Travis B.

employee since 2010

The Zappos Culture, to me, is a fun, different way to get through a long day at work.

Travis C.

employee since 2007

Smiles. Singing. Dancing. A good time. Letting the love in. Keeping the dark out. That about says it all.

Travis R.

employee since 2008

The Zappos Culture is unlike anything at any previous job I have had. Everyone treats everyone else like they are somebody, because ... well ... we are special. Zappos cares about its people and the environment. I can't say enough good things about Zappos because I would fill this book up. To keep it short, I love my job and truly enjoy everyone with whom I work.

Trevor B.

employee since 2009

I love Zappos. It's a home away from home and the employees are just like a family. I couldn't ask for a better place to work.

Tyler H.
employee since 2010

What makes me happy at Zappos is everyone has a positive attitude. I haven't found anyone in a bad mood, and I think the reason for that is because Zappos goes out of its way to make employees happy.

Tyler S.
employee since 2009

I've been at Zappos for two years and I love working here more and more every day. The company is growing so fast and changing so much that every day is exciting and full of new challenges. The one thing remains the same is the people, who love their job and love working for Zappos. I still see them every day!

Val A.
employee since 2010

I am pleased with the way Zappos management relates to the teams. We are given many ways to better ourselves while helping the company grow. The motivation is in front of us on a daily basis, with ways to train to advance in each job and make sure we learn safety as well as skills. I give Zappos an A-plus and I will focus each day on achieving my goals with the help of each person on my team.

Valerie L.
employee since 2011

Zappos is a wonderful place to work. It's exciting and sometimes crazy, but we are all like one big family. We each strive to be the best and in our own ways. We have fun and work hard at the same time, and it is one of the best places if you want to work with hard-working, sometimes crazy, but fun people.

Valerie M.
employee since 2010

The Zappos Culture means family to me. After my son passed away, the people from the entire warehouse came out to support my family and me. From the first night to this very day, if someone sees me having a rough day, they take the time to try to make mine better. You might expect this from some of your closer friends or people in your department, but I have received this compassion from people throughout the warehouse. Soon after his death I had to have surgery and leave work. I was gone a total of ten months. The first day back, I had hello and hugs from someone in every department. It made it feel like I had come home.

Vanessa D.
employee since 2007

The Zappos Culture encourages us to communicate with one another. I feel free to share my thoughts and feelings with my friends, and I'm grateful for their concern. Also Pipeline classes and All-Hand meetings are great benefits, with fun and challenging discussions. Thank you for providing interpreters so we deaf can enjoy classes and meetings too. :o)

Vickie P.
employee since 2010

I have worked for Zappos for almost a year now and this is the most awesome company I've ever worked for. I love coming to work and I enjoy the company of other crazy people like myself. The benefits are super and the people are my family when I'm not at home. Thanks, Zappos, for a wonderful place to work. Zappos rocks in my heart!

Walter A.
employee since 2010

What I like most about Zappos is working with different types of people and the overall work environment. People work as a team to help make the company profitable and productive and this keeps people in a job when times are tough.

Wanda M.
employee since 2011

One of the things I like most about Zappos is being able to ask questions without people getting mad. They are very helpful and patient. I like that we all work as a team. They make it fun.

Warren E.

employee since 2010

Zappos is unlike any other company I have worked for. I have never encountered a company that cares so much for its employees. They want to make sure we stay happy, and they meet that goal. Since coming to this company, I have grown so much. Everything I have today I owe to Zappos!

Wayne C.

employee since 2011

Zappos is an exciting place to work with a lot of different personalities. Plenty of free drinks and snacks. Plus free lunch.

Wesley P.

employee since 2009

For me, the Zappos Culture is the reason I wake up and look forward to going to work every day. I am motivated to give my best effort and to develop my career and grow within Zappos. I couldn't ask for a better place to work and I am so thankful for the opportunity they have given me. Much love, Zappos!

Wesley S.

employee since 2010

The Zappos Culture, to me, means happy employees. We enjoy doing our work and have a fun, comfortable working environment. It also means that if there are any problems or conditions that need to be considered, the leads or co-workers are ready and willing to help out at any time.

William A.

employee since 2010

Working at Zappos is a fun, rewarding job. We all share a sense of belonging to a group throughout the Zappos community. My manager always makes sure we are happy. Things are done in a positive way. The support given to each team member is amazing.

William B.

employee since 2010

The Zappos Culture means that I am part of a large family of other people striving to better themselves and the community around them. Getting others work together to help improve the quality of everyone's lives is unusual, and it is essential to get the entire community involved.

William B.

employee since 2011

So far, I love Zappos! It is a fun company to work for that offers job security and great benefits! I really like the way it is managed and the fact that they thank you and appreciate the hard work that we do.

William C.

employee since 2011

A very friendly and fun atmosphere. Full of laughter and pants-wetting activities . This is the only place I've ever been where, on my days off, I look forward to clocking back in.

William M.

employee since 2010

Besides being the best company that I've ever worked at, Zappos also gives me an opportunity to advance in the company to any level I wish, or to just be the best I can be for the Zappos family.

Yohance H.

employee since 2010

The Zappos Culture Revolution: "WOWing the World One Customer at Time!"
P.S. Everyone is a customer!

Zachary B.

employee since 2011

This isn't just a job; it's an opportunity have a great career. I hope to be here for a long while. Just think positive about everything. I'll work my hardest to continue going where I want to go in my life.

Zackery P.

employee since 2011

Zappos is a respectable work environment and the people are great. I can't wait to receive the wonderful benefits they have to offer. I haven't been here long, but I'm ready to make a long-term commitment. I enjoy being a part of the Zappos family.

A WORD FROM THE CEO AND *Chief Happiness* OFFICER OF DELIVERING HAPPINESS, LLC

Zappos means so many things to me, but when it comes down to it, he's like my best friend's little brother.

Back in my high school days, I'd always get a kick out of my friend's little sibs. They'd run up to me, hug my thigh and I'd think "Oh too cute..." Then, just a few years later, I'd run into them on the street, look up and wonder, "Whoa. How'd you get so BIG?"

That's my relationship with Zappos. When I first met him, he was just a tiny little startup. Twelve years later, I still catch myself shaking my head, in disbelief of how much he's grown.

So, Zappos, what do you want to be when you grow up?

Zappos, Age 1 – *The biggest online shoe retailer in the world!*
Zappos, Age 4 – *A service company that happens to sell shoes!*
Zappos, Age 6 – *A company led by culture and core values!*

And finally, at the dear age of 10, Zappos knew exactly what its purpose really was... to deliver happiness to the world.

I've been consulting at Zappos for almost nine years now, and being a part of its journey has been a bit surreal at times. Looking back, it was probably a mix of luck, timing, curiosity and passion that gave me the chance to grow with the Zappos family.

Whether it was creating the Zappos Culture Book over the years, or helping them relocate to Las Vegas, it was always an adventure. Many times, we'd embark on things we've never tried before, but that was all part of the fun – figuring it out.

So when Tony asked if I wanted to work on the book *Delivering Happiness* together, it was a familiar feeling – we've never done it, but it sure sounded fun to give it a try.

It was Labor Day 2009 when we locked ourselves up in a cabin in Lake Tahoe. We only had a few weeks before our deadline, so we experimented with all sorts of things to keep ourselves as awake and productive as possible. We stocked our cupboards with junk food to reenact our college days of cramming for finals. Tony made chicken soup that he left simmering on the stove until the end of our trip (by then it was so dense, you could stand a knife in it). We tried ingesting all kinds of concoctions – Excedrin, tea, coffee, vodka – even coffee beans in vodka – until our time was up. A couple long weekends later, the book was done.

When the stork dropped *Delivering Happiness* off at bookstores, we didn't know what to expect. Before long, we found out we hit #1 on the *New York Times*, *Wall Street Journal* and Amazon.com. It didn't feel real at first, but that changed with one thing: hearing people's responses upon reading it.

On one end, we anticipated businesspeople to react to it (since it was marketed as a business book). But what we didn't expect was the response from the non-business community – people working in education, hospitals, nonprofits, and government... even moms and dads wrote to tell us they were inspired to make a change – big or small – in their lives because of the book.

Then, as the book was translated into different languages, we started hearing from around the world. With every email or story that came in, it felt like a chord had been strum – regardless of background, ethnicity or age – people were not only ready to consider happiness as a model in business and in life, they were ready to do something about it. Even though we didn't know what to expect going in, this was beyond what we ever imagined.

When it came time for the tour, we hit the road on a 23-city, 3-month cross-country bus tour. For us, it was less about selling books, it was about sharing a message we believed in. Again, we didn't know what we were getting into, but we did know this – with every email we got from around the world, and every person we met, we were inspired to do something about it. This gave birth to the name of our tour (and a mantra we still live by today): **Inspire And Be Inspired**.

After the tour ended, the emails and stories continued to pour in. It was as if we hit a tipping point and we had to do something about it. First it was a book, then it was a bus tour, and now, we're the Delivering Happiness Movement. We've evolved into a company with a cause – to spread and inspire happiness at work, in communities and everyday life.

How are we doing it? With a cool, frosty cup of ICEE:
I – Inspiration
C – Community
E – Education
E – Experience

Whether it's our online and offline communities growing around the world, DH@Work (helping companies apply happiness as a business model), the DH Shop (selling inspirational gear and goods, and eventually experiences), DH@School (integrating happiness into education), or content to inspire people to be true to themselves, follow their passions and find their higher purpose... everything we do comes back to our belief that, together, we can nudge this world to a happier place.

And to think, it's just the beginning. So much has happened in so little time, it makes me wonder if Zappos is going to look at DH in ten years and think, *Wow. How did you get so...*

Guess we'll have to wait for the 2021 Culture Book to find out :]

Jenn Lim
CEO and Chief Happiness Officer
Delivering Happiness, LLC

DELIVERING HAPPINESS
... with Music
IN KENTUCKY

IN A
Balloon
STATE OF MIND

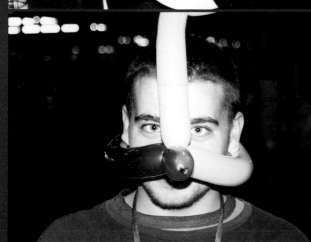

Zappos Core Value #4

Be
Adventurous, Creative, and Open-Minded

(I knew I took a risk wearing this outfit today,
but it was worth it...I feel fabulous)

Alex T.

UPS

As I enter my ninth year as Zappos' UPS representative, the Zappos Culture now means Delivering Happiness to employees, vendors and customers. Tony has always touted Culture as the number one priority. If you get it right, everything will naturally fall into place.

First, the unique, great Zappos Culture delivers happy employees. Compared to the cultures at my other clients' companies, only Zappos empowers employees to deliver WOW through service. They are happy and enthusiastic with all internal and external customer interactions during work and off-work hours. Zappos is more than just a job; it is a way of living, validated by Fortune's inclusion of the company in its list of "100 Best Companies to Work For."

Second, the Zappos Culture also delivers happiness to vendors. Not too many companies acknowledge and appreciate the importance of a positive vendor relationship. Zappos has done many things (such as vendor appreciation parties) to cultivate it. Over these wonderful years, Zappos has treated me like a member of the family. Based on my interactions with your other vendors, they all feel the same. Working with Zappos is definitely a privilege and honor. As the physical and metaphoric conduit between Zappos and its customers, UPS will continue to creatively provide the best service, so we can collectively WOW and deliver happiness one customer at a time.

And third, when you have a dynamic culture that fosters happy employees and vendors working collaboratively, you will deliver happiness to customers. Happy customers will (and they do) tell their friends, families, and business associates through word of mouth, Twitter, and other social media outlets about their positive Zappos experiences, which leads to more business and brand growth.

Ardee O.

Skechers Work

To me, the Zappos Culture means:

a. Mutual respect.

b. Life/work balance.

c. A chance to enjoy work and have fun doing it without losing sight of the objectives.

d. A standard that needs to be emulated.

Dan S.

IMG College/West Coast Conference

The partnership between Zappos and IMG College, of course, has different business goals and objectives for each entity. However, at the core of this partnership are the beliefs and values the West Coast Conference shares with Zappos, spelled out in two of Zappos' Core Values – "Deliver WOW Through Service" and "Do More With Less."

Both of the above-mentioned Core Values are exhibited by Zappos and the West Coast Conference in an important component of this partnership – the shoe drive at the Zappos Men's and Women's Basketball Championships in Las Vegas.

Performed in conjunction with the 2011 Zappos West Coast Conference Basketball Championships in Las Vegas, this shoe collection, donation and subsequent distribution delivered more than 10,000 used and new shoes to the international non-profit organization Soles for Souls, as well as to underprivileged youth in Las Vegas. The actual distribution to Las Vegas youth on the day of the final game was particularly telling of Zappos and the WCC's shared belief to WOW with service. Approximately 150 Zappos employees, along with WCC personnel, bands, cheer, and even mascots went above and beyond to make sure every child who came through the line, was fitted and 'WOWed' with their new Zappos-donated shoes and other goodies.

While the shoe drive certainly demonstrated Zappos' and the WCC's commitment to "Deliver WOW Through Service," it also is a small part of both entities' commitment to "Do More With Less. Both Zappos and the WCC have built their brands and established a niche in their respective industries by doing more with less. This shoe drive, carried out by the WCC at all eight member institutions before culminating with the Las Vegas distribution had minimal costs yet affected the lives of thousands.

This event is just a microcosm of the overall belief that there is no limit to what can be accomplished in any industry, no matter what resources are available. The West Coast Conference competes at the highest level of intercollegiate athletics with a budget that pales in comparison to the six BCS conferences, while Zappos has established itself as an industry leader, relying most heavily on its most valuable "resources" – people and hard work.

In an era when the terms "partnerships", "core values," and "ideals" are thrown around rather loosely, Zappos and the West Coast Conference have developed a foundation of a relationship that tries to live the true meaning of these words, where employees on every level of each organization are intimately involved. That is what the Zappos Culture means to me.

Dorothy V.

Indecomm/FuseSource

The Zappos Culture means Nerf Gun Battles and awesome support solving problems; drinking contests and coding contests; playing hard and working harder; friends that are like family. It means caring about coming to work; caring about being at work; caring about what we're doing and how we're doing it. The Zappos Culture is a passion shared and multiplied.

Dusan M.

SAP

The Zappos Culture extends not just throughout Zappos itself but into its vast ecosystem as well. Being a partner of Zappos encourages us to always bring the highest level of service possible and to always remember the end goal of a memorable experience.

Katie D.

Columbia Sportswear Co.

I have had the privilege of working with Zappos for six years. When I think of the Zappos Culture I instantly think of Chris P., Bill J., Marisa R. and Braden M. I just love them: they ooze the Zappos Culture, day and night. The Zappos Culture, to me, is about doing your best 100% of the time, always challenging yourself, striving to grow and being passionate about everything you do. It's about being your true self. It's about working hard and playing even harder. Chris, Bill, Marisa and Braden challenge me every day to be the best at what I do. They are my partners in business and my friends once the computer has been turned off.

I am privileged to be a part of the Zappos Culture. Cheers to Chris, Bill, Marisa and Braden for BEING Zappos Culture!

Kel K.

Kel & Partners

To K&P, the Zappos Culture illuminates all the attributes you love about your best friend on the planet: happy, fun, crazy hysterical, risk taker, honest, inspiring, humble, accountable, kind-hearted, loyal, trustworthy and "wicked smaht" (as we say in Boston). The Zappos peeps are the kind of people you want to have a drink(s) with, and since 2008, Kel & Partners has done this many times. We love, love, love working with the Zappos team. Booyah!

Kelly T.

CIGNA Healthcare

I have only had the pleasure of working with Zappos since October of 2010, although they have been a client of CIGNA's for about four years. They have inspired me to think differently and have encouraged me to be creative in delivering "insurance" to their employees. It's inspiring (especially considering today's economic conditions) to enter a Culture that is willing to go against the grain. Most employers are looking for solutions to the increasing cost of providing health care to their employees by reducing benefits or shifting the cost, but Zappos is looking at ways to improve their employees' coverage and their experience. Working with them makes my job FUN and FUN is contagious.

Mark & Elli

Proforma Printing & Promotion

"Thanks SO much for being SO on top of it! You two WOW me on a daily basis."

From the very first conference call, we knew Zappos was special. The energy, enthusiasm and pride were bursting out of the receiver. After the call, we were speechless for a few moments. Then we went straight to work for them and it has been the most enjoyable and rewarding customer/vendor relationship we've ever experienced. Our first visit was beyond amazing. (The cold draft beer was pretty darn good, too!) As the owner of my company, I was beyond impressed with the Zappos team and their amazing culture. We returned to Boston with a motivation, drive and energy to "capture" some of that culture; that uniqueness; that inexplicable feeling of wanting to be "more like Zappos!" Months later, we received an email containing the quote from above. Again, we were momentarily speechless. If Zappos ever creates a Boston office, we might just be first in line for a job! Thanks for sharing this one-of-a-kind thing you call the Zappos Culture. In due time, we hope to have our own Culture Book at Proforma. In the meantime, we're proud (and grateful) to be part of yours!

Mark L.

SAP

Zappos is an awesome partner. On behalf of SAP Retail, and myself personally, we are really proud to have such a great company as part of our Retail family. Zappos' enthusiasm, commitment, and quirkiness are what make it unique and I hope this never changes. We look forward to working together for a long time to come!

Mike B.

Adidas

The Zappos Culture is a great example of how companies and people can improve society through integrity, open and honest communication, service and fun. This is a business model that should be recognized and rewarded by Wall Street.

Mullen

Mullen & Co.

The Zappos Culture is the mystery flavor popsicle. You don't know exactly what to expect, but you know it will be good. We love that our job is to tell that story.

Rich J.

RD Johnson Consulting Group

As a consultant looking at Zappos Culture from the outside in, I've never felt like I was on the outside looking in. I think that says a lot about the Culture. Also, having been around many companies throughout my career, I can say that I have never seen a company that works really, really hard and plays really, really hard the way Zappos does. This says a lot about the Zappos Culture also.

But here's one of the telling signs of the Zappos Culture: When there is an issue and people have to jump into solving it, no matter what it takes and no matter what time of the day it is, it's "all hands on board" without anybody complaining, during or after the fact. What this tells me is that working at Zappos isn't about the job. It appears to me that everyone truly wants and cares that Zappos succeeds, not just so everyone can keep getting a paycheck. It's the same pride watching someone in your family succeed. This may sound strange to some people but I've been at many companies where you didn't get that feeling ... Zappos Culture = Pride in Zappos = Pride in job = Pride in Colleagues.

Ron K.

Superior Vision Services

As an Account Manager, I have the privilege of working with many companies on an intimate level. Zappos is, without a doubt, on the VERY top of my list of "Best Companies to Work With." I literally get a smile on my face every time I get an email from any one of the several Zappos employees that I work with.

Not only does Zappos go out of their way to make their employees happy and fulfilled (both professionally and personally), they also go out of their way to make their vendors and other business partners feel like we are a part of the Zappos family.

Thank you, Zappos!

Sandy P.

Axis Promotions

Downtown, amazing to consider the impact a company can make for the common good. Fairness, consideration, it's life, it's real ... so proud to be a partner of the Zappos Culture. Who knew "business" could be this much fun and all encompassing?

part of the Zappos family!

This is me and my daughter Jayla showing how much we LOVE Zappos!
- Desiray Flint

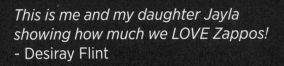

CUSTOMER *Appreciation*

Hey Zapponians!!

Thanks for Delivering Happiness to me and my humans.

I love Zappos and really want to be a Zapscot...I live and bark each and every Zappos Family Core Value (ok...I am working on the "do more with less" value, but my humans kind of spoil me...so I donate a lot of my toys to other barkers as my way to do more with less...but I have all the other values nailed :-))

Anyway, I'll keep living the values... you keep Delivering Happiness...and maybe one day I'll get to visit my fellow Zapponians!

Love you forever...
- Roxie Wolf

Was so cool to meet Tony in ATL and find out he was just a cool approachable guy....this photo made Elizabeth Fallon (on the button) smile. Sadly we lost Elizabeth to cancer. - Michael Gibbons

One of my passions is serving. Here I am on my first trip to Haiti. Can't wait to go back!! - Richard L. Berry, III

What I think of when I hear "Zappos"
"WOW"
"Fun"
"Happiness"
        - hedgehog smile

CUSTOMER *Appreciation*

Dear Zappos!

Thrilled by the possibility that I may be in the culture book as a longtime loyal Zappos VIP Customer. In this picture I am holding up a "Wish" for TEDxChange Conference which was focused on the Millennium Goals and held last fall here in Seattle, WA.

This Fall we are honored and proud that Zappos Culture Book author, Jenn Lim, will be joining us by speaking at TEDxRainier on the Delivering Happiness Movement! ... Let us Deliver Us Some Happiness! - Jeris JC Miller

CUSTOMERS
AROUND THE
World

ANOTHER YEAR PASSES,
ANOTHER YEAR OF
LIVING, BREATHING
AND LIVING
Zappos Culture

TIL
Next Year
DON'T FORGET TO KEEP LIFE...

FUN

AND

A LITTLE

WEIRD

PEEP
YA
LATER...

2011 Culture Book